To my husband, James Francis Keller,
without whose financial, emotional,
and intellectual support none of the research
would have been possible.

FREEDOM *of the* SCREEN

FREEDOM
of the
SCREEN

Legal Challenges to State Film Censorship, 1915–1981

Laura Wittern-Keller

THE UNIVERSITY PRESS OF KENTUCKY

Publication of this volume was made possible in part by a grant from the National Endowment for the Humanities.

Scholarly publisher for the Commonwealth,
serving Bellarmine University, Berea College, Centre College of Kentucky, Eastern Kentucky University, The Filson Historical Society, Georgetown College, Kentucky Historical Society, Kentucky State University, Morehead State University, Murray State University, Northern Kentucky University, Transylvania University, University of Kentucky, University of Louisville,
and Western Kentucky University.

Editorial and Sales Offices: The University Press of Kentucky
663 South Limestone Street, Lexington, Kentucky 40508-4008
www.kentuckypress.com

12 11 10 09 08 5 4 3 2 1

Library of Congress Cataloging-in-Publication Data

Wittern-Keller, Laura, 1951-
Freedom of the screen : legal challenges to state film censorship, 1915-1981 / Laura Wittern-Keller.
p. cm.
Includes bibliographical references and index.
ISBN 978-0-8131-2451-3 (hardcover : alk. paper)
1. Motion pictures—Censorship—United States—History. 2. Motion pictures—Law and legislation—United States. 3. Motion picture industry—Law and legislation—United States. I. Title.
PN1995.62.W58 2008
344.7305'31—dc22 2007037997

This book is printed on acid-free recycled paper meeting the requirements of the American National Standard for Permanence in Paper for Printed Library Materials.

Manufactured in the United States of America.

Member of the Association of
American University Presses

Contents

Preface and Acknowledgments

This project grew out of one of those innocuous "hi how are you" conversations in the hallway. Ivan Steen stopped me outside his office in the history department of the University at Albany to tell me about a trip with his public history class to the New York State Archives. He had just listened, he said, to archivist Bill Evans practically beg the students to use the state's massive collection of film scripts and other records from the state's forty-three years of censorship bureaucracy. Evans had made the same appeal to Steen's classes for years, to no avail. I decided that I'd go down to the archives to see what Evans was so eager to reveal. What I found was a massive repository of more than seventy thousand film scripts and other censor records. A conversation with Evans got me thinking about the censors and why they never wondered, after watching so many of these supposedly dangerous movies, that they themselves were not crazy, drug-addicted, alcoholic, adulterous, murderous sex addicts. I wanted to find out who these censors were and how they worked. I quickly learned, though, that most of the personnel records of the New York State Motion Picture Division had been culled before being turned over to the archives. So, searching for a research topic, I looked to see which of those seventy thousand files were the fattest, and then I had it. The research bonanza I was looking for was in the files of the movies whose distributors had sued. That tack brought me to long-forgotten distributors of foreign films who earnestly fought to allow their movies to be shown—men like Joseph Burstyn, Ronald Freedman, Edward Kingsley, and Richard Brandt. I was hooked.

None of the ensuing research would have been possible without the assistance of the New York State Archives staff, specifically Dr. Jim Folts, and the now retired Bill Evans and Dick Andress. Generous support of the New York State Archives Partnership Trust allowed me to spend as much time in the archives as I could for two years running. The New York State Library staff also provided much-needed help as I struggled to understand the complexities of the New York legal system.

Then I got to thinking about the other states that censored movies, and that led me to the Maryland State Archives, the Pennsylvania State Archives (and the knowledgeable, helpful Rich Saylor), the Virginia State Library, the Ohio Historical Society, the Seattle Municipal Archives and Municipal Library, Columbia University's Oral History Research Office and Rare Book and Manuscripts Library, and the ACLU records at the Seeley G. Mudd Manuscript Library at Princeton.

And then I looked to see what had been written about these censors and their challengers. I found out quickly that there was not much. But there was a master's thesis that looked intriguing. I read it with great interest and contacted the author, Andrew James Driggs. Not only was Andy, who had become a lawyer, still interested in censorship; he also sent me his original research materials, including tapes of interviews he'd conducted with Lillian Gerard. His generosity still amazes me.

Equally generous with time, expertise, and encouragement was Richard Brandt of Trans-Lux. One of the intrepid film distributors profiled in this book, Brandt generously shared his considerable knowledge. So, too, did Ronald Freedman, another one of the challengers to state film censorship. Florence Perlow Shientag, one of the attorneys who battled through the state courts and on to the Supreme Court, not only shared her memories but became a wonderful friend in the process. Michael Mayer, executive director of International Film Importers and Distributors Association, also gave me a generous and helpful interview. Each of these helped to flesh out the dry archival records with their memories and memorabilia.

Approximately half of this book started as a history dissertation. At the University at Albany, I was more than lucky to have as my mentor Richard Hamm, a fine legal scholar and dedicated teacher. Richard once told me that the advisor-advisee relationship should be like a marriage: a lifetime commitment. Luckily for me, he really meant it. Long after the dissertation was done, he was offering advice on the book project. And my equally supportive readers, Julian Zelizer (now of Princeton University), Nadia Kizenko, and Ivan Steen, were great sounding boards for ideas, most of which they wisely managed to persuade me to forget.

I must also thank the librarians at Castleton State College and the University of North Carolina at Wilmington. Both of these colleges are blessed with incredibly patient, diligent, and friendly interlibrary loan staffs.

For seemingly endless conversational time and emotional support while working on our dissertations, I want to thank my good friends and

University at Albany colleagues Susan Goodier, Candy Murray, Mary Linane, and Lizzie Redkey. I often feel so fortunate to have undertaken my graduate program where I did and when I did.

Then to wind up at UNC Wilmington while turning the research into a book was too lucky for words. I must thank the entire warm and welcoming history department at UNC Wilmington, particularly my good friend Taylor Fain and my supportive department chairs, Kathleen Berkeley and Sue McCaffray.

Leila Salisbury, the film acquisitions editor at the University Press of Kentucky, and her assistant, Will McKay, have been marvelously helpful through the long publication process. This book is not straight legal history, nor is it film history or cultural history or a straight policy study, but a combination of all. That made it challenging to pigeonhole, but Leila saw the need for such a study and wanted to make it happen. For helping me bring to light the story of the intrepid independent film distributors who fought against governmental film censorship, I am forever grateful.

Someone who has helped me think through this story and what it has meant to society is cultural historian Ray Haberski. Lengthy phone conversations and conference presentations with Ray both reinforced my ideas and, more important, made me rethink assumptions.

Finally, and most important, there's my family. While it may sound hackneyed, I can't imagine completing this manuscript without their support. My parents, Hildegard and Herman Wittern, were my first and most important intellectual role models. My daughter, Amanda Pavlick, who has just completed her master's degree in classical archaeology, is always up for a good academic conversation and will be publishing her own books soon. And my husband, Jim Keller, who burst into my life fifteen years ago, made everything related to this research possible—my PhD studies, my research trips, and my mental health during the many months of manuscript revisions. He even acted as my research assistant, cheerfully making copy after copy and scanning files for interesting tidbits. To him, for his financial and emotional support and most especially for his never-ending cheer and cheerleading, this book is lovingly and gratefully dedicated.

Introduction

Historians, lawyers, and journalists have debated for several decades whether the United States has had a "legacy of suppression" (as first phrased by Leonard W. Levy in 1960) or whether it has fostered freedom of expression. The arguments have gone back and forth for almost forty years. But whether the nation has suffered from constraint of speech or whether it has nurtured free expression, when movies burst onto the cultural scene at the start of the twentieth century, the scales tipped decidedly toward suppression.[1]

Even in the heyday of Anthony Comstock in the late nineteenth century, material deemed unwholesome was suppressed only after publication or circulation.[2] But when moral reformers (loosely defined here as anyone concerned with public morality) began to comprehend the magnetic power presented by the new movie medium at the turn of the twentieth century, they demanded greater control than after-the-fact prosecution. The concern over immorality in media, evident throughout the Victorian era and embodied in the career of Comstock, came to a full rolling boil with the new technology of moving pictures in the early years of the twentieth century. The fear of movies was so great that previous methods of control could no longer suffice. Worried about the impact of movies on children, immigrants, and the uneducated, reformers turned to the government for help in controlling film content. At this point, efforts at suppression of speech in the United States took a decidedly more calculating turn.

Motion pictures became a target in this ideological battle for several reasons. First, they contributed in a highly visible way to the advancing decline of the private sphere so valued by Victorians. With nickelodeons cropping up seemingly on every urban street corner, the new film craze became a clear culprit in moving leisure activity from the domestic, controlled, proper world of the parlor. Second, by showing on a larger-than-life screen the intimate details of people's relationships, movies questioned Victorian norms of propriety in favor of mass voyeurism.

Third, the movie theater indiscriminately mixed male and female, immigrant and native, young and old, all in close proximity in the dark. And, fourth, many movie themes openly questioned or mocked traditional Protestant values of propriety and privacy. Take, for example, the 1896 film *The Kiss*. Although it is hard for today's viewers to imagine, this snippet of two mature people kissing was considered shocking, inappropriate, and dangerous to morals. Kissing, at the turn of the twentieth century, was considered a private affair. That the act could be made public by filmmakers was the problem.

Movies with larger-than-life figures and tradition-challenging themes, shown in the dark to a mixed audience, spawned what political scientists call a "moral panic," which in turn caused a disproportionate reaction as people grasped for some sort of control.[3] Censoring of motion pictures reflected the willingness of many Americans to restrain seemingly dangerous or threatening ideas for the good of society. The early to mid-twentieth century offered fertile ground for such cultural control as well-intentioned people were struggling to comprehend the massive societal changes caused by rapid urbanization, industrialization, and immigration. Many of the bewildering changes going on all around could not be easily addressed. But movies offered an expedient, hittable target.

During the first two decades of the twentieth century, a time usually referred to as the Progressive Era, many activists encouraged governmental action to better the lives of all Americans. To the progressives, control of a possibly damaging new mass communication medium like motion pictures fit naturally with other concerns about impure food and drugs, prostitution, child labor, and unsanitary, unsafe working and housing conditions. Individual rights to expression (particularly of minority viewpoints) had little currency in progressive America.

Societal changes were so substantial and concerns so well publicized in turn-of-the-century America that reformers were able to reverse the legal culture's long-standing deference to property rights, advancing instead corporate regulation to benefit society. In such an ideological atmosphere, the economic rights of the new film industry were unimportant in comparison to the societal benefit to be gained from decent movies. And between 1907 and 1926, the legislators of seven states—Pennsylvania, Ohio, Kansas, Maryland, New York, Virginia, and Massachusetts—as well as one hundred cities, adopted some sort of prior restraint on motion pictures.[4] By midcentury, this control directly affected more than 60 percent of all city dwellers and at least 41 percent of all Americans.[5] It also indirectly affected virtually all American movie patrons, because filmmakers were not likely to cut one version of a movie for one location and offer a different version for others. Well-intentioned as it was, this was censorship that not only said "thou shalt not" but also had the legal authority of the state behind it.

Prior Restraint

Beyond the power of the state to regulate societal ills, governmental censorship of motion pictures carried a far more powerful ability to repress. Unlike the prosecution of indecent books, the censoring of motion pictures was what legal scholars call *prior restraint.* In all its legislatively authorized power, prior restraint places the burden of proof of content propriety on the creator, effectively reversing the usual legal process. Literature, art, photography—even theatrical productions—were usually subject to control only after release to the public. When progressive and religious pressure groups began demanding state control of motion pictures, virtually every state had indecency laws on the books that allowed prosecution of harmful movies. But for those fearful of movie influence, this was not enough: the potential harm of a movie before prosecution could get underway was considered too great. So reformers demanded that movies be examined before exhibition. Because few progressives considered movies a part of the press or legitimate vehicles of speech, appeals to First Amendment rights were out of the picture.

Movies were fair game for prior restraint not possible over other forms of media. If Mr. X had a book that was considered dangerously obscene, no governmental body could keep him from publishing it. He could be prosecuted for obscenity after the book's appearance, but he could not be stopped before his book had become part of the "marketplace of ideas," something that could be discussed.[6] Then, if he were prosecuted for obscenity, the state would have to prove that the book was indeed legally obscene. But if Mr. X put the same content into a motion picture in one of the censoring localities, it would be subject to prior restraint and would never see the inside of a movie theater. It would not become part of the marketplace of ideas, and no one would even know about it. Moreover, because the government had no burden of proof, Mr. X's only recourse would be to bring suit against the censors and then try to convince a judge that his film was not objectionable. Add these circumstances to a prevailing judicial climate prior to World War II that considered the legislatively empowered experts of most bureaucratic agencies to be virtually infallible, and the picture of what the motion picture industry was up against becomes apparent.

Prior restraint of movies, which first attracted the progressives, found a later proponent in the Catholic Church in the 1930s and gained additional momentum from the anti-Communists of the 1950s. Though the supporters changed over the years, they shared the belief that when a conflict arises between society and the individual, the greater good must always win. In their quest for the greater good, though, they ran into opposition. During the "rights revolution," often attributed to the 1960s, another ideology came to the fore: that the individual has the right to be free from restrictions on the basic liberties of the Bill of Rights. Governmental constraints on political speech, news media, and artistic expression started to fall in the 1920s and 1930s, but movie censorship lived on, declining only in the 1960s. How the judiciary became more receptive to the right to communicate freely through motion pictures and those who pushed that idea on the judiciary are the twin foci of this book.

The Nature of Censorship

A discussion of censorship compels some attempt at definition since the word carries a host of connotations, all of them value laden and most of them negative. But defining censorship allows about as much precision as describing freedom or love or a good Beaujolais. And, in the case of motion picture history, the term carries even more imprecision because of the varying methods used to control content. In the Progressive Era, when motion picture control began, censorship carried positive connotations for many. Censorship was something that would benefit society by keeping profit-driven movie producers from eroding the proper division between the private realm and the public world, destroying young or impressionable minds in the process and demeaning intimate personal relationships.[7] Aside from a few civil libertarians, most people would not have seen censorship of threatening ideas as a free speech issue. Today, however, with an expanded ideology of free speech rights, censorship carries connotations of repression, authoritarianism, and intolerance. That radical change owes much to public perceptions of the fascisms of World War II and the communism of the cold war and to an evolving jurisprudence over the meaning of the First Amendment. Today, generally only obscenity, libel, and words that carry an immediate, direct incitement to violence remain outside the free speech protections of the First Amendment. But in the early to mid-twentieth century, First Amendment jurisprudence was far more circumscribed, a situation that allowed judges to deny free speech and free press arguments when considering the constitutionality of movie censorship.

Beyond the change in connotation over time lies further ambiguity about the word *censorship*. Looked at broadly, censorship can mean any action that inhibits or changes expression, and that is how it is often used in current discourse. But in a more narrow view, one that I favor, censorship means the outright restriction or prohibition of expression. Motion pictures have been subjected to censorship on both levels.

Motion pictures have also often been victims of self-censorship. As concern over film content grew alongside the new motion picture industry, those in the film business found themselves faced with both massive lobbying from various pressure groups and a continual threat of ever more governmental censorship as more and more state legislatures and the U.S. Congress considered film censorship bills. In defense, the industry created several trade groups to lobby against censorship and experimented with a number of in-house cleanup schemes, which proved wholly unsatisfactory to reformers. Then, in 1934, faced with a threatened boycott by Catholics, the industry created its own control mechanism, the Production Code Administration (PCA). The keepers of the code had great authority over film content. By the end of the 1930s, political message films had all but disappeared from American screens.[8] In the mid-1950s, civil libertarian Elmer Rice, as chair of the ACLU's National Council on Freedom from Censorship, worried that the Production Code was "strangling freedom of expression to a degree that no political censor would dare attempt."[9] This "self-censorship," as it was called, exerted unknown influence on film.[10]

Yet *self-censorship*—the restriction of content that a person places on his own work out of fear or financial concern—does not suitably reflect the work of the PCA. Standard dictionaries define *censor* as one who has the authority to suppress or remove objectionable material, but Hollywood's "censors" had no legal power to do either. The administrators of Hollywood's Production Code recommended deletions or additions before and during the production of films. They negotiated with studio heads and producers. But they had no legal authority to restrict content or the exhibition of films containing material they requested be removed. The PCA administrators had colossal economic clout, to be sure, and they shaped the content of America's movies for decades, but their actions should not be confused with the legislatively empowered bureaucrats of state and municipal censor boards who had all the weight of law behind their pronouncements on motion pictures (and whose restrictions were the basis of Hollywood's content regulation in the first place). Jon Lewis offers a more accurate term than *self-censorship* for the PCA's activity: "content regulation."[11]

Unlike governmental censors, who utilized prior restraint, the PCA chose to regulate the content of its member studios' product, a process that recent scholarship reveals was based largely on negotiation before and during production—quite different from the actions of state agencies with broad power to restrain completed films. This book concerns legal censorship, not the intrigues of studio politics and internal code negotiations. In this text, a censor is a person who determines whether a film can be legally exhibited, and to censor a movie is to review and restrain its content.

Although they were different in their legal stature, in several ways the governmental censors and the Production Code administrators shared a symbiotic relationship. First, the Hollywood studios would probably not have instituted their own control mechanism were it not for the existing governmental censorship and constant threats of its expansion. Both Janet Staiger and Nancy Rosenbloom have revealed that by 1910, the movie industry was already thinking about how it might control its own product.[12] Second, Hollywood's regulators constantly monitored the activities of state and local censors to ensure that their members' studios would face little interference once film canisters left the warehouse. Finally, both the censors and the content regulators influenced what would and would not be seen on movie theater screens. So American moviegoers may not have been aware that their entertainment had been tampered with, but it is certain that all films of the era were shaped both by profit-driven concerns of the studios and by restrictions imposed by bureaucrats.

Beyond the activities of the PCA and the governmental censors, there was a third type of control, what Richard Randall calls "informal censorship." Motion picture exhibitors were frequently harassed by local pressure groups, who made phone calls in the middle of the night, sent threatening letters, requested spot checks by the fire department, and picketed outside theaters. In areas without governmental censorship bodies, these tactics were (and still can be) devastatingly effective. Faced with threats like theater license revocation, blue-law enforcement, and boycott, exhibitors almost always backed down. Indeed, Randall argues, informal censorship was even more effective in shutting down film content than the PCA and the state censors.[13]

The Fight against Censorship

It might be expected that Hollywood producers would have fought back against their industry-wide regulation, yet filmmakers accepted this set of circumstances for decades without mounting any legal or political fight against it. In many ways, the Hollywood studios welcomed censorship, both their own content regulation and governmental controls, as protection against public criticism and potential box office losses from boycotts. Censorship also calmed the easily jangled nerves of bankers who controlled production funding. By adding some degree of predictability, it kept the funding channels open for increasingly bloated film budgets.

Studios did not fight against censorship in their heyday of near-monopolistic control because they found it easier, less expensive, and even profitable to do what the censors wanted. Studio heads learned early that complying with the demands of moral reformers worked to their advantage. Not until after World War II did the studios' trade organization, the Motion Picture Association of America (MPAA), consider aiding challenges to governmental censorship, and even then it entered the arena hesitantly. Most challenges to state and municipal censors arose from foreign films, independent productions, and individual exhibitors.[14]

Those who fought against governmental censorship of motion pictures were not named Goldwyn or Fox or Warner. Their names would not have been recognized by filmgoers. They were a small, unorganized number of independent film distributors with very little funding or support from their peers. The first challenge to governmental censorship came in 1915 when Mutual Film Corporation mounted a three-state challenge by appealing to the free speech and free press guarantees of the First Amendment. But that attempt was denied by the U.S. Supreme Court. In the next three and a half decades of film censorship—the 1920s through the 1940s—distributors who challenged censorship conformed to the hostile judicial atmosphere created by the *Mutual Film Corp. v. Ohio* decision and backed away from First Amendment claims. As businessmen, they needed to get their films licensed, so they avoided sweeping constitutional arguments sure to fail. Moreover, a political culture hostile to free speech ideals in the 1940s, one marked by congressional investigations into the mass media, kept a wise film distributor from making waves with the public. By the end of the 1940s and the beginning of the 1950s, however, those who bucked state censors sensed a change in the judiciary—a demand for greater specificity in statutory language and a more sympathetic reaction to claims of First Amendment violations—and they changed their tactics, using free speech and free press language to attack the constitutionality of vague prior restraint statutes.

Although most did not start out as free speech ideologues, these challengers and their lawyers became effective advocates for the expansion of free speech rights. In their fight against prior restraint of films, these distributors combined a normally healthy desire for profit with what sounds like principled opposition to government intrusion into individual rights. Without their film distribution businesses, these men (and they were all men) would very likely not have become First Amendment warriors. However, when motivated by a governmental mechanism that interfered with their trade, they adopted the rhetoric of an idealistic anticensorship position that expanded legal interpretation of First Amendment rights to new levels. Joseph Burstyn, Edward Kingsley, Jean Goldwurm, Richard Brandt, and Ronald Freedman (among others) refused to acknowledge the legitimacy of the legislatively empowered film censorship bureaucrats. They joined a small but vocal group of civil libertarians who thought governmental censorship wrong. And though it might be easy to discount these small businessmen as mere capitalists—many of them were just that—once they got into the legal wrangling over film content, they expressed concern for the constitutional rights of all Americans to speak and to hear. Whether this was sincere and idealistic or not, their efforts helped to reshape and broaden First Amendment jurisprudence.

As small businessmen with few financial resources and no political clout, these independent distributors were unable to seek legislative repeal, so they fought censorship through the courts. Although some postmodern free speech theorists argue that the judiciary has usurped control of the public discourse, this was not the case in terms of movie content. Rather than judges seizing legislative power and determining what could be seen on American movie screens, it was the lawmakers of seven states and hundreds of municipalities who abdicated their roles and invited the judiciary to direct public discourse. Because the lawmakers left appeal to the judiciary as the only relief provided for arbitrary censorship rulings, that is exactly what these independent distributors did. They did not choose litigation over other avenues; it was their only recourse, a situation intentionally created by legislators.

The distributors who challenged censorship were men who made their living in a risky business, who gambled whatever they had on a few movies, and who could be ruined by an adverse censorship determination that could delay their films for months or even years.[15] While censorship publicity might have helped to sell books or theater tickets, the distributors who fought against the censors before World War II rarely received any publicity. Their cause was a quiet one, fought far away from the front pages of newspapers. When, after the war, some Americans began to question restraint on films, publicity was still nearly impossible since governmental censors could keep any film within their jurisdictions from being seen. Even for films that sailed through the review process unscathed, submission to censor boards was time consuming and expensive, a major factor for an industry with time-sensitive products like movies.

Why did some independents challenge the censors in court? Unfortunately, this question cannot be definitively answered because most of the independents did not leave papers behind and all but two are now gone. All we know of their motivation comes from public statements, a few interviews with the press, a few interviews that I have conducted many years afterward, and some guesswork based on their actions.

Not every distributor who challenged governmental censorship was fighting for idealistic reasons. Some, like the exploitation filmmakers of the middle twentieth century, fought censors purely to make money. But the majority of the challenge cases came from men who spoke repeatedly about freeing the screen from what they considered an un-American prior restraint.

Most of the challengers' Hollywood counterparts remained silent until the late 1950s. Even then, they entered the anticensorship ranks haltingly. With bankers scrutinizing each project's profitability, the major studios could ill afford protracted court battles or negative publicity. So, rather than fighting, they decided to work with the censors, and their goal became production of uncensorable films. Social message films, boundary-pushing themes, and controversial topics evaporated. As the influential civil liberties authority Zechariah Chafee put it in 1941, "The maxim of the industry is said to be: 'Thou shalt not offend any one, anywhere, at any time.' And so it has almost ended by boring every one everywhere."[16]

In this midcentury era of sanitized films, though, some independent distributors spied a new market—one for more daring films—and they set out to deliver. Post–World War II European film producers, like the Italian neorealists, were creating a new style of filmic reality. Importation of these new films placed distributors squarely in conflict with state and local censors. While some independents did make the required cuts, others refused. They hired lawyers, planned strategies, and challenged censor boards, hoping to overturn statutes. Those who were able took their cases to the U.S. Supreme Court, hoping the justices would validate their free speech arguments.

Most of the distributors whose cases are profiled in this book exemplified true commitment to the principles of free speech. They fought for the right to deliver more mature themes, the kinds of movies that Hollywood had failed to supply. The new, more realistic movies that they used to fight censorship were not pornographic. *The Miracle*, the movie that led to the landmark Supreme Court case in film censorship jurisprudence in 1952, was neither salacious nor violent. Seven years later, another major Supreme Court case turned on a much toned down film adaptation of a novel now considered a literary classic, *Lady Chatterley's Lover*. Ronald Freedman's 1965 Supreme Court case came from a film about the Irish rebellion of 1916. Jean Goldwurm brought two cases to the Supreme Court, neither of which dealt with an obscene film. And Richard Brandt, who brought the 1965 case that knocked out New York State's censorship, simply thought that the time had come for Americans to choose their own film entertainment, an idea shared at the time by many film critics.

But the story of the legal battles against governmental prior restraint is not one of good guys versus bad guys. Many procensorites believed sincerely that control of movie producers and directors was necessary to protect women, children, and society in general. Who is to say they were not correct, particularly about the children? Because Hollywood sought the widest possible audience for every film, it refused to accept age classification. Thus making movies that could appeal to more and less mature audiences was not possible in the United States. That meant that any child could see any movie, a situation understandably worrisome to many people.

The question of whether society needs censorship of mass media, however, is beyond this study. This book concerns neither right and wrong nor good versus bad. This book looks at the intersection of laypeople's rights consciousness and the judiciary's constitutional interpretation: at those who wanted to statutorily protect society against certain individuals versus those who thought society should protect itself through open communication—and who were willing to fight to secure the unfettered transmission of ideas. Along the way, the rights consciousness of ordinary people pushed and prodded constitutional interpretation into new areas. A society based on control shifted gradually to a society based on "expressive individualism"[17] or, some might argue, on *excessive* individualism.

While this study answers how and why governmental censorship ended—not coincidentally at the same time as the demise of the Production Code—it raises new questions about how governmental censorship came to be in the first place. This book starts in the first two decades of the twentieth century by looking at the origins of statutory film censorship and suggests that if the educators and organized club women who spoke out so clearly against the movies had presented a united front in favor of censorship, more states might have hosted censor boards; it then examines a distributor's first legal attack in 1915, which was slapped down by an unreceptive judiciary; it next moves through a series of unsuccessful challenges in the 1920s and 1930s; it then focuses on the increasing number of cases brought in the post–World War II era as First Amendment jurisprudence began to transform; it then examines the final cases during the rights revolution of the 1960s, when state film censorship entered its terminal phase; and it finishes with a look at the Maryland State Board of Censors, still censoring into the beginning of the 1980s.

Hollywood Begins to Fight Censors

While independent distributors were sporadically fighting back against the state censors through the 1920s, 1930s, and 1940s, Hollywood stayed quiet. It was simply too expensive for a studio to have a big-budget, heavily leveraged film lying about, waiting for court cases to be resolved.[18] Having welcomed the safety of censorship under the PCA since 1934, the industry's trade group, the Motion Picture Producers and Distributors of America (MPPDA), found it difficult to rally behind the idea of opposing censorship, even when society's sexual mores began to change and the national legal climate began to expand individual liberties. The MPPDA was a trade organization, devoted to improving the economic situation for its members. Only when economic necessities—like the need to compete with the new television medium and decreased box office numbers after World War II—sent Hollywood scrambling for new ways to attract ticket buyers did state censorship begin to look like a burden worthy of resistance.

The industry's road to an anticensorship position was long. In the 1940s, the MPPDA became the MPAA and joined a few cases as amicus curiae (friend of the court), but these challenges were carefully chosen not to embarrass or disturb the association's members. In the 1950s, the MPAA began to make public statements opposing governmental film censorship. But not until 1965–1966, almost two decades after the major studios had been forced to give up their monopolistic control of exhibition, two decades after it had begun to face significant competition from foreign films, and fifteen years after the battle against television had commenced, did the MPAA begin its own legal action against a governmental censor board.

Similarly, the American Civil Liberties Union, which did not consider silent motion pictures as speech, announced opposition to film censorship only with the advent of the talkies in 1929, and then did little to aid the independent distributors. The civil liberties organization that so doggedly pursued rights challenges in the 1930s and 1940s and was responsible for so many of the early civil liberties decisions did not get involved in a meaningful way with state film censorship. It made anticensorship public pronouncements but participated in only four of the eleven prior restraint film cases that went before the U.S. Supreme Court. The ACLU did, however, monitor the censorship situation at both the state and national levels, staying on the lookout for promising test cases. But its limited resources, split among a bevy of competing rights issues, meant that the ACLU could not mount a full-scale campaign against motion-picture censorship.

More important, the ACLU was also hampered by division within its ranks on how far the First Amendment should go to protect speech. While it made statements about fighting censorship in the 1930s, most of its members believed that only political speech should be protected. Even those who believed that entertainment speech should be protected stopped short of thinking that obscenity deserved free expression. In the 1930s, 1940s, and 1950s, the only cases the ACLU would consider joining were those of demonstrably nonobscene films. Only in 1962, after a three-year debate, did the ACLU assume an absolutist position on free speech issues. So for most of the time that independent distributors were fighting against censorship, they were on their own, with no help from the big studios of Hollywood and only some help from the ACLU.

Movies' Capacity for Evil

Whoever mounted the attack, any fight against film censorship involved the tricky proposition of convincing judges that the film medium was not necessarily different from other methods of communication. The belief that movies carried a special capacity for evil (an idea stemming from their mass appeal) grew as the movie industry grew. In 1915, this concern received judicial approval when the U.S. Supreme Court considered freedom in the mass media for the first time in *Mutual Film Corp. v. Industrial Commission of Ohio* and decided that movies did not qualify for free speech and free press protection. In 1930, concern about movies' capacity for evil gained even more momentum when a group of social science studies revealed deleterious effects of movie viewing on children. The belief that movies were capable of greater influence and therefore greater damage, which I call the *harmfulness concept*, was still routinely accepted in the 1940s and in some jurisdictions into the 1960s.

But World War II set in motion the beginnings of an ideological change that would eventually help the independent distributors in their incremental fight against censorship. As Americans witnessed the repression of totalitarianism, liberals began to abandon their Progressive Era and New Deal era "celebration of the state," turning instead toward "concern for personal freedom."[19] Then, opposition to governmental censorship begin to look like a democratic value. But progress in this new direction was slow. Massive fear of Communists kept these new liberalizing tendencies at bay for a while. Ardent anti-Communists, the Catholic Church in particular, kept the censoring impulse alive and well. Even into the late 1950s, the capacity-for-evil theory resonated in state courts, making censorship challenges uncertain at best. A Pennsylvania Supreme Court justice in 1959 sounded more like his progressive forebears from a half century before when he insisted that regulation to protect "moral health" was no different from governmental inspections of food, medicines, water, and automobiles.[20] But by the 1960s, a new focus on the individual's rights and liberties began to erode the legal rationale behind governmental censorship. Even so, the belief in the special ability of movies to negatively influence society was so pervasive and so tenacious that the U.S. Supreme Court never abandoned it. Films are still controlled today. Seventy-five years after instituting its content-regulating Production Code, the MPAA still classifies films for content suitability.

Production Code historian Gregory Black suggests that to fully understand movies, we need to understand censorship. He notes in *Hollywood Censored* that the control mechanisms were "first and foremost a censorship of ideas. The intent of the censors . . . was to prevent mass entertainment films from challenging the moral, political, and/or economic status quo. Pro-censorship movements began with moral crusades against Hollywood but quickly became instruments for suppressing thought."[21] Hollywood's homogenized and sanitized films of the 1940s and 1950s illustrate Black's point. But although censors would become arbiters of idea worthiness, that is not what many of the early procensorship forces wanted. Many who were concerned about movie morality did not envision thought police; they wanted "better films," uplifting stories without devious displays of nudity or criminal behavior. What they got, however, were censors who worked without public input or supervision, slashing films without concern for artistic integrity or entertainment value.

Often, those who write about censorship and civil liberties focus on the Supreme Court. While that kind of study gets to the result quickly, it ignores several basic realities: that the decisions of lower courts often affect individuals' lives and actions more directly than Supreme Court pronouncements; that lower courts have a much more direct influence on the legal culture within a state; and that Supreme Court edicts can be ignored by both lower courts and state bureaucracies. Similarly, although much has been written about the Hollywood Production Code, necessarily painting the history of censorship with a national brush, there has been very little work on the state and municipal censor boards, which are also important to understanding the motion pictures of the mid-twentieth century. Only two book-length studies have examined the decades of state film censorship: Ira Carmen's 1966 *Movies, Censorship and the Law* and Richard Randall's 1968 *Censorship of the Movies*. Nothing has been written about the individual state censorship bureaucracies, much less those who challenged them in court. Outside contemporary law reviews, only a few articles touch even tangentially on the end of state film censorship.[22]

This lack of attention may have something to do with the relative invisibility of censors in their own time. As New York's chief censor, Hugh Flick, remarked in 1955, "People hardly know we exist. . . . We're only in the news when we blunder."[23] At the time, there were few journalistic reports on the state censors, and today many people seem unaware that movie censorship was carried on for so many years. This book examines both the process used by states to keep supposedly harmful motion pictures from the public and the legal arguments against it. As such, it is meant to serve as a reference work, a compendium of the cases, their arguments, and their outcomes.

The fight against film censorship did not progress in a straight line. As film critic Bosley Crowther put it in 1961, the fight against the censors was "full of holes and stumps." There often seemed to be no real progress, "just movement around in circles."[24] Even in the postwar years, when the First Amendment was broadening to encompass movies, the anticensorites won cases, but they also lost many. Considering that film censorship was never knocked out by the Supreme Court or a state legislature, Crowther was right—the anticensorship cause never came to a climax. But it did make inroads: it hamstrung governmental censorship of motion pictures, and it advanced free speech rights by revealing the inequity of prior restraint and granting to film the right of expression under the First Amendment.

1

The Origins of Governmental Film Censorship, 1907–1923

With the advent of moving pictures at the turn of the century, Americans experienced a totally new phenomenon. For the first time, new and sometimes unwelcome ideas could be transmitted quickly and easily to anyone, regardless of education, age, or economic status, and without the usual communal filters imposed by family, church, and civic groups. The burgeoning film industry threatened traditional values of modesty, propriety, and lawfulness, and it did so in a most public fashion.[1] It particularly attacked the Victorian boundary between public and private behavior, once quite well defined but gradually melting at the turn of the century. Many social critics railed against what they saw as a retreat of decency, sounding alarm bells over the insertion of private matters into public discourse. A "party of reticence," as they have been sympathetically dubbed by Rochelle Gurstein, had been worrying over popular novels, intrusive journalistic techniques, and sex education for decades. They believed that the advancing trend toward openness, pushed by a "party of exposure," was debasing public life and making normal, healthy, intimate relationships impossible.[2] In 1865, Congress had entered the discussion of private and public when it enacted the first national antismut law, which authorized the U.S. postmaster to intercept obscene photographs. Eight years later, Congress appointed antivice crusader Anthony Comstock as a special agent of the postal service and charged him with intercepting "obscene, lewd, or lascivious" books, postcards, pamphlets, and pictures, a job he spiritedly pursued for forty years, until his death in 1915.[3] The reticent had been battling invasive journalistic practices, realistic novels, and unauthorized advertising practices for decades when, in 1900, they got a new target: movies.

Movies were an entirely new medium—far more graphic, more widespread, and more rapid in delivering realistic, riveting instruction in the ways of romance, seduction, and crime. Moralists worried about movie content they considered to be "social sewage"—films about straying spouses, wild "dancing daughters," gun-crazed gangsters, hard-drinking youths, and seductive foreigners.[4]

The arrival of movies provided all the necessary ingredients for a "moral panic"[5]—a level of public concern disproportionately high considering the potential harm—and a full-blown conflict over moral values. As James Morone has shown, the reticent typically demand governmental action to control a medium if they perceive in it a dangerous other who lazes about, drinks or takes drugs, or acts violently or sexually uninhibitedly.[6] Movies and their makers easily fit the category of *other*. The movie men were responsible for encouraging large numbers of people to drop productive activities in favor of sitting idly in movie theaters. The characters in their movies often drank or took drugs. They could be violent. And many were seducing or being seduced by someone. So it was a natural reaction for moral guardians to demand policy changes both to control the dangerous other and to protect the virtuous, which in the case of movies was verbalized as "the children."

The moralists' response to motion pictures had as much to do with the rapid changes of society as it did with the content of the films themselves. Industrialization and urbanization of the mid-nineteenth century took farm sons and daughters away from home to the wicked city and led to panic over issues like masturbation, prostitution, and a male "sporting culture."[7] Several decades later, the "flickers" became the damnable vehicles that hastened what was already perceived as a moral breakdown by bringing dangerous ideas to millions of society's most impressionable—uneducated workers, unassimilated immigrants, and unchaperoned, impressionable youths.

That moral guardians (a neutral term in this study) turned to censorship of this new, supposedly threatening medium should not be surprising, nor was it so to people at the time. Americans had long accepted the idea of censorship for the theater, starting in the colonial era and continuing through the nineteenth and early twentieth centuries. While English law, upon which much of American law was based, condemned prior restraint on the press, it had no problem with such restraint on theatrical productions.[8] Prior restraint on a new medium, then, especially one that was similar to staged productions, was not likely to be considered either unconstitutional or un-American in the Progressive Era.

Pressure Groups Push for Censorship

The moral panic that greeted movies was more than a knee-jerk reaction to a new medium, or a reaction to a new, dangerous other, or the next logical step in efforts to contain smut: this backlash also had religious roots—specifically Protestant. Protestants saw their values (thrift, hard work, individual achievement) threatened by the massive cultural and social changes of the early twentieth century. Biergartens, vaudeville, amusement parks, and dance halls had all caused the Protestant establishment great concern, but it was movies that seemed the epitome of what was wrong with the changing culture.[9] Long dominant in American life but declining in cultural authority at the turn of the century, Protestants saw in movies a manifestation of the very social and political changes that they found so threatening.[10] Movies bypassed the normal communal filters—parents, pastors, teachers—so Protestant progressives wanted a substitute filter that could weed out the bad movies and send forth the good ones with a recognizable label of purity.

The intensity of the Protestant reaction only grew as the new medium became popular among middle-class audiences and as movie theaters cropped up seemingly on every street corner. More people were going to movie theaters each week than to church.[11] And when it became clear that most of the new film companies were Jewish owned, Protestant progressives found another reason to question the movies' morality. It was no longer merely what was in the movies and who was watching, but also who was creating them and with what motivation. Paul Starr attributes much of the negative reaction against filmmakers in this early period to a religious dichotomy: Christian reformers demanding control of Jewish filmmakers.[12]

Moral guardians had two powerful justifications that they used in their campaign to control the movie industry: the effect of movies on the innocent (children and the uneducated) and the growing societal concern about juvenile delinquency. These trepidations formed a mighty foundation on which the procensorites built their case for film control. To use historian Frances Couvares's term, reformers spotlighted the "vulnerable viewer." It worked. As Andrea Friedman has shown, wherever progressive reformers could persuade legislators that vulnerable viewers were being harmed, they succeeded in getting legislative protection. Vulnerable viewers could certainly be found in the cheap movie theaters of every neighborhood.[13] In New York, by 1910, fully one-quarter of the city attended at least one movie each week. Forty thousand children went to the movies daily, and many working-class mothers were using movie theaters as babysitters.[14]

What kinds of movies were these children and illiterates watching? According to Sharon Ullman, early film content represented "an important shift in cultural imagination," commodifying female bodies by displaying women disrobing, or initiating romantic contact, or engaging in sexually suggestive exercise.[15] Titles like *His Naughty Thought* (1917), *His One Night Stand* (1917), and *Her Purchase Price* (1919) helped sell tickets. Films and their advertising were frank in matters of sex compared to cultural norms. For progressives, the potential of such films to cause moral disorder made an afternoon in a darkened theater no different from other societal menaces like sausage or patent medicine. All needed regulation for the public good.

These progressives were earnest reformers working to cure the societal ills that came in the late nineteenth and early twentieth centuries from the triple blow of overwhelming immigration, explosive urbanization, and unrestrained industrialization. While progressives varied so widely in their beliefs that defining their philosophy is impossible, most of them would have agreed that the worship of individual property rights condoned by the U.S. courts of the nineteenth century led to most of America's social problems—worker abuse, impure food, substandard housing, moral decay. In the progressive mind, it was the excessive individualism of industrial capitalism that caused societal problems. According to civil liberties historian David Rabban, "Progressives believed the promise of American democracy could only be realized by replacing an outmoded attachment to individualism with a commitment to an activist state."[16] Protection of the individual's right to make money had caused the great urban woes, progressives argued, so Americans needed to focus on the greater good, sacrificing the rights of the individual if necessary to achieve a just result for the majority.

Pushing for movie regulation, pressure groups used the same language that was used in the campaigns to regulate child labor and housing conditions. The Society for the Prevention of Crime called for the "moral equivalent of a state board of health to protect us from the moral pestilence which lurks in the attractive, seductive motion-picture."[17] The magnetic quality of movies also worried many women's reform groups. Since activist women were often concerned with the socialization (or Americanization) of poor urban children, the content of movies shown in urban neighborhoods quickly became a major anxiety.

Yet even though these activist women agreed on the need to control film content, they split over who would make the better referee—dedicated, enlightened volunteers (like them) or governmental agencies. The two largest women's organizations exemplified this schism. The Woman's Christian Temperance Union (WCTU) pushed for governmental regulation—preferably federal—of movies.[18] The General Federation of Women's Clubs, a national umbrella organization of women's self-improvement and civic clubs, was less certain about governmental censorship. Before 1918, the federation's clubs were so divided on the issue that the group could take no national stand. At their 1918 meeting, a close vote pushed the federation to endorse a drive for federal censorship. But because the decision was so contentious and the group was so far from unanimity, its newly adopted procensorship stance was weak. Like many other groups that worried over movies, the General Federation of Women's Clubs agreed there was a problem but disagreed on the solution. Just four years later, it withdrew its call for federal censorship.[19]

Another group that was vocally critical of movies' influence was the education community. Like the women's groups, educators saw themselves as guardians of American morality who suddenly were competing with the visual stimulus of the movies. And like the women's groups, teachers' organizations began pleading for some sort of censorship by 1918. Yet they mounted no organized lobbying effort for censorship. Thus the clout of another large group was nullified because it could not decide whether movie control belonged with a governmental agency, a voluntary agency, or parents.[20]

Those moral guardians who did favor governmental censorship set to work and began lobbying for censorship laws, achieving some success at both the state and local levels. The political atmosphere of the Progressive Era—which reflected a growing belief that government could and should work for the betterment of society—and the new modernist philosophy of scientific management in government combined to provide a good fit between organized procensorship reformers and the legislators they lobbied. Moral reformers of all sorts agreed that movies needed to be cleansed for the moral health of the nation, but the mostly Protestant groups pushing for governmental censorship wanted that cleansing carried out by experts within administrative agencies. Seven states answered the call.

Censorship Begins and the Moguls Respond

The City of Chicago enacted the first moving picture ordinance in the United States in 1907. Chicago vested control of its movie screens in its police commissioner, who in turn was empowered to hire such censors as he saw fit. This first censorship victory, in a major city filled with immigrants, encouraged the procensorites and flustered the movie industry. The Chicago market represented millions of dollars of potential revenue, and this ordinance could snowball into other cities. So the beleaguered industry set out to cleanse its image. The public's faith in governmentally sanctioned expert control, however, meant that any halfhearted effort to elevate movie content by the industry itself would satisfy no one for very long.

While some purity groups busied themselves lobbying for governmental motion picture control, the movie industry considered its options. It might have responded with one outraged voice, but those in the movie trade were rarely in agreement when it came to censorship. This discord was in part due to the fractured nature of the industry. People now refer to the industry as Hollywood, a term that implies a monolith. But the movie industry has never been anything of the sort; it actually comprises three separate yet interrelated parts: producers, distributors, and exhibitors. Since exhibitors were on the front lines in the neighborhoods, they often welcomed censorship because sanitized content defanged any local protests. Those who made and distributed films also realized that governmental regulation could bestow an unassailable mark of purity and thwart further criticism, but they feared the absolute control of a federal censorship agency. And they feared the prospect of a chaotic city-by-city censorship, in which local boards in the enormously profitable urban markets would each impose differing requirements. For an industry that relied on the creation of a single product for national distribution, that would be disastrous. Whatever their individual reactions, by 1907, with the establishment of the Chicago censor board, the moviemakers realized that more censors would soon appear.

The next scene in the censorship struggle was the immensely significant market of New York City. On Christmas Eve 1908, New York City mayor George McClellan revoked the license of every nickelodeon in his jurisdiction after a raucous public meeting about film decency and theater safety. So many citizens had been railing against film content that McClellan's action was widely hailed not as interference with legitimate business (despite the era's strong laissez-faire attitude) but as a child-saving achievement.[21] The exhibitors took action on two fronts: they asked the courts for an injunction against the mayor's action, which they received,[22] and they sought help to forestall further criticism. Recognizing that the calls for protection of the city's youth via movie censorship were widespread, the exhibitors asked the People's Institute (the adult education division of the Cooper Institute) to form a volunteer censoring body that would make recommendations, encourage elimination of immoral and violent material, and sanction films for exhibition. Just three months later, the National Board of Censorship (renamed the National Board of Review in 1915) began reviewing movies.

The board not only reviewed completed films but also managed to convince some film producers to cooperate in advance of production. With such collaboration, the board could do more than just issue approvals or condemnations of films; it could also influence the content of movies before they were shot.[23] As the board became better known, theater owners began to demand that any film brought in by a distributor have the board's seal of approval stamped on the first few feet of the movie. This helped the board to coerce compliance from film producers: no seal, no theaters. Many producers welcomed this approval process because it created greater uniformity, and hence business stability, through "the exercise of peer pressure."[24] And, of course, the exhibitors were happy because their theaters could play movies with an insurance policy of sorts.

Although the National Board of Censorship started work amid great fanfare, many procensorship groups soon became disenchanted. Financed by the movie industry, the board never escaped allegations that it answered to the industry's needs first. And in truth, the board's goal was not to ban bad films but to raise the level of taste in American movies and to keep governmental film censorship at bay by proving that volunteer cultural guardians could better serve the public than bureaucrats. (A similar board set up in Great Britain in 1912 and still functioning today has escaped such criticism by remaining conspicuously independent of the British film industry.) In its first five years, the American board reviewed twenty thousand films, rejecting almost 20 percent. But it also approved many films that others decried. The Chicago censors, for example, banned many more films, making the national board look ineffective. And when the board approved a spate of exploitative white slave films in 1913, criticism grew shrill.

The real problem, however, was differing expectations. Moral guardians wanted objectionable scenes and language cut out. The board, however, took a more holistic view of each movie's overall effect. It also had a different view of what constituted immorality in film. Most of its reviewers considered nudity neither obscene nor immoral, and since white slavery was a real issue, the board had no trouble approving the films.[25]

This discrepancy in viewpoint can be explained by looking at who was doing the censoring for the board. Made up of cultural liberals, the board preferred enlightened persuasion to a more heavy-handed, "thou shalt not" type of censorship. And as the original rosy glow of consensus over the national board faded, it became clear that a significant split existed in America's procensorship faction. As Andrea Friedman puts it, two "competing visions" of progressive censorship arose. One side, the dominant voice in procensorite agitation, insisted that all films must be suitable for children—the most vulnerable viewers—and that only a statutorily empowered expert could be entrusted with such work. On the other side were the supporters of the national board, who believed that a private, voluntary regulation system that could adjust as culture evolved would better mediate between society and the film industry.[26] To this end, the national board's most basic goal had been to prove that enlightened censorship by educated progressives could handle the nation's moral needs without reverting to governmental interference. After its first few years, the industry's first attempt at placating moral critics had received at best only mixed reviews. Moral guardians, insistent on protecting children, were not mollified, and calls for governmental censorship grew louder and more insistent.

States and Cities Adopt Censorship

Unimpressed by the work of the National Board of Censorship and disagreeing with its philosophy, many New York procensorites continued to seek legislation for a professional, governmental censor board. Although they claimed that they wanted to protect innocent youths from the vile influences of the movies, several historians believe that they were more interested in controlling immigrant behavior.[27] What is certain, however, is that many procensorites were driven by a genuine desire to protect all children, immigrant and American born.

In the background, the battle between the "party of reticence" and those who favored open discourse continued. Comstock and others of the reticent persuasion felt that the home's sanctity was invaded whenever sex was openly discussed. They worried that what should remain private was becoming public. The "party of exposure," on the other hand—sex education reformers, journalists, novelists, moviemakers, and free speech advocates—fought against what they saw as puritanical Victorianism, hoping to move the public discourse into a more modern, open realm where ideas could be freely debated. As the century moved forward, the argument became increasingly polarized, and the meanings of private and public continued to change. That the privacy advocates were sincere is undeniable. Many thoughtful people were convinced that movies could cause children to commit all sorts of hideous acts. The *New York Times* reported that seeing a film of a man being burned at the stake had caused some young boys to reenact the torture, severely injuring the boy chosen for the starring role.[28] Many people believed that the motion picture theater was more "far-reaching than the schoolhouse," and they set out to protect, in the words of one censor, "children of immature years," the "great army of mental defectives," and the "vast number of illiterates and the ignorant."[29] Even though these views smack of elitism and those who favor free speech over censorship have long dismissed this work with insulting terms like *Comstockery* and *Puritanism*, the reticent deserve to have their anxiety over the fate of American society examined within its historical context and acknowledged as genuine.

In 1909, regardless of the motivation, moral reformers were able to convince New York authorities to make it a misdemeanor to "advertise or present any obscene, immoral or impure drama, play, exhibition, show or entertainment which would tend to the corruption of youth or others." This ordinance is often referred to as a censorship law, but in reality it did little. Lumping together all performance arts, the law was inconsistently enforced[30] and did nothing to prevent questionable movies from coming to the screen.

Pennsylvania's legislators took up the cause of the reticent in 1911. They believed that their state's citizens deserved more protection from immoral movies than they were getting from the National Board of Censorship.[31] The concern about immoral films in Pennsylvania was so great that both houses unanimously passed a bill creating a censorship board, making Pennsylvania the first to establish statewide film censorship (though its censors did not begin work until 1914). Pennsylvania's censors got negative marching orders from their legislature: they were not to approve films but to disapprove those that were "sacrilegious, obscene, indecent or immoral, or such as tend, in the judgment of the Board, to debase or corrupt morals."[32] As the pioneer of state censorship, Pennsylvania's statute became a model for other states. Just two years after Pennsylvania's legislation, censor boards sprang up in Ohio and Kansas.[33] Only Ohio's statute directed its censors in positive terms, requiring them to approve "only such films as are in the judgment and discretion of the board of censors of a moral, educational or amusing and harmless character."[34] In each statute, *immoral*, *obscene*, and *indecent* were left undefined, in accordance with the Progressive Era's norm of statutory vagueness. Judges routinely remarked that men of ordinary intelligence understood what was immoral and what was obscene, and beyond the quotation of a dictionary definition, no further discussion was necessary. Britain and France passed similarly vague censorship laws.[35]

Like that of Pennsylvania's law, the language of Maryland's statute, passed in 1916, was negative. And, like the other boards, Maryland charged distributors a fee for the privilege of having a film examined. In practice, all the state boards turned hefty profits for their state treasuries. Through World War II, New York's censor board never earned less than $58,000 annually, with one year's (1939) overage hitting $200,000 (nearly $3 million today). Tapping some revenue from the new, highly profitable film industry may have been the extra incentive legislators needed when deciding whether to answer the call from their constituents of the moral guardian persuasion.

In states where censorship statutes had not yet been passed, haggling continued in legislative committees. This was true especially in New York, the single largest movie market, with its large, multiethnic audiences. The story of motion picture censorship there deserves a full examination.

The New York legislature began a long flirtation with statutory censorship in 1911 with the unsuccessful introduction of a bill that would have given a three-member censorship board sweeping powers. The following year another unsuccessful proposal tried to give each town the right to set up a censorship board made up of local officials. The state assembly also flirted with the imposition of a department of morals for New York City, a five-member board with its own special police force that could impose a moral code on the movies.[36] When that bill failed, procensorites settled for the establishment of a city license commissioner who could shut down any theater for showing an "immoral" film.[37] Like his censoring counterparts in Chicago, Pennsylvania, Kansas, and Ohio, New York City's license commissioner had no guidelines or standards by which to judge offenses against morality.[38] Considering that early-twentieth-century judges gave wide latitude to the discretion of administrative officials, the new commissioner could work virtually unchecked. Over the years, he and his successors did just that, and the commissioner's power was consistently upheld by state courts and federal courts.[39] Such judicial invincibility must have had a sobering effect on any theater owner thinking about exhibiting a questionable film.

Along with a newly empowered license commissioner, New York City also adopted a movie theater licensing ordinance in 1913. The license fee to operate a movie theater was raised from $25 to $500 in the hope that a higher fee would encourage theater owners to seek middle-class clientele that would, theoretically, raise movie standards. But just as high liquor license fees did not aid the Prohibition cause, the increased theater license fee did not rid the movies of undesirable elements. The law was, however, a true progressive offspring in its concern about movies' effect on the young: children under sixteen were to be admitted only with a chaperone. On paper, at least, reformers had achieved their goal of keeping impressionable New York City children from darkened theaters. In practice, though, the law was openly defied.[40]

The license commissioner, the high license fees, and the ineffectual child-restriction provision affected only the theaters in New York City. But many of the state's most ardent film censorship proponents were rural, upstate members of the General Federation of Women's Clubs, so pressure for statewide censorship continued. It only gained strength in 1915 when the U.S. Supreme Court sanctioned Ohio's state film censorship by specifically denying that motion pictures deserved First Amendment protections of speech and press (see chapter 2). Momentum from this Supreme Court decision spurred the New York legislature to pass a bill setting up a three-member board to accept or reject films for exhibition. But Governor Charles Seymour Whitman, bothered by constitutional issues, vetoed the bill in 1916. This close call ramped up the procensorship forces, and during the next four years, they hit the legislature with a stack of bills.[41] Each went down to narrow defeat until 1920, when the New York State Conference of Mayors, after studying the issue for several months, decided to mount an all-out defense against statewide censorship. "Legalized censorship of the film is a dangerous departure in a free country," they argued. "It is no less dangerous than a censorship of the press or the stage, for it places a ban upon ideas."[42] The mayors, obviously fearing loss of control to New York's rural upstate legislators, insisted that the National Board of Review was sufficient and managed to kill the censorship bill.

The next year, however, the cultural climate in New York had grown decidedly more hostile to the mayors' plan to keep censorship local. A widely disseminated series of investigative reports in the *Brooklyn Daily Eagle* critical of the National Board of Review's lax standards and possible corruption encouraged many civic, religious, and social groups to lobby for a statewide film review commission.[43] When a new bill was introduced in 1921, hearings displayed the views of a wide range of groups, both in favor and opposed. Headlining the antis were the American Federation of Labor, the mayors, and the National Association of the Motion Picture Industry (NAMPI), an industry trade group largely devoted to fighting censorship. Their position, though eloquently stated (D. W. Griffith testified that "censorship is the weapon of autocracy"), was nullified by political maneuvering when the bill's sponsor, the immensely powerful Senate leader, Republican Clayton R. Lusk, rushed the bill to a vote at midnight the day before it had been scheduled.[44] According to *Moving Picture World*, the Republican senators were "whipped into line like slaves of old . . . aware that this is a pet measure of Senator Lusk, right-hand man of Governor Miller."[45] While it is true that state censorship was attractive to many in New York State, the passage of the bill was clearly politically wrangled. Senate Minority Leader James J. Walker accused Lusk of railroading "the most un-American thing . . . ever brought into the New York State Senate."[46] But it was done. The loss of New York State and its important market to the procensorship forces was a major blow to the movie moguls. It caused them to dissolve the ineffective NAMPI; create a new industry trade group, the Motion Picture Producers and Distributors of America (MPPDA);[47] and hire a new leader, Will Hays, to rally the industry against more governmental censorship.

Florida tried to piggyback on New York's censorship when it enacted a motion picture censorship statute that political scientist Ira Carmen has called "bizarre." This 1921 statute required any commercially exhibited film to be approved by either the National Board of Review or by the New York State motion picture censors. Florida thus vested its censoring power in two agencies—one private, the other governmental, both in other states. Although this was ostensibly a measure to protect its citizens from dangerous movies, Florida was clearly not in the censoring business, and in 1937, this strange law was overturned by a state circuit court.[48]

Virginia followed the next year, copying verbatim New York's statutory standards (which had originally come from Pennsylvania's statute).[49] However, the Virginia censors had a slightly different, unwritten mandate. They were expected to keep from the screen any portrayal of an African American that did not reflect current racial sensibilities in the Old Dominion. While Pennsylvania, Kansas, and Maryland screened for scenes that might prove racially divisive, Virginia went further, making sure that its moviegoers saw only false stereotypical African American images: blacks as maids, butlers, fools, or criminals.[50]

Over the next two years, thirty-four more attempts were introduced into other state legislatures. All were defeated.[51] One of those defeats came in 1923, when, after several failed legislative attempts, Massachusetts attempted to institute censorship by popular referendum. Intense lobbying efforts by the leader of the new MPPDA kept Massachusetts free from prior restraint. Will Hays, hired to improve Hollywood's image and keep censorship at bay, skillfully coordinated every anticensorship group he could find and saved Massachusetts for the moguls.[52] Just three years later, however, Massachusetts found a way around Will Hays. The legislature dusted off and put into effect a colonial-era Lord's Day observance law that permitted the exhibition of only those entertainments considered by the commissioner of public safety or local mayors to be "in keeping with the character of the day."[53] Since no profit-minded distributor was likely to cut a film just to be shown on Sunday, Massachusetts ensured that the same safe film would be shown midweek as well. Massachusetts became the only state to provide for censorship not by establishing a censor board but by empowering local officials based on blue laws. This jerry-rigged, localized structure stood for thirty years before it was struck down by the state supreme court.

All these state censorship statutes shared more than words. The open-ended statutes' lack of definition—in the scope of their authority as well as in the qualifications of the people who would administer them—bespeaks the typical progressive reformers' zeal at getting legislation passed without much concern over implementation. They also betray, in their vagueness, the reformers' belief that experts could be trusted to make difficult policy decisions. A tightly drawn statute would have left little room for experimentation or discretion. A loosely drawn statute, however, particularly in an era when judges typically deferred to administrators, gave the option to grow or constrict the administrator's dominion as needed.

The censoring states had one final commonality. All embraced motion picture censorship despite having free speech protection clauses built into their state constitutions. Movies were not considered worthy vehicles of communication.

Why Only Seven States?

If film censorship was such a popular, progressive notion, backed by influential Protestant and civic groups, why did only seven states embrace it? Why, when so many Americans were worrying over the shift of previously private affairs into the public discourse, did more governments not work to restrict movie content?

First, as we have seen, many of the pressure groups in favor of censorship remained divided on the best method—whether censorship should be entrusted to local, state, federal, or voluntary censors. Such division weakened their ability to pressure legislators. Second, by 1926, movies were subjected to preexhibition censorship not only in seven states but also in at least one hundred municipalities in twenty-three other states.[54] The presence of censorship in so many large metropolitan centers, like Chicago, Memphis, Dallas, Atlanta, and Detroit, helps to explain why other states declined to enter the censoring business. There were about thirty film exchanges, most serving two or more states, so a film cut for a state or city with censorship was distributed in its stripped-down version to neighboring cities and states as well. The energetic censors of Chicago, for example, probably made Illinois legislators confident that their rural constituents were also adequately protected. Adding the states with municipal censorship to the censoring states makes it clear that at least thirty of the forty-eight states were directly covered. Moreover, since production was centralized (and became more so as the decades went on), and because the seven censoring states often shared information, the film industry was subject to a national censorship of sorts that has gone mostly unrecognized.

That censors in different locales could object to different elements made the censorship that much more restrictive. The result of the years of procensorite lobbying was the creation of local and state censorship boards that operated—some haphazardly, some diligently—throughout the United States, interfering with the profitability, intellectual freedom, and artistic output of America's most visible industry. A third factor has to do with public relations. After a two-thirds majority voted down the censorship proposal in Massachusetts, Hays and others could claim that censorship was unpopular. And, finally, the public housekeeping campaigns that Hollywood undertook in 1922, 1930, and 1934 helped convince legislators that there was no longer any real reason for concern, and the moral panic passed. Bills continued to be introduced on a regular basis, but Virginia was the last state to create a censorship board.

Although all of these bills were passed in the name of the people and what was best for them, it is important to note that there is no evidence of a strong groundswell of opinion favoring motion picture censorship.[55] But pressure groups, religious organizations, and social welfare clubs demanded censorship. And there were many of them, including the New York Society for the Suppression of Vice, the WCTU, the YMCA, the Christian Endeavor, the Protestant Church, the Catholic Church, the League of American Mothers, the National Congress of Mothers, the Society for the Prevention of Cruelty to Children, the General Federation of Women's Clubs, the Watch and Ward Society, the National Association of Colored Women, and the International Reform Bureau.[56] It is difficult to imagine that legislators would have come to the decision to start censoring films without these groups' activism.

Motion Picture Distributors Are Left Holding the Bag

Progressive reformers may have preferred general statutes for maximum flexibility of application, but this meant that film distributors faced laws whose enforcement they could not accurately predict. This was a new problem for the legal culture. Motion pictures were like no other products being regulated because they dealt with abstractions, very difficult concepts to nail down for control purposes. The need for statutory specificity would not be recognized in the courts until the mid-twentieth century, and it would come to light then largely because of free speech arguments put forth by religious groups, public speakers, publishers, and movie distributors.

Not only were distributors facing uncertainty in the early censoring years, they were paying for the privilege. License fees were paid not by the studios or the exhibitors but by the distributors—the central characters in the story of film censorship. Early in its development, the industry adopted an independent distribution system to satisfy the demand for rapid turnover of motion pictures in the nation's theaters. Studios had little interest in peddling their films to thousands of individual theaters. And local theater owners needed lots of films for frequent marquee changes. Entrepreneurs soon stepped in and began buying motion pictures from studios to rent to theaters. Renting them to theater after theater, these distributors could continue to make money from films until they wore out.[57]

This early distribution system, in which a film exchange bought a film and the rights to rent it out within a certain territory, was called *states' rights*. It was a fixed-fee system—the producer got the same amount whether he created an excellent film or rubbish—so there was little incentive to improve the quality or increase the appeal of films. Paramount, owned by five distributors who together controlled 80 percent of the nation's market, instituted a new system in the 1910s, charging a percentage of the ticket sales as rental. Films that sold more theater seats put more money back into distributors' and producers' pockets. This system of independent distribution exists today with minor modifications. While a distributor handles getting the actual reels of finished film into theaters' projectors, he can also invest in independent productions, boosting the budget available for those films, taking a percentage of the rental fees up front, and then sharing the remainder with the producer.[58]

In the early years, distributors were well situated to make money. Exhibitors needed distributors' films, and producers needed to get their films into theaters. As downtown theaters became more lavish in their construction and amenities in the 1910s and 1920s, distributors categorized them by profit potential. The most elaborate theaters got the most expensive productions first. After the first-run theaters were done with them, the films were released to smaller theaters in poorer neighborhoods. As this system grew, so too did the importance and the power of the distributors.

Adolph Zukor, of Famous Players–Lasky Corporation, innovated another surefire way of making money: block booking. To dump lower-quality, more cheaply made productions on theater owners, Zukor packaged the lesser films with sure seaters like Mary Pickford features. Under block booking, the theater owner had no choices. He took the whole batch of the distributor's films, often as many as ten, or he took none. Since Zukor had so many of the era's most popular stars, large theaters were forced to do business with him.[59]

When Zukor began to buy up theaters, other companies followed suit. By the 1930s, five of the eight major studios were approaching complete vertical integration, controlling production, distribution, and exhibition. The major studios bought and constructed so many theaters that they soon controlled 70 percent of the nation's box office.[60] The distribution system tied exhibitors' hands: those theaters affiliated with studios had to take their productions, while independent theater owners were beset by the strictures of block booking, forced to rent unwanted films or to lease ones they had not seen in order to get the heavily publicized star vehicles they needed to fill their seats.

The block booking system of the major studios also left the producers far less concerned about the quality of the product and the impact of governmental censors on film content. Producers could afford to create films that complied with most censor dictates without worrying about lessened artistic content, a situation that goes far toward explaining why major Hollywood studios acquiesced in the governmental censorship practiced across the country.

Conditions were quite different for independent filmmakers and distributors, however. Shut out of the majority of first-run theaters until the 1950s, independents had little chance to strike it big with any picture. Independent distributors were left with B movies—films made on low budgets with low profit expectations—or foreign films that had slim audience appeal until the 1950s. Stiff licensing fees cut into all distributors' profits: three dollars per reel (a typical feature film was about ten reels) in the large New York market, a bit lower in Virginia, somewhat higher in Ohio. And this cost covered only the first copy of the movie—additional prints of the film cost more.

Large distributors, such as those owned by the Hollywood studios, had large numbers of duplicate prints for simultaneous openings. This meant that they paid a large percentage of the state's overall censorship fees. But smaller distributors, some with fewer than ten films per year to market, paid a much larger percentage of their budgets to the state for censorship fees. For example, a small distributor in New York State in 1936 would have paid seventy dollars for three prints of a ten-reel film, equivalent to more than one thousand dollars today. A major distributor could toss off the censorship fee as "a negligible burden,"[61] but his smaller, independent competitors would not echo that sentiment. The feeling that they were paying more than their fair share may account for some of the independent distributors' dedication to fighting censorship.

Seven States, Seven Censorship Boards

While some exhibitors welcomed governmental censorship as a buffer against local patron protest, those who worked in the national marketplace—studio heads, producers, and distributors—found themselves facing seven different state boards with seven different viewpoints. While all the boards operated under similar mandates—censoring film scenes that were immoral, inhuman, sacrilegious, obscene, indecent, or likely to incite viewers to crime—all the state mandates were undefined. What constituted immoral content in a Kansas censor's mind might be perfectly moral to a censor in New York. How was a film producer to know for certain what an Ohio censor meant by *harmful*? Moreover, when censors resigned or were removed from office in patronage turnovers, how could movie distributors predict the reactions of the censors who replaced them? It is difficult to imagine other businesses in the United States accepting such an uncertain regulatory environment, yet Hollywood acquiesced. The uncertainty with censorship was preferable to the certainty of pressure group action without it.

Occasionally, a director of the censors granted an interview or made a speech that shed some light on their interpretations of the statute. In 1928, for example, New York State Motion Picture Division director James Wingate tried to clarify the meaning of the statutory language for a reporter. Wingate defined *inhuman* as "those scenes in which even the realism or authenticity of the action does not warrant their exhibition." He gave as an example "an ancient slave ship or galley in which the slaves or other prisoners were indecently treated or brutally beaten; a scene that might add materially to the realism of the film but would hardly meet with the general approval of the public."[62] So any film producer considering a scene on a slave ship was forewarned, but everyone else was still in the dark.

Most state boards consisted of three appointed censors with support staffs of salaried reviewers who were state employees. Except in New York and Ohio, the censors were political appointees. Positions on the political censorship boards became valuable patronage plums, usually given to people with little or no expertise in the film industry—not the administrative experts at judging film content that earnest procensorites had envisioned. Censors in Pennsylvania, Maryland, Virginia, and Kansas were often friends or neighbors of the sitting governors. Dr. Ellis Oberholtzer, the head of the Pennsylvania censor board during its formative years, openly admitted that that he knew "little indeed" about movies when his friend, the governor, offered him the position of head censor.[63] Three decades later, not much had changed. A Pennsylvania censor admitted that "the only requirement in the [censorship] act is that the censors be 'decent, moral people.'"[64]

Because the positions did not require special qualifications, it was easy for most state legislatures to pay censors low salaries. The jobs were usually taken by politically connected women. In Kansas, where salaries were the lowest, only one man served during the board's fifty-year history.[65]

Only New York and Ohio required their censors to be civil servants with specified qualifications. Although both states originally utilized political appointees, in the late 1920s, they reorganized their boards and placed them under the control of their education departments. There they became civil servants, and they became faceless. As bureaucrats, the censors went underground, with only the chief censor remaining publicly visible. Virginia also reorganized its system, abolishing its original board and reinstating the censors under its department of law, supervised by the state's attorney general. But the censorship jobs remained patronage plums for the governor to award.

Personnel records on most state censors are unavailable, but the files kept on each film reviewed in New York provide a paper trail of sorts.[66] New York censors were mid- and low-level civil servants with college educations and "knowledge of history, literature, and a foreign language." They were to have "high standards of morality without intolerance, a good sense of justice, mature judgment, good address, and the ability to deal impartially with motion picture producers and distributors without arousing antagonism." Knowledge of film or psychology or educational theory, which might have informed their decisions, was not required. The remarkably low turnover suggests that reviewers found the work tolerable. And on those rare occasions when vacancies did open, the position attracted hoards of job seekers.[67] During the 1930s, the New York board was composed of four reviewers, all women, and two theater inspectors, both men. All but one of those reviewers and inspectors were still there at least as late as 1948. Of the six employees, five remained on the job for more than sixteen years.[68]

Tenure records in Ohio are even more impressive. By 1954, the Ohio board's last full year of operation, chief censor Susannah Warfield had been on the job for thirty-one years, and her assistant had been with her for twelve.[69] Warfield was both exceedingly loyal to the censor board and exceptionally energetic. The *Columbus Dispatch* described her in 1954 as a "Puritan" who believed it her duty to "see to it that no movies are shown in Ohio that would lead a single child astray."[70] The last censors of Virginia, Mrs. Wagers, Mrs. Whitehead, and Mrs. Gregory (all well over the age of sixty), had a total of thirty-seven years of censoring experience when that board was shut down in 1966. According to the *Roanoke Times*, no Virginia censor had ever retired.[71]

Even though censor turnover was generally low, we cannot assume that the censors exercised any degree of consistency in evaluating material. Film review slips note only the physical locations of objectionable passages on the reels. Since the originals of these films are long gone, it is impossible to assess the quality or the uniformity of censoring.

In the early years, censors were neither particularly well qualified nor necessarily enlightened about their work. When the *New York Times* asked the first chairman of New York's censor board, George H. Cobb, what the principles of censorship were, he replied, "So far, I haven't been able to find any."[72] Ironically, the ineffective and voluntary National Board of Review had far more definite guidelines for its work than did the legislatively empowered experts of these state censor boards. When, in 1925, one movie distributor wrote the New York board for clarification of what was censorable, Cobb haughtily declined the request, responding only, "Each picture is judged on its merits and if you have any pictures on which you want our opinion, we would suggest that you apply to have them licensed and pay the customary fee and you will receive our decision."[73]

Movie distributors thus could face differing reactions to the same movie. In the 1930s, the Ohio board refused to license a harmless movie called *Springtime for Henry* because a character in the film mentions that in France it is not illegal for a wife to shoot her husband. Massachusetts decreed that a scene of two people lying on the ground could not be shown on Sunday. Pennsylvania would not allow women to be shown pregnant or engaged in knitting baby booties.[74] Kansas required deletion of a speech that turned out to be paraphrased from an actual speech delivered by Pope Pius XI. Ohio censored a 1937 Russian film, *A Greater Promise*, because "the picture encourages social and racial equality, thereby stirring up racial hatred. . . . All the above doctrines are contrary to accepted codes of American life."[75] With pronouncements like this, it is no wonder that film distributors had trouble predicting what would pass and what would have to be cut to get a license.

Even the types of materials that were subject to censorship were not uniform. Newsreels, for example, were censored in all the states at first but were exempted in New York by 1926. Pennsylvania and Ohio gave up on newsreels only when forced to do so by state court decisions (in Ohio's case not until 1952).[76] In most states, only commercially exhibited films were subject to censorship, but Ohio considered even films shown in public schools and church basements fair game. Pennsylvania censored *Felix the Cat* and all other premovie cartoons.

This jumble of regulations made business difficult for producers, but it was the distributor who faced economic losses when a censor board held up a film by ordering that certain "eliminations" be made or rejected the film "in toto." When eliminations were ordered, the distributor was invited to return the edited film for further screening before a license was issued. The cuts were always made at the distributor's expense. The independent distributor who had a few copies of a film to rent around the state could ill afford the expense and time lost in reediting a film for further review by a censor board.

If a distributor's film was rejected in toto, he had several routes of appeal. In New York, for example, he could request a rescreening by the director of the motion picture division. If he failed to charm the director into a different determination, he could then appeal to the censors' overseers, the Board of Regents of the University of the State of New York. A committee of three regents would then view the film and take legal arguments pro and con. If the distributor had no luck with the regents (which was routinely the case until the 1950s), he could bring suit against the censors in the New York State Supreme Court, Appellate Division. If the appellate division justices disagreed with him (which they always did until the 1950s), he could then try his luck with New York's highest court, the court of appeals. Failing there, his only recourse was to apply to the U.S. Supreme Court. Four intrepid distributors took this long route trying to get their films shown in New York. Many other distributors, however, appealed to the board of regents, and they usually gave up afterward. Other states had similar appeals procedures, proceeding first to a rescreening by the chief censor, then to the board's supervisors, and then to the courts.

In all the states, the appeals process reversed the usual burden of proof of the American legal system, placing it on the distributor—the person who wished to communicate—rather than on the government. It was up to the distributor to prove that his film was worthy—a difficult, expensive, and time-consuming burden.

If the distributor was successful and the film was found to have been incorrectly judged by the censors, no provision existed to compensate the distributor in any way, either for his lost time or his legal expenses. For the few who fought state censors, the delay could run into years, and an appeal could rack up tens of thousands of dollars. On top of that, the distributor had an investment tied up in a film that he could not rent. By the time the film was released, it could be years old and worth little.

Aside from the obvious economic losses it forced the distributor to incur, the system of prior censorship interfered with the public discourse. First, it kept censored ideas from reaching the marketplace of ideas. Second, since such decisions were made behind the scenes, only egregious cases of abuse had any chance of being brought to public attention. Closed-door decisions about what people could see effectively kept the public from having any input. For example, by 1940, New York had forced changes in more than three thousand movies, yet only seven distributors had publicly questioned the censors' determinations by litigation.[77] Prior restraint certainly succeeded at keeping censorship issues from the light of public scrutiny.

The provision of an appeal process allowed the censors to wrap themselves in a mantle of fairness. After all, if the censors made a mistake, the distributor could appeal. But, in reality, the appeals procedure, with its cost and inevitable delay, operated as a powerful disincentive to challenge the censors' actions. And the courts would provide no relief for decades.

2

The Courts Provide No Relief, 1909–1927

America's first movie censorship law—Chicago's—became the first challenged in court. And the judiciary welcomed movie regulation with open arms: America's legal culture was right in step with those who wished to control movies. The courts accepted the potent harm-to-minors arguments that had been used by the procensorites to get statutes like Chicago's passed. Prevailing legal doctrine on obscenity at the turn of the twentieth century still rested on an 1868 British ruling (*Regina v. Hicklin*) that had carved in legal stone the idea that anything corruptive of youth (even if found in an isolated part of a work of fine art) should be banned for all.[1] American courts did not begin to reconsider this enduring legal construct of obscenity until 1915, and the Supreme Court made no substantive change until 1957.

The City Council of Chicago had not specified what types of obscenity its police chief was to ban. But specificity did seem necessary to film distributor Jake Block, who, in 1909, argued that the ordinance was too vague because it offered no way to test the police chief's determination that a film was immoral or obscene. The answer Block got from the Illinois Supreme Court did not augur well for the new film industry. Chief Justice James H. Cartwright unveiled the argument that censor opponents would hear repeatedly from the courts when he told Block, "The average person of healthy and wholesome mind knows well enough what the words 'immoral' and 'obscene' mean and can intelligently apply the test to any picture presented to him."[2] Cartwright's judicial philosophy, that definitions and standards were unnecessary, prevailed in the courts for forty-four more years.

Motion picture censorship took root in an era when faith in legislatively empowered public servants was so pervasive that their judgments were rarely overturned in American courts. Moreover, the judiciary had little sympathy for free speech claims, especially if there was any hint that the speech in question might lead to criminal behavior. Speech was seen as an individual right and as such always subservient to society's right to public order. So any speech that could be deemed offensive or potentially inflammatory was outside the pale of protection. Before 1925, judicial concern over speech restriction was so minimal that despite the Fourteenth Amendment's protection of liberty against arbitrary state action, the Supreme Court did not apply the provisions of the First Amendment to any state statutes. Only in 1925 did the Court begin the process of forcing state laws to conform to the constitutional guarantees of free speech and free press, and even then, the only speech the Court considered worthy of protection was political speech that did not incite to crime. Commercial speech, obscenity, blasphemy, profanity, and libel were excluded from First Amendment protection.

Few Americans were troubled by this interpretation. Even those few legal scholars and political activists who advocated for a more expansive interpretation of speech rights were perfectly comfortable with restrictions on obscenity, sacrilege, and profanity.[3] Some constitutional scholars have argued that the founders never intended the First Amendment to apply to the states; indeed, that the First Amendment was specifically intended to encourage the states to regulate speech.[4] If that was true, then motion picture censorship was a proper and expected exercise of the state's power to protect its citizens. In any event, the courts were uninterested in First Amendment claims against state restrictions of speech, and, as David Rabban has shown, prior to World War I, no court was less interested in free speech and free press claims than the U.S. Supreme Court.[5]

That did not stop another film distributor, Mutual Film Corporation, from trying to get a case before the Supreme Court. Mutual set out to test the normative view of free speech before a historically unreceptive judiciary. It would learn that in 1915, even a national industry like the movies could expect no protection from the First Amendment.

Started by Hollywood pioneer Harry Aitken, Mutual Film was a consortium of independent film studios, a producer of newsreels, and a well-financed national distributor. Aitken's company was profitable, with sixty local film exchanges across the country. Its profitability rested on a marketing strategy that released new films on the same day in many states. But with censorship review a reality in Pennsylvania, Ohio, and Kansas,

Mutual was concerned that films in these states would be delayed, ruining their carefully orchestrated openings. Moreover, Mutual was forced to pay for the privilege of having its films delayed. The company decided to take legal action. Aitken was clearly worried that censorship would spread to every state. "It would be nearly impossible to run a film distribution concern profitably," he complained. "For what pleases one censor displeases another, and the manufacturer cannot possibly meet the varying requirements of them all."[6] In a gutsy display of corporate defiance, Mutual filed suit against all three states as well as the City of Chicago. Other film distributors were watching, worried that a court defeat would mean the spread of movie censorship along with its licensing fees and inevitable delays.[7]

Mutual's case against Pennsylvania foreshadowed many of the later film censorship challenges. Borrowing an argument from the liquor interests fighting against dry laws in the pre-Prohibition era, Mutual tried to use the original package doctrine to argue against state censorship.[8] Since film reels were manufactured outside Pennsylvania and shipped into the state in their original containers, Mutual argued, they should be subject only to regulation under the federal government's interstate commerce powers. In a legal tour de force, Mutual also charged that Pennsylvania's license fee imposed an excessive tax; that the statute violated due process by keeping companies from freely renting their merchandise; that by imposing arbitrary determinations on their films, the legislature had incorrectly delegated legislative powers to an administrative body; and that the review of films restrained "the right of plaintiffs to freely write and publish their sentiments, guaranteed by the Constitution."[9] This last contention was daring. As legal scholar John Wertheimer has pointed out, Americans had long accepted governmental restraints on theatrical exhibitions. During the nineteenth century, many states restricted performances by requiring them to be approved in advance.[10]

However impressive the scope of Mutual's arguments, the Pennsylvania Supreme Court was not moved. Motion picture censorship was a valid exercise of the police power of the state, "enacted to conserve the morals and manners of the public," the court said. Mutual's appeal to the federal interstate commerce power fell flat when the judges held that laws to promote the "peace, safety, good order, [and] health interests of the State" could not be superseded by the federal government. In effect, the film exchanges learned that attempts to use the U.S. Constitution's protections of free speech, free press, and due process would not work in

Pennsylvania as long as the state legislature was acting to protect the morals of its citizens. Since the Bill of Rights restricted only the actions of the federal government and not those of state legislatures, these film distributors could find no redress within the U.S. Constitution for the business they did within Pennsylvania. In a refrain that would become familiar as film censorship challenges dragged on, Mutual heard that "the promotion of public morals and public health is a chief function of government . . . and the largest legislative discretion [should be] allowed."[11]

Mutual also confronted Ohio, but there it chose a federal district court rather than a state court, perhaps hoping that its interstate commerce argument—and an added appeal to the First Amendment—would receive a warmer reception. Appealing to the First Amendment was truly innovative, for it would be another decade before the Supreme Court began to consider that the Bill of Rights could be applied to any laws except those passed by Congress. This venue shopping reveals the savvy of Mutual's attorneys and the seriousness of the attack they mounted. Since Mutual was not only a film distributor but also a newsreel producer, the Mutual attorneys argued that Ohio's censorship offended the free press guarantee of the First Amendment as well as the Ohio constitution's provision against restraint of the press. But the federal judges rejected all of Mutual's arguments. The original package contention was summarily dismissed: the judges ruled that when films were removed from their shipping containers and placed upon projectors, they became intermingled in the state's commerce. The judges also rejected Mutual's First Amendment claim and insisted that the State of Ohio was fully within its rights to regulate the "public evils" that "grew" out of motion pictures. "What court can rightfully say," the judges asked, "either that such evils do not exist, or that the measures adopted are not reasonably designed to correct the evils?"[12] Thus the federal court was unable to find any merit in Mutual's assertions, and Ohio's censoring law, like Pennsylvania's, passed constitutional muster.

Mutual had one more state to go. As it had in the other state cases, Mutual attacked Kansas's statute as a burden on interstate commerce, a restriction on free speech, and an unlawful delegation of legislative authority.[13] The Kansas judges were not impressed with Mutual's arguments, either. But their opinion was not to be the last word. Mutual's request for review by the U.S. Supreme Court was granted. The highest court in the nation was about to consider, for the first time, the issue of freedom and mass media.[14]

The U.S. Supreme Court Confronts Motion Picture Censorship

The censor statutes of Pennsylvania, Kansas, Ohio, and Chicago had all passed their first judicial tests, but the U.S. Supreme Court had not yet spoken. In the lower courts, Mutual had used both economic and free speech arguments, but when the company prepared its arguments for the U.S. Supreme Court, it decided that the free speech issue was paramount. More than 80 percent of Mutual's brief argued infringement of free speech. Considering the hostility of the Supreme Court toward free speech claims, this was either amazingly courageous or downright foolish.

First, Mutual questioned the interstate commerce burdens and statutory vagueness, but the justices rejected both of these claims outright. As in *Block v. Chicago*, the justices held that imprecise terminology was no basis for overturning a law. Mutual next contended that Ohio's statute violated the Constitution's protection of property rights. Since the Ohio censors reached a determination about each film without a public hearing or judicial action, Mutual maintained, the denial of an exhibition license meant that the company had been deprived of its property (i.e., the film's potential to earn money) without due process of law, a violation of the Fourteenth Amendment. The property-venerating judiciary would be more likely to hear this argument sympathetically. Finally, Mutual got to the heart of its argument when it asserted that movies as "publications of ideas" should be considered part of the press and should enjoy the free speech and free press protections of the Ohio constitution. The company argued that newsreels, which were nonfiction, were clearly part of the press and therefore entitled to freedom from prior restraint.[15] While Mutual was clearly concerned with its bottom line, its attorneys also pulled out all the constitutional issues they could muster, including an impassioned appeal to free speech values. Their suits, a creative and fervent attempt to expand free speech rights, wound up striking a major blow to the motion picture industry.

Writing for the unanimous Court in 1915, Justice Joseph McKenna found the free speech argument inconsistent with both "judicial sense" and "common sense." Since movies could be used for evil as well as for good, he wrote, their examination prior to exhibition was a necessary control.

> It cannot be put out of view that the exhibition of moving pictures is a business pure and simple, originated and conducted for profit, like other spectacles, not to be regarded, nor intended to be regarded by the Ohio constitution, we think, as part of the press of the country or as organs of public opinion. They are mere representations of events, of ideas and sentiments published and known, vivid, useful and entertaining no doubt, but, as we have said, capable of evil, having power for it, the greater because of their attractiveness and manner of exhibition.[16]

The *Mutual* decision was a major victory for the censors; it stamped their legislatively empowered status with new judicial legitimacy. In their first at bat with film censorship, the justices had come down squarely on the side of governmental control (perhaps not surprisingly—player piano rolls in 1908 and telephone privacy in 1928 also lost their first appeals for judicial protection[17]). Although some historians have criticized the 1915 ruling as wrongly decided, it was made by a unanimous bench and was widely endorsed at the time by the legal community.[18] Those who look back at *Mutual* and see a reactionary judiciary fail to consider its context. First, the legal culture was not ready to consider entertainment as speech (i.e., as expression worthy of protection). Others who had tried to expand the Court's horizons on protected speech—including ministers, government employees, and crime reporters—had failed.[19] It would not be until 1946 that the Supreme Court expanded the concept of speech to include entertainment.[20] More specifically, the Court was not ready for arguments that movies deserved First Amendment speech protections. Second, Americans and their courts had long accepted restrictions on theatrical performances. As we have seen, state and local laws allowed for the prior restraint of exhibitions. The justices would have found little evidence to convince them that films were any different. Third, since Supreme Court justices are never immune from public opinion, widely publicized moral panic over movie content at the time would have encouraged a vote to restrict movie content. Movies made by men who had little allegiance to any ideals of high culture were enjoying a popularity that looked to many people like "an epidemic utterly out of control."[21] Fourth, progressives of the early twentieth century had a strong belief in the ability of legislatively empowered experts, like film censors, to protect society. These progressives believed that the good of society was more important than the rights of any individual. With their concerns about film content, their acceptance of controls on other exhibitions, and their belief that censors could benefit society, it is little wonder that Mutual Film lost. That the case stood as precedent for almost four decades, however, is another matter.

The decision is understandable but is also easily criticized. It is probably most vulnerable in its argument that movies are a business and therefore not entitled to free speech protections. Such a stance seems indefensible because newspapers and magazines, both of which were businesses conducted for profit, were free from prior restraint. Moreover, the courts were highly sympathetic to complaints that business regulation violated property rights. That the Supreme Court permitted infringement on the property rights of the movie business reveals an inconsistency possible only because the justices believed that movies carried an extraordinary capacity for evil. There is little question that the Ohio statute interfered with Mutual Film and would cost the company a great deal of money and wasted time. The Court's acceptance of such interference in a business enterprise reveals both the justices' belief in legislative wisdom and their concern that society was being led astray by amoral, politically motivated movie producers. Since early silent films were not only daring but also more political than films at any other time in motion picture history, the decision may have been motivated by the desire (of conservative, elite judges) to slap down an overtly message-filled medium (made by non-elites).[22]

A small but vocal group of eminent legal scholars who argued against prior restraint on speech began to question *Mutual* not long after the opinion was read. Ernst Freund, Roscoe Pound, Henry Schofield, Thomas Cooley, and Theodore Schroeder all wrote tirelessly in favor of speech rights, hoping to affect state, local, and federal judges. Although they were mostly ignored, they represented the growing number of intellectuals who questioned the restrictions on free speech, a group that continued to push for a more expansive interpretation of the First Amendment.

Nevertheless, *Mutual* became a longstanding precedent, the kind that justices are loath to overrule. Starting with the New York State Supreme Court, which eagerly adopted the special-capacity-for-evil mantra seven years later, judges held up the decision as precedent. It was cited in thirteen Supreme Court cases and twenty-one federal district court cases, and it was repeatedly cited as justification for upholding the censors of every censoring state.

The Mutual Film Corporation had gambled in a high-stakes legal game and lost. But the stakes were even higher for those who followed. The decision gave to prior censorship bodies "an aura of judicial approval"[23] that lasted for decades, and pressure groups like the WCTU, still hoping for federal censorship, gained new momentum. Movie moguls began considering self-regulation of movie content because the *Mutual* decision left them vulnerable to attack by all sorts of antimovie lobbies. And one of the moguls' anticensorship arguments was seriously weakened: hereafter they would stand on unsure ground if they characterized new censorship proposals as un-American, since the concept now had the high court's blessing. Between 1916 and 1922, a reenergized censorship movement went on the attack. Film men had to mobilize against congressional proposals for federal oversight of movie content seven times by 1920[24] and against state bills dozens more. Immediately after the *Mutual* decision, Maryland joined Pennsylvania, Kansas, and Ohio as the fourth censoring state. Each time the motion picture industry claimed that movies were no different from other media, reformers intoned the *Mutual* decision as legal proof that movies were indeed different—and harmful.[25]

The true weight of the *Mutual* decision, however, was neither in the decision itself nor in subsequent statute enactments but in later courts' reluctance to tamper with it. Decided in 1915, when motion pictures were still primitive, *Mutual* controlled the legal discussions on prior restraint of film long after the arrival of talkies and even color.

Mutual's Influence

Mutual's long career as a precedent began in 1921 when a national film distributor tried to challenge it in the New York state courts. Having existed for only three weeks, the New York State Motion Picture Commission (as the board of censors was known until 1926) found itself challenged by Pathé Exchange over a newsreel about a new type of portable bath house for public beaches. One of the young ladies in the newsreel appeared in a one-piece bathing suit (rather than the standard bathing dress), and for this, the censors refused a license.[26] Pathé's attorneys, recognizing that censorship of newsreel footage would be a constant irritant to their client's business, chose to go straight to the heart of the matter. The company questioned the constitutionality of New York's prior restraint of a news medium. It ignored the easier, narrow issue of whether the specific newsreel in question was immoral.

New York's appellate division ruled against Pathé eleven months later, dismissing the argument that newsreels, like newspapers, should be entitled to the free press guarantees of the First Amendment. The New York justices declared that they found the Supreme Court's logic in the *Mutual* decision compelling. A newsreel was different from a newspaper, the justices agreed, because it was more "spectacle or show" than a medium of opinion. The justices intoned the oft-repeated concern that children and illiterates might be harmed by the moving picture's allure and transparency. "Nothing is left to the imagination as with the printed page," the opinion read. "The picture creates its own atmosphere so vividly, so attractively, that even the child and the illiterate adult may see and learn."[27] Not satisfied, Pathé decided to try the state court of appeals. But without further opinion, New York's highest court confirmed the lower court.[28] Considering the U.S. Supreme Court's position just eight years earlier in *Mutual*, a further appeal would have been foolhardy. Pathé retreated, presumably to more acceptable subjects. The *Mutual* precedent was daunting, and for thirty more years, even trained constitutional lawyers would not try to win film censorship cases by pleading First Amendment protection.

The weight of the *Mutual* decision was felt not only in lower courts, legislative halls, and hearing rooms but also in Hollywood. The year following the decision, Hollywood created the National Association of the Motion Picture Industry. Trying to present a unified front against its critics, NAMPI included all the segments of the trade—producers, distributors, exhibitors, supply companies, trade papers, actors, insurance companies, and advertising agents. One of NAMPI's first concerns was finding a way to deal with *Mutual*. It first considered a constitutional amendment to guarantee freedom of the screen, but the proposal went nowhere in Congress. Thwarted constitutionally, NAMPI turned to image enhancement. During World War I, the moviemakers coordinated efforts with George Creel's Committee on Public Information, the wartime propaganda agency. Hollywood began turning out patriotic movies and using theater lobbies for recruitment and bond drives. The effort was so spectacular that Hollywood succeeding in winning friends all over the hostile political and social landscape as the United States entered and fought the war.[29]

But while NAMPI's patriotic war efforts won the industry new friends, the National Board of Review, always suspect among moral reformers for its lenience, was gaining new critics. Revelations about the board's Hollywood-based funding crippled the reviewers, and it could no longer help the moguls stave off criticism of movie content. NAMPI came up with a brilliant solution that enabled it to quell the carping while keeping its studios out of trouble with governmental censors. It marketed the Thirteen Points—a list of subjects that were to be proscribed in the interest of the greater good—as a major housecleaning, a plan to create only wholesome pictures. The list included sex (which actually meant seduction or kissing), nudity, white slavery, crime, gambling, drunkenness, narcotics use, ridicule of public officials and governmental authority, disrespect for religion, and gratuitous violence[30]—all subjects that state and local censors had repressed. By trumpeting this new self-cleaning mechanism, the movie moguls were able both to mollify their critics by appearing virtuous and simultaneously to warn members away from governmental censors' hot buttons.

Thus began a long parade of lists, proscriptions, committees, and other attempts by Hollywood to make itself appear respectable whenever its moral critics rose up in complaint. Throughout this dance between moviemakers and moral guardians, Hollywood persistently bowed to the dictates of others. More concerned with the business of making films than the art of making films, the studio heads could ill afford to butt heads with vocal and organized critics. But the independent distributors who had purchased the rights to single films could not so easily acquiesce to the wishes of others without major financial losses. Hollywood bent to the cultural winds; independent distributors did not.

Early Challengers

Most of the early censorship challenge cases came in New York: the state found itself challenged in court four times in the first three years. The distributors lost every case but one. As they began a losing streak that would last through World War II, the distributors found themselves not only spending a great deal on legal expenses but also enduring major delays. In most censoring states, appeals of censors' decisions went first to a local court and then to a statewide appellate court. New York's court system was different, with two levels of appeals courts rather than one supreme court. Film censorship appeals beyond the board of regents in New York bypassed local courts and went first to the appellate division of the state's supreme court. If either party chose to appeal further, the case then proceeded to New York's highest court, the court of appeals. Only after a ruling by the court of appeals could the losing party petition to be heard by the U.S. Supreme Court. Seven of the cases against censorship in New York State appealed beyond the appellate division to the court of appeals, and four cases went to the U.S. Supreme Court.

New York's first legal challenge came from its newsreel censoring, in the Pathé case described above. Before the New York censors had issued their first eight hundred licenses, they found themselves facing another challenge, this time from a feature film. Goldwyn Distributing Corporation took issue with the censors' refusal to license *The Night Rose* (1921) on the ground that it "might tend to corrupt morals or incite to crime." Starring Lon Cheney, this crime drama about "the evils of political corruption" contained several scenes of police bribery and official corruption as well as illegal drunken reveling, complete with nude dancers.

Other producers and distributors closely watched Goldwyn's appeal over *The Night Rose*. If it succeeded, others planned to challenge their license refusals both in New York and in other states.[31] But the appellate division justices viewed the film (which later benches would refuse to do) and pronounced it just as the censors had determined: hazardous to morals and a motivator to crime.[32] Since Goldwyn Distributing had not raised any constitutional issues and the decision was unanimous, the distributor had no further legal recourse in New York State.[33] *The Night Rose* was never shown there.[34] The censors cheered the decision and assured the public that the precedent would fend off many future challenges through its "moral force."[35]

The next film to challenge the New York censors came to the state with plenty of bad advance publicity. *Fate* (1921) had two significant problems as far as censors were concerned: it was a true story about a deplorable murder, and it starred the actual murderer. Clara Hamon, the film's star and producer, had been acquitted of killing her husband even though she freely admitted shooting him and the murder had been publicized in newspapers across the country. When Hamon decided to make and star in a movie about her story, the public was outraged. Although the scenarist took great pains to remove any salacious details and play up the lessons to be learned from the story, many censors and government officials refused to watch the picture.[36] It arrived in New York complete with testimonial letters from Jewish, Protestant, and Catholic clergy who had been impressed by the moral of the story, but the censors were not swayed, and they refused to issue the license. The distributor appealed to the appellate division, which ruled six months later without opinion that the motion picture commission's determination had been correct. For the third time, the New York court had upheld its censors.[37]

The last of the four early challenges suggested that New York's appellate division had a better appreciation for comedy than the state's censors. A short feature from producer Hal Roach and Pathé Exchange, *Good Riddance* (1923), was censored on the ground that it was "inhuman" and "would incite to crime." According to a *New York Times* editorial, the comedy's gags included tying a stick of dynamite to the tail of a dog that was then thrown out of an airplane. "No doubt a good many of our restless and inciteable youth might imitate these things, if they could get hold of the airplane and the dynamite. . . . Anyhow, these scenes were plainly humorous, and the producers have taken the case to the courts to see if Judges are as dull as censors."[38] Without opinion (although, one would hope, with a chuckle), the appellate division reversed the commission.

This win for a distributor (the only one until after World War II) did not open a floodgate of producers and distributors challenging censorship determinations, even though many films were cut or rejected outright during the 1920s. In 1924, the year after the *Good Riddance* overturn, the censors rejected thirty-four films in toto. Over the next three years, they banned thirty more.[39] Still, no film distributor challenged the New York censors for another six years. The number of distributors requesting review of an adverse decision dropped each year until 1928, after which it dropped again until 1931. The percentage of films required to make changes, though, remained relatively constant. It seems likely that the studios were realizing that appeals were pointless.[40]

For the distributors who handled independent productions and foreign films, however, censorship meant more than just expense and delay; it posed a major threat to existence by taking a large part of their inventory out of circulation. Few independents were willing to take on New York State and its bureaucracy, but after 1928, six chose to fight protracted battles despite the censors' earlier legal victories. Those challengers battled the censors in an exceedingly unfriendly legal culture with judges who routinely deferred to the "legislative will" concerning administrative actions. In a 1937 case, the Pennsylvania Supreme Court provided a perfect explanation: "However much we prize liberty, we must value democracy no less. The General Assembly of the Commonwealth of Pennsylvania—representative of the people—has found censorship desirable, and the courts have frequently sustained this expression of the popular will."[41] In such a legal culture, individual rights would continue to take a back seat to the majority view, expressed by the passage of legislation.

3

Hollywood and the Legion of Decency, 1922–1934

As successful and influential as the states' censoring was, the push for national censorship persisted into the 1930s. The major studios were willing to accept some censorship as a necessary component of doing business, but they lobbied against any further governmental censorship, rallying forces whenever federal legislation loomed. Although it might seem that a federal agency would have been easier to deal with than a myriad of state and local boards, the moguls feared that a federal censorship agency might lead to broader regulation of their product,[1] including their greatest fear: antitrust action. From the start, the American movie industry had had centralizing tendencies, and by the late 1920s, it had achieved a near monopoly over the major cities' screens through vertical integration.

The first serious attempts to establish federal censorship had failed to garner enough congressional votes in 1914 and again in 1916. But more legislative attempts were to come, mostly thanks to the movie colony's own behavior. State censorship satisfied some moral reformers, but others, some newly emerging in the late 1920s and 1930s, distrusted secular control and demanded nothing less than control at the source: that the studios police their own products before and during production. For these reformers, governmental censorship would not suffice. For still others, only governmental control at the national level would do. When the Thirteen Points did not work, Hollywood's trade organization adopted several types of content regulatory schemes, attempting to forestall any further governmental censorship and answer the demands of both its old and its new critics.

Some of the new criticism stemmed from the emerging star system.

Fan magazines fed by Hollywood publicists eager to promote their clients' every move and newspapers thirsty for shocking details about how the stars lived and played contributed to a new, voracious fan base.[2] But the publicity machine that was the industry's marketing friend in good times became its affliction in bad times. Fans were stunned to learn that America's sweetheart, Mary Pickford, had run off to Nevada for a quick divorce so she could marry her lover, Douglas Fairbanks. Popular comedian Fatty Arbuckle was charged and tried three times for the rape and murder of young starlet Virginia Rappe. He was never convicted, but the sordid rumors about the drunken party that led to Rappe's death ruined Arbuckle's career. Public outcry against him was so intense that many theaters voluntarily pulled his movies. Even the censorship-phobic Committee for Better Films of the National Board of Review authorized the banning of all Arbuckle films.[3] Then director William Desmond Taylor was found shot, possibly the victim of a love triangle, and the popular, clean-cut actor Wallace Reid died of a drug overdose. Relentlessly publicized across the nation, these scandals provided evidence for reformers' contentions that America needed protection from profit-hungry, amoral producers and their immoral actors.

Facing these new crises that needed aggressive handling, and smarting from its inability to stop the loss of the New York market to a censorship board, NAMPI disbanded, and the industry created the Motion Picture Producers and Distributors of America. Taking a cue from the baseball industry, which had also undergone a widely publicized scandal, movie moguls sought a politically connected, high-profile leader who could convince legislators and the American people that the movie industry could clean its own house (a cliché often used by the industry at the time). They chose Will Hays, a Washington insider with immaculate credentials: he was an elder in the Presbyterian Church and the former chair of the Republican National Committee, and he had agreed to resign as postmaster general of the United States to take the new position. As "movie czar," Hays immediately announced that "public censorship" would soon become unnecessary because the industry was on its way to enlightenment. "Too many people who know nothing about the business are named to censorship boards," he said. "We are going to obviate the necessity of censorship."[4]

In 1925, Hays faced a federal censorship proposal that contained worrisome provisions. The proposal gave a federal censor board the power to set film rental and theater ticket prices and established a national film distribution system in an attempt to extend the influence of the censoring states to the entire nation. Congress gave the bill extensive consideration but did not pass it.[5]

Recognizing that the Thirteen Points were no longer deflecting criticism, the MPPDA began sweeping itself up again amid great fanfare. A new list of banned topics to replace the Thirteen Points, called the "Don'ts and Be Carefuls," looked like a sincere blueprint for wholesome films, but in reality it was just another compilation of topics refused by state and local censors. Hays sent a copy of the list to every newspaper in the country, promising a new beginning.[6] It took just two years to see that Hays's plan was not working: 1929 saw a new high-water mark in governmental, censor-mandated cuts.[7] Clearly, the Hays Office was not doing a good job of helping producers anticipate the types of cuts that state censors were demanding, and many Protestant antimovie activists claimed that it was giving their concerns only lip service. In 1925, convinced that films were the number one moral decay issue, the WCTU had begun focusing all its censoring activities on film.[8] By 1929, the women of the WCTU were not impressed with either Hays or his list; they continued their calls for national censorship. In their temperance crusade, they had learned that it made no sense to cooperate with brewers; collaboration with movie producers, they now realized, was also futile.[9]

With the advent of talkies about the same time, Hollywood discovered more ways to get itself into trouble through the seductiveness of the human voice, the double entendre, and the veiled, sexually charged joke. Gangster movies became far more shocking when gun shots rang out, panes of glass shattered, and bodies thudded on sidewalks. By 1932, at least forty civic and religious organizations were seeking federal censorship of movies.[10]

As if this were not enough, Hays was also learning to deal with a new adversary, the Catholic Church. While concern about the capacity of films to inspire evil seemed to remain relatively constant, the identity of those who demanded control of movies changed over time. Censorship appealed to those who believed that communal good was more important than individual liberties. As religious groups moved into and out of that orbit, the prime movers of censorship changed. Protestants, Jews, and Catholics had all at some point railed against what they saw as the immoral Hollywood product, yet each group proposed a different solution. During the Progressive Era, with its emphasis on societal improvement, Protestants led the movie censorship battle, some hoping that voluntary control by enlightened censors could suffice and others pushing for governmental control. As progressivism faded during World War I, especially after the federal government exposed the warts inherent in speech regulation when it went on a rampage of speech-restrictive excess during the 1919 red scare, Protestants began to shift their concern from the progressives' communal ideal to individual rights. At this point, many Protestants began to lose interest in censorship. Censorship existed in many major cities and in seven states, and Protestants seemed satisfied with that. Moreover, many of the women's groups who had spearheaded the agitation for governmental censorship were losing their influence as it became clear to politicians that women would not vote as a bloc and the demands of women's lobbies could be ignored.

While many Protestant groups shifted back toward concern for the individual, those raised in the teachings of the Catholic Church maintained a different view. Like the progressives, Catholics were communitarians: they believed that the individual's autonomy was trumped by the greater good. The decline of progressivism and "internecine warfare" among women reformers left the field open for Catholics to move in as the head cheerleaders for movie control. This meant the substitution not only of Catholic for Protestant but also of men for women. In the early 1930s, the maternalists of the Progressive Era were replaced by priests and prominent laymen of the Catholic Church.[11]

Unlike the procensorite Protestants, the Catholics who wanted something done about movies did not want to involve the government, since statutory regulation meant secular control.[12] Because Catholics were not willing to share their moral authority with civil authorities (Protestant dominated in many areas), they favored "aroused public opinion,"[13] a phrase earlier used by other groups that wanted better films without governmental interference: the Protestants of the National Board of Review and many clubwomen. Like their publicly "aroused" forebears, Catholics put their lobbying efforts not into state or federal legislators but into the movie industry, insisting that it improve its output from within.[14]

Despite its new code of moviemaking conduct, the "Don'ts and Be Carefuls," the MPPDA found itself failing to appease any of these reform groups for very long. The movie moguls faced an unremitting clamor for change: demands from Catholics, from purity crusaders, even from independent exhibitors, coupled with a barrage of negative media attention and the new threat of antitrust investigation. From pulpits across the nation came thundering denunciations of the movie industry. A Buffalo,

New York, priest spelled the word *movies* for his congregation this way: "M—means moral menace, O—obscenity, V—vulgarity, I—immorality, E—exposure, and S—sex."[15] That so many moguls were Jewish and desperate to prove their legitimacy to Christian critics only added to the angst that caused Hollywood to admit that its product was bad and needed to be restrained for the good of the nation. Further, the movie industry was facing a financial predicament—the result of overextension of credit for theater building, retrofitting for sound, and declining audiences of the Depression—that made it more susceptible to the demands of pressure groups.

When Catholic priest Father Daniel Lord, who had just finished serving as religious consultant to the production of *The King of Kings*, and Martin Quigley, publisher of the *Motion Picture Herald*, offered to write a code for movie producers—one that would set clear standards for content acceptable to Catholic sensibilities—the MPPDA lunged at the offer. What better way to silence critics than to embrace their criticism? The industry accepted a draft presented by Lord and Quigley without substantial change,[16] and in 1930 Hollywood had a new set of rules to live by: the Production Code. Unlike the open-ended state censorship statutes, the Production Code specifically listed proscriptions under the headings Crime, Brutality, Sex, Vulgarity, Obscenity, Blasphemy, Costumes, Religion, National Feelings, and Cruelty to Animals.[17] The MPPDA summed up the general outlines of the code this way:

1. No picture will be produced which will lower the moral standards of those who see it. Hence the sympathy of the audience should never be thrown to the side of crime, wrongdoing, evil or sin.
2. Correct standards of life, subject only to the requirements of drama and entertainment, shall be presented.
3. Law, natural or human, shall not be ridiculed, nor shall sympathy be created for its violation.[18]

Since not every film could deal with the joys of family life, the code left room for some antisocial conduct, but only if such "immoral" or criminal behavior was overridden at the end with what came to be called "compensating values." Six reels of felonious, reckless, or debauched behavior could be accepted provided the criminal ended his life behind bars, the adulteress lived out her days alone, or the alcoholic turned teetotaler. Even though the code would become the butt of much joking by the 1950s, film historian Thomas Doherty points out that at the time it was written it was seen as an enlightened document that protected women and children, demanded respect for immigrants, and "sought to uplift the lower orders and convert the criminal mentality. If its intention was social control, the allegiance was on the side of the angels."[19]

In accepting this code, the industry was tacitly acknowledging the harmfulness concept, the long-lived idea that movies carried a special capacity for evil. The code specifically drew a distinction between art that could be represented in book form and art that could be presented in film. "Movies are primarily to be regarded as ENTERTAINMENT," the code began. Because movies reached every class and every area of the country, the latitude given to books could not be extended to movies. In an explicit comparison with books and newspapers, the code denigrated the seriousness of film art, which reached the eyes rather than the mind, bypassing the imagination necessary for interpretation of literary or intellectual works. "Hence," the code continued, "many things which might be described or suggested in a book could not possibly be presented in a film." And it was only right that motion pictures be more constrained than staged drama because they could reach mixed audiences in "communities remote from sophistication" and because film audiences were unable to distinguish between screen events and real life. Remarkably, then, the motion picture industry had accepted, in an official document, that its product was neither as legitimate nor as uplifting as other forms of art because of its reach, vividness, and directness. The mea culpa begun with NAMPI's Thirteen Points—an attempt to placate critics—had become, with the adoption of the code, an outright act of contrition.

The movie industry's reception of this Catholic interference might seem self-defeating, but new media "almost invariably yield to pressure" and institute some sort of internal regulation to ease pressure from outside groups.[20] From dime novels in the Comstock era to comic books in the 1950s, rock music in the 1980s, and videogames in the 1990s, media industries have hamstrung themselves with internal restrictions to stave off boycotts and possible governmental controls.

With Lord and Quigley's new code in place, hope sprang again that Hollywood would cleanse the screen of undesirable elements. That hope was dashed, though, when enforcement of the code turned out to be less stringent than many moral reformers would have liked. It did not take producers and scriptwriters long to figure out that the double entendre and sly dialogue that had become so popular could slip easily through the code. Its first two enforcers, Jason Joy and James Wingate (formerly New York State's chief censor), were, in relation to many state censors, quite enlightened. They believed that the code should concern itself with the overall message of a film, not individual sentences or scenes.[21] For example, Wingate allowed this dialogue between two female roommates from *Red Headed Woman* (1932):

> Jean Harlow: Why, you son of a sea snake. Have you got on my pajamas?
> Una Merkel: Well, uh . . .
> Harlow: Well, you shake right out of 'em, Hortense.
> Merkel: All right.
> Harlow: I'm too important these days to sleep informally. What if there'd be a fire?
> Merkel: You'd have to cover up to keep from being recognized.

And this dialogue from *Parlor, Bedroom and Bath* (1931), when a poolside gigolo attempts to pick up a young woman:

> He: You can't judge a man in a bathing suit.
> She: No, but you can get a rough idea.[22]

This type of indelicacy, raised to a high art by Mae West, mocked the code, disillusioned reformers, and shortened the honeymoon between the Catholics and the code. Joy and Wingate were stuck in a cinematic no-man's-land: caught between Depression-hammered studios, who knew that audience titillation meant increased sales, and the MPPDA, which knew that sex and crime stories meant pressure group ire and censor cuts.[23]

Far more important than sneaky dialogue and barely hidden meanings, though, was Hollywood's increasing penchant for violence. Films like *Little Caesar* (1931), *Public Enemy* (1931), and *Scarface* (1932) portrayed gangsters as glamorous heroes. And the "fallen women" cycle of films showed all manner of prostitutes, kept women, and degraded virgins.[24] "Is there nothing interesting about a good woman?" asked an Atlanta censor.[25] Numerous code violations occurred between 1930 and 1934.[26]

With Hollywood seemingly running amok again despite its vaunted code, publicity-hungry congressmen routinely introduced new national censorship legislation, often more to promote their own careers than to accomplish any meaningful reform. Particularly for congressmen with rural constituents, appearing a champion of movie morals held political capital. A 1932 *Variety* headline griped, "Congress Has 11 Legislative Film Bills Including the Usual Nut Stuff."[27]

The Payne Fund Studies

But routine federal censorship threats were just the beginning of the movie industry's troubles in the early 1930s. From the start, procensorites had stressed the harmful impact of movies on children. The arrival of the talkies only heightened reformers' concerns about controlling children's viewing. Literally hundreds of studies were conducted around the world, including three by the League of Nations.[28] But the most influential came in 1933, with the publication of an exhaustive, nine-volume scholarly study. Commonly known as the Payne Fund studies, they were undertaken by the Motion Picture Research Council to investigate the effects of movies on American children. Though their intention was to discredit movies, the social scientists who undertook the massive project actually came to much more nuanced conclusions about the effects of movies on children's behavior. The studies' conclusions were "about one-third unfavorable to the movies, about one-third favorable, and about one-third neutral."[29]

The Motion Picture Research Council asked a writer, Henry James Forman, to summarize the results in one volume for popular consumption. The abridgment, *Our Movie Made Children*, was more a polemic than an accurate digest of the study. It twisted conclusions, omitted facts, and used inflammatory language to conclude that children's mental attitudes were changed by their viewing choices and that youths everywhere imitated what they saw in movies.[30] *Our Movie Made Children* held films responsible for juvenile delinquency, promiscuity, and disrespect to parents.[31] Widely read, the summary was also popularized in a series of articles in magazines like *Christian Century* and *Parents*. The *New York Times*, like other publications, was taken in by the book's seeming objectivity. The *Times*' reviewer suggested that parents looking for answers about their children's viewing habits could learn all they needed to know from the book: "The importance of these answers lies in the fact that they are authentic, the results of extensive, scientific investigation. . . . [Forman] does not try to make a case against the movies, he merely sets forth the facts."[32]

Forman had done much more than simply set forth facts, however. He had given massive intellectual authority to the position of the procensorship forces and reinforced the belief that movies were capable of evil. Although some of the social scientists who conducted the research tried to distance themselves from Forman's book,[33] it was the popularized version that stuck in the minds of policymakers. As late as the mid-1950s, legal briefs routinely referred to the "titanic" capacity for evil held by the movies.[34] The U.S. Supreme Court never completely rejected the harmfulness concept.

The anxiety caused by *Our Movie Made Children* was only part of the antifilm atmosphere of the 1930s. Critical articles flowed into the public discourse. When it came to movies, negative articles consistently outnumbered positive ones until 1997, but journalistic hostility reached a peak in 1933 and 1934, not to be surpassed until 1991—when there were significantly more magazines in existence.[35]

The National Board of Review struggled to promote freedom of the movies in spite of such antimovie propaganda. Clearly worried about *Our Movie Made Children*, the board adopted a resolution that urged parents "not to indulge in loose thinking about motion pictures and their alleged effects."[36] The board's constant pleas for a free screen may have been encouraged by the introduction in 1934 of a bill to repeal New York's censorship statute. This repeal effort, no doubt emboldened by the repeal of national Prohibition the year before, had some high-powered support—former governor Al Smith, New York's City Fusion Party, a well-known Methodist bishop, and the chancellor of New York University.[37] Not only did the bill fail, but the following year the legislators considered (but tabled) a proposal to strengthen the state's censorship authority by authorizing the director to work with religious leaders to determine standards of immorality.[38]

By 1934, then, Hollywood had five incentives to police itself more carefully: the never-tiring threat of national censorship, reediting costs from governmental censorship that were now running about $500,000 per studio,[39] concerns about antitrust litigation, the barrage of negative articles given new life by the Payne Fund studies, and worries over financing. Heavily indebted to New York bankers for the conversion to sound, moguls faced intensified scrutiny for each new script and its profit potential. As if that were not enough, the industry confronted yet another problem: the newly passed New Deal National Industrial Recovery Act, which required major American industries to draw up codes of fair competition.

Like tire manufacturers and tuna canners, the movie moguls adopted their own code. But the movie industry, "sitting over a volcano," as the *New York Times* noted, created the only New Deal code to include a morals clause.[40] And the man in the hot seat, Will Hays, was coming to realize that the public relations campaigns that had worked in the past would not work now.

There was someone who could help, though: Martin Quigley, who had roots planted in both the Catholic Church and Hollywood. A prominent lay Catholic, Quigley often used the *Motion Picture Herald* to rail against the immorality of the movies. Recognizing that Hollywood had again "built an enormous amount of ill-will," the worried Hays told Quigley that the Catholic Church "could have anything it wanted."[41] All Hollywood asked in return was the right to continue monitoring itself without federal censorship. If the church helped forestall more governmental censorship, Hollywood would police its member studios.

But Catholics like Father Lord had heard all this before. Furious at Hollywood's disregard of his carefully written rules, Lord reported to an Episcopal committee that in the previous six months, no fewer than 133 Hollywood films had violated the Production Code. The bishops decided that a lay organization dedicated to encouraging decent films (but actually assembled to boycott the indecent ones) was the answer. The new organization was called the Catholic Legion of Decency. Catholics signed up in door-to-door campaigns or joined by taking a pledge at Sunday Mass. The pledge bound each person to "condemn vile and unwholesome motion pictures," to attend only those pictures that did not "offend decency and Christian morality," and to work to prevent the "filthy philosophy" of criminals from becoming "something acceptable to decent men and women." Children declaimed the pledge in parochial school classes; diocesan magazine articles reminded everyone else of their duty to join.[42] It is impossible to know for certain how many Catholics took the pledge, but estimates range from 7 to 11 million.[43] When some Protestants and Jews were also encouraged to join, many did. Hays and the MPPDA knew it had real trouble on its hands with all three groups aligned, Catholics in the forefront.

Hollywood now faced a tsunami of pressure: from its bankers (threatening to withhold financing of indecent pictures); from Catholics (threatening to boycott); from politicians (threatening national or harsher state censorship); from rising reediting costs; from increasingly negative articles, books, and scholarly study; and from the constant threat of antitrust action, all in the midst of a national depression and declining box office receipts. The movie industry was highly visible, heavily criticized, conveniently centralized, and under attack seemingly from all sides.

With great fanfare and the blessing of the newly formed Legion of Decency, the industry vowed to clean house again, to enforce its own regulations, and to produce more wholesome entertainment. To save the code, Hays's subordinate, Joseph Breen (a "professional Catholic," according to code historians Leonard Leff and Jerold Simmons[44]), recommended the creation of an enforcement department, the Production Code Administration. Appeals would be handled by the MPPDA's board of directors, mostly financial men. The PCA was empowered to levy $25,000 fines for the production, distribution, and exhibition of any noncode film. Since the major studios owned most of the first-run metropolitan theaters, which generated much of the industry's profits, and since many smaller theaters and independent theaters used the code as a guide, a film denied a seal would be "dead in the water."[45] Hollywood accepted the PCA as its penance. It made all the difference. For nearly twenty years, no member studio attempted to defy the PCA by distributing an unapproved film.[46]

Hollywood's Production Code, now with its own police, was different from governmental censorship. The code could not legally prevent films from being shown, but Hollywood's vertical integration provided a built-in mechanism against nonconforming films. Producers soon learned that adherence to Breen's demands also meant fewer problems with the state and local censor boards.[47] The price for this decrease in censor trouble, of course, was loss of artistic freedom, which sometimes bordered on the inane. Walt Disney was forced to cover the udders of cows.[48]

As time went on and societal mores evolved, the keepers of the code proved reluctant to tamper with its provisions. Like the state censorship statutes, the 1930 code remained substantially unchanged for more than two decades. As late as 1956, code administrators were still requiring that digression from moral norms be punished. Crime still could not pay; divorce or adultery or moral turpitude of any kind could not go unpunished. Infractions of societal norms (as interpreted by the code) had to be followed by degradation, incarceration, or death. Many topics were simply unthinkable. In 1948, a frustrated scriptwriter placed this anonymous classified ad in the trade publication of the Screen Writers Guild: "Wanted, An Idea: Established writer would like a good up-to-date idea for a motion picture which avoids politics, sex, religion, divorce, double beds, drugs, disease, poverty, liquor, senators, bankers, wealth, cigarettes,

Congress, race, economics, art, death, crime, childbirth and accidents. . . . Noncontroversial even amongst critics, if possible."[49] Indeed, even "an expressive 'Oh God' was considered blasphemy, and a generation of screenwriters ground their teeth as they typed 'Oh boy!'"[50]

The Many Sources of Interference

Like a garland of garlic around the neck of the movie industry, the PCA succeeded not only in warding off the vampire of federal censorship but also in reducing the number of eliminations required by the state censors. From 1930 to 1934, New York's problem films hovered between 17 and 19 percent. The rate dropped to 14 percent in 1935, the first full year of the PCA; to 10 percent in both 1936 and 1937; and then to an all-time low of 7 percent in 1938.[51] Whereas governmental censorship boards, whether municipal or state, played a purely negative role by denying content after it had been created, the content regulation of Hollywood attempted to play a positive role by making a significant dent in the number of films deemed offensive. The PCA under Joseph Breen was so successful that no code-approved film was banned in New York for five years.[52] Content regulation was "simply good business," according to Gregory Black. Between 1936 and 1940, not one film was condemned by the Legion of Decency.[53] The code provided a "haven of refuge" from what a group of 1950s film men called the "censoriousness of the American public."[54]

But the PCA was just the first stop a film had to make on its way to the projection booth. Once approved by the PCA, films were sent to New York for duplication and distribution. There they faced review and categorization by the Legion of Decency.[55] The legion's categories included "approved for all, "objectionable in part," and "condemned." Film critic Andre Sennwald realized right away that while the Legion of Decency's recommendations were binding only on Catholics, the widespread publication of its ratings gave it influence over the film viewing choices of others. This worried Sennwald, because many of the films the legion condemned in 1934 were the most artistically meritorious of the season, including *Catherine the Great*, *One More River*, and *Of Human Bondage*. Nevertheless, Sennwald, like many others, saw hope. "Since Joseph Breen's board of control began to operate," he wrote, "there has been an obvious improvement in themes and a noticeable diminution in the kind of appalling cheapness and unintelligence which filmgoers deplore without regard to private allegiances of faith or creed."[56] Although the Legion of Decency claimed to be only a film classification group—and only for its own adherents—behind the scenes, its leaders brought much pressure to bear on Hollywood producers and exerted great influence over the content of films.[57]

The 1930s and 1940s have been called the golden age of Hollywood, when Bette Davis, Katharine Hepburn, and Humphrey Bogart reigned as box office attractions and when parents could send their children to the movie theater unaccompanied, without fear of inappropriate content. It was also an era, though, when scriptwriters and producers were restrained in topics, characterizations, and dialogue, when many fine novels failed to make it to the screen because their content was considered too dangerous, and when other novels were hacked beyond recognition to get scripts past layers of interference and censorship.

Yet the major studios were still in business, having answered calls for their reform. Many foresaw a bright future as the MPPDA walked off into the sunset hand-in-hand with the Legion of Decency. For independents, however, the situation was quite different. Although there were few nonstudio producers in the United States before World War II, there were some independent distribution companies who, as non-MPPDA members, did not abide by the Production Code. Their only interference before exhibition came from the state and local censors. In the prewar era few of them challenged the restrictions, yet those who did set the stage for challenges to come.

4

Early Challenges to State Censors, 1927–1940

The judicial system was central to the control of movie content, both in upholding the censors' legality and in legitimating censorship as fair and reasonable. Censorship statutes would have appeared draconian if they had not allowed recourse to judicial review. Permitting appeal of censor determinations gave prior restraint the appearance of equability. Recourse to the courts, however, the very thing that validated the censors, eventually proved their undoing.

Between the initial New York challenges of the 1920s and World War II, fourteen distributors (all independents) legally challenged state censors. Almost half of those challenges were filed against New York's censors.[1] But Pennsylvania's board also found itself repeatedly challenged, usually when it was trying to extend its reach. The first cases came from Fox Film and Vitagraph, which questioned Pennsylvania's censoring of dialogue in the new talkies. The Pennsylvania Supreme Court had no trouble extending the censors' authority over spoken dialogue. The statute was elastic enough, the court said, to encompass spoken dialogue. Other state courts were satisfied with Pennsylvania's pronouncement, and the matter ended there.[2] This decision represented a significant victory for the censors.

A second important issue arose in Pennsylvania over censoring for political messages. Because of their lack of accountability, many censor boards in the 1930s abused their discretionary use of the term *indecent* by quashing what they considered dangerous political messages.[3] Ohio in 1937 disallowed *A Greater Promise* and *A Fighter against Fascism* as pro-Soviet propaganda.[4] Two feature films ran into trouble with the Pennsylvania board when they portrayed a foreign power in an unflattering light. *Spain in Flames* (1937), which also encountered trouble with the Ohio censors, was a pro-Loyalist semidocumentary about the Spanish civil war. Pronouncing censorship "presumptively bad" but "tolerated as a necessary evil," Pennsylvania judges refused to overrule the censors and deferred to the legislative will: "Every reasonable doubt must be resolved by us," the court said, "in behalf of the administrative action, lest we arrogate to ourselves the functions of legislator and administrator."[5]

The backdrop for the second Pennsylvania challenge was the rapidly spreading war in Europe and the national debate over isolationism in the late 1930s. On the side of intervention was *The Ramparts We Watch* (1940), a joint venture of RKO Radio Pictures and Time Inc. produced by Louis de Rochemont, the well-known producer of the popular and often controversial *March of Time* news programs. Pennsylvania banned the film because it contained scenes from a Nazi propaganda film that showed a "Hitler-like figure" denouncing Americans as weaklings. The Pennsylvania court agreed with its censors that *Ramparts* might inflame resentment against German Americans and concluded that its ban was well within the proper authority of the censor board.[6] In the prewar legal culture, films could be censored not just for indecency or obscenity but for political messages the censors found dangerous.

In these challenge cases, the plaintiffs questioned, at least perfunctorily, the censorship statute's violation of free speech rights. But in New York, where most of the 1930s challenges came, none tested the statute on the nature of prior restraint, the restrictions on free speech, or the infringement of due process. Instead, they squabbled over definitions, differences of opinion, and nuances of connotation. Faced with such subjective arguments, the New York courts consistently refused to overturn the legislatively empowered body charged with interpreting statutory opinions and definitions. Because judges routinely practiced judicial restraint of administrative decisions, and because they usually protected only mainstream political speech, New York distributors were forced to attack on more prosaic grounds. And so began a long series of unsuccessful challenges, each questioning the censors' determinations, each upheld by the state's courts.

Although newspapers had been freed from prior restraint by a 1931 Supreme Court decision (*Near v. Minnesota*), prior restraint of motion pictures continued. The harmfulness concept excluded movies from any serious consideration of First Amendment rights, and there the matter stood as far as the MPPDA was concerned. The farthest any major studio went in questioning the censors was to appeal to the New York censors' immediate overseers, the state's board of regents.

The censors were so well entrenched in the legal culture between the late 1920s and World War II that in New York, only thirty-eight of the hundreds of films denied licenses on their first application bothered to avail themselves of their right to appeal to the board of regents.[7] Of these, only six distributors went over the regents' heads and challenged in court. These six cases had much in common: every film was an independent production or a foreign film released by an independent distributor, and every one lost. In at least one case (a semidocumentary about childbirth produced and sanctioned by the American Medical Association), the censors clearly overreacted. Yet they never reversed themselves, nor were they overruled by the courts. In only one case in the pre–World War II years did the board of regents overturn a censor ruling, and that decision came only after a protracted court battle.

While each loss added to the pile of precedents working against the distributors, each also managed to put a dent, however small, in the censors' dominance. Each helped to shed some light on the closed-door clout wielded by the censor boards.

The Naked Truth

In 1927, the New York censors refused to license a film called *The Naked Truth* despite its claim to be a vital public service message about venereal disease.[8] It tells the story of three young men, each of whom takes a different path in life. Bob, a young attorney, refrains from premarital sex and faces a happy future when he marries. Bob's friend explores sex with a prostitute and contracts a venereal disease. He must postpone his wedding and face a difficult medical treatment. Another friend also contracts a venereal disease but plows ahead with his marriage plans, eventually losing his mind and killing his wife. The virtuous Bob comes to the rescue, successfully defending the third young man from murder charges with an insanity plea.[9]

Public Welfare Pictures applied for a conditional license that would allow *The Naked Truth* to be shown in commercial theaters to sex-segregated audiences over sixteen, but New York had no statutory provision for age-related classification of film. When its request was denied, the distributor appealed to the board of regents, which also rejected the request. Public Welfare Pictures then appealed to New York's appellate division, arguing that the film was neither immoral nor indecent but was educational and taught "a great moral lesson." New York was being "arbitrary and unreasonable," Public Welfare argued, since Virginia, Ohio, Maryland, Memphis, Detroit, Chicago, and Newark had all shown the film with audience restrictions.[10]

The motion picture division responded that the statute's appeal provision was not intended to turn the appellate division into a "super motion picture commission." Earlier, both the Pennsylvania and Kansas supreme courts had dealt with this issue and had come to the same conclusion. The appellate division deferred to the censors because the case revolved on "a question of fact, the determination of which has been committed to the Education Department." The justices refused to watch the film, setting a precedent that would stand for eleven years.[11]

The decision limited the chances of any sort of venereal disease film. For the next twenty years, every picture dealing with syphilis was rejected; finally, in 1949, the Army Signal Corps got approval to show one of its training films.[12] The MPPDA also frowned on the topic of venereal disease. Under the PCA, no mention of syphilis was allowed, even for a 1940 Warner Brothers biopic about the scientist who discovered its cure.[13] Not until 1952 would the New York censors allow sex education films to be shown in theaters.[14]

A Prolonged Case of *Ecstasy*

In 1936, just as censorship controversies were starting to settle down thanks to the imposition of the PCA, the New York censors were faced with what they considered a completely unacceptable foreign film, the controversial Czechoslovak-German production *Ecstasy*. Its tortured licensing attempt covered six years and ten court appeals. Before this case file closed, its American distributor, Eureka Productions, labored mightily to overturn the motion picture division by dragging *Ecstasy* through state and federal courts, raising both constitutionality questions and federalism issues.

Ecstasy's long battle with New York actually began in 1934, when its first incarnation, *Ekstase*, appeared for review.[15] With sexual frustration as its central theme, this film was bound for trouble. The lead character, Eva (played by Hedy Kiesler, who later changed her name to Hedy Lamarr), has married an older man who turns out to be impotent. Frustrated and unhappy, she returns to her father's house, where she takes long horseback rides. One day, while she is swimming nude in a nearby pond, her stallion, scenting a brood mare in heat, runs off carrying Eva's clothes with him, leaving her little choice but to chase desperately—and nakedly—after. A young, virile engineer working on a nearby construction project spots the horse and runs to catch it. He gallantly returns Eva's clothing when he finds her cowering in nearby bushes. Their attraction is instant (made painfully obvious by intercut shots of the lusty horses and a flower being pollinated by a bee). The engineer and Eva fall in love. In the most famous (or infamous) scene of the movie, the lovers retreat to the engineer's cabin. The camera discreetly pans away from their bodies but indiscreetly focuses on Eva's face as she achieves the satisfaction her husband has been unable to provide. A short time later, Eva's husband learns of his wife's affair and travels to the hotel where the young couple has planned to spend the night before running away to build a new life together. Eva's husband commits suicide in a room one floor above where the lovers have been dancing. When Eva learns of her husband's death, she feels such guilt that she abandons the engineer. In the end, Eva's adultery causes great misery for all involved.

New York's censors ordered eliminations, but the distributor, Elekta Productions, never came back for rescreening. The film went back to its Czech producer, who made changes, dubbed it into German, and then sold the film's U.S. distribution rights to Eureka Productions. Eureka tried to bring the film back into the United States as *Ecstasy* but ran afoul of the censorship provisions of the Tariff Act of 1930, which denied entry of any obscene matter. According to film distributor Arthur Mayer, an apprehensive customs inspector assigned to watch *Ecstasy* called for guidance from his boss, the secretary of the treasury, Henry Morgenthau. Morgenthau did not know what to do either and suggested that they call in an expert. The "expert" turned out to be Morgenthau's wife, who insisted that *Ecstasy* not enter the country.[16]

When Eureka challenged customs, it came face to face with valiant opposition from U.S. Attorney Martin Conboy, a prominent lay Catholic who had previously served as Anthony Comstock's lawyer. President of New York's Catholic Club and director of the National Council of Catholic Men, Conboy zealously argued that *Ecstasy* was both obscene and immoral. At trial, the judge's inane instructions—"Immoral means anything which is inconsistent with good morals as good morals are understood by the community"—set a tone that would make Eureka's case impossible. It took a jury of "middle-aged businessmen" only thirty-five minutes to agree with customs officials that *Ecstasy* was obscene.[17] Eureka promptly appealed, and when the court reversed the decision on technical grounds, *Ecstasy* made it back to the screening room of New York's motion picture division.[18]

Resubmitted in March 1936, the remade *Ecstasy* was rejected in toto.[19] Eureka made several more changes, hoping to appease the censors. To avoid the adultery problem, it added a scene showing a divorce decree being ripped from a typewriter and inserted another scene to indicate that Eva and her lover got married before the sex began. But the censors found that neither addition was enough to offset the film's obsession with physical satisfaction.[20] Having lost an appeal to the board of regents, Eureka sued in U.S. district court, asking for an injunction against New York for encroaching on federal power over foreign commerce. Mutual Film Corporation had played the federalism card in 1915 without success, but that case had involved interstate commerce. This was a case, Eureka argued, of a state's interfering with the federal government's power to determine the acceptability of foreign commerce. Since federal authorities had censorship authority and had admitted the film, state authorities should not be able to prohibit its exhibition. The district court did not accept, however, that Congress had intended the Tariff Act of 1930 to supersede the police power of a state. The judgment of a federal court in admitting the film, then, did not prevent state officers from arriving at a different decision. Citing *Mutual*, the court held that New York's censorship statute violated neither interstate commerce nor foreign commerce powers.[21]

Losing its constitutional-federalism argument in federal court, Eureka decided to appeal to the New York appellate division again, arguing that the motion picture division had no "reasonable basis or apprehension that public morality, decency, or welfare would be endangered by [the film's] exhibition." Eureka's lawyers tried to argue that the movie should be considered only as a whole. "The proper test," they argued, "was not whether certain scenes taken from their context and judged by themselves alone may be offensive, but whether the dominant effect of the picture as a whole is obscene." Here the lawyers were clearly attempting to convince the court to apply new case law. Three years earlier, federal judge Augustus Hand had tried to update the definition of *obscenity*, urging that artistic works be considered as organic entities rather than individual parts.[22]

Eureka also appealed on the precarious ground that the critics had "unanimously acclaimed [*Ecstasy*] as a work of art." This was the first time that a film distributor had used artistic merit and the evaluations of film critics as arguments in censorship disputes. In the middle 1930s, films were not recognized as art except by a few forward-thinking film critics and museum personnel.[23] Most people, and indeed many critics, viewed the moving picture as nothing more than a form of entertainment, and a potentially harmful one at that. Still, Eureka's attorneys pointed to *Ecstasy*'s first prize at an international film festival the year before, as well as to the other jurisdictions whose censoring boards had approved. (The film in various versions had been shown in most parts of the United States, including Washington DC and Boston.[24])

Then Eureka arrived at the crux of the argument: "We submit that many films out of Hollywood contain more objectionable scenes." Here, however, the attorneys were trying to buck precedent. In *Public Welfare Pictures* eight years before, the New York court had definitively stated that it would not substitute its judgment for the determinations of the censors. Perhaps Eureka's attorneys hoped that enough time had passed and the new justices on the bench would see things differently. They further claimed that their client had based its purchase of the film rights on the motion picture division's conditional acceptance of the original *Ekstase* and that New York's determination would probably cause refusals in other states and thus harm their client's business.[25]

The motion picture division responded that *Ecstasy* had been rejected because the entire concept of the picture was immoral, not just individual scenes, although it also objected to the many symbols of sexuality, such as the mare in heat and the bees pollinating flowers. To buttress its case, it reminded the court that a federal jury had also pronounced the film obscene. The appellate division, not surprisingly, upheld the motion picture division.

By this time, the scandalous film had become an international cause célèbre, denounced by the pope, the Catholic Legion of Decency, and even the Nazis. But negative publicity made Eureka bolder. In 1936, it hired Jewel Productions in Los Angeles to submit *Ecstasy* for a PCA seal. Breen, not surprisingly, declined, calling the film "highly—even dangerously—indecent."[26] He refused even to consider a totally reedited film as long as it carried the same name.[27] Failing to get a PCA seal, *Ecstasy* could not play in any major studios' theaters and would remain a low-grossing, art-house film. Worse, if *Ecstasy* could not get a license to be shown in New York, even that small distribution would be impossible.

The film was running into trouble in other censors' jurisdictions, too. Pennsylvania rejected it outright. Maryland required numerous cuts, including scenes of condoms and aphrodisiacs, full-length views of Eva reclining on her bridal bed, her nude scenes at the pond, and even the nature shots of the brood mare and the pollinating bees.[28]

In the late 1930s, a new player entered the censorship wars as film critics began to question state regulation. One month after Eureka's state court defeat in New York, Thomas Pryor of the *New York Times* noted that *Ecstasy* was being shown in many other states and wondered whether the New York censors had gone "off the deep end in their efforts to be puritanical, or whether there [was] something radically wrong with the moral standards of the rest of the nation." He concluded that while critics disagreed on the film's artistic merit, they agreed that it was neither immoral nor obscene.[29]

Eureka had now invested a great deal of money in legal challenges. Although the film was being shown in some areas of the country, it was being kept from the most lucrative market. Seeing the intransigence of the New York censors, Eureka decided to "reconstruct" the film to make its overall concept more palatable; it submitted this revised version to the motion picture division in 1939. According to the application, "The reconstruction of the story of *Ecstasy* is different from the original story in that we explain the unhappiness between the bride and bridegroom due to the difference in age and temperance [*sic*]. In the reconstructed story, the girl is divorced and then married to the engineer, changing the theme of the story."[30] But the motion picture division, recognizing this story as not much different from the second version, rejected the application. The board of regents then also rejected an appeal, and once again Eureka asked the appellate division justices for help. Eureka's attorneys, learning that two new men had been appointed since the last suit, hoped for a more favorable outcome.[31] But they lost again.

Eureka, amazingly, refused to give up. When it showed up again in April 1940 with yet another version, motion picture division director Irwin Esmond had had enough; he refused to even look at it.[32] Back in court, Eureka asked the appellate division to view both the 1936 and the 1940 versions. In keeping with previous decisions, the justices declined to view the film, but, in a victory of sorts for Eureka, they did order the motion picture division to screen the movie again.[33] Again (for the sixth time) the censors refused *Ecstasy* a license. When Eureka appealed to the board of regents in this war of attrition, the board reversed the motion picture division, finally allowing *Ecstasy* to be released to New York theaters in November 1940.

With only three hundred words of dialogue, *Ecstasy* should have the thinnest file at the motion picture division archives. It has the fattest. Its long court career carried major implications for the film industry. First, the film's legal history reinforced the court's position of refusing to overturn any motion picture division finding unless the appellants could prove malfeasance. Any appeal using the position that the motion picture division acted arbitrarily or capriciously was unlikely to succeed. Second, as we will see, the case provided precedent against a concurrently litigating film, *Remous*, that had a similar theme. Third, appeals based on artistic merit and the opinions of film critics would be fruitless. Fourth, the censors would continue to view motion pictures by individual scenes rather than as organic entities. Finally, and most important, it demonstrated that the motion picture division would not be cowed into changing a determination even after protracted legal battles.

Tomorrow's Children Meets *Our Movie Made Children*

In the midst of the *Ecstasy* battle, the censors faced another challenger, *Tomorrow's Children.* Judicial unfriendliness toward advocates of movie freedom was compounded by the socially hostile mood from the recent publication of *Our Movie Made Children* and the Payne Fund studies. Into this negatively charged atmosphere stepped the producers of *Tomorrow's Children.* Its topic was not adultery or sexual gratification but sterilization, birth control, and eugenics. In the early 1930s, more than thirty states still had eugenics laws on their books. New York was not one of them, having repealed its eugenics law fourteen years earlier. New York's censors may have been reluctant to license the film for that reason alone. They may also have lumped *Tomorrow's Children* with other "exploitation" films like *The Naked Truth.*

But whether seeking quick profits or trying to publicize the plight of those in danger of involuntary sterilization, *Tomorrow's Children* pushed some judicial hot buttons. It depicts a judge indifferently ordering sterilization for a feeble-minded man, a convicted sex offender, a criminal, and an entire family. The criminal is saved by the intercession of his congressman. A daughter of the supposedly defective family is dramatically dragged off for sterilization before her marriage, though she objects strenuously and piteously. Just as the surgeons are poised to cut, her mother bursts in to admit that the girl is a foster child, not a blood relative. Only then is she spared.

New York rejected *Tomorrow's Children* because it was "immoral" and would "incite to crime and to corrupt morals." The rejection letter told the distributor, Foy Productions, only that forced sterilization "was not decent for screen presentation to general audiences." After a revision and second rejection, Foy appealed.[34]

Foy chose a former judge, Jonah J. Goldstein, as lead counsel. A well-respected criminal lawyer, Goldstein based his appeal memorandum for Foy on recent court decisions concerning obscenity in publications that could be prosecuted only after publication. Goldstein argued against the motion picture division's use of the censoring term *indecent* by pointing out that the court of appeals had recently interpreted indecency as "lewd, lascivious and salacious or obscene publications, the tendency of which is to excite lustful and lecherous desire." Latching onto this last phrase, Goldstein argued that *Tomorrow's Children* was hardly likely to excite anyone's desire and charged that the motion picture division was operating without accountability. Then he went after the director personally, accusing Esmond, who had now been chief censor for two years, of using the term *immoral* "as meaning something that was offensive to him." As further evidence of the motion picture division's wide latitude in interpreting indecency, Goldstein pointed out that Esmond had considered indecent the film's portrayal of a judge influenced by political concerns.[35]

Esmond replied that the entire film was immoral, especially "the final scene of the surgeons hovering over the unfortunate girl like harpies prepared to rob her of the most precious thing in life, namely the ability to reproduce life in her body. . . . Even when animals are sterilized, they are not brought out into the public square to be operated on for public amusement or edification." Referring to the New York Penal Law, which in 1934 forbade the advertising of contraception, he argued, "Some women . . . will find in [the film] an easy way to accomplish a permanent release from the fear of conception and subsequent motherhood. . . . To those in the audience who may be susceptible to this suggestion, the picture serves as an advertisement of a method of providing complete relief."[36]

"No woman without the aid of a physician can make herself sterile," Goldstein exploded in reply. "Birth control is as different from sterilization as is the Equator from the North Pole." Echoing the pleas of the attorneys for Public Welfare Pictures in the case of *The Naked Truth*, he concluded, "The picture presents in clean, dramatic form a social problem from a scientific and educational viewpoint. It would be a sad day indeed when this subject, discussed in the press, in magazines, in published works, in legislative halls, adopted by 31 states, should be tabooed on the screen in New York."[37]

But taboo it would remain; Foy's appeal to the regents was unsuccessful. When he brought the matter to the appellate division, Goldstein convinced the court to view the film to decide whether the motion picture division had acted arbitrarily or capriciously—something no New York court had done since the early 1920s. This decision was a turning point, indicating that the court would now consider matters of fact relating to New York censorship as well as matters of law. If Goldstein thought, however, that the justices would overrule the legislatively empowered censoring body, he was wrong. The court's opinion of the film that the "perversion" of reproductive organs was the sole subject matter did not augur well for the appellants. The three-man majority was clearly offended by the film, describing it as "a studied creation to teach the corruption of courts." Esmond had been wise to point out the film's disparaging treatment of the bench. *Tomorrow's Children* would get no license from this majority.[38]

But a potent dissent by the presiding justice reflected the influence of the totalitarianism threatening Europe that year. American newspapers in 1938 were full of stories detailing the rise of Hitler and Mussolini. New Yorkers seemed spellbound by the consequences of strong central governments gone mad.[39] The widespread concern about creeping totalitarianism that affected popular thought about governance is evident in Justice James P. Hill's dissent. Comparing the motion picture division to "ministers of propaganda" in their authority to determine which information should be given to the public, Hill concluded that the disagreement among the justices demonstrated the "dangers of censorship entrusted to men of one profession." Implying that public opinion should have some influence in censorship decisions, he suggested that juries would provide more equitable determinations than judges. He agreed with Foy Productions that the motion picture division had presented no "finding of facts" to prove that the film was indecent. He found the motion picture division's allegation that the film would incite to crime preposterous. "The film no more suggests sterilization as a means of birth control than a film showing the amputation of a leg would suggest that as a means to prevent persons from walking into danger."[40]

Encouraged by the appellate division's three-to-two vote and by Hill's vehement dissent, Foy Productions appealed to the court of appeals, which upheld the lower court but offered no opinion.[41] After three years of appeals, *Tomorrow's Children* received no license for exhibition in New

York. Eight years earlier, sex education had been removed from the definition of obscenity in book publication,[42] but sex education in film would remain unmentionable. Not only was film subjected to prior restraint, but the special-capacity-for-evil concept kept movies from dealing with subject matter available to other media.

Although judicial screening of *Tomorrow's Children* did not help Foy Productions, the case did at least provide a victory of sorts for the industry. An important precedent had been set: no longer could the censors work completely in secret—at least not if they were challenged in court. Their determinations of what was obscene, immoral, indecent, inhuman, and sacrilegious could now be appealed for judicial interpretation. The case also showed the beginnings of a crack in the previously unified courts. Whereas other challenges had resulted in unanimous rulings, *Tomorrow's Children* split the justices. They were never again unanimous in dealing with prewar challenges to the motion picture division.

Remous

While the motion picture division was busy defending its rulings on *Tomorrow's Children* and *Ecstasy*, a French film, *Remous*, showed up to challenge the New York censors. *Remous* and *Ecstasy* have remarkably similar plots, both dealing with impotence, adultery, and despair. In *Remous*, an automobile accident leaves a honeymooning bridegroom impotent. His young wife struggles to remain faithful but finally succumbs to another man. She regrets her infidelity, and when her husband learns about the affair, he commits suicide.

Depicting another unfulfilled, adulterous wife, *Remous* inevitably met the same censorial fate. But this was no exploitation film or social hygiene ruse. Described as a "beautiful French film" by free speech activist Morris Ernst,[43] *Remous* was an artistic production unlike anything being produced in Hollywood. Nevertheless, the motion picture division reviewers objected to the entire film, writing in an internal memo, "Impotency of the husband and its effect upon the sex life of the wife, resulting in her adultery and the husband's suicide, is not regarded as a decent theme for screen portrayal. . . . Her action was immoral and would tend to corrupt morals."[44] But the distributor, Burstyn and Mayer, was not told why the film had been rejected. As standard practice, when the motion picture division ordered eliminations in a film, it explicitly stated the offensive parts. But when it rejected a film in toto, it provided no such information.

The reader of this book knows more about why *Remous* was rejected than did its distributor.

Burstyn and Mayer, a respected film importation partnership, pleaded by letter, noting that "members of the Catholic Clergy" had approved the film as an ethical "preachment against marital infidelity." The distributors asked for justification of the motion picture division's ruling. "If you can point out a line of dialogue or any footage which violates any one of your regulations," their letter promised, "we shall examine even more thoroughly the dialogue or the footage in question." The motion picture division seems to have had little sympathy for this request.[45] After major revisions and a second submission, however, the censors gave *Remous* a license in February 1937. Later that year, Burstyn and Mayer had a change of heart and came back, this time requesting a license for a second revised version, apparently with some of the excised scenes reinserted. The distributors may have felt that the approved film's artistic message was unclear or that as an art film, *Remous* had been damaged by the revisions. Or they may have reinstated the condemned scenes to create a test case for the courts. When the motion picture division refused to license the film with the scenes restored, Burstyn and Mayer appealed to the board of regents and then to the appellate division.

Before taking the case to court, Burstyn and Mayer arranged representation by one of the nation's foremost civil liberties experts and corporate attorneys, Arthur Garfield Hays, well known for his participation in the Scopes "monkey trial," the Sacco and Vanzetti appeal, and the Scottsboro case.[46] Hays, who also served as counsel to the ACLU, had a long history of passionately opposing censorship in all forms. He once remarked, "Whenever you fight for liberty, you sometimes win, but you never lose!"[47] His experience in fighting censorship of stage dramas included representing the producer of *The Captive*, a 1926 Broadway play about lesbianism, and bringing Theodore Dreiser's suit against Paramount Publix Corporation in 1931 over changes the studio had made to Dreiser's screenplay for *An American Tragedy*.[48]

For the *Remous* offensive, Hays and New York University film studies professor Russell Potter compiled ammunition on public attitudes toward the film. After screening the film in class, the professor asked his students whether they liked the picture, whether they would censor any part of it, and which scenes should be cut. Of sixty-three in the group, forty-five said they liked it, fifty-eight said it should not be censored, and most failed to select the scenes the censors had actually cut.[49]

Armed with this focus group research and represented by one of the leaders of the civil liberties bar, the case of *Remous*'s license came before the appellate division in 1939. Hays argued that the term *immoral* had no legally defensible meaning. "Every murder is immoral," Hays insisted; "every dishonest act is immoral; every cruel act is immoral; every act frowned upon by present-day society is immoral." The first attorney to tackle the special-capacity-for-evil concept, Hays insisted that any connection between onscreen immoral conduct and incitement to that conduct was illogical: "It cannot be said that the portrayal of such themes necessarily 'tends to corrupt morals.' If any such theory were applied, the motion picture public would have to be content with pictures portraying Mother Goose Rhymes and even some of these would have to be barred." Hays characterized the actions of the motion picture division director as "sublime naiveté" and suggested that the eliminations required would be beneficial only "if the audience were made up of morons." He justified Burstyn and Mayer's restoration of some scenes as necessary and said that the cuts required by the motion picture division made the film "silly," a position taken also by three New York film critics. In fact, Hays argued, the changes required to get the first revised version licensed made the film more immoral. Hays charged that the motion picture division was notorious for disallowing anything "which might give some moron the slightest provocation for misconstruing or distorting the action depicted."[50]

Unfortunately, all of these allegations merely recounted the difference-of-opinion argument, on which the courts had consistently refused to rule, and avoided matters of law and constitutionality, on which the court could rule. Hays's contention did not move beyond the definition question. The motion picture division said the film was immoral; the appellants said it was not immoral; and the courts were left to decide. More than a decade earlier, *The Naked Truth* had proved that this approach would not work. While the decision about *Tomorrow's Children* hinted at some incipient flexibility on this point, it offered little on which to build a case. The courts were still hesitant to interfere with a legislatively appointed body whose job was to determine immorality, obscenity, and indecency. Rather than directly attacking the unfairness of the vague terminology or the motion picture division's refusal to be forthcoming with its applicants, Hays merely argued that the censors were wrong. Even if the justices agreed with him, he gave them no legal grounds on which to challenge the statute or its operation. On the other hand, his first duty was to his clients; if Hays had gotten the court to agree that the film was not immoral, *Remous* could have been shown. More important, had the court overturned on the facts, it would have been a major victory that would have left the censors vulnerable to attack on the grounds that their judgment was faulty.

Hays may have thought he had a better way to challenge the motion picture censors. He used arguments similar to the ones he used in his theater cases. "If we judge *Remous* by the standard laid down [in the theater], it is clear that the censors exceeded their powers. . . . No person either normal or abnormal could possibly be excited to lustful and lecherous desire by anything depicted in the picture. . . . To object to showing a married couple in a bedroom without accompaniment of any improper action is an indication of the narrow-mindedness of the censors." The censorship statute, he continued, should not be construed to give the censors "the power of life and death over thought." Arguing for censorial change to match societal change, his brief concluded that the standards applied "are not only harsh, they are absurd in this day and age."[51]

But while he wanted more enlightened censors, Hays stopped short of questioning the undefined discretionary power that allowed them to apply their own personal standards to film determinations. He never mentioned the First Amendment. Perhaps most surprising, he ignored the prior restraint issue even though, eight years earlier, the U.S. Supreme Court had disallowed prior restraint in newspaper publishing. In the legal milestone of *Near v. Minnesota*, Chief Justice Charles Evans Hughes had tried to remind American legislators that the First Amendment made clear that Congress could place no previous restraint on publication. Hughes asserted that the "security of the freedom of the press requires that it should be exempt not only from previous restraint by the executive, as in Great Britain, but from legislative restraint also."[52]

True, motion pictures were not yet considered part of the press, but it is surprising that an attorney of Hays's stature would take the case of a relatively insignificant foreign film if not to try to set new legal ground with it. In all likelihood, Hays did not consider that the New York censorship statute might violate the First Amendment or the New York State constitution's guarantee of free speech. As Mark Graber argues in his 1991 book on free speech, even civil libertarians of the post–World War I era often failed to consider obvious violations of free speech rights as First Amendment issues. Graber shows that even activists like Clarence Darrow viewed speech infringements more as economic issues than as expression issues. When Eugene V. Debs was famously enjoined from urging workers to leave their jobs, Darrow defended him on the right-to-strike issue rather than on First Amendment grounds.[53]

This still seems less than satisfactory as explanation for Hays's legal strategy, however. Twelve years before the *Remous* case, he had successfully argued that H. L. Mencken's *American Mercury* deserved to be released from prior restraint because the Boston Watch and Ward Society had been acting as "censors of our business," which, according to Hays, it had "no right to do."[54] Why would Hays refuse to accept prior restraint for a magazine client yet accept it for a motion picture client? Even more puzzling, Hays failed to mention two recent, promising developments for civil liberties proponents. Two years earlier, Justice Benjamin Cardozo had argued that certain parts of the Bill of Rights were so fundamental to personal liberty that the Court should move beyond oversight of congressional infringement to watch for state legislative infringement as well. The justification for doing this was the Fourteenth Amendment, which prohibited states from taking "life, liberty, or property" without due process. If the states were prohibited from taking liberty without due process, then *liberty* needed to be defined. Which liberties were the states not allowed to legislatively take? Building on Cardozo's idea, one year later Chief Justice Harlan Stone suggested that courts should closely scrutinize any statute that limited personal liberty and that certain liberties were so basic that they deserved special attention.[55] Acting on Stone's "preferred freedoms" argument, over the next few years, the Supreme Court would overturn many state laws that had infringed the rights of radicals, labor organizations, and minority religious groups to speak and organize freely. Had Hays taken advantage of this new direction, or the route provided by the *Near v. Minnesota* precedent against prior restraint, he might have argued for an overturn of the New York statute that kept the film industry from speaking freely. But he gave the court an easier route. If someone like Hays failed to appreciate that making films free from interference was a right, then certainly the courts were not ready to recognize that right either.

To answer Hays's brief, the motion picture division simply maintained that the film "unduly emphasized the carnal side of the sex relationship" and that both *Ecstasy* and *Remous* taught "the proposition that a wife cannot remain chaste where the husband . . . is impotent."[56] After viewing the film, the court upheld the censors "beyond question."[57] A lone dissent, however, found the picture "unobjectionable" by the standards of the board of regents and called the excised scenes "trivial." It offered small comfort to Burstyn and Mayer, but it displayed another splinter in the previously unified court.

After further cuts, *Remous* was licensed in 1940, but it was not the same film. *New York Times* critic Bosley Crowther lamented the obvious impact on the film's integrity.

> The perils lying in store for a film which attempts to fly in the face of providence after a thorough and obvious job of censorial wing-clipping has been done upon it are clearly and pathetically revealed in the case of the French film *Remous*. . . . For whatever emotional impact this tortured psychological drama may have possessed before the public's guardians had at it has been manifestly impaired by the most tantalizing interruptions, cuts of critical scenes and a consequent series of blank transitions which leave one groping desperately for the thread. . . . Scenes which obviously should have been emphasized . . . have been cut away in chunks.[58]

Critics from the *New York Sun* and the *New York Herald Tribune* agreed.[59] Other fine foreign films like *Club de femmes* (1936) and *La maternelle* (1933) had faced similar expurgation, which made them seem poorly made and choppy. Most viewers of these films had no idea that they were watching hacked-up versions of films that had been exhibited around the world in far different forms.[60] This wholesale chopping of foreign films for supposedly moral purposes became a turning point as critics began to take notice of the artistic interference inherent in censoring. In the next few years, critics would move toward becoming vocal opponents of the state film censors.

But artistic merit was no consideration in New York's motion picture division offices (or on any of the other censor boards). Censors in this prewar era failed to consider artistic merit in making decisions about eliminations and rejections. They ignored the aesthetic consequences of the required cuts on the integrity of the work. But because motion pictures were still not considered a legitimate art form, none of the pre–World War II cases questioned the censors' lack of expertise in film or drama or challenged the artistic damage done to films by cutting. The story lines of both *Remous* and *Ecstasy* were enfeebled to get New York State licenses. Film critics of the time found the results disappointing. Their opinions, however, were no match for those of the legislatively empowered censors.

The Birth of a Baby Unnerves the Censors

The last significant film case before the cease-fire in the censorship battles brought on by World War II was an educational film, *The Birth of a Baby* (1937), sponsored by the American Medical Association, the U.S. Public Health Service, the American Hospital Association, and a plethora of other medical and social organizations. This film was intended to spread much-needed information to would-be parents at a time when 150,000 American mothers and children were dying in childbirth each year. With support from so many organizations as well as from critics from the *New York Times*, the *Nation*, and the *New York Herald Tribune*, it should have been a shoo-in.

But the situation was not so clear cut for the censors of New York, Virginia, and Pennsylvania in the mid-1930s. They hewed to the social mores of the day, and in pre–baby boom America, pregnancy was a topic only for private discourse. The euphemism for pregnancy, *confinement*, meant exactly that: pregnant women were expected to disappear from polite society until their babies were born. Secrecy abounded, even between mothers and daughters, and few women knew what to expect when they prepared to give birth to their first child. This veil of secrecy over pregnancy was in part the reason the United States had one of the highest infant mortality rates in the industrialized world. Lifting that veil, though, meant yet another assault on the province of the reticent, and the film became a major controversy in the continuing debate over public versus private.

When baby food manufacturer Mead Johnson and Company decided to produce an educational film about pregnancy and birth, it wanted to blend drama and documentary. The film centers on a young woman named Mary who is ignorant of the facts of life and who believes that she might be pregnant. Her mother-in-law encourages Mary to see a doctor right away. At the doctor's office, she is examined (discreetly) and instructed in the development of the fetus with explanatory diagrams. Months pass, and Mary gives birth at home. The film includes a twenty-second scene of the baby's head being delivered (although Mary is so well draped that the baby seems to be born from a towel). The camera moves back to give a long shot of Mary receiving the baby to nurse, but with no view of the requisite breast. Mary's husband enters, and all is well.

Although the film was originally intended for distribution to doctors as a teaching aid, the American Committee on Maternal Welfare, a subagency of the National Academy of Sciences, set out to distribute the film to American theaters. Unimpressed by the film's long list of organizational supporters and even an endorsement from First Lady Eleanor Roosevelt, the New York censors rejected *The Birth of a Baby* in July 1937. Irwin Esmond characterized the movie as "a medical treatise . . . in pictorial form. . . . Its presentation to general audiences at places of amusement is objectionable. . . . The picture is 'indecent,' 'immoral' and 'would tend to corrupt morals.'"[61]

The New York censors were soon joined by their colleagues in Pennsylvania, who banned the film despite numerous letters requesting its release and additional pressure from the media and medical associations. Virginia also rejected it, resulting in the first challenge to Virginia's censorship law (*Lynchburg v. Dominion Theatres*, 1940) and the last until 1965. The state censors were not unanimous, though, in this battle over public and private: Ohio licensed *The Birth of a Baby* without hesitation.

The American Committee on Maternal Welfare appealed to New York's board of regents, explaining that it would have preferred an entirely factual presentation, "but the picture can attain its objectives only if it is seen by the public. . . . Without the facilities of the motion picture theatre, any educational effort of this nature must necessarily be circumscribed." To demonstrate the sincerity of their educational purpose, the producers offered to submit all advertising in advance and to agree to any age restrictions required by the motion picture division. The picture was not obscene, they insisted: "It appeals to the noblest sentiments of humanity and there is no incident, word or act in the entire picture which could be construed as indecent, immoral or tending to corrupt morals."[62] Nine regents reviewed the film and rejected the American Committee on Maternal Welfare's argument.

Unlike so many censor decisions that remained unknown, this one set off a firestorm in the form of nationwide censorship debate. The April 11 issue of *Life*, which carried thirty-five still photographs from the film, was banned by local authorities in several states. *Life*'s publisher, Roy E. Larsen, arranged to have himself arrested for selling the magazine in the Bronx, where the magazine had been banned as "obscene literature."[63] Four local court cases stemmed from the *Life* photographs, but judges dismissed them all.[64] All of the controversy was based on the actions of government bodies, either on the state level, as in the case of the New York, Pennsylvania, and Virginia censors, or on the local level, as in the case of the Bronx. Trying to thwart discourse, the reticent had unwittingly created conditions under which the unmentionable became the center of attention.

This controversy and the public forum that resulted became a victory of sorts for the American Committee on Maternal Welfare. Because the press picked up on the litigation in New York, people across the nation got a glimpse into the workings of the state censor boards. Editorials in the *New York Times*, the *Nation*, the *New York Herald Tribune*, and the *New York Post* all called for the movie's release. The *New York Times* criticized the censors' obsolescence, reminding readers, "Novels, plays, books on the social sciences discuss sex with a frankness that would have seemed incredible at the turn of the century. Endorsed as it is by the foremost medical and civic organizations, *The Birth of a Baby* merely follows the trend of the times."[65] This editorial points out the major dilemma for censors. They were expected by the public and by critics to "follow the trends," yet they were set to work by legislatures and town councils primarily to serve as a brake. Because censors' work was overseen by traditionally conservative judges, film censorship remained one of the last hopes of the party of reticence (to use Rochelle Gurstein's phrase).

After the *Life* controversy, the motion picture division found itself the butt of media criticism and sarcasm. Another editorial in the *Nation* dismissed the allegation that the film could incite to immoral behavior. "This quiet, serious treatment . . . can be no more incentive to lust than a plate of lamb kidneys or a motor car accident." The most disparaging comments came in Ernest L. Meyer's column in the *New York Post* under the headline "Those Odd Censors: Murder Approved, Maternity Taboo." Meyer had watched the film as part of a test group.

> You can vision the forty of us being corrupted by a movie so monstrous that we left the projection room with lecherous urges and climbed on a bandwagon headed for the nearest bawdy house. . . . The movie censors who banned "The Birth of a Baby" . . . should change their name to the Society for the Perpetuation of the Stork Legend. Curious people, these censors. They approve films showing crimes of violence, manslaughter, shootings by gangsters and G-men, scenes of lynching and wars—all the terrifying techniques by which life is destroyed. They do not approve of a film depicting the constructive and comparatively beautiful technique by which life is created. . . . Strange that this film which is intended to preserve life should be scuttled while films which glorify the destruction of life should receive official benediction.[66]

American Committee on Maternal Welfare, backed by the AMA and represented by retired New York justice Ellis J. Staley, brought suit in the appellate division based on the novel legal position that "the test of indecency lies in public opinion." Staley pushed the public-private boundary when he argued that a charge of indecency was "impossible" since sex instruction had become "recognized and accepted as part of our authorized and legalized educational program."[67]

The motion picture division responded that childbirth could not be decently presented as "public entertainment." Since a live birth scene would not be allowed on stage, the motion picture division argued, it should not be allowed on film.[68] Although this argument was clearly spurious (how could a live birth be presented on stage?), it was the position maintained by New York censors for another sixteen years. No scenes of birth would be allowed in New York movies, not even of animal births. In 1954, Walt Disney would be stunned to learn that his Academy Award–winning documentary *The Vanishing Prairie*, which was already approved by the Legion of Decency and every other state censor board, was banned by New York's motion picture division as indecent because it showed the birth of a baby buffalo. The motion picture division's acting director, Helen Kellogg, wrote to the Disney studio to explain: "It has been the policy of the Motion Picture Division over the years to take out views of actual births."[69] Disney apologized if his film had given offense, but, he wrote, "It would be a shame if the New York children had to believe the stork brings buffalos, too."[70] Kellogg was reversed by her boss after the ACLU filed a complaint.

But such open-mindedness was years in the future. In 1938, the American Committee on Maternal Welfare still needed to get *The Birth of a Baby* before theater audiences. After dismissing the state's comparison to live births on stage as impossible, Staley struck at the vagueness of New York's law. In a valiant attempt to question the censors' lack of accountability, he argued that the motion picture division should have to furnish more information when a license was refused than a few words from the statute, such as *immoral*, *indecent*, or *obscene*. "The condemnatory words of the statute," his brief continued, "are merely characterization. They express the ultimate conclusion, not the reasons for it. . . . Matters of mere personal opinion cannot be weighed and tried before courts of justice."[71] After seventeen years of censorship without standards, a film distributor had finally legally questioned the basic operation of the motion picture division.

The appellate division, however, rejected, three to two, the American Committee on Maternal Welfare's case. The majority opinion, ignoring Staley's allegation that the motion picture division failed to give sufficient reason when rejecting a film, sounded like all other film censorship opinions in its assertion that "there is only a difference of opinion as to the character of the picture. . . . The determination should not be disturbed."[72] The motion picture division had won again. But the decision came with another strong dissent by Presiding Justice Hill, who had previously dissented on *Tomorrow's Children*: "The film will give vital and needed information. . . . To limit the exhibition to educational and clinical groups will defeat the worthy purpose of the sponsors of the film."[73] A last step to the court of appeals took almost a year, and then the judges refused to overturn, offering no opinion. The producers of *The Birth of a Baby* revised the movie sufficiently to pass the censors in 1941. From inciting a nationwide debate on indecency in motion pictures, the issue raised by the film became a lost cause in the war years.

The American Committee on Maternal Welfare had tried to bring the motion picture division to greater accountability, but to no avail. The film's producers had tried to update the censoring activities to take into account public opinion and changing mores, but that had failed also. But the case did succeed, with the help of *Life* and other publications, in focusing attention on the secretive work of New York State's censors, the vagueness of their standards of censorship, and the types of films they were keeping from the people of the state.

The controversy also shed light on the rigidity of the motion picture division's decisions. The Legion of Decency faced the difficult decision about how to handle *The Birth of a Baby*, a film that portrayed a proscribed subject yet was capable of effecting so much societal good. The legion responded by creating an entirely new category, "separate classification." Taking its cue from the distributor's willingness to attach conditions to the exhibition of the film, the legion, unlike the governmental censors, realized that not all films would fit prescribed categories. Although "separate classification" was used very sparingly over the years, the legion had recognized the varieties of film effects and purposes.[74]

The Birth of a Baby was the last film to challenge the motion picture division until after World War II. All of the distributors who challenged the censors in the 1930s had lost in New York, yet each succeeded in shining some light on the workings of the motion picture division. Although the ACLU's National Council on Freedom from Censorship had in 1933 published a list of the eliminations required by the New York censors in a pamphlet, *What Shocked the Censors*, the average moviegoer was probably not reading such esoteric fare.[75] The public would have remained unaware of the censors' edicts were it not for the challenge cases that put the issue of movie censorship into the newspapers. Without these challenge films, New York's censoring would have remained camouflaged, protected by its secretive methods, statutory ambiguity, and "aura of judicial approval."

Beyond airing the issue, two of the 1930s challenges had also managed to split the previously solid courts, chipping away at the solid legal front that was the legacy of the *Mutual* decision. Indeed, by 1939, in all the censoring states and cities, only three challenge cases had succeeded—two on procedural grounds and one substantive reversal in Virginia, where a lower state court overruled its censors' ban of *The Birth of a Baby*.[76]

While Hollywood acquiesced in prior restraint of its product and simultaneously submitted to internal content regulation, nine independent producers and distributors had resisted state interference. Those independents questioned the censors' opinions, the secrecy in which they made their decisions, the vagueness of the statutes, the lack of accountability, and the disregard for public opinion. Yet none questioned the qualifications of the people who acted as society's guardians, none attacked the issue of prior restraint, and none attacked on the grounds of the free speech provisions of their state constitution[77] or the First or Fourteenth amendments to the U.S. Constitution. The *Mutual* precedent set in 1915 still stood. No film distributor took the risky road of questioning the state's limitations on the constitutional rights to free speech. Because movies were believed to be more dangerous than other media, they had been singled out for prior restraint. Other areas where prior restraint had been applied—theater and tabloid newspapers—had been freed by the 1930s. Books could still be controlled by after-publication prosecution, but only for obscenity. Radio escaped state control because its regulation was claimed by the Federal Communications Commission. But movies could be stopped for many different reasons, all of them at the censor's say. This discretionary area opened the possibility for litigation, which seemed the only way to eliminate censorship, since legislators showed no interest in depriving their state budgets of the income from movie review. Prior restraint on movies would continue as long as the courts upheld the censors.

Constitutional challenges to censorship would not surface until after World War II. The censors and the dissident distributors took a break during the patriotic fervor of the war years. The war also ended importation of foreign films, removing one of the sources of contention between distributor and censor. But this was just an intermission; act two in the censorship legal struggles would soon begin.

5

The First Amendment Resurfaces, 1946–1950

After 1915, when the U.S. Supreme Court refused to accept free speech and free press arguments for motion pictures, censorship challengers dropped any attempt to invoke movies' First Amendment rights and took a more pragmatic route, arguing findings of fact. The approach narrowed from "*All* movie censorship is wrong" to "Censorship of *this* movie is wrong." During the 1930s, however, freedom of political speech became the subject of much debate in the legal community, assuming, according to Richard Steele, "the proportions of a national cause." Only a decade removed from the speech-restricting excesses of the post–World War I years, civil libertarians were still worried about the potential power of governmental control. In the late 1930s, they were joined by businessmen, newspaper publishers, and radio broadcasters who, seeking relief from New Deal controls, turned to the First Amendment.[1] As World War II loomed and the American public witnessed the antidemocratic excesses of fascism, new groups joined those already questioning centralized controls on speech.

Those who favored free speech began to make some progress in the courts. By World War II, four more justices had adopted Stone's preferred freedoms philosophy. The only political speech restrictions that would survive Supreme Court scrutiny in these years were those that were designed to prevent a "clear and present danger." Statutes infringing on the right to make nondangerous, nonthreatening political speech would likely be struck down.

Still, the special-capacity-for-evil construct made any attacks on movie censors' decisions almost unthinkable and invariably futile. Moreover, Chief Justice Stone died in 1946 and was replaced by the more reticent Fred Vinson; then Justices Frank Murphy and Wiley Rutledge—two of the dependable civil libertarians—died in 1949 and were replaced by moderates Sherman Minton and Tom C. Clark. It looked as if Stone's philosophy of preferred freedoms would be weakened considerably. Some Court watchers worried that the justices would move from the "clear and present danger" test to a "possible and remote danger" test.[2]

Even so, there were some major speech protection breakthroughs in the immediate post–World War II years. In 1945 and 1946, three nonfilm cases testing the limits of free speech reached the U.S. Supreme Court, each one expanding the scope of the First Amendment's protections of freedom of speech and press and holding out new promise for film censorship challenges. The first case, *Hannegan v. Esquire*, restricted the postmaster general's power of censorship (the source of Comstock's power). The Supreme Court enjoined the postmaster from refusing second-class mailing rates to publications that he personally found to be indecent. The second case, *Thomas v. Collins*, disallowed state laws that could require a speaker to gain permission from civil authorities in advance for speech (provided the speech supported a lawful organization). The third case, *Pennekamp v. Florida*, extended First and Fourteenth Amendment protections to newspaper editorials.[3]

Each of these three cases stretched the First Amendment to fit new speech circumstances. Nonetheless, protections of speech and press were still limited by the courts' sharp distinction between economic rights and noneconomic rights. As long as the production and exhibition of movies was regarded by judges as an economic activity, a "business pure and simple," as first phrased by Justice McKenna in the 1915 *Mutual* case, motion pictures would not be seen as a legitimate exercise of free speech. As free speech became a matter of public discussion and judges began to expand the realm of free speech concerns, though, movies slowly began to look less like a business and more like an art form. But not until the economic activity of movie distribution became secondary to the art of moviemaking in the minds of the justices would courts extend speech protection to film.[4]

Nevertheless, the First Amendment was dusted off and called back into service by film distributors in 1947 and again in 1951. Although the two challenge films, *The Outlaw* and *The Miracle*, were dissimilar (one domestic, the other foreign; one pure entertainment, the other artistic), they shared two unusual traits. Both attracted the ire of the New York

City commissioner of licenses after being passed by the censors of New York's motion picture division, and both were condemned by the Catholic Church. The cases also reflect the growing involvement of the ACLU as some midcentury Americans began to think about extending the reach of free speech rights.

During the 1940s and 1950s, the ACLU's involvement in fighting film censorship was sporadic. Most members adhered to legal scholar Alexander Meikeljohn's distinction between political speech (which was to be absolutely protected) and entertainment speech (which could be restricted for obscenity). Some members, like Arthur Garfield Hays, argued that the ACLU should adopt an absolutist position on free speech issues, but this idea did not prevail in the organization until changing societal norms and the sexual revolution of the 1950s and 1960s made literature and entertainment that dealt with sex socially acceptable.[5]

Local affiliates of the ACLU might have sympathized with film distributors who wanted to challenge censor boards, but with limited resources and many other civil liberties issues demanding their attention, most chapters were not actively soliciting test cases.[6] The National Council on Freedom from Censorship and the New York Civil Liberties Union, however, were on the lookout for a promising litigant. The proponents of censorship, the largest and most vocal of which was the Catholic Church, were also looking for a test case—one that would extend their reach to imported films. The early 1950s was ripe for a showdown between the ACLU and the Catholic Church.[7] In this confrontation, the Catholics' arsenal of arguments included propriety, morality, and anti-Communist patriotism. The ACLU appealed to the ideals of free speech, a free press, and open democracy.

The First Postwar Challenge

Having been quiet throughout the war, film distributors began to question censor determinations again once the war ended. The first challenge came in 1946 when New York denied exhibition to a twelve-year-old French film, *Amok*. Dealing with adultery, abortion, and obsessive love, the film carries unmistakable overtones of misery and damnation for characters who stray beyond society's norms. *Amok* is set on a French colonial island. The main characters are a doctor and his unrequited love, the wife of an absent landowner. When the woman has an affair with another man and becomes pregnant, she begs the doctor to perform an abortion before her husband returns. The lovesick doctor agrees to perform the abortion, but only if she becomes his mistress. She refuses and finds a local quack, who botches the abortion, causing her death just as her husband returns. He is determined to have her body autopsied in France, but as her coffin is being lifted onto a ship, the distraught doctor cuts the ropes and then plunges into the harbor to drown beside her body.[8]

Surprisingly, the New York censors had no problem with the film's adultery, but they had a big problem with the abortion. Taking *Amok* to the appellate division, Distinguished Films, like most previous challengers, argued opinions. The censors said the film was immoral; the distributor said it was not. The distributor said that the motion picture division had licensed far more objectionable films; the motion picture division said it had not. And the appellate division of the New York State Supreme Court did what it had been doing for twenty-five years: it refused to substitute its judgment for that of the legislatively empowered bureaucrats whose job it was to decide such matters. The NYCLU, which had been watching the case, decided against involvement when Distinguished Films failed to sue on constitutional grounds.[9] So the first postwar challenge to New York's film censorship agency sustained the legal status quo of the prewar years: no one mentioned prior restraint or freedom of speech. These issues remained dormant until Howard Hughes's *Outlaw* rode into New York City the following year.

A Tempest in a Teapot

In 1945, after thirteen years as head censor, New York's motion picture division director, Irwin Esmond, retired. He was replaced by Ward Bowen, an audiovisual specialist from the New York State Education Department who had pioneered the use of visual aids in the classroom. Unusual among censors, Bowen had a background in film and a strong belief in its inherent instructional benefits. He had been on the job just a few months when he was faced with what would become one of the motion picture division's highest-profile cases, that of Howard Hughes's infamous film *The Outlaw*. The world-famous aviator, manufacturer, and millionaire had been dabbling in films since 1926. By 1940, when he decided to make a film loosely based on Billy the Kid, Hughes had already produced nine films, including *Hell's Angels* (1930), *Front Page* (1931), *Cock of the Air* (1932), and *Scarface* (1932). Along the way he had developed a flare for annoying both the PCA and the state censors. Both *Cock of the Air* and

Scarface had endured serious cutting from the PCA and even heavier slicing by some state and local censors.[10]

Hughes began production in 1940 on *The Outlaw*, knowing that the film would inflame another censorship debate. His new project depicted a love triangle: Rio, an extraordinarily well-endowed "half-breed" played by newcomer Jane Russell; Billy the Kid, played by another discovery, Jack Buetel; and Doc Holliday, played by Hollywood veteran Walter Huston. Rio's blouse always seems to be at the center of attention, and the screenplay is peppered with dialogue that makes it clear that both Billy and Doc have had a sexual relationship with her. Late in the movie, for example, Doc Holliday declines Billy's invitation to take up with Rio again, saying, "I don't want her. Cattle don't graze after sheep."

Hughes was so intent on making a splash with this film that, even before shooting a single foot, he hired the highest-powered Hollywood press agent he could find to begin promotion. Hughes told the publicity man, Russell Birdwell, fresh from his monumental promotion of *Gone with the Wind* the year before, that *The Outlaw* was more about sex than gunplay.[11] So Birdwell made Russell a sex symbol by posing her at ship launchings, at baby beauty contests, and as the centerpiece of sensational ad layouts. Hughes and his project were clearly on a collision course with the full gamut of censors in the PCA, the Legion of Decency, and the state boards.

Hughes began filming without submitting the shooting script to Joseph Breen at the PCA. Breen requested a copy and immediately objected to more than one hundred scenes. Hughes made some of the required revisions, but Breen was not satisfied when he saw the final film. Hughes agreed to make several more changes, and *The Outlaw* earned the necessary seal late in 1941. But the approval came with a catch. Figuring that Hughes would exploit *The Outlaw*'s approval troubles to lure patrons, the PCA made a special point of reminding Hughes of the requirement that all advertising and publicity materials be submitted to its advertising council. Hughes was put on notice that the MPAA would be watching his promotional campaign closely.

Hughes also submitted the film to the censors of New York and Maryland. Both ordered eliminations, but Hughes did not resubmit. He decided not to release *The Outlaw* until he could mount another publicity blitz. Birdwell went to work again, plastering much of the country with advance publicity built around Russell's endowments.[12] Months before the film finally hit the screen in 1943, Russell had become a national celebrity, famous not for her acting ability—no one had seen that yet—but for her physique. After a feverishly promoted but not very successful eight-week run in San Francisco, Hughes withdrew the film for the remainder of the war.

He decided to rerelease in 1946 and dutifully followed the PCA's requirement concerning advertising by submitting 202 photos and twenty-one newspaper ads for review. The advertising division found fault with 20 of the photos and all but one of the ads. Some of the ads falsely claimed that the film was "Exactly as Filmed: Not a Scene Cut." One ad depicted Russell and Buetel horizontal in the hayloft, while another showed Russell wearing a low-cut blouse and a high-cut skirt, reclining on a hay bale, with the caption "How Would You Like to Tussle with Russell?" Hughes refused to have his artists raise the neckline or lengthen the skirt. Another shot of Russell from the waist up asked the reader to identify "the TWO reasons for Jane's rise to stardom."[13]

Acting quickly, before the MPAA had the chance to move against him, Hughes opened the film to long box office lines that helped him recoup his $1.2 million production budget. Critics were not kind: a disappointed *New York Post* film critic wrote, "The movie has never been made that would live up to the inferred combustibility of [this] picture."[14] Finally, the MPAA caught up with Hughes and revoked *The Outlaw*'s seal. Without it, the best he could hope for was three thousand theaters and about 25 percent of theater locations.[15] The MPAA put Hughes on notice that he was about to be expelled, so he decided to withdraw, filing a $5 million lawsuit on his way out.

Hughes resubmitted the film to the Maryland censors in 1946, and they promptly refused him again, bolstered by moral support from 2,200 citizens who had signed a petition demanding the film not be shown.[16] Never fazed by negative publicity, Hughes brought suit in the Baltimore City Court but lost when the censor-sympathetic judge found that Jane Russell's breasts "hung over the picture like a thunderstorm spread out over a landscape."[17] Hoping for the New York market, Hughes also tangled with the motion picture division again in 1946. More forgiving than their Maryland counterparts, the New York censors asked for a few more deletions (including the "cattle don't graze after sheep" line), and *The Outlaw* was free to open.[18]

But the New York openings did not go well for *The Outlaw*. New York City's license commissioner, Benjamin Fielding, took issue with Hughes's ads and petitioned the motion picture division to yank its license. It refused. Fielding then took matters into his own hands and threatened New York City theater owners with license revocation if they showed the film. Hughes responded with a string of lawsuits, the first of which tried to compel theater owners to show the picture despite the license commissioner's warning. This got the attention of the ACLU, whose National Council on Freedom from Censorship called Fielding's ultimatum "the most vicious attempt at pre-censorship made in this city in the last 20 years." The council worried it could lead to the closing of any movie that was offensive to whoever happened to be license commissioner, even if it had been passed by the motion picture division.[19] Even so, the ACLU let Hughes fight the case alone. Making a public pronouncement against Fielding's quasicensorship held far more appeal for the ACLU than helping Hughes exhibit his infamous film.

Hughes received no help from the New York State Supreme Court, either. On October 23, 1946, the judges, later backed by the appellate division, refused to force the city's theater owners to honor their contracts with Hughes because to do so would have left them open to criminal prosecution.[20] With a relatively simple contract issue as their resolution, the justices did not need to consider the license commissioner's authority to interfere with the exhibition of a state-licensed film.

Then the situation grew complicated. A "condemned" rating by the Legion of Decency caused many theaters across the country to remove the film from their screens. Several cities, including Boston, Tacoma, and Bridgeport, Connecticut, banned *The Outlaw*, and theater owners in Texas, Washington DC, Minneapolis, Chicago, Syracuse, and Seattle voluntarily withdrew it under the Catholic pressure. At Sunday Mass, Catholics across the country were repeatedly directed not to see *The Outlaw*.

Failing to budge Maryland or New York City, Hughes went forward with his $5 million lawsuit against the MPAA, pulling out every conceivable argument, including an appeal to the film's free speech rights under the First Amendment. It had been thirty-one years since *Mutual*, and only one film challenge since then had been based on abridgment of free speech.

Hughes's attorneys began by tackling the monolith of the MPAA, showing that the organization rigidly controlled film content in 90 percent of American theaters, either through ownership or through the economic intimidation of block booking. This was the issue the MPAA most wanted to hide. Indeed, the need to deflect attention from its monopolistic practices was one of the main reasons that Hays and company had been so willing to embrace the institution of the PCA in 1934. But the ploy had not fooled the Justice Department's antitrust division, which had brought a suit against the MPAA that was still dragging on when Hughes sued, enabling him to jump on the Justice Department's bandwagon and complain that the industry was clearly violating the Sherman Antitrust Act by unfairly restraining trade. Hughes's attack was the first significant legal challenge from within the industry to the MPAA's lockdown on movie content. (The Justice Department's case would not be settled for another two years.)

Trying to deflect attention from the monopoly that Hollywood had so carefully constructed and maintained for years, the MPAA's new president, Eric Johnston, issued a statement that came as a big surprise to member theater operators: they were free to show *The Outlaw* despite its lack of code seal.[21] The Justice Department continued its case, however, and Johnston probably regretted the statement a few years later, when other producers began opening movies without the code seal, weakening the PCA's enforcement power.

Hughes also claimed that the MPAA's advertising code administrators had deprived him of property without due process of law. He finished with an appeal to the First Amendment, claiming that both governmental censors and the MPAA were withholding "a large body of information, knowledge, and understanding of controversial topics against the wishes of individual producers, distributors, and exhibitors and to the great detriment of the public."[22] It was a good argument, but *The Outlaw* was not the best vehicle for it.

Federal district court judge John Bright showed little patience with any of Hughes's contentions and dispatched them one by one. Bright had no sympathy for Hughes's struggle against the MPAA because he had used rejected materials, amplifying their effect by slapping "censored" across the front. Bright saw the code as Hollywood's attempt to "maintain the highest possible moral and artistic standards" and chastised Hughes for accepting the Hays seal to gain entry to the eighteen thousand MPAA member theaters in the United States yet refusing to accept the contractual limits that would have allowed him to keep the seal. He also discarded Hughes's claim of protection under the First Amendment. "Even if plaintiff in this case is in a position to invoke the First Amendment relating to freedom of speech, and of that I have grave doubt, he can hardy succeed where the speech which has been rejected is not the truth." Aware of the Justice Department's ongoing investigation into the antitrust complaint against the industry, Bright would have been foolish to rule further on Hughes's monopoly claims. So he found the restraint inherent in the MPAA's censoring of movies "reasonable," since its goal was to maintain high moral standards. Finally, dismissing the worthiness of Hughes's case, Bright concluded, "The whole matter is a trivial one, a tempest in a teapot. In fact, it seems more an effort on the part of the plaintiff to add this case and its peregrinations through the courts as additional publicity and advertising in promotion of the picture."[23]

Attempting to weaken the PCA, Hughes had accomplished just the opposite. He had started as an outsider and finished as an outcast. He had not learned to play along with the PCA or the Legion of Decency, as his Hollywood colleagues had. Able to force-feed the majority of first-run theaters in the United States through its block booking, and enjoying box office sales still at record levels, the industry had little reason to struggle against censorship, either its own or the government's. Hughes challenged both and succeeded only in confirming the legality of the former and the acceptability of the latter.

Hughes requested a stay pending his appeal but got no sympathy from Judge Learned Hand, who suggested, "The plaintiff can avoid the whole difficulty by changing its advertisements to meet the defendant's requirements. That the necessary changes will in any substantial way lessen the plaintiff's audiences is the merest speculation."[24]

Hughes was not through; he took on License Commissioner Fielding again. But this time he asked a good legal question: whether the exhibitor of a duly licensed motion picture could be prosecuted under the New York Penal Law for presenting "an immoral exhibition" and whether a theater's license could be revoked for such exhibition. This was a question of law rather than of fact, and it deserved an answer. In 1940, a Virginia court had ruled that such conflicting police powers could not coexist. That court ruled against local censorship in favor of state censorship as a matter of common sense.[25] But judicial precedent in New York concerning the license commissioner's authority was not on Hughes's side. The commissioner was statutorily empowered to revoke theater licenses that showed "immoral" films, and numerous similar attempts to curb the commissioner's powers had failed.

Hughes brought in some heavy hitters for this court appearance, including former lieutenant governor Charles Poletti, but to no avail. Supreme Court justice Bernard Shientag held that because the state's censorship law left no opportunity for public review in court, local police power was the only possibility for public input. "In the last analysis," Shientag held, "what is proper to be shown to the public must be decided by the public." Prosecution and conviction under a local ordinance, Shientag declared, was one "possible and not unreasonable method . . . of reviewing . . . the fitness of the film to be shown." In the court's view, then, Fielding had acted properly and with the people's interests in mind. Hughes had lost again.[26]

He appealed, and by early 1948, the case was slated for review by the New York State Court of Appeals. Although the ACLU had declined involvement before, some of its members now considered taking part, not to make a free speech case but to limit the license commissioner's censorship powers. A disagreement arose between ACLU general counsel Osmond Fraenkel and Clifford Forster, lead attorney for the National Council on Freedom from Censorship. Forster believed that without a challenge to a censorship board, the case had no merit. Fraenkel argued that the ACLU should fight any extension of administrative censorship authority: "A threat by a license commissioner . . . is itself a form of censorship," Fraenkel wrote, "and it seems to me we would have an interest in any limitation on his powers in this respect."[27] Fraenkel prevailed and the ACLU filed an amicus curiae brief for the final appeal in *The Outlaw* case, but the only signatures it carried were his and coauthor Emanuel Redfield's. (Normally when the ACLU drafted an amicus, it would circulate it among sympathetic attorneys for their signatures.) The brief started by distancing the ACLU from Hughes, whose main point was that a motion picture division license immunized *The Outlaw* from any action by the license commissioner. This position philosophically accepted governmental censorship, a stance with which the ACLU could not agree. The amicus brief made only two other points: that the license commissioner's powers were "vague" and that they violated freedom of speech. The "field of censorship should not be widened . . . to extend beyond the present controls of the Education Department." The brief suggested that an attack on the *Mutual* decision would be made "at the appropriate time"—but clearly not in this case and not at this time.[28] Both the appellate division and the court of appeals affirmed Judge Shientag's original opinion. Hughes had lost once more.

In the end, Howard Hughes had spent much time in court and had irritated many judges. But he did not take even a tiny step forward in shaking off censorship of film. In fact, his legal maneuverings with film advertising set back the cause of anticensorship, and bills introduced in

1947 sought to close a loophole concerning film advertising. The motion picture division's censors recommended amending the law to give them the power to review "any medium or means reaching the people of the State." Industry columnist Sherwin Kane, writing in *Motion Picture Daily*, worried that "the entire industry, in its important operations in New York State, stands in danger of having its advertising subjected to political censorship hereafter. Conceivably, if [the proposal to close the loophole] is enacted, a producer-distributor could suffer the loss of the lucrative state market through the withdrawal of his picture's state license simply because some misguided exhibitor overstepped the bounds of decency in advertising the production."[29] Regardless, the amendment was signed by the governor and took effect immediately.

Ending the Monopoly

The constitutionality of motion picture censorship in the United States hinges on four decisive turning points. The first was the affirmation of prior restraint in the 1915 *Mutual* decision. The second, thirty-three years later, came in an unlikely package, the antitrust case brought by the Justice Department—*United States v. Paramount Pictures, Inc.*

As we have seen, one of Hollywood's main reasons for wearing the hair shirt of the Production Code was to keep its movies at a low profile, lest attention be focused on how Hollywood was getting movies into theaters in the first place: by monopolistic business practices that allowed enormous profits. Without the reward of guaranteed theater bookings, the PCA's censors would hold little authority over motion picture producers. So when the Justice Department instituted proceedings against the studios' monopolistic control of film exhibition, the MPAA's worst fears came true. The delicate balance between the carrot of maximum theater bookings and the stick of content regulation could be maintained only if the industry controlled the business environment. Hoping to maintain the status quo a bit longer, the industry entered into a consent decree in June 1940 that allowed the movie moguls to continue their distribution practices relatively unchanged for a three-year trial period.[30] When the consent decree expired in 1944, a new attorney general, Tom Clark, revisited the studios' business methods and instituted a new suit, joined by the American Theatres Association, the Conference of Independent Exhibitors' Associations, and the Society of Independent Motion Picture Producers (all hoping the majors would be forced to sell off their theaters, opening the market for competitive pricing and opening theater screens for independent productions), as well as the ACLU, which argued that the MPAA's business practices had reduced film quality.

The Supreme Court considered the situation in 1948. In a striking show of juridical agreement, Justice William O. Douglas wrote a single opinion for a court united in its condemnation of an industry "whose proclivity to unlawful conduct has been so marked." The ruling boiled down to four main points. First, whether the movie industry intended to restrain trade had no relevance; the only thing that mattered was that its practices had stifled competition. Second, to violate the Sherman Antitrust Act, the industry needed only to maneuver to prevent competition—successful destruction of competition was not necessary for the activity to be considered illegal. Third, the acquisition of any theater, if intended to stifle competition, was fair game for antitrust action. And, fourth, block booking and price fixing combinations were illegal. The justices sent the case back to the federal district court to reconsider divorcement.[31] One year later, the district court ordered the majors to sell off their theaters. With new competition from other sources, however, selling theaters was not easy, and the process took until 1957.[32]

While the *Paramount* decision had major ramifications for independent production and distribution of films, it held more than the hope of free competition; it also contained words of comfort for the opponents of film censorship. The opinion came with an aside from Justice Douglas, who wrote, "We have no doubt that moving pictures, like newspapers and radio, are included in the press whose freedom is guaranteed by the First Amendment."[33] Since this was a monopoly case and not a speech case, the words carried no weight as precedent. But they did hint that the Court might be ready to reexamine the status of film freedom. More important, the words carried recognition that the MPAA's economic monopoly, its content regulation, and film freedom were inexorably linked. Hollywood's monologue was about to end.

Things looked glum for the MPAA. Its hegemony had been weakened, ticket sales were down, television was gaining popularity, and foreign distribution revenues were dropping as European film industries recovered after the war and began supplying overseas audiences. The moguls needed to find new ways to compete now that their guaranteed outlets—both domestic and foreign—would soon be gone. The industry faced another threat: real competition for ticket admissions from foreign films in American theaters. With the game changing so rapidly, some in

Hollywood began to question the restrictions of the Production Code and the domination of the Catholic Church. In previous hard times, movie moguls had turned to sex and violence to turn up box office draw. In the late 1940s, realistic, message-filled films from Europe were taking away patrons who were hungry for more serious, artistic fare. Beset on all sides, Hollywood had to rethink its old ways.

The industry had to figure out how to compete. With block booking gone, the studios could no longer control screen time, which they had been packing with cheaply made, highly profitable B movies. The decrease in guaranteed theaters forced the major studios to reduce production, leaving exhibitors scrambling to fill screen time. They increasingly turned to independent producers and foreign film distributors, none of whom were interested in abiding by the code. Production by independents so increased that by 1957, they could claim half of all major films made.[34] Within two years, desperate for new sources of profit, all the major studios save one had begun distributing productions of their former competitors, the independents.[35] The studios' own distribution companies were now balking at content regulation—certainly not good news for the PCA's administrators.

The *Paramount* decision that had initiated so much of this change must have worried governmental censors as well. If the Supreme Court had "no doubt" that movies were part of the press, how long could governmental censorship hold on? The ACLU's National Council on Freedom from Censorship sensed blood in the water and, in June 1949, made a public plea for any exhibitor to assist with a test case.[36] The perfect test, the council believed, would come if an exhibitor were fined and jailed for showing a banned film or if a banned film appeared on television.[37] But no exhibitors volunteered, and no banned films were broadcast on the small screen.

The showing of uncensored films on television did, however, become a legal issue in Pennsylvania, a case watched closely by the censors in the other states. When television began to appear in Pennsylvanians' homes, the state's censors sought to extend their power of review. But several companies with television broadcast interests brought suit, claiming that the censors had no authority over broadcast programs since the federal government had already staked out the territory when it established the Federal Communications Commission. A federal district court agreed.[38] But chief Pennsylvania censor Edna Carroll was determined that her board would decide what could be shown on TV. She pursued the case, but a court of appeals panel agreed that Congress's intention in setting up the powers of the FCC was so clear that the state could not have any jurisdiction.[39] Undeterred, Carroll tried to appeal to the U.S. Supreme Court, but the justices found the argument so clear and so correctly decided that they denied certiorari.[40] All the state censor boards took note and went back to theatrical releases.

The ACLU was keeping tabs on the Court's attitude toward freedom of speech. The justices had overruled a number of long-standing speech-restrictive precedent cases in recent years. As Justice Douglas put it, the Court was "slowly removing from constitutional doctrine excrescences produced early in the century."[41] One year after Douglas issued his *Paramount* dictum that movies deserved First Amendment protection, Justice Hugo Black added new hope for those interested in movie freedom when he insisted in *Kovacs v. Cooper* that films should "be free of governmental censorship or prohibition." But anticensorship optimists got a quick dose of reality when in the same case Justice Felix Frankfurter intoned once more the deeply rooted argument about the "special problems" presented by movies that justified governmental control.[42]

Nevertheless, a possible attitudinal shift on the Court, competition from television, and declining profits combined to convince the MPAA that it might be time to think about backing censorship challenges. Nothing would change quickly, though. MPAA president Eric Johnston, a businessman and former president of the U.S. Chamber of Commerce, was not likely to lead a frontal assault on movie censorship. But Johnston was also a board member of the NAACP, and the censoring of race-themed movies in the South seemed to stick in his craw. Two race-censored movie cases were up for certiorari review in the Supreme Court's 1950 term. The first was *Curley* (1947), a comedy banned in Memphis, and the second was *Lost Boundaries* (1949), a serious film about race relations banned in Atlanta. Both were refused licenses on the grounds that they might negatively impact race harmony. A year later, another banned race movie, *Pinky*, also got the MPAA's attention. Under Johnston's leadership, the MPAA saw these films, particularly the dramatic *Lost Boundaries*, as promising tests that could be used to challenge the 1915 *Mutual* decision.[43] If the MPAA was hoping to show that its members' movies had grown up and deserved to be treated like serious art with serious messages, *Lost Boundaries* and *Pinky* were good choices. The harmless *Curley* was also a good choice because its ban was outlandish.

A Hal Roach Studios production distributed by MPAA member United Artists, *Curley* was a rehash of the Our Gang comedies that Roach had made so popular in the 1930s. Like its predecessors, the gang in *Curley* was integrated—a condition that offended Lloyd Binford, Memphis's censor since 1928. Binford wrote to United Artists that he could not approve the picture "as the south does not permit negroes in white schools nor recognize social equality between the races even in children."[44] This was too much for the MPAA and the Screen Actors Guild, who jointly protested Binford's "intolerance and prejudice."[45] Johnston claimed that Binford's actions provided "conclusive evidence that political censorship of any medium of expression—the press, the radio or the motion picture—cannot be tolerated if we expect American democracy to last." But, while forcefully attacking Memphis's municipal censorship, Johnston went to great lengths to differentiate the work of his own content regulators from that of the government censors. "Political censorship," Johnston wrote, "has no place in America."[46] At that time and for the next eight years, Johnston straddled the issue, criticizing governmental censors and aggressively defending the content regulation of the code.[47]

Despite the MPAA's interest, *Curley* was unpromising as a test case—something Johnston would surely have known. Both a trial court and the Tennessee Supreme Court had used technicalities to avoid overturning Binford,[48] leaving the U.S. Supreme Court with no real controversy on which to rule. When United Artists attempted to take the case further, the Supreme Court declined to review the case.[49]

The second case that Johnston and the MPAA were watching was RD-DR Productions' fight against the Atlanta censor over *Lost Boundaries* (1949). Hollywood had good reason to follow the fate of this movie. The film represented a new, promising direction that the moguls hoped would help shore up sagging profits: realistic treatment of serious social concerns. After many actors and directors came home from service in World War II, they wanted to make more "mature films."[50] A prime example was the 1946 Samuel Goldwyn production *The Best Years of Our Lives*. Dealing with the psychological aspects of the postwar experience, the film appealed to almost everyone even though it had no happy ending, no solutions. It was an extraordinary success, winning the Golden Globe award for best picture, the New York Film Critics Circle award for best film, and seven Oscars, including best picture, best director, best supporting actor, best lead actor, and best screenplay. Other serious movies followed and did well at the box office.

Before the war, fear of losing the southern box office had effectively kept stories about racial and religious bigotry from the screen, but after the war, as Americans came to appreciate serious films and as the movie industry came to realize that the South claimed only 8 percent of movie revenues (whereas New York alone accounted for 14 percent), exploring the dramatic potential of segregation and discrimination became less risky.[51] Bigotry first showed up in movies about anti-Semitism like *Crossfire* (1947) and *Gentleman's Agreement* (1947) and spread to racial problems in *Home of the Brave* (1949) and *Intruder in the Dust* (1949). The success of these movies made Hollywood realize that if governmental censors could interfere with *Lost Boundaries*, it might lose its ability to compete with European films.

Lost Boundaries was the work of Louis de Rochemont, famous for his *March of Time* newsreels. After World War II, he decided to return to his New England roots and shoot what he called a nonfiction film about a light-skinned African American family passing for white in New Hampshire. After twenty years of complete community acceptance of the couple and their two children, the family's secret is revealed when the father is rejected for military officers' training because he is black.

When the film was banned in both Memphis and Atlanta, the fiery, combative de Rochemont had his company, RD-DR, sue in federal court, claiming that the Atlanta censorship ordinance violated the First and Fourteenth amendments and infringed on motion pictures' right to freedom of expression as organs of the press. According to newsreel historian Raymond Fielding, who knew de Rochemont, fighting against censorship would have been almost second nature for this principled, passionate filmmaker. Certain that the Supreme Court was ready to overturn *Mutual*, RD-DR urged the U.S. Court of Appeals for the Fifth Circuit to administer an "anticipatory coup de grace." But the court emphatically refused; in fact, Chief Judge Joseph Hutcheson Jr. was convinced that, given the chance, the Supreme Court not only would refuse to overturn *Mutual* but would emphatically reaffirm it. Highly annoyed, Hutcheson slapped down RD-DR's contentions, saying that it was not the court's duty to "consult crystal ball gazers or diviners . . . to base a decision on a prophesy [*sic*]."[52]

Hutcheson's view, while condescending, was correct: only two justices, Black and Douglas, had expressed the opinion that the First Amendment should be applied to state action against movies; the majority on the Court had shown no evidence of tilting in that direction. And, as we have seen, the makeup of the Court had moved rightward. The 1949 deaths of staunch civil libertarian justices Murphy and Rutledge gave President

Harry Truman two appointments, which went to his friends, Minton and Clark. Minton favored order over individual rights and deferred to legislative will almost reflexively. And Clark was a moderate who would go on to reject 75 percent of the civil liberties claims that came before him.[53] This effectively cut in half the bloc that had repeatedly voted in favor of the preferred freedoms concept. So the 1950s were opening with a Supreme Court that looked less than promising for those who hoped to overturn state film censorship. By rejecting United Artists' request for certiorari for *Curley* in May 1950 and RD-DR's request for *Lost Boundaries* five months later, the Supreme Court showed that it was indeed still unwilling to revisit the issue of film censorship. The *Paramount* hint two years earlier that movies were part of the press remained nothing more than a tease. It was not just Jane Russell's cleavage that hung over the movie landscape like a thunderstorm. It was *Mutual*. First Amendment protection was still beyond the reach of any movie producer, exhibitor, or distributor at the midcentury mark.

6

The Strange Case of *The Miracle*, 1950–1952

In December 1950, when Americans first heard about Roberto Rossellini's forty-one-minute film *The Miracle* (*Il miracolo*), New York State had been censoring all films commercially exhibited within its borders for twenty-seven years. Most New Yorkers gave little thought to this restriction on their entertainment. The country had more important issues, many of them focused on the cold war. It was clear that the five-year uneasy postwar peace was unraveling. The United Nations had censured the Communists of North Korea in June, President Truman had sent in American forces, and by December the news from the front was all bad. The Soviet Union had exploded an atomic bomb, and Truman proclaimed a national emergency to ready the country's economy for war.[1] And it was not just external Communists who were of concern: FBI director J. Edgar Hoover claimed that there were fifty-five thousand Communist Party members within the United States. The Senate had just legitimized the charges of Joseph McCarthy about Communist influence in the State Department by appointing an investigating committee. And, as in the past, a time of national stress was used to justify censorship. After the Senate held hearings on immorality and violence in comic books and criticism from moral guardians rattled the new television networks, both industries adopted content regulation codes modeled on Hollywood's Production Code.[2] The National Office for Decent Literature (a Legion of Decency for books) stepped up a nationwide campaign against obscene literature to intimidate booksellers into dropping any title deemed offensive to Catholics.[3] Meanwhile, governmental censors of film continued to reign supreme over what was considered obscene, indecent, or harmful.

Into this environment of fear, aggressive Americanism, and unchecked censorial power, Joseph Burstyn (who had tangled with the New York censors over *Remous* in the late 1930s) brought *The Miracle*, a film that he considered of great artistic merit. Packaging it with two other short films—Marcel Pagnol's *Jofroi* and Jean Renoir's *A Day in the Country*—Burstyn titled his trilogy *Ways of Love*, submitted it to the censors of New York, received his exhibition license, and prepared for a profitable run at New York City's Paris Theatre (a new and highly regarded art theater built especially for foreign films).

Burstyn probably never imagined, as he waited for the critics' reviews, that the film would be seen as godless, Communist propaganda, but that is just what happened. Over the next two years, he would assault New York State's wall of censorship, and his name would become synonymous with anticensorship at the Supreme Court. Although the Supreme Court decision that came from *The Miracle* would not overturn censorship statutes, as Burstyn and others hoped, it would specifically grant motion pictures the protection of the First and the Fourteenth amendments, something they had been denied since the 1915 *Mutual* decision. An emancipation of sorts, *The Miracle* was, according to ACLU historian Samuel Walker, "the beginning of the end of film censorship."[4]

This beginning had a great deal to do with slowly expanding ideals about free speech rights. During the Depression, as millions of previously self-sufficient Americans turned to the government for assistance, government had come to be seen as a force for good. During World War II, however, some Americans came to question the New Deal era's "celebration of the state" as they learned of the abuses of individual rights in Fascist countries.[5] Even after the Fascist threat had been eliminated, some Americans' suspicion of governmental benevolence continued to grow as they observed the Soviet system. The authoritarianism of the Soviets made controls on speech and press in the United States look less than democratic. Censorship was slowly coming to be seen not so much as a democratic ideal—the role it had played since the Progressive Era—but as the archetype of arbitrary interference. But when Joseph Burstyn imported *The Miracle* in 1950, censorship's hold was still very strong. Ironically, fear of communism contributed greatly to the censors' appeal, and *The Miracle* came to bear the full brunt of its clout.

With a Federico Fellini script, *The Miracle* starred Italy's most beloved actress, Anna Magnani, as a mentally unbalanced peasant girl who is seduced by a stranger she mistakes for Saint Joseph. When her neighbors learn she is pregnant, they ridicule her innocent belief that she will bear a divine child. Cast out, she retreats to the mountains and gives birth in a deserted church, where (according to Rossellini) she is transformed by love for the child she has just delivered.

The Miracle arrived to a particularly contentious reception because of its director. While filming *Stromboli* earlier that year, Rossellini had committed an unforgivable sin in the eyes of many American Catholics: he seduced their favorite film star (and favorite film nun), the married Ingrid Bergman. After the news broke that Rossellini and Bergman were having an affair and the pregnant Bergman was leaving her husband, many groups wanted *Stromboli* banned, and censors everywhere were under pressure to respond. Some, like the Seattle Board of Theatre Supervisors, banned the film. The Ohio board intended to ban *Stromboli* but was restrained by its attorney general.[6] The Rossellini-Bergman liaison, like the Fatty Arbuckle scandal of the 1920s, so incensed many Americans that one powerful senator introduced a bill in Congress that would have certified all film actors, producers, and directors with licenses rescindable for moral turpitude.[7] The bill's sponsor, Colorado senator Edwin C. Johnson, chairman of the Interstate Commerce Committee and a Joe McCarthy emulator, demanded "a method whereby the mad dogs of the industry may be put on a leash to protect public morals." He called Rossellini "vile and unspeakable" and Bergman an "apostle of degradation."[8] *Film Daily* predicted that Johnson intended to make the secretary of commerce a "morals commissar."[9]

While this bill had little chance of making it out of committee, it gave political voice to yet another wave of outrage over movies' immorality. Hackles raised further in Hollywood when the Interstate Commerce Committee hired Stephen S. Jackson to "sift movie morals."[10] Jackson had impressive credentials for such a job: he had been a judge and two years earlier had served as the acting head of the PCA.[11] Many in Hollywood were incensed not just at the prospect of political scrutiny from the Interstate Commerce Committee but also at examination by one who knew the industry so well. But they need not have worried.[12] Jackson's proposed investigation lasted just one week; it folded when the PCA agreed to monitor advertising practices more stringently.[13] Once again, the movie industry had turned on itself to avoid governmental intervention. Senator Johnson withdrew his proposed bill a month later, claiming that he had never intended it seriously except to draw attention to the "exploitation of immorality to get people to attend picture shows."[14] Indeed, the bill focused enough attention on Hollywood's supposed immorality to encourage the lawmakers to pass a "sense of the Senate" resolution that films produced by "totalitarian-minded persons" (Rossellini was believed by many to be a Fascist) should be excluded from interstate commerce.[15]

Not only had Rossellini affronted millions of Catholics by corrupting their favored actress, but *The Miracle* also presented a view of Catholic behavior not seen on the screen before. American Catholics had grown accustomed to seeing sympathetic, even heroic portrayals of their priests, nuns, and parishioners on the screen. Not only had Catholics influenced what was kept off the screen, but their considerable heft had encouraged the mostly Jewish studio executives to depict any religious leader as a heroic Catholic. Films like *Going My Way* (1944), *The Bells of St. Mary's* (1945), *Boys Town* (1938), *Angels with Dirty Faces* (1938), *On the Waterfront* (1954), and *Fighting Father Dunne* (1948) practically canonized the priesthood. The Hollywood priest archetype became the "'superpadre,' virile, athletic, compassionate, wise."[16] Accustomed to heroic portrayals in movies, the Catholic community did not look favorably on any movie that suggested Catholic imperfection, especially one by a suspected Fascist adulterer like Rossellini.

Some people, however, had grown tried of Catholic pressure on censors and responded with pressure of their own. After Seattle banned *Stromboli*, the censor board received twenty-five irate letters. One group letter tried to take back the anti-Communist high ground from the Catholics: "The first thing we know you will be baring [*sic*] Republican or Democratic actors on the same ground—in fact there is just no limit to such a policy. This type of action is just the type advocated by the communists." Another woman wondered if Seattle's citizens were "such morons that their personal tastes must be dictated to them by the city administrators? Are you such intellectual giants? Are you God?" Seattle's mayor was not swayed. *Stromboli*'s "background" made it both immoral and indecent.[17]

Into this overtly pro-Catholic and anti-Rossellini environment came *The Miracle* in late 1950. Although foreign films were not yet de rigueur, they were becoming more popular each year. Ticket buyers who were drawn to serious films represented a new type of film fan: the intellectually curious who had grown weary of code-strangled fare. Those who valued movies like *The Best Years of Our Lives* also began to appreciate the new foreign films. *Open City* (*Roma, città aperta*, 1945) and *The Bicycle Thief* (*Ladri di biciclette*, 1948) drew audiences hungry for cinematic realism. But these were productions that no Hollywood director would have dared undertake in the late 1940s.[18] After a few years working in Hollywood during the war, the famous French director Jean Renoir returned to Europe and told his boss, Darryl Zanuck, how much he had enjoyed working for "Sixteenth Century Fox."[19] The new foreign films, with their gritty realism, filled the need of a postwar generation that no longer wanted a steady diet of happy endings, moral rectitude, and "compensating values."

The growing appeal of foreign films, the critical success of movies like *The Best Years of Our Lives*, and the rising importance of film critics who judged films' artistic value encouraged Hollywood to question its methods, its product, and its cash flow. The exceptionally influential *Life* magazine recognized the new stirrings in Hollywood and in 1949 organized a summit meeting of critics, stars, scholars, and moviemakers, then devoted thirteen pages of its June 27 issue to the future of the movie industry. The discussants concluded that Hollywood needed to produce less formulaic, "more adult" films that were the work of a single "man" rather than the committee productions of Hollywood. (Here the influence of European auteurs like Rossellini was clearly visible.) But that might not be so easy, the panelists warned, because the "censoriousness of the American public" could trouble unconventional productions.[20]

The American people's censoriousness was about to burst forth in New York City, ignited by *The Miracle*. Opening at the Paris Theatre on December 12, *Ways of Love* received some positive critical reaction. Writing for the *New York Times*, Bosley Crowther found the trilogy "judged by the highest standards, on either its parts or the whole . . . fully the most rewarding foreign-language entertainment of the year."[21] Wanda Hale of the *New York Daily News* called *The Miracle* segment "forty-one minutes of unrelieved tragedy . . . artistic and beautifully done."[22] Seymour Peck of the *New York Daily Compass* found *Ways of Love* "an unusually intelligent and fascinating experience. . . . We are all beholden to Mr. Burstyn for two hours of uncommon fare."[23] And Frank Quinn of the *New York Daily Mirror* praised *The Miracle* as the best film in the trilogy, raving about Magnani's "phenomenal performance" as the half-witted peasant girl.[24]

A few critics warned viewers to be prepared for offense. *Newsweek* prophesied that *The Miracle* would be "strong medicine for most American audiences."[25] Even the supportive Crowther was concerned, noting that the story's "symbolic parallels might by some be considered a blasphemy of the doctrine of the Virgin Birth." But for the non-Catholic

Crowther, it was a "vastly compassionate comprehension of the suffering and the triumph of birth."[26]

At this point, New York City had a controversial but obscure foreign film. Film buffs looking for the reviews in the morning papers had to wade through pages of bad news: American troops retreating in Korea, the draft quota increasing, the building of new military training camps, rationing looming again, and foreign affairs assistant W. Averill Harriman warning of another world war. Communists seemed to be infiltrating New York City's classrooms; eight teachers were dismissed. Truman was clearly worried about the Soviets and their bombs: declaring that the American "full and rich life" was threatened by the Communists, he called for sacrifice and a "mighty production effort" for defense.[27] Little did Burstyn know that the national anti-Communist passion would be used as a weapon against his latest film import.

The cultural obscurity of *The Miracle* was soon to end, courtesy of another New York City license commissioner, Edward T. McCaffrey. Tipped off by the Legion of Decency, McCaffrey had gone to see *The Miracle*. Horrified, he collared new motion picture division director Hugh Flick and asked him why the film had not been censored. (Flick had not seen the film; the director usually viewed only problem films, and both *The Miracle* by itself and the *Ways of Love* trilogy had passed without a hitch.) An open-minded man, Flick agreed to see *The Miracle* with McCaffrey. But he must have disappointed the license commissioner when, as the credits were rolling, he told McCaffrey that he saw no blasphemy or sacrilege; he saw a film that was "a good illustration of man's inhumanity to man," a film that deserved its license.[28]

When he saw that he was not going to get any help from the motion picture division director, McCaffrey, like Fielding before him, took matters into his own hands. He told the Paris Theatre that he found *The Miracle* "officially and personally blasphemous" and ordered it deleted it from *Ways of Love* or, he threatened, the theater would lose its license.[29] Then he notified all other New York City theaters that if they dared to play *The Miracle*, they too would lose their licenses.[30]

Twelve days after the film's opening, the Legion of Decency pounced, officially pronouncing the film "sacrilegious and blasphemous" and rating it C for "condemned."[31] Neither McCaffrey nor the legion gave specific reasons for these actions, but the vehemence of their reactions may have stemmed more from how *Ways of Love* was assembled than from the content of *The Miracle* itself. To put his three short movies together,

Burstyn settled on a common theme: love. Since the films dealt with love in entirely different ways, he stitched them together by introducing each with a dictionary definition. *A Day in the Country* (about the beginning of a love affair) was introduced with a definition of *love* as "tender and passionate affection for one of the opposite sex, also an instance of love, a love affair." The second film, *Jofroi* (about a farmer's passionate attachment to his land and his orchard), was introduced as "love of country, love of the soil, deep attachment." The third, *The Miracle*, defined love as "ardent affection, passionate attachment, man's adoration of God, sexual passion, gratification."[32] The use of this last definition might explain why some, like McCaffrey, interpreted the movie as an intentional comparison between the Virgin Mary, who bore the son of God, and a demented, seduced woman who bore a bastard.

Whether the words Burstyn chose accentuated the possible sacrilege of the plot or the film was offensive in itself, priests warned their parishioners to stay away, as they had with *The Outlaw*. Faced now with both unofficial and official interference, Burstyn decided to act. He took License Commissioner McCaffrey to court to challenge his authority to revoke the theater's license based on personal opinion. From a nonlegal standpoint, Burstyn's position was reasonable. After all, McCaffrey's job was to license bowling alleys and electrolysists, not to act as the city's censor.[33] From a legal standpoint, however, Burstyn's position had precedent to overcome. Just three years earlier, when Howard Hughes had asked the court to set aside another license commissioner's ruling, the court had upheld the commissioner's authority to interpose his moral judgment on state-licensed films.

The commissioner had thrown down the glove, and the ACLU was ready for the challenge. It jumped in with an offer to aid any theater willing to bring a test case of *The Miracle*. It also wired the mayor on behalf of the "eight million people of the city whose intelligence is insulted when one man tells them what they may see. Even if he and some of our citizens regard it as 'blasphemous,'" the ACLU wrote, the mayor should "recognize that other equally religious citizens, including reputable film reviewers, had reached the exactly opposite judgment and that banning any film because it is for or against any religious doctrine violates the First Amendment to the Constitution, which guarantees freedom of religion and speech."[34] The next day, the New York City Film Critics Circle named *Ways of Love* the best foreign film of 1950 and sent a resolution to the mayor condemning McCaffrey's "suppressive action . . . [as] symptomatic of a growing tendency toward a dangerous censorship of the content of films."[35] The entertainment trade publication *Variety* reported that "industryites were unanimous over the long Christmas weekend in promising support to the theatre and Burstyn in a 'full-scale legal fight.'"[36]

With *The Miracle*'s distributor now suing the city's license commissioner, and with the ACLU and a host of film critics diving in, New York City's newspapers began pumping out editorials about *The Miracle* and the commissioner. In an editorial titled "Civic Censor," the *New York Post* wrote, "The issue is not whether the film is a triumph or a turkey; the issue is whether the city License Commissioner is empowered and/or qualified to decide what films are fit for the eyes of New York. . . . This city hasn't elected anybody to select its movie programs and to bar controversial films. . . . McCaffrey may prefer westerns; the rest of us have the right to do our own movie-shopping." The *Post* was full of the *Miracle* controversy that day, also running a column by Max Lerner dramatically titled "The Shadow on the Screen." Lerner questioned which was more offensive, the film or the action of the license commissioner. "The real blasphemy," Lerner wrote, "is that of a little man who seems for the moment to have blundered into assuming godlike powers of decision for the rest of us."[37] In the *New Republic*, Robert Hatch took exception to McCaffrey's allegation of blasphemy by offering him a vocabulary lesson: "To blaspheme is to revile or curse the Deity, and *The Miracle*, whatever its shortcomings, is a powerful statement of the mercy and peace that God bestows on his most unhappy and forsaken children. If the Commissioner is setting himself up as a one-man inquisition, he should consult a dictionary before handing down any more bulls."[38]

Not all parts of the press aligned against the license commissioner, however. The Catholic press had long taken a strong anti-Communist stance, and it energetically encouraged the public to see a link between communism and obscenity.[39] The *Miracle* controversy was tailor made for Catholic journals. "Conspicuous among those who seek to destroy religious belief are the Communists and their collaborators," wrote the *Catholic News*, "because the spread or containment of Communism depends ultimately on their success or failure in this regard."[40] And the *Brooklyn Tablet*, one of the more influential Catholic newspapers, linked the ACLU with communism because it was encouraging theaters to test the censorship authority. The paper suggested, "Isn't it time we put an end to nursing red treason at home in the name of the Constitution and of liberty?"[41]

The Catholic Church and the Movies

The clash over *The Miracle* was not the first time the Catholic Church and the ACLU had butted heads. Catholics became politically active internationally in the 1930s. But just as they were discovering their political legs, an intellectual atmosphere hostile to Catholic thought was building, and not quietly. Tensions reached a high point in the interwar period when international Catholicism seemed to support Fascists and American Catholics sided with labor unions and sometimes with anti-Semitic groups. High-profile Catholics like the radio priest Father Charles Coughlin and New York's Francis Cardinal Spellman added fuel to the growing opinion that Catholics were assuming too much cultural and political authority. To a nation that prided itself as democratic, classless, and tolerant, the church seemed authoritarian, hierarchical, and intolerant.[42]

Paul Blanshard's *American Freedom and Catholic Power* rose to the best-seller list of 1949 by arguing that Catholic teachings were antithetical to American freedom. Blanshard's second treatise, *Communism, Democracy, and Catholic Power*, published two years later, identified communism and Catholicism as the greatest threats to American liberty. Intellectual leaders like John Dewey, Albert Einstein, and Bertrand Russell all praised Blanshard's anti-Catholic polemics. Lewis Mumford and Reinhold Neibuhr had earlier warned that the monolithic Catholic hierarchy could interfere with the separation of powers, the core definition of American political authority. Anti-Catholicism became a main component of midcentury liberalism.[43] It thus seems inevitable, given the prevailing atmosphere of liberal thought from the late 1930s into the 1950s, that the ACLU should clash with the American Catholic Church. As the ACLU stepped up its anticensorship, anti–pressure group activities in the early 1950s, the Catholic Legion of Decency was ramping up its efforts to halt *The Miracle*. The turmoil over the film placed the two groups face-to-face in the cultural debate.[44]

Of course, the American Catholic Church had been closely tied to Hollywood for years. The church had been instrumental in writing the Production Code, and the Legion of Decency was actively involved in the preapproval of scripts from 1934 through 1954. Because the legion could brand any film "condemned," it forced producers to change content and was, in effect, a national board of censorship. As Gregory Black has clearly shown in *The Catholic Crusade against the Movies*, from 1934 until Joseph Breen's retirement twenty years later, it was impossible to separate the PCA from the Legion of Decency.[45]

Not all Catholics agreed with the work of the legion, though. In 1951, just a few months after *The Miracle*'s premiere, an article denouncing the legion's interference was published in *Commonweal*, a liberal weekly edited by Catholic laymen. Even though *Commonweal*'s film critic had found *The Miracle* sacrilegious, the magazine deplored the church's interference, calling it "semi-ecclesiastical McCarthyism." *Commonweal* criticized the "odious methods" used, particularly "guilt by association" and "hysteria . . . a spectacle which many of us, as Catholics, can view only with shame and repulsion."[46]

In the wake of all the rhetoric, the New York State Supreme Court heard Burstyn's arguments for stopping the license commissioner. Recognizing that *The Miracle* presented an excellent test case, the New York Civil Liberties Union composed a brief (the first of four it would file on behalf of Burstyn's *Miracle*) that, unlike its brief for *The Outlaw*, bypassed the issue of the license commissioner's authority and went straight to the heart of the constitutional issues of free speech, prior restraint, and freedom of religion. Justice Aron Steuer granted Burstyn a temporary injunction against McCaffrey on January 5, 1951, overturning several precedents by ruling that the state censors had sole authority to decide the fitness of any film and that the license commissioner had overstepped his bounds.[47] The situation was easier for Steuer than it had been for Justice Shientag three years earlier in the similar case brought by Howard Hughes because the legislature had amended the penal law to prevent prosecution of a duly licensed motion picture. Nevertheless, Steuer's ruling was a stunning reversal of the commissioner's powers, the first time in thirty-five years that a commissioner's decision to interfere with a film had been overturned.[48] The city appealed, but in the meantime, *The Miracle* went back to the Paris Theatre to resume its place in the *Ways of Love* trilogy. The Paris's managing director, Lillian Gerard, had been on the front lines of the struggle over *The Miracle* since the beginning. She remarked some years later, "I never could have anticipated what a decision in our favor would mean: what ugliness, what fury, what duplicity would envelop us, all in the name of patriotism, all rooted in puritanism, an Armageddon to prove the inviolability of censorship."[49]

So far, *The Miracle* had faced a frontal assault and won. But then came a major blow—not from a censor board or a government official but from the Archdiocese of New York. A pastoral letter written by Cardinal Spellman and read in all four hundred parishes of the vast archdiocese on January 7, 1951, called on all American Catholics to stay away from *The*

Miracle and any theater showing it. *The Miracle*, Catholics were told that Sunday, could "divide and demoralize Americans so that the minions of Moscow might enslave this land of liberty." More than just a danger to society, the film was "subversive to the very word of God," railed Spellman. *The Miracle* was an insult to Italian women, and the motion picture division should be "censured for offending and insulting millions of people."[50]

On the job as head of the motion picture division for only a few months, Hugh Flick had already disappointed McCaffrey with his reaction to *The Miracle*, and he would go on to disappoint Spellman repeatedly. An intellectual, cultured man, Flick held an undergraduate degree in philosophy and a doctorate from Columbia in U.S. history. Before becoming New York's chief censor, he had served as state archivist and state historian. During the war years, he had been chief archivist for the U.S. Army. Well-traveled, well-read, and well-respected, Flick would come to be considered by many, including the ACLU, as America's most enlightened censor, hardly the kind of moral guardian Spellman wanted in charge of New Yorkers' film viewing. Flick was always more worried about violent messages in films (particularly violent acts against women) than with sexual depictions or culture wars like the *Miracle* controversy.

Like many people in the early 1950s, Flick held ambivalent views about film. He was convinced that censorship was abhorrent to American principles yet concerned that films could incite to crime.[51] Even so, in a 1955 opinion piece in the *New York Times*, Flick volunteered his view that the impact of movies had lessened over time. "Our concept of control must grow with the art of the film, which is now mature," he told a *New York Herald Tribune* interviewer the same year.[52] He believed that the film industry needed neither more nor less control but a sociological study to determine the actual effects of movies on American viewers. Whereas Spellman wanted to continue the Legion of Decency's unilateral evaluation of sexual and moral matters in film, Flick wanted to analyze audience reaction. Flick hoped to move the discussion about films beyond the 1930s studies that had culminated with the overwrought *Our Movie Made Children*. Only with scientific information about movies' effects could legislators choose the best path concerning the films that their citizens saw.[53] Flick did not like the word *censor*, and he preferred to think of his work as guardianship. Like the progressives before him, he compared censor statutes to pure food and drug laws. And like those food inspectors, Flick would not "pass upon whether the product tastes good, or whether it will make you fatter or thinner, but simply upon whether it is poisonous or non-poisonous."[54] He never advocated complete freedom of exhibition, although he did favor using the censors to implement age classification in place of licensing. Such moderate views in a censor, coupled with increasingly strident demands for restriction from the leader of New York's Catholics, made for a volatile mix. The Legion of Decency might still have had immense power over the PCA in 1950, but its influence on state censors was not so certain.

After denouncing both the censor board and *The Miracle*, Spellman moved to motivate not only the faithful but "all good Americans," asking them "to unite with us in this battle for decency and Americanism." Like moral reformers at the turn of the century who criticized deficient law, Spellman urged both immediate and longer-term action. "If the present law is so weak and inadequate to cope with this desperate situation, then all right-thinking citizens should unite to change and strengthen the Federal and state statutes so as to make it impossible for anyone to profit financially by blasphemy, immorality and sacrilege."[55] In other words, since the laws of New York did not ban movies that offended Cardinal Spellman, they needed to be changed. The *Nation* snidely suggested, "We must plug the loophole that permits this shocking affront to clerical omnipotence."[56] Spellman, an immensely powerful man (nicknamed the Powerhouse by politicians[57]) with connections throughout city government, next turned to the most potent weapon in the church's arsenal—the boycott—and again asked all Americans to join in.

On the evening of Spellman's pronouncement, pickets barricaded the Paris Theatre with signs that read, "Don't enter that cesspool!" and "Don't look at that filth!"[58] The picketers belonged to Catholic War Veterans, a group that had earlier convinced a local television station to ban Charlie Chaplin's films because of his alleged Communist leanings. Later that week, the picketers moved beyond any semblance of subtle persuasion, handing out catechism-like handbills to passersby. Included were the following:

> Question: Can you give me one good reason why I shouldn't go see the picture?
>
> Answer: What now happens to us may some day happen to your Belief. If you give your O.K. to anti-religious pictures by patronizing them, then don't be surprised if a picture is made attacking your own religion.

Question: I saw the picture and I didn't see anything wrong with it.
Answer: Nobody knows the Catholic religion better than Catholics themselves and they are therefore better able to know what is attacking their Belief.

Question: I am a Catholic and I like the picture.
Answer: You are evidently either ignorant of the teachings of our Church or you are actually defying our Church and are then not a real Catholic. Since the Church has condemned the picture, you are therefore disqualifying yourself as a Catholic by acting contrary to what the Church has told you.[59]

But moviegoers got more than one flyer at the Paris Theatre. A small group of counterpicketers, urging everyone's right to see *The Miracle*, also handed out leaflets. One sign read, "Jesus taught compassion and not condemnation."[60] Even the management of the theater got into the act, handing out more reading material, complete with legal citations backing up its position.[61] Before a prospective viewer could get close enough to buy a ticket, he had amassed a stack of propaganda from all sides.

The picketers remained for three weeks. To Bosley Crowther, a long-time censorship opponent who had championed the cause of *The Miracle* from its debut and would continue to use his weekly *New York Times* column to support it, the picketing was "among the most distasteful and disturbing aspects of the case. An ugly and fanatic spirit was often apparent among the marching men as they shouted in the faces of the people."[62] By the middle of January 1951, there were two hundred picketers per night. Some estimates placed the number of people on line as high as one thousand. Fifteen thousand Catholics and their supporters offered to take turns on the picket line.[63]

A few weeks into the picketing, with box office sales high, the signs began to change. Unable to intimidate the theater management, the picketers had begun a letter-writing campaign intended to force the board of regents to rescind *The Miracle*'s license. Placards read, "Write to the Board of Review [*sic*] in Albany to remove the license of this picture."[64]

The Catholics' were not the only voices raised. The day after Spellman's pronouncement, Joseph Burstyn called a press conference. Burstyn was no ordinary film distributor. Highly regarded by the critics, he imported only the finest foreign films. Film critic Alton Cook called him "a small man with small fame outside movie trade circles. But within them he is regarded with a combination of amazement and awe."[65] The entertainment industry periodical *Cue* called him "a genius in this difficult business . . . responsible for bringing to America multiple prize-winning importations."[66] Those imports had given Burstyn an impressive résumé; four out of five years, a Burstyn presentation won the best foreign film award from the New York Film Critics Circle: *Open City* in 1947, *Paisan* in 1948, *The Bicycle Thief* in 1949, and *Ways of Love* in 1950 (*Miracle in Milan* would win in 1952).[67] Burstyn had an uncanny knack for picking winners, but his real success lay in his method of marketing films. He would bet his entire season on one or two films of artistic merit, then work them with "100 percent effort."[68] His former partner, Arthur Mayer, described Burstyn as becoming "overwhelmingly and monogamously (temporarily) enamored of [a film] to the exclusion of everything else in the world."[69]

Along with his love of the films, Burstyn also had a heavy financial investment in *Ways of Love*.[70] The New York City market was crucial to the success of any foreign film in the early 1950s. A ban in New York based on Catholic protests could influence municipal censors in key cities like Chicago and would often intimidate theater owners in censor-free cities. Burstyn could not count on all theaters' being so courageous as the Paris Theatre in New York. After Spellman's boycott call, Burstyn had to fight back for economic as well as ideological and emotional reasons.

Burstyn's press conference was well covered by the New York City press, indicating both the level of interest and the significance of the controversy. In prepared remarks, Burstyn pointed out that *The Miracle* had been passed by the Italian censor board (which was responsible to both the Catholic Church and to Italy's 99.6 percent Catholic population). "In the twenty years that I have been engaged in the distribution and presentation of foreign motion pictures to the American public," Burstyn said, "my primary consideration in the selection of films has been the artistic merit of the picture. That was my sole criterion in the selection of *The Miracle*." His assessment, he said, had been seconded by the film critics. He praised Justice Steuer's decision against the license commissioner because it freed producers and distributors from the threat of "one-man rule," and he concluded, "If we permit one person or one group to direct us what to see or not to see, then our basic constitutional liberties will have been abridged."[71] During questioning, Burstyn insisted that both Spellman and the Legion of Decency had the right to express their views on any picture, but, he said, they did not have the right to demand increased governmental censorship or to set themselves up as censors. "There seems to me to be a motive behind this big ado," Burstyn continued. "The Legion has been quite harsh—quite tough—on films coming in from Europe. It is my impression that the Legion is trying to establish itself as the official censor of the City of New York."[72]

After Burstyn had his say, it was the Protestant clergy's turn to speak out. Whereas earlier the Protestants and the Catholics had worked together in their call for movie reform, all such comity broke down over *The Miracle*. Some churchmen insisted that the Catholic Church had no right to dictate terms of conscience to others. The Reverend Chworowsky of the Flatbush Unitarian Church released a statement carried by the *New York Times*: "As a Protestant and as a religious liberal of the Christian persuasion, I resent a public statement calling the Catholics of the nation 'the guardians of the moral law,' and I further and deeply resent the insinuation of the Cardinal that everyone not sharing his opinions regarding *The Miracle* is thereby classified as an indecent person."[73] Two days later, prominent Protestant clergy and laymen sent the motion picture division a telegram insisting that "the Roman Catholic Church has no legal or moral right to attempt to force its views on the state as a whole."[74] Playwrights, novelists, theatrical producers, and members of the Authors League of America (including Eugene O'Neill and Henry Steele Commager) also sent a telegram to the motion picture division, urging the censors to stick with their original determination on *The Miracle*.[75] Another telegram, from the ACLU, asserted support from luminaries like Oscar Hammerstein, Moss Hart, Frederick Lewis Allen, and Richard Rodgers.[76]

So far the battle over *The Miracle* had been all words and picket signs, but now the New York archdiocese began direct action to affect policy. The Catholic Welfare Conference, the lobbying arm of the church, announced that it would ask the legislature to strengthen the existing censorship law. The Catholic Press Institute (with four hundred members) unanimously adopted a resolution calling on Governor Thomas Dewey to ask for *The Miracle*'s license revocation.[77]

Feeling the heat of public criticism, Hugh Flick sent a lengthy memo to Regent James E. Allen justifying the censors' original verdict on the film. On first screening, he wrote, three of the four reviewers had interpreted the film as a portrayal of man's inhumanity to man rather than as a mockery of the divine birth—indeed, that was how Flick himself had viewed it. After the public protests, though, Flick changed his mind. He used this memo to justify his reversal based on several complicating factors: Rossellini's personal life and political affiliations, the film's problematic title, its debut during the Christmas season, the negative publicity that had kept the theater filled, and the "public pronouncements and news coverage" that had blown the issue out of proportion. Flick concluded by calling for statutory change, suggesting "some appeal procedure [for] the public in such cases where there is sufficient evidence to warrant the assumption that the Motion Picture Division may have made an honest error in judgment due to the existence of one or more interpretations of a picture." Flick told his boss, "The Division would welcome and recommend the establishment of such a procedure."[78] At the least, he was willing to reexamine the film based on the public outcry. As the only public figure at the motion picture division, Flick was on the hot seat and was clearly reacting to public pressure.

Nine days later, on January 19, Burstyn was ambushed by the state. He received notification from the regents of a show-cause hearing to determine why *The Miracle*'s license should *not* be rescinded, placing the burden of proof that the movie was not sacrilegious on Burstyn. An unprecedented move by the board of regents, it was a major blow to Burstyn's hopes; now his troubles had spread from the license commissioner of New York City and the Catholic Church to the overseers of the statewide censor board. The regents reported that they had received hundreds of complaints about *The Miracle*. In other words, they were admitting that they could be swayed by pressure groups. Cultural critic Gilbert Seldes, in his usually succinct fashion, summarized the situation well. "What the picture actually is becomes less important than what people think it is, and those who have seen the picture become less influential than those who have been simultaneously directed not to see it but to protest against it."[79] The regents failed to admit that along with the protest letters, they had also received many letters supporting *The Miracle*'s right to be shown, many from prominent Protestant clergy.[80] However, the regents were also feeling political heat: a letter from Assemblyman Thomas Duffy urged revocation,[81] and Assemblyman Samuel Roman was pushing Governor Dewey to intervene with the state censors to revoke the film's license.[82]

Because no provision within the statute or the Rules of the Board of Regents allowed for the rescission of a license,[83] the state's lawyers set to work to find some basis for reconsideration of *The Miracle*. Since the original 1921 statute had provided for the revocation of a license, they could easily have argued that such power was automatically transferred to the motion picture division when the censors were reorganized under the New York State Education Department in 1927.[84] Eventually, the attorneys decided that since the board of regents oversaw the censor board, the regents were authorized to review the acts of its employees and to hold hearings on anything that affected the department of education. Thus legitimized, the hearing was set for eleven days later, January 30.

While Burstyn and his lawyers prepared for this unique proceeding, protests turned nasty. On the night of January 20, a bomb threat cleared the Paris Theatre.[85] A fire department lieutenant happened to find fire code violations at the theater, then alleged that the theater management had tried to bribe him. The management in turn filed harassment charges against the fire department. The *New York Post* smelled a rat: "When fire chiefs become movie censors, we can all start running, not walking, to the nearest exit."[86]

Cardinal Spellman's biographer, John Cooney, finds none of the fire department's newfound administrative zeal surprising. After all, Spellman wielded immense influence in city government. Moreover, the license commissioner was Catholic, the mayor was Catholic, and the fire commissioner was Catholic. After Spellman's boycott command, these city officials, in Cooney's words, "toed the Cardinal's line." They "flew to Spellman's causes like pigeons to bread crumbs." Although New York City's Catholic population was large and politically well situated, they still suffered from what Cooney calls a "siege mentality" and viewed themselves as "a beleaguered minority standing bravely against Protestant onslaughts." The nation's intellectual climate against Catholics was surely taking a toll, but they need not have worried about their political influence in New York. Catholics had been in control of city government "for as long as anyone could remember."[87]

They now pressured *The Miracle* on a different front. The New York Film Critics Circle had already announced the selection of *Ways of Love* as its foreign film of the year, to be recognized at an awards ceremony at Radio City Music Hall in February. A telephone caller to the venue threatened a Catholic boycott. When questioned by the *New York Times*, Monsignor Walter P. Kellenberg refused to deny that Radio City Music Hall would incur the disfavor of the New York archdiocese for allowing the ceremony to proceed. The New York Film Critics Circle, not wishing to injure New York's most famous theater, withdrew to a private ceremony at the much smaller Rainbow Room.[88] At the awards ceremony, Burstyn said, "I accept this award as a tribute to the integrity of people who really care about films, as a symbol of the truth cherished by all Americans."[89]

One member of the film critics' association had had enough of the intimidation tactics of the Catholic Church. Bosley Crowther was so intent on bringing the pressure to light that Frank Beaver has called him "a servant in *The Miracle*'s cause."[90] In his Sunday *New York Times* column, Crowther lobbied for an end to censorship (both Hollywood's and the state's) and declared *The Miracle* a perfect test case. Crowther wrote, "The constitutionality of all motion picture censorship stands to be brought to a showdown on the singular and significant issue in this case. . . . Sacrilege is a matter on which theologians do not agree. . . . If ever there was a clear case on which to challenge censorship, this is it."[91] Crowther also set to work on an article for the *Atlantic Monthly* titled "The Strange Case of 'The Miracle.'" He described how the Legion of Decency had locked down the American film industry over the previous two decades through its collaboration with the PCA. Through a face-off on *The Miracle*, Crowther claimed, the Catholics hoped to extend their reach to all films shown in the United States. Arguing that the attempts to suppress *The Miracle* were neither isolated nor "spontaneous," he maintained that the film had become "the recognized issue for a calculated test of strength."[92]

The ACLU was ready for a showdown, too. It had been actively searching since at least 1947 for a test case to overturn film censorship, but both of its earlier cases, *Lost Boundaries* (Georgia) and *Curley* (Tennessee) had been denied hearings before the Supreme Court the year before. The ACLU had offered to help the MPAA pursue a challenge over the race relations film *Pinky*, but that case had gotten bogged down in the Texas courts.[93] Still searching for a test case, the NYCLU had jumped on *The Miracle* when it was a localized conflict within New York City. But when the struggle grew beyond the issues that had been presented by *The Outlaw*, swelling into a state controversy and involving the authority of a state censorship body and the Legion of Decency, the civil liberties group had found its test case.

Moreover, the timing looked good. The backdrop to the *Miracle* controversy was the rapidly escalating cold war and its anti-Communist rhetoric, but the early 1950s were not just a period of speech intimidation. Beneath all the talk about hunting Communists, a burgeoning legal culture of individual rights was gaining strength. In 1937 and 1938, a pair of Supreme Court cases had begun the move toward a more stringent scrutiny of state laws that infringed civil liberties in the interest of the public good. More cases continued in that direction, striking down the postmaster general's right to censor, prosecution of newspaper editorialists, restrictions on speech in public parks, the power of state authorities to grant licenses for public speech, and the state's right to prohibit certain types of magazines.[94] In New York, the ACLU had just helped overturn a statute that had given open-ended licensing authority over speech to an administrative official.[95] The ACLU saw a strong parallel between this case, *Kunz v. New York*, and the possibilities offered in a case prompted by *The Miracle*. If the *Kunz* ordinance was invalid as a previous restraint on the exercise of First Amendment rights, then any interference by the board of regents on behalf of a religious group might also be unconstitutional. Even though the U.S. Supreme Court bench seemed to be moving rightward, the overall legal culture was becoming more interested in eliminating speech-restrictive legislation. As Burstyn's lawyers prepared to meet the board of regents, the NYCLU prepared to do battle on First Amendment grounds.

The Miracle's Legal Merits

For the ACLU, *The Miracle*—and the conditions surrounding its exhibition—held great potential in several significant ways. First, it was a film of unquestioned artistic merit, complete with the honorific title of best foreign film of 1950. Second, its distributor was highly regarded and well respected as an importer of fine films; he was not out to make a quick buck from a sensational film. Third, with new threats of federal censorship, seeking a decisive court pronouncement that would restrict movie censors was now more compelling to the ACLU. Fourth, a test in New York presented the biggest potential reward because its motion picture division was also influential in other states. Fifth, Hollywood was now starting to move against censorship. Sixth, some members of the Supreme Court had dropped hints that they were ready to extend First and Fourteenth Amendment protection to the movies. Finally, and perhaps most important, *The Miracle* presented two solid constitutional issues: freedom of speech and separation of church and state.

In January 1951, Joseph Burstyn had little interest in questions of church and state, although he would become more interested in succeeding months. At this point, he was focused on maintaining his film's legally granted exhibition license. At the show-cause hearing ordered by the board of regents, no one had to prove that *The Miracle* should be banned; Burstyn had to prove that *The Miracle* should not be banned.

But the game was even more skewed than it seemed. Before the hearing was called to order, the regents committee charged with sorting out the *Miracle* controversy (one Catholic, one Protestant, and one Jew) had stated on record that they believed the film to be sacrilegious.[96] Burstyn's attorney, John Farber, insisted that the regents committee disqualify itself on the grounds that it had prejudged Burstyn's film. When the committee refused, Farber walked out, calling the board's actions "unprecedented and unauthorized."[97] Farber's dramatic exit was a shrewd legal move—if he had spoken at the hearing, he would have given legal standing to what he planned to later claim was an extralegal proceeding.

Though the published intent of the committee was to gather evidence from Burstyn's company, Burstyn himself, and interested community members, the committee refused to allow Burstyn's personal attorney, the well-respected, well-connected Ephraim London, to speak on his behalf.[98] The committee also refused to allow a group of twelve Protestant clergy and divinity professors to speak. It agreed to accept only written testimony from Bursytn's attorneys and from the public at large. Burstyn submitted eighty-two documents attesting to the nonsacrilegious nature of his film; he claimed that he received no evidence from the regents to the contrary. Eight groups and twenty-four individuals filed statements with the committee and expected to speak at the hearing but were not heard.[99] The Paris Theatre's managing director, Lillian Gerard, later wrote, "The committee seemed to contradict itself without any hesitation whatsoever. It had earlier promised to 'hear' all interested parties. . . . Now the committee was proceeding without 'listening' to anyone."[100] Frustrated, Protestant ministers delivered a petition to the board of regents' office. They argued that since a wide divergence of opinion existed over sacrilege, even among religious leaders, "For anybody, public or private, religious or non-religious, to seek to deprive the public of its right of judgment in the matter is to seek to violate basic civil and religious liberties."[101]

Two weeks later, on February 16, *The Miracle*'s license was rescinded by the board of regents[102]—an action that was, as Farber had suggested, totally unprecedented. But more important, the regents' action was logically unsound: they had received as much mail supporting *The Miracle* as opposing it. Indeed, Flick later revealed that the only commendation letters the censors had ever received from the public came as a result of their initial approval of Rossellini's film.[103] But the board of regents bent to political and social pressure from the Catholic Church. In its revocation statement, the board conjured up America's "priceless heritage of religious freedom" and then, in the same paragraph, used that religious freedom to reject *The Miracle*. Somehow, the regents failed to appreciate the considerable irony of suppressing *The Miracle* in the name of religious freedom.

Following the decision, Burstyn told the *New York Times*, "This is a sad day not only for us who are connected with the film business, but for every free citizen of the great state of New York."[104] In a formal statement, he said, "Conceding every right to any religious minority to voice its opinion on anything pertaining to artistic or cultural expression, we must, nevertheless, come to the sad conclusion that an organized minority is dictating through various pressure tactics to the entire citizenry of this state what it may or may not see in the movies, and eventually this will happen to books and other artistic media."[105] Burstyn repeated this refrain often. Considering the cultural atmosphere of the early 1950s, it was not just fear mongering.

Reaction to the regents' decision came swiftly from the ACLU. Its press statement blasted the regents' action, calling it "a shocking instance of raw censorship" and a "serious blow to the First Amendment." It accused the regents of "illegal and unconstitutional" handling of *The Miracle* and warned that the decision could lead to "restriction of expression and thought, which is totally un-American." The ACLU urged film distributors and exhibitors "not to be intimidated or cowed into silence" and offered its attorneys to help challenge "these attacks on the First Amendment."[106]

Crowther worried about Hollywood's being cowed, too. In his February 25 column, he reprimanded the industry for not coming forward. But it would have been extraordinarily difficult for Hollywood to take up this fight. The MPAA would have had to ditch its long-standing alliance with the Legion of Decency if it fought the Catholics over *The Miracle*. Moreover, Hollywood was still licking its wounds from the House Un-American Activities Committee hearings and thus understandably shied away from confrontation with Communist-hunting Catholics like Spellman.[107] Besides, MPAA president Eric Johnston considered the currently litigating *Pinky* a more promising test case—and an obviously safer one for his organization. Finally, *The Miracle* was a foreign film, in competition with the American-made films that the MPAA was in business to promote.[108]

The NYCLU offered Burstyn moral support through amicus participation, which it would continue through each round in the New York state courts. Thus it happened that a film intended to illustrate religious irony engendered far greater public irony. This little Italian film—made by a Catholic director, starring Catholic actors, untouched by Catholic censors in its homeland—became the football kicked around in a contest of wills in the United States. *The Miracle* would come to be seen as the means to an end for both Catholics and civil libertarians, each side intent on using the movie to advance a broader agenda. Round one came in the appellate division of the New York State Supreme Court as Burstyn brought suit against the board of regents.

As Burstyn's attorneys worked on their briefs, they knew they faced an uphill battle. The only way to overturn a censorship ruling in any state was to prove abuse of "discretion."[109] But that would be difficult for Burstyn to do. Since New York had legislatively authorized its censors to suppress sacrilege, the regents were well within their legal discretion to consider religious sensibilities, and the likelihood of a state court's reversing the body charged with making that determination was low. Judicial restraint and the specter of *Mutual* stood in the way.

In the New York Courts

Burstyn's attorneys filed two briefs at the appellate division of the New York State Supreme Court, one for Burstyn personally and one for Burstyn's company. Burstyn's personal petition took advantage of the disagreement among New York's censors: the motion picture division's approval—twice—proved that there was doubt as to whether the film was truly sacrilegious. Because there was no consensus—there were in fact diametrically opposite views among the public—Burstyn wanted the court to recuse itself from any decision about whether it was "a mockery of religious faith." A proper area for the court's consideration, though, was whether "those who want to see it shall have the *right* to do so or whether they shall be denied that right" because "a minority group" was lobbying to shut it down. The regents' revocation was "arbitrary, unjust, unreasonable and unwarranted, and unconstitutional," Burstyn claimed, and the action deprived him of property rights without due process in violation of the First, Fifth, and Fourteenth amendments and the constitution of New York State.[110]

The brief for Burstyn's business rested on three further points. First, the regents had no statutory authority to rescind a license. Second, the state's censorship statute violated the right to free exercise of religion and the separation of church and state by taking the religious views of one group in society and fastening them "with the force of law on the backs of all citizens." Ten years earlier, the Supreme Court had struck down an "astonishingly" similar censoring of a sacrilegious phonograph record (in *Cantwell v. Connecticut*), and Burstyn wanted that case's precedential value considered against New York's motion picture censorship. Finally, the brief declared that censorship was prior restraint, which violated the free speech guarantees of the First Amendment and of the New York State constitution. Citing Douglas's dictum in *United States v. Paramount Pictures* that movies should be included in the press freedoms guarantee of the First Amendment, Burstyn tried to kill off *Mutual* by arguing that "its force . . . [has been] utterly destroyed and overruled by half a hundred decisions."[111] Such attacks would become a familiar refrain in the Burstyn briefs. As long as *Mutual* stood, *The Miracle* stood little chance of overturning New York's censorship. Overturning *Mutual* had become Burstyn's holy grail.

Counsel to the regents Charles Brind argued the case for the state, a role he would reprise in every succeeding motion picture censorship case in New York State. A dedicated anti-Communist, Brind sincerely believed that film censorship bettered society, a position that the *Miracle* case and later challenges would not cause him to reconsider. In 1953, he gave a speech that probably reflected the attitudes of most censors of the period. Suggesting that thirty years of state censorship had given people a "false sense of security," he reminded his listeners how bad films had gotten in the precensorship days. The need for vigilance remained high, he warned, and he asked his audience to consider, "What would happen if the statute were declared unconstitutional?" Playing on the fears of Communist influence in Hollywood, Brind pointed to a New York statute outlawing the teaching of subversive doctrines in school. What good would such a law do, he asked, if schoolchildren could watch subversive films in theaters? "We stand at some crossroad. Whether we go ahead under present statutes in those states having them, whether we find it necessary to amend those statutes either to attempt to define standards or otherwise, or whether we must set up an entirely new program for motion picture review presents an enigma." The new program Brind had in mind was a proposal to allow state censors to cut "'subversive' content."[112] Here he was being more censorious than the state's chief censor, Hugh Flick, who had gone on record in favor of replacing the current system with age-based classification of movies. Flick was rethinking censorship, but Brind never lost his faith in its rectitude.

For the *Miracle* case, Brind began by asserting, as had all censor defenses before, that there was no ambiguity: everyone knew what was meant by *sacrilege*. Ignoring all the public disagreements over *The Miracle*, he declared that "common agreement" made the picture "sacrilegious *per se*." Second, he argued that the regents did have jurisdiction to rescind the license because of their constitutional duty to administer the workings of the motion picture division; indeed their failure to do so would be "inconceivable." Then he moved to contradict Burstyn's briefs. Responding to the contention that *Mutual* was antiquated, Brind reminded the court that just the year before, the Supreme Court had upheld a local censorship statute in Georgia by refusing certiorari (in the *Lost Boundaries* case). Addressing Burstyn's point that the Supreme Court was moving in a new direction, Brind quoted from a concurring opinion by Frankfurter in a case just two years earlier: "Movies have created problems not presented by the circulation of books, pamphlets or newspapers, and so the movies have been constitutionally regulated."[113]

There was one more brief for the court to consider. Two of the NYCLU's most successful attorneys, Osmond Fraenkel and Herbert Monte Levy, had filed an amicus brief for Burstyn. They wanted to convince the appellate division judges that the Supreme Court was moving away from judicial restraint when it considered speech-inhibiting statutes. The appellate division justices watched the film and withdrew to deliberate.

Despite the best efforts of Burstyn, Farber, London, and the NYCLU, on May 8, 1951, the justices returned a unanimous decision upholding the regents. State courts in 1951 were still unlikely to overturn actions of state agencies, and this court also had been asked to take on a constitutionality issue that it not surprisingly wanted to avoid. Indeed, as Brind had pointed out, the U.S. Supreme Court had avoided the issue just the year before when it refused to hear the *Lost Boundaries* appeal (as well as the *Curley* appeal). Writing for the appellate division, Justice Sydney F. Foster maintained that it was not appropriate for an intermediate court to "reexamine the issue" of film censorship's constitutionality in view of the Supreme Court's recent refusal to do so. He asserted that the state could bar a film because of sacrilege because movies were not, like the press, legitimate "organs of expression." He dismissed Burstyn's contention that the regents had no statutory authority to rescind a license, claiming such authority as inherent in the general oversight position. He did accept one of Burstyn's arguments, that there was disagreement on the sacrilege of *The Miracle*, but used it against him, claiming that the "conflict of views is proof that the issue is one of judgment to be resolved by the administrative body which has it in charge."[114]

Burstyn was not about to give up, and both sides readied for New York's highest court, the court of appeals. The briefs were similar to what had been argued at the appellate division. But the NYCLU used the opportunity to appear before the state's highest court to step up the attack on *Mutual*. "It is now the duty of this Court to . . . lay the ghost of that precedent, and to vindicate the fundamental constitutional principle *that every vehicle of ideas is shielded from such censorship*." *Mutual* was an anachronism, it argued, since both the movie as a means of communication and the First Amendment had "undergone constant refinement" since 1915. The NYCLU was correct: when *Mutual* was decided, the First Amendment had not yet been interpreted to apply to state actions against free speech. The NYCLU further argued that since the majority of criticism had been from the Catholic Church, with Protestant and Jewish clergy expressing no concern, New York's ban on sacrilege was essentially a pro-Catholic action. "If there is any fixed star in our constitutional constellation," the brief quoted Supreme Court justice Robert Jackson, "it is that no official, high or petty, can prescribe what shall be orthodox in . . . religion or other matters of opinion."[115]

Burstyn's list of amici curiae had grown with the addition of the Metropolitan Committee for Religious Liberty (the New York chapter of Protestants and Other Americans United for Separation of Church and State). The committee's brief minced no words, calling the Catholics who protested *The Miracle* "holy rollers" and insisting that no religious group should be allowed to bar a film because of its supposed sacrilege. Also joining were Artists Equity Association and the American Jewish Congress, both adding little to the arguments but lending their names in support of Burstyn's position.[116]

Again, a New York court upheld its board of regents, but this time the judicial facade betrayed a crack. In the ruling against Burstyn, two judges emphatically dissented. The five-man majority still clung to the belief that movies were purely entertainment with the potential for evil. Accepting the regents' determination of *The Miracle* as sacrilegious, the majority opinion cited an 1892 Supreme Court case: "We are essentially a religious nation of which it is well to be reminded now and then." The majority wanted to remind Burstyn and other anticensorites that the recent First Amendment cases they had cited as expanding speech rights also showed that freedom of speech "is not absolute but may be limited when the appropriate occasion arises."[117]

Even though he had lost, Burstyn could take comfort in a lengthy dissenting opinion by Judge Stanley Fuld, who agreed with the NYCLU that the U.S. Supreme Court had been moving toward removal of restraints on speech for several decades. This was movement that Fuld applauded. He believed that law was a living thing that should take its direction from the mores of the times. He had little sympathy with the idea that judges should defer to the legislature in all matters. Since legislators did not review all of their statutes each year, it was perfectly sensible, he thought, for the courts to do so when a litigant pressed an issue.[118] Burstyn's issue, for Fuld, was a valid one. "I just favor free speech," he later told the *Albany Times-Union*, "and I oppose any limitation on it."[119] But Fuld was no radical; in fact, his views were so conventional that a few years later, he would win the endorsement of all four major political parties when he ran for reelection.

In Burstyn's case, Fuld insisted, "Invasion of the right of free expression must find justification in some overriding public interest, and the restricting statute must be narrowly drawn to meet an evil which the state has a substantial interest in correcting." New York's censorship statute was not narrow enough for Fuld. "On the contrary," he wrote, "it imposes a general and pervasive restraint on freedom of discussion of religious themes in moving pictures, which cannot be justified on the basis of any substantial interest of the state." Fuld agreed with the NYCLU that *Mutual* should be "relegated to its place upon the history shelf."[120]

At the U.S. Supreme Court

The history shelf would have to wait until Burstyn could get his case heard by the U.S. Supreme Court—by no means a certainty. Of 1,107 cases filed with the Supreme Court in its 1951 term, only 200 were accepted.[121] Since the Court had just turned down both of the ACLU's other possible test cases, *The Miracle* was its last chance in the 1951 term. And it did not seem promising with such an enigmatic bench. Despite the unpromising context, Burstyn announced that his request for Supreme Court review had the support of various religious, civil liberties, and entertainment organizations (although he did not specify which ones).[122]

One entertainment organization would not lend its support: the MPAA. Ever since the 1948 *Paramount* decision, which parenthetically classified film as part of the press, the MPAA had hoped that the Supreme Court would declare movies deserving of First Amendment protection once and for all. Facing declining revenues (between 1946 and 1948, the industry had lost half its overall profits[123]), the MPAA was slowly and cautiously coming around to the idea that movies could best counter increasing competition by offering more adult content. But MPAA president Eric Johnston, who had gone on record several times as being in the market for a new test case and who had gotten nowhere with the *Lost Boundaries* and *Curley* cases, was having trouble convincing the major production companies' attorneys to sign on with any case in 1951. The time was not yet ripe for Hollywood to fight back enthusiastically. Film historian Garth Jowett's research shows that the industry typically responded to three basic threats: censorship, competition for box office revenues, and moral indignation from the public. But before the industry took any meaningful steps toward change, it had to face all three threats simultaneously, like a "three-bladed Sword of Democles [*sic*]."[124] If Jowett's formula is correct, the 1950s were not the right time for the MPAA to move against state censorship. State and municipal censorship, the first blade of the sword, was still operating, but it had become relatively predictable and not much of a threat. And although the second blade—competition—was present in the form of television and foreign films, the necessary third blade, organized protest over movie morals, was not present as it had been in the Progressive Era and the early 1930s. The MPAA would continue to mouth platitudes about censorship and freedom, but the industry never wholeheartedly jumped on the free screen bandwagon.

As the 1950s began, industry insiders and columnists openly discussed producers' growing restiveness under both the Production Code and governmental censorship. After the challenges of *Lost Boundaries* and *Curley* fizzled, the MPAA had two films to choose from: *Pinky* and *The Miracle*. Johnston and his group had many reasons to choose *Pinky* over Burstyn's film. Produced by Darryl Zanuck and directed by Elia Kazan, *Pinky* was the product of a member studio and, like *Lost Boundaries*, represented a new vogue in the late 1940s, the social consciousness film. Like *Gentleman's Agreement* and *Home of the Brave*, *Pinky* questioned the status quo with a bold treatment of race relations and class distinctions in the South. The title character, a light-skinned mulatto woman who has passed for white in the North, moves back to her Mississippi hometown, where she experiences discrimination. It would be easier to go back to Boston, but she decides that she can do more good if she remains in Mississippi and fights for racial equality. *Pinky*'s daring treatment of American racism had offended the censors of Marshall, Texas.

In addition to Hollywood's new interest in social message films and Johnston's personal interest in race relations, *Pinky* presented other compelling reasons for attention. The MPAA was typically interested in censorship challenges if profitability of a member film had been threatened.[125] *Pinky* was a major production, distributed by a member studio, and its profit potential was jeopardized. Although theater revenues from Marshall, Texas, would not have been of great concern, that *Pinky*'s troubles were caused by a local censor was. Local censors had always been more unpredictable than state boards, so the MPAA needed to thwart local censorship wherever it could. *Pinky* was ideal for that task.

On the other hand, many of the industry's attorneys advised the MPAA to stay out of the *Pinky* battle (*Gelling v. Texas*), because an adverse ruling might backfire and spawn more statutes, even perhaps the long-dreaded federal censorship.[126] The Court's two new members, Minton and Clark, were headed the wrong way for those who wanted film freedom.[127] The 1951 bench seemed less likely to sympathize with the free speech rights of movies than had been the 1948 bench, which decided *Paramount*.

Nevertheless, the MPAA continued its halfhearted participation in the *Pinky* appeal,[128] providing an excuse for not helping with the *Miracle* case. Although Johnston thought Burstyn had a good chance to win, industry attorneys took a short view of the case; they believed that "there'd be nothing gained from an industry standpoint other than that *The Miracle* would be permitted to play in New York."[129] But the case surrounding *Pinky* became bogged down in the Texas courts, and Gelling was not able to petition for certiorari until January 30, 1952. The MPAA was not able to convince the justices to consider the merits of its case until after they had heard arguments in the *Miracle* case. Thus Burstyn and the MPAA faced the Supreme Court in the same term, but not together. Burstyn had on his side the NYCLU but not the industry trade organization or any of Hollywood's guilds of writers, producers, and directors.

Burstyn did have the moral support of the Italian film industry, for what that was worth. He had done so much to encourage the American market for Italian films that the Italian version of the MPAA gave Burstyn a major award in the spring of 1951. Accepting the honor, he said that on his trips to Italy to purchase films like *Open City*, *Paisan*, and *The Bicycle Thief*, he had picked up a bit of Italian. He had learned, he said, that *citta aperta* meant "open city," that *paisan* meant "countryman," that *ladri di biciclette* meant "bicycle thief," and that *il miracolo* meant "trouble."[130]

The sign that the Supreme Court was finally willing to reconsider the *Mutual* decision came with the grant of certiorari for Burstyn's case. What the justices would do with that decision, however, was by no means certain. Burstyn and London proceeded on the assumption that they would have amicus support from the ACLU (which had taken over for the NYCLU), the American Jewish Congress, the Metropolitan Committee for Religious Liberty, the International Motion Picture Organization, and the National Lawyers Guild.[131]

As it turned out, New York State was allowed only one amicus, from the Catholic Welfare Committee, and Burstyn was allowed only two amicus briefs, from the ACLU (and whoever would join it) and a newly formed splinter group, the Catholic Committee for Cultural Action, whose support London desperately wanted to prove that even Catholics disagreed about the sacrilege of *The Miracle*. London's hopes went unfulfilled, however, when the New York archdiocese suddenly reined the new group in.[132]

Movie freedom advocates finally had a case before the Supreme Court, but the burden rested on a small businessman and his young attorney. Why was Burstyn willing to risk so much on one short movie? The evidence indicates that he was a committed civil libertarian, although he probably would not have seen himself that way, at least not at first. He had, of course, a financial stake in *The Miracle*. But it is clear that he was also motivated by noneconomic interests. Burstyn's life story reads like the American entrepreneurial dream. After starting a career as a diamond polisher upon arriving in New York City from Poland in 1921, he moved on to publicity work for a Yiddish theater. He got his big break when the owner allowed him to rent the theater for $500 and Burstyn sold $2,500 in tickets. That seed money enabled him to open a film importation and distribution business.

Burstyn developed a distaste for New York State's censorship when he and partner Arthur Mayer tangled with the censors over *Remous* between 1936 and 1939. Mayer, also well respected in the film business both as an exhibitor and a distributor, described Burstyn as "a very courageous little man"[133] who would not give up on *Remous*. A decade later, Burstyn found himself locked in two battles over *The Bicycle Thief*. Even when local censors in Oregon attempted to shut it down, Burstyn refused to allow any scene to be cut.[134] In New York, from the first struggle over *The Miracle* with McCaffrey through this final round in the Supreme Court, Burstyn maintained his commitment to a free screen. "We, the small independent people who import pictures from Europe have to fight the censors. Those good films, they're frank—that's what's good. And Hollywood can't afford to fight anyone because they've got too much real estate to protect."[135]

But Burstyn also had a business to run, and he sometimes put his censorship troubles to good marketing use. In 1945, he and Mayer tweaked a *Life* magazine quotation to promote *Open City*, advertising it as "sexier than Hollywood ever dared to be" (which it was not).[136] Leonard Leff and Jerold Simmons describe the lengths to which Burstyn went to embarrass the PCA into granting *The Bicycle Thief* a code seal so he could play it in mainstream theaters.[137] But their take on Burstyn seems too cynical. He told *Time*'s Hollywood reporter, Ezra Goodman, "Sure, I am a businessman. But freedom is the life blood of business. The movies, I think, are in such bad shape because they allowed themselves to be stifled in their freedom of expression. . . . I insist on presenting films as freely as a writer writes a book or a painter paints a picture."[138] Like many of the other independent distributors described in this book, Burstyn was a small business owner, struggling to make a living in a field dominated by giant companies. He lashed out at the systems, both private and governmental, that kept him and others like him from operating their businesses as they wanted, that interfered with the rights of their potential customers to see their product, and that kept ideas and art from the American moviegoer. On the eve of the Supreme Court's acceptance of the *Miracle* case, Burstyn called his next move "a step forward in the long struggle to free the American screen."[139]

London's motivations are clear. He demonstrated a lifelong interest in civil liberties, especially First Amendment rights. When he represented Burstyn's *Miracle*, he was thirty-nine, just beginning a distinguished career before the Supreme Court. He would go on to argue and win nine civil liberties and personal freedom cases before the high court.[140] Devoted to ending film censorship, London also worked to keep the First Amendment issue before the public by writing magazine articles and granting interviews. One of his earlier articles, "Freedom to See," maintained that the argument used to justify censorship—that films had broad appeal—should be seen as the argument against censorship. "In a democratic society," London wrote, "the greater the audience reached by any medium of communication, the greater the need to keep it free."[141] He became general counsel to the Independent Producers and Distributors Association, representing it in several court battles, including a 1954 case that led to the demise of film censorship statutes in Ohio and Pennsylvania and caused the remaining censoring states to strike *immoral* from their censorable categories. Active for many years in the NYCLU, London represented many artists who had been touched by censorship. Not only was he idealistic, he was also a superb advocate. Michael Mayer, attorney and executive director of the International Film Importers and Distributors Association, described him as "attractive, tall, well-spoken, articulate . . . one of the most effective attorneys I've ever heard."[142]

The ACLU attorneys who joined Burstyn's case in the Supreme Court—Arthur Garfield Hays, Osmond Fraenkel, Morris Ernst, Emanuel Redfield, and Shad Polier—were also distinguished and well respected. Hays, who had represented Burstyn in the *Remous* case a decade earlier, was still considered one of America's foremost corporate attorneys. Fraenkel had appeared before the Supreme Court fifteen times and was considered by the ACLU to be its best Supreme Court litigator. The ACLU's historian describes him as "one of the best constitutional lawyers of all time."[143] Ernst, best known for his influential argument that exonerated James Joyce's *Ulysses* from obscenity charges, had shared the general counselship of the ACLU with Hays for many years.[144] Redfield was the NYCLU's leading expert on obscenity law and had made many appearances before the Supreme Court.[145] And Polier was a noted civil rights attorney and counsel to the American Jewish Congress.[146] In contrast to the ACLU's amicus brief for *The Outlaw*, signed by only two attorneys, its brief for *The Miracle* carried ten well-known names.

Oral arguments for *Burstyn v. Wilson* were set for April 24 before Chief Justice Fred Vinson and Associate Justices Hugo Black, William O. Douglas, Stanley Reed, Robert Jackson, Felix Frankfurter, Harold Burton, Tom Clark, and Sherman Minton. London's arguments boiled down to two questions for the Court: was the New York State statute an unconstitutional abridgement of the right of free communication, and was the standard (sacrilege) applied unconstitutional? London insisted the *Mutual* decision had been "all but explicitly overruled" and that even theologians could not agree as to the sacrilege of *The Miracle*. New York's authorization of prior restraint, London said, violated the "main purpose" of the First Amendment. Frankfurter, wondering whether London was suggesting that motion pictures should be completely freed, asked, "You do not judge that an exhibitor of an obscene or sacrilegious film could not be prosecuted after the showing, but that a system of prior licensing must fall?" London answered, "Yes, your Honor, such a system must fall." He explained that films should be subject only to the same regulation as books, magazines, and plays. London then tackled both the vagueness issue and church-state separation concerns, arguing that determination of whether a motion picture is sacrilegious requires judgment based on religious beliefs. "Any state law requiring a government official to pass on substantive matters of religion is a law respecting the establishment of a religion." Brind directly contradicted London, asserting that the statute was, as judicially required, a "very narrow one." Since the prohibition against sacrilege did not apply to any one religion, he said, it did not involve religious opinions by the censors. Frankfurter jumped on this, asking whether sacrilege could be "mechanically determined," to which Brind answered yes. Then Black asked how sacrilege could be determined. He asked Brind whether a church group (whose exhibition of a film would be exempt because it was noncommercial) could exhibit a film that might be deemed sacrilegious by another religion. Brind was forced to answer yes. Jackson tried to sum it up, asking whether New York law prohibited "sacrilege for pay but not sacrilege for its own sake?" Brind sidestepped the question.[147]

New York's solicitor general, Wendell P. Brown, argued the rest of the state's case. He began by contradicting London's contention that *Mutual* no longer applied. Chief Justice Vinson asked Brown about the Court's recent statements contrary to *Mutual*. Brown answered that the *Paramount* language was merely dictum, which it was, but Vinson, reluctant to let the point drop, added, "But the statement was made." Brown tried to paint Burstyn and *The Miracle* as renegades by alluding to the motion picture industry's failure to join the case as amicus curiae. But here Jackson came to Burstyn's aid, forcing Brown to admit that the issue at stake mattered substantively only to foreign films and to independent distributors, since domestic productions submitted their films to industry-imposed content regulation. Brown also tried to argue that the sacrilege standard was sufficiently definite, pointedly reminding the justices that they had no authority to disagree with the finding of a state court about a statutory definition. (The New York State Court of Appeals had accepted a *Funk and Wagnalls* dictionary definition, and there the matter had to rest.) On church-state separation, Brown tried to convince the justices that the state's prevention of sacrilege in a film was "the very neutrality for which appellant argues."[148]

Having watched the film (a first for the Supreme Court), the justices retired to consider their decision with the aid of two amicus briefs, one from the ACLU and American Jewish Congress (for Burstyn) and another from the Catholic Welfare Committee. The latter argued that if the Court were to accept Burstyn's line of reasoning, a sacrilegious film would occupy a "privileged constitutional position." It pointed to governmental recognition of religion, such as the use of the Bible for the swearing in of witnesses and elected officials.[149]

The ACLU, joined by the American Jewish Congress as co-amicus, had honed its previous arguments to two that would complement and augment London's brief. First, representing the American Jewish Congress's point, the brief argued that the statute crossed the line into state support of religion. Second, it begged for the overturn of *Mutual*, calling it "as anachronistic as the nickelodeon." As if appealing to the justices' sense of modernity, it warned that to "permit pre-censorship of motion pictures would be to render nugatory the First Amendment, to hold that the Constitution cannot keep pace with modern technology."[150]

On May 26, 1952, the Supreme Court handed down a unanimous decision that turned the tide of film censorship litigation. The opinion was written by Clark, a surprising choice for a case that overturned a long-standing precedent on civil liberties grounds. Clark was a Texas Democrat who had helped Truman win the 1944 vice presidential nomination. In 1945 he became Truman's attorney general (where he oversaw the federal antitrust action that culminated in the *Paramount* decision), and in 1949 associate justice of the Supreme Court. In both posts he had shown little interest in free speech arguments for Communists; he was more interested in the "nuts and bolts" of justice than its "grand designs" and philosophical ramifications.[151]

Clark's pragmatic judicial philosophy was evident in his majority opinion, which was crafted to find in favor of Joseph Burstyn's movie in the narrowest possible terms. Clark began by declaring that the only issue the Court would consider was New York's abridgment of free speech and free press rights (discounting the church-state issue). First, he wrestled with the ghost of *Mutual*. He scrapped the idea that because filmmaking was a commercial enterprise, it deserved no First Amendment protection. Next, he addressed the harmfulness concept that had kept movies captive to prior restraint systems. Though perhaps "relevant in determining the permissible scope of community control," the possibility of societal harm presented by movies was not so imminent as to "authorize substantially unbridled censorship such as we have here." Clark was unwilling to discount entirely the idea that movies carried greater danger than other media, but he would not allow that concern to justify open-ended censorship, either.[152]

Then he wrote the words eagerly awaited by anticensorites: "Expression by means of motion pictures is included within the free speech and free press guaranty of the First and Fourteenth Amendments." Just to be sure that no one would misunderstand, he explicitly overturned *Mutual*: "To the extent that language in the opinion in *Mutual Film Corp. v. Ohio Industrial Comm'n* is out of harmony with the views here set forth, we no longer adhere to it."

So far, all seemed to be going Burstyn's way. But Clark and the Court stopped short of the definitive decision desired by the independent distributors, the MPAA, the ACLU, and other anticensorship forces. Clark took the narrowest route: "Since the term 'sacrilegious' is the sole standard under attack here," Clark continued, "it is not necessary for us to decide whether a state may censor motion pictures under a clearly drawn statute designed and applied to prevent the showing of obscene films. . . . We hold only that under the First and Fourteenth Amendments a state may not ban a film on the basis of a censor's conclusion that it is 'sacrilegious.'" At this point, the opinion's clarity ended. That the Court "would no longer adhere" to *Mutual* did not mean that it would mandate "absolute freedom to exhibit every motion picture of every kind." In the case of *The Miracle*, it was censoring for sacrilege that was the problem, not censorship per se. Clark explained,

> In seeking to apply the broad and all-inclusive definition of "sacrilege" given by the New York courts, the censor is set adrift upon a boundless sea amid a myriad of conflicting currents of religious views, with no charts but those provided by the most vocal and powerful orthodoxies. New York cannot vest such unlimited restraining control over motion pictures in a censor. Under such a standard, the most careful and tolerant censor would find it virtually impossible to avoid favoring one religion over another. . . . The state has no legitimate interest in protecting any or all religions from views distasteful to them which is sufficient to justify prior restraint.

Contemporary and later commentators have remarked on the Court's refusal to throw a knockout blow to overturn film censorship once and for all, but throughout its history, with few exceptions, the Supreme Court has hesitated to decide cases on broad constitutional grounds. Even when it has done so, it has often used the narrowest possible terms. While the opinion did squarely place motion pictures under the protection of the First Amendment, it also left much legal debris. For example, what constituted the sufficiently narrow statute that Clark described under which governmental agencies could continue to chop and ban obscene films? And just what was obscene? More important, was the Court saying that only obscene films could now be censored?

Justice Reed's concurring opinion, which has been largely overlooked (perhaps because of its brevity, just seventy-five words), was remarkably prescient, offering a glimpse into what the Court's answers to these questions would be. Since the Court was leaving some censorship still constitutional, Reed predicted that the justices would have to decide whether the First Amendment had been violated in "each case." He foresaw that the Court would have to become a board of supercensors, or as Burstyn later called them, "the nine supreme critics."[153] Over the next thirteen years, the Supreme Court, accepting several more motion picture censorship cases, became just what Reed had predicted—autocrats of censorship determination.

Even for Frankfurter, who had consistently fallen into the capacity-for-evil camp, censoring movies for sacrilege went too far. The New York censors, the board of regents, and the New York courts had interpreted *sacrilege* to mean something close to blasphemy. Frankfurter spent twenty-two pages in his concurring opinion detailing the history of the word, concluding that it meant only the physical desecration of sacred property, not the *Funk and Wagnalls* definition accepted by the New York courts. Although the Supreme Court was legally bound to accept the New York high court's definition, Frankfurter thought the New York court wrong (and told it so) and was convinced that such disagreement was enough to prove that the statute offended due process by its vagueness. This strike at the vagueness of the New York statute was great news for the anticensorites. But of even greater importance to the motion picture industry was Frankfurter's lengthy statement about film critics. It mattered to Frankfurter that most critics had praised *The Miracle*, and he quoted from nine reviews. For three decades, the censors of New York and other states had demanded revisions to motion pictures with no concern for art. By 1952, at least one Supreme Court justice had come to believe that the art of a film mattered and that the artistic merit could be determined by professional film critics.

The next day's *New York Times* story carried a five-line headline that neatly summarized the opinion: "Court Guarantees Films Free Speech:

Ends 'Miracle' Ban—Opinion Unanimous—High Tribunal Reverses State Appeals Bench in Sacrilege Case—Overturns Own Decision—Denies, as Held 37 Years Ago, That All Motion Pictures Are 'Business Pure and Simple.'"[154]

The Heavy Burden Starts to Shift

Burstyn had won. *The Miracle* would be shown in New York State. *Mutual* had been overturned. *Burstyn v. Wilson* overturned the use of *sacrilegious* as a censorable term and extended free speech and free press protections of the First and Fourteenth amendments to films. But the suspicions of the Hollywood lawyers had proven to be well founded: the opinion was not a sweeping destruction of prior restraint. According to the opinion, a well-drawn statute could still be used to prevent obscene movies. The opinion was ambiguous enough to be cited as precedent by both procensorites and anticensorites over the next thirteen years as the film censorship battle continued.

On the other hand, *Burstyn* was a true landmark decision. It overturned the thirty-seven-year stranglehold of *Mutual* and extended constitutional protections to the movie industry that it had never before enjoyed. The decision placed a serious dent in state sanctioning of religious beliefs, and it dealt a blow to the influence of pressure groups. By striking out *sacrilege* because it gave too much discretion to the censor, it also forced the reconsideration of impossibly ambiguous statutory language. Most significant, though, the decision reversed the burden of proof, placing it squarely on the censors. Clark's opinion levied "a heavy burden" on the states to prove that a film censored prior to exhibition represented an "exceptional case." Although, in practice, state courts did not require this until well into the 1960s and the Supreme Court itself did not make good on enforcement of the burden shift until 1965, *Burstyn* did provide the precedent that eventually trickled down to lower court levels. As legal commentator Anthony Lewis noted, *Burstyn* was "the first real breakthrough" in censorship litigation.[155] A *Times* editorial the day after the decision noted that the nine justices of the Supreme Court, "so widely divergent in their political, economic and social thinking, united in the view that the Constitutional guarantees of free speech and free conscience must be preserved."[156]

Two theories exist in historical and legal circles about the unanimity of the decision. The first theory is that the majority of the Court wanted to declare all prior restraint unconstitutional, but the more liberal members sacrificed that sweeping position for the indefinite one written by Clark to achieve unanimous agreement. According to this view, Clark added the problematic paragraphs (leaving the possibility of censorship under clearly drawn statutes) to get the support of the more conservative Justice Burton.[157] The second theory, which comes from Ephraim London, contends that Vinson asked Clark, one of the more conservative members of the Court, to draft the opinion, hoping to sway him and other members to a more liberal position.[158] Clark may also have been tapped to write the opinion since he had some experience with the motion picture industry during his tenure as attorney general. Whatever the reason, the unanimity helped to bolster the legal authority of the decision, as it overturned a long-standing precedent.

In reaction, the MPAA gathered positive press comments from around the country and printed the responses in digest form for redistribution.[159] The ACLU's press release exulted, calling the decision "the most striking blow the courts have dealt censorship in years." The ACLU had a second reason for celebration. Having long battled the influence of what it called pressure groups, it interpreted the opinion as a warning to all such groups "that bans on expression of opinion will not be defended in a democratic society because they run counter to democracy's fundamental concept of unfettered free speech."[160] In all likelihood, it was the potential to strike at the Legion of Decency that had prompted the ACLU's strong support of Burstyn's case. Executive Director Patrick Murphy Malin called the decision a "warning to all pressure groups, whether they be racial, religious or political." Burstyn, having endured eighteen months of legal maneuvering and virulent public controversy, called the decision a "victory of the first magnitude . . . clearing the way for the motion picture to take its rightful place as a major and adult art form and as a medium of expression and communication of ideas on all facets of our life and society."[161] What may have appeared as rhetorical excess at the time would later prove correct. Motion pictures were not set free by *Burstyn*, but the unrestrained reign of the censor was over.

Spellman declined comment,[162] but the Catholic press despaired. The *Brooklyn Tablet*, which a year before had accused the ACLU of aiding communism by supporting *The Miracle*, called the decision "a victory for the vendors of smut. . . . The vicious assailants out to destroy the Christian religion are free to go and do their worst." The paper wailed, "All legal redress and governmental protection are denied."[163] Film critic Richard Corliss recognized *Burstyn* as the beginning of the end of Catholic power over movies, "the first great defeat of Catholic motion picture pressure." The Legion of Decency had learned, Corliss wrote in a 1968 article, "that a simple massing of the laity in front of a theater might not be enough."[164] The legion had wanted the State of New York to adopt its Catholic vision of what was acceptable in movie fare. The state was willing to go along, but the U.S. Supreme Court was not. Though the *Burstyn* ruling did not specifically address the separation of church and state argument, by refusing states the ability to censor for sacrilege, the Court denied the church some of the influence that it had exercised for so long.

Legal professor Zechariah Chafee wrote in 1941, "Stamping on a fire often spreads the sparks."[165] The story of the *Miracle* litigation proves the point. Before the censorship controversy and boycott, *The Miracle* had drawn only moderate attendance, but in the midst of the hubbub, it sold out every day. After its reinstatement by the Supreme Court, it again drew lines that snaked around the block. After five weeks, though, the crowds dropped, and the film closed without much fanfare.

Afterward, the International Motion Picture Organization honored Burstyn at a luncheon in New York City with 310 people attending. Speaking to the group, Burstyn explained why he had gone to so much trouble over this one little movie. "Every time I had to submit a film for censorship," he explained, "I felt that I was in an illegitimate business and that being in this business was a crime. So, I felt that it was about time to try to restore a little dignity." Arthur Garfield Hays, also being honored, spent much of his speaking time extolling Burstyn: the ACLU members had merely been "back-seat drivers," he said, and the movie industry "with all its money couldn't accomplish what Burstyn and London did."[166]

The litigation cost Burstyn between $60,000 and $75,000 (roughly equivalent to a half-million dollars today).[167] If Burstyn was motivated by money, he was surely fooled, having spent far more than the film could have been expected to earn. But he refused financial help from "major figures in and out of the business" because they would not lend their names to the fight. "I could use their money," Burstyn said, "but if they would not stand up with me, I would rather be without it."[168] Lillian Gerard described Burstyn as "often afraid and always deliberative, sometimes overly so. He would worry himself into acute anxiety before he made a move, and when he did move, he moved like the chess player who always expects defeat."[169] Yet worried as he must have been, he would not allow himself or his movies to be bullied. He later remarked, "You can't give in to censorship; you must stand up for your self respect. When they picket me, I fight back."[170]

That Burstyn, with the help only of his attorney, the NYCLU, and the management of the Paris Theatre, carried this fight at the height of the McCarthy hysteria makes his courage even more admirable. As Gregory Black remarks, "Ignored in his day and now largely forgotten, Joseph Burstyn deserves recognition for helping to bring freedom of expression to an industry that had grown comfortable with its cozy relationship with censors and clerics."[171] Burstyn acted independently and courageously at a time when many others in the film industry were surrendering to the demands of more strident voices.

Burstyn was not finished, by any means. In June 1953, he notified the Kansas State Board of Censorship that he intended to institute legal proceedings against its statute in light of the Supreme Court's addition of film to the protections of the First Amendment. He would pay the Kansas license fees only under protest, and he insisted that such fees "violated the constitutional guarantees of expression and communication and are, therefore, void."[172] He tackled the Ohio board as well when it required that he remove one line from his next film, *Fugitive*. He refused, and the Ohio board acquiesced.[173]

The Emancipation Proclamation of the Film

The *Paramount* decision had been the first indication of a shift in a legal culture that had endorsed governmental censorship for thirty-three years. Four years after *Paramount* came *Burstyn*, the second major transition. In their 1982 book *Banned Films*, Edward de Grazia and Roger Newman see the decision as "radically" altering "the course of freedom of the screen." Ira Carmen uses *The Miracle* decision as a dividing line between the early days of censorship and what he terms "the modern period," in which censorship and free expression came into conflict. Gregory Black notes that "it was a stunning decision for freedom of the screen." Garth Jowett comments that this historic decision placed films within the category of a "significant medium" worthy of free speech protection. Richard Randall attributes to the *Miracle* decision a turnabout in government's willingness to bend to pressure groups on the control of film. Lillian Gerard calls it "the Emancipation Proclamation of the film in America."[174] Her analogy is more than hyperbole. Just as Lincoln's proclamation did not free any slaves or end racial prejudice on January 1, 1863, the *Burstyn* decision did not open the door for full freedom of the screen. That process, like ending slavery, would take more time. But the *Miracle* decision did both reflect and effect the beginnings of an attitudinal swing. As legal historians Michael Klarman, Peter Irons, David O'Brien, and others have pointed out, Supreme Court doctrines usually reflect societal attitudes. The Court's hesitance to knock out prior restraint in 1952 reflected society's enduring belief in the "vulnerable viewer" who needed protection from the evils of money-grubbing, amoral movie producers. In questioning censorship, however, the Court was also reflecting the legal culture that was beginning to adopt closer scrutiny of any statutory infringement of individual liberties. The *Miracle* case also shaped the legal atmosphere, clearly shown by the forty-seven cases that have cited *Burstyn v. Wilson* as precedent.

Burstyn became the first in a five-round knockout of many long-standing film censorship statutes. The second round came just one week later, when the justices handed down a frustratingly ambiguous per curiam decision in the MPAA's test case, *Pinky*. The entire text of the *Gelling v. Texas* decision was as follows: "The judgment is reversed. See Joseph Burstyn, Inc. v. Wilson." Such brevity was particularly disappointing because the industry had hoped that *Burstyn* was the warm-up act for the total overturn of statutory film censorship to come from *Pinky*. *Gelling v. Texas* had overturned the local Texas ordinance that banned movies that were "injurious to the public interest" but had not cleared any of the judicial fog left from *Burstyn*. Frankfurter did attach a short concurrence explaining that he had found Marshall's ordinance overly vague.

In short succession, then, another set of governmental censors had been overruled, but in the most frustratingly limited and ambiguous way. One thing was clear from *Gelling*, however. At least one of the justices was ready to overturn all motion picture censorship. William O. Douglas (who had written the *Paramount* dictum) attached a brief concurring opinion centering on "the evils of prior restraint." The act of censoring, Douglas wrote, was injurious to constitutional liberties. "If a board of censors can tell the American people what it is in their best interests to see or to read or to hear, then thought is regimented, authority substituted for liberty, and the great purpose of the First Amendment . . . defeated." But Douglas was writing alone. It seemed that the majority still found film censorship standards invalid only if vaguely drawn.[175]

The legal atmosphere after *Burstyn* and *Gelling* was confused. It had taken the Supreme Court thirty-seven years to reconsider freedom of expression for movies, and when it finally spoke, the message was mixed.

Constitutional commentators were perplexed; even the states' attorneys general did not agree on what the rulings meant for their censor boards. In Maryland, the state's highest legal officer notified the censors to stop banning anything but obscenity and indecency. When, five days later, the New York State appellate division upheld its censors' ban of the French film *La ronde* for immorality, the Maryland censors took heart, ignored their attorney general, and went on censoring as usual.[176]

There were ramifications from *Burstyn*, but it would take years to see them. The *Burstyn* decision would be used to end state censorship in Pennsylvania and Ohio and would help tear down statutes in Kansas, Virginia, New York, and most municipalities by 1965.[177] It would also have a parallel legal effect. According to Leonard Levy, after the *Miracle* decision, "No state blasphemy act could survive the appellate process if challenged on free-speech grounds." The legal separation of blasphemy and obscenity was complete. Maryland's blasphemy statute, the last remaining one in operation, was finally voided in 1958, "inaugurating a new age: the end of blasphemy convictions in the United States."[178]

Sadly, Joseph Burstyn did not live to see the end of film censorship. He boarded a trans-Atlantic flight on his way to Europe to purchase his films for 1954, but he never made it. The Polish immigrant who had made his living by bringing European influence to the American screen died of a coronary thrombosis somewhere between the two continents. In a last tribute to Burstyn on December 13, 1953, when censorship's grip was still evident but loosening with each court challenge, Bosley Crowther headed his column "The Fight on Film Censorship Goes On, in an Honorable Name." He wrote, "Though Mr. Burstyn is no longer here to see it done, the case he singly and bravely carried . . . may yet spearhead full freedom for the screen."[179]

After all the politicians and priests, fire department captains and license commissioners, editorialists and picketers, and the ACLU and regents had spoken, it had taken one litigant with a good test case to extend the boundaries of free speech. But to achieve full freedom for the screen, more distributors like Burstyn would need to step forward, forcing the American judiciary to question further the constitutionality of prior restraint.

7

La Ronde, 1951–1954

In 1953, the U.S. Supreme Court agreed to hear another case against the censors of New York State. The film was *La ronde*, a saucy, satirical, cynical treatment of seduction and casual sex. By the time Robert and Raymond Hakim of Commercial Pictures Corporation brought *La ronde* to the United States in late 1951, it had played for two years in Paris and for ten months in London, where it had passed the British censors with no cuts. Even though British censoring was considered "heavy handed," the board there had begun to make allowance for artistic license.[1]

U.S. Customs censors had no problem with *La ronde* when it arrived in 1951, and it began playing in many states—with the single exception of New York. The motion picture division refused to grant an exhibition license, claiming that the film was "immoral" and "would tend to corrupt morals." After failing to move the board of regents, Commercial Pictures appealed to New York's appellate division. Losing there as well, it then appealed to the New York State Court of Appeals, and finally to the U.S. Supreme Court. Only by taking the film to the nation's highest court were the distributors finally able to give the people of New York State the chance to view *La ronde*.

The *La ronde* case has been seen by historians and legal commentators as nothing more than a footnote along the way to the inevitable demise of governmental film censorship, perhaps because the historiography of film censorship tends to look only at a teleological march to overturn censorship at the Supreme Court level. Yet the rulings of the U.S. Supreme Court map out only the general boundaries of any legal point; it is up to the state courts to interpret and apply these boundaries. Studies of Supreme Court cases miss the major point of the *La ronde* case, which was its considerable effect on state courts. In light of the state court decisions that followed the Supreme Court ruling, the *La ronde* case deserves credit as a major step in the fight of the anticensorship forces.

The Film

La ronde was a faithful adaptation of a famous Arthur Schnitzler play, *Reigen.* Schnitzler had intended the play as a dramatic preachment against the dangers of venereal disease contracted through casual sex (its plot could function as an AIDS awareness play today). Set in 1900 Vienna, the scenario depicts ten connected vignettes of seduction. In the first scene, a streetwalker propositions a soldier. They depart the scene together, but nothing of what happens next is shown, although the outcome is certainly not in doubt. In the second scene, the same soldier seduces a servant girl. Next, the servant girl seduces a bookish young man, who then seduces a married woman, who next seduces her husband. Her husband then seduces a young gold digger, who seduces a poet, who seduces an actress, who seduces a count, who winds up in the apartment of the streetwalker from the original vignette. The film's narrator, an elegant and sophisticated man on a merry-go-round, appears whenever Schnitzler wants to make some wry commentary. The narrator, played by Anton Walbrook, even appears in one scene with scissors, suggesting censorship (as noted by several film reviewers). While there can be no doubt about the off-screen culmination of each seduction, no display of sexual intimacy appears. Everything beyond the emotional foreplay is left to the viewer's imagination. The film's innovative camera techniques, elaborate sets, magnificent costumes, pleasant Oscar Straus waltz theme music, and witty dialogue lead to a charming, wry, and slightly sardonic tone.[2] Within the context of the evolving sexual mores of the 1950s and the continuing expansion of the previously private into public discourse, some were bound to find the film acceptable adult fare. Others were bound to find it immoral.

La ronde's well-known stage antecedent, its famous author and director, and its distinguished cast assured that it would be widely distributed throughout Europe.[3] Indeed, in London, it played to rave reviews. The *Daily Mail* described it as "wickedly witty" and "visually enchanting":

> In one cynical lesson and nine easy seductions, it makes the point that the pattern of love always repeats itself. There must be a conqueror and a conquered, and next time the conqueror becomes the conquered. The point is illustrated by a sort of game of amorous

> consequences in Vienna 1900. . . . Such a theme could be ruptured by a single indelicacy, and you must take my word for it that no error is committed. Perfectly handled by Max Ophuls, it floats like a cloud of ping-pong balls on slender jets of champagne, the jets being provided by ten stars.[4]

The *London Sunday Express* called the film "a deliciously cynical exposure of love. Here is love without humbug—but also without offensiveness."[5] The London *Times* summed it up as "elegantly sophisticated. . . . Desire is the mainspring of the amoral motives and actions of everyone and all is played out in the shadow of the bed, and yet it is never offensive."[6]

The film industry was also impressed with *La ronde*. The British Film Academy named it best film for 1951, ranking it ahead of *An American in Paris* and *The Red Badge of Courage*. *La ronde* also took best scenario and best screenplay awards at the Venice Film Festival that year and was nominated for a best screenplay Academy Award in the United States in 1952.[7]

Unlike most other foreign films, which began their American distribution in New York City to get favorable reviews to help bookings in other cities, *La ronde* was first viewed in Washington DC, Los Angeles, and a few smaller cities. Only months later did Commercial Pictures apply for a New York State license. Thus the film had been seen and reviewed in the United States before it was brought to the attention of the New York censors. If this was the plan, it was clever: it ensured that any censor problems in the New York market would get a public airing, which most New York–censored films did not.

The Hakim brothers of Commercial Pictures must have been happy to see that the American critical reaction was as positive as the European had been. *Time* magazine called *La ronde* "an audacious, world-wise comedy of sex . . . certain to delight adult audiences. . . . It is never prurient, smirking or pornographic. . . . It spoofs sex rather than exploits it."[8] Popular gossip columnist Dorothy Kilgallen called it "naughtee,"[9] an adjective sure to sell some extra seats. The reviewers of the Catholic Legion of Decency, however, did not find anything appealing about the film and in early November rated *La ronde* C for "condemned."[10]

The Hakims submitted *La ronde* to New York's motion picture division, which promptly refused a license.[11] Needing the New York City market, as all foreign films did, Commercial Pictures edited the film and sent it back for another try. Again, the censors refused. Motion picture division director Hugh Flick, however, was not altogether comfortable with his board's ruling. He later admitted that *La ronde* was a "well-meant and a well-made movie. . . . We did not, could not, issue it a license, and all the various cuts the distributor was almost overeager to make still didn't get it to the point where we felt we could legally pass it." The basis of morality for the motion picture division, Flick explained, was the sanctity of the family. Any film that challenged that convention and that could be seen by the "weak and depraved" and children needed to be banned. All six of Flick's reviewers had enjoyed the film but found that it contradicted the "standards of normal family life."[12]

Since *La ronde* could not be shown, most New York City film critics were silent. But *New York News* film critic Kate Cameron was bothered about the ban and wanted to find out why New Yorkers could not see it, so she arranged a private screening, a request that the Hakims must have been only too happy to accommodate. Cameron headlined the resulting article "Banned Comedy Is Enchanting." She noted with no little disdain that a recent British satire of murder had not caused the state censors to blink, but *La ronde* had to go. She wrote, "The New York censors believe that a satire on murder is not apt to corrupt the morals of our citizens, but that one based on the lighter side of love may do so."[13]

La Ronde Meets the Board of Regents

Commercial Pictures hired Florence Perlow Shientag, a high-profile former judge, to represent *La ronde* when it appealed to the regents. A pioneering lawyer in New York City, Shientag graduated from the New York University School of Law in 1933, at a time when many law schools, including Columbia University, were refusing to admit women. She became a law aide in Thomas E. Dewey's famous organized crime unit in the late 1930s, then law secretary to Mayor Fiorello LaGuardia from 1939 to 1942. She was appointed a justice of the domestic relations court in 1941 and served as assistant U.S. attorney from 1943 to 1951. She was the widow of Justice Bernard L. Shientag, the New York State appellate division judge who had ruled against Howard Hughes's claim against License Commissioner Fielding in the *Outlaw* case. She was a founding member of the New York Women's Bar Association and served as its president. Shientag was well connected in New York City society, and as the first woman in the criminal division of the U.S. attorney's office, she got lots of publicity. The Hakim brothers of Commercial Pictures decided to hire her after reading about her in the newspapers (and perhaps after seeing her picture—she was a most attractive forty-year-old).[14]

Shientag's argument for Commercial Pictures centered on four points. First, she insisted, the film was not immoral and had, in fact, "earned highest acclaim for its artistic integrity." Second, she claimed that the film's famous French actors would not have risked their reputations on a questionable film. Third, she argued that the film should not be taken "seriously or literally." It was, as Kate Cameron had noted, a satire. And fourth, the picture had already been heavily edited to remove anything that might be offensive to New York sensibilities. Shientag quoted British film reviews that admitted the film's sexual irreverence but affirmed that it was harmless.[15]

In answer, the motion picture division asserted that the film was indeed immoral because sex was the dominant theme. The censors found the film emblematic of the "gulf which exists between the generally accepted standards of morals and behavior as they exist in France and in the State of New York." The regents predictably agreed and refused Commercial Pictures' request for a license: "Promiscuity is the central theme and although the actual consummation of the amorous adventures is in no instance presented on the screen, the conclusion is inescapable. . . . Presentation of such a film in theatres in this State is 'immoral.'"[16]

La Ronde Goes to Court

As Shientag prepared for the appellate division in May 1952, the U.S. Supreme Court had already heard oral arguments in the highly publicized *Miracle* case but had not yet handed down its decision. The precedent of *Mutual* still reigned. Motion pictures were still an unworthy method of communication as far as the First Amendment was concerned.

At the appellate division, Shientag encouraged the justices to heed the evaluation of critics, invoking the rising authority of independent experts in both American society and in the courts.[17] But on that point her case was tenuous. The U.S. Supreme Court was then considering the issue in the *Miracle* case, and the judicial value of film critics' opinions was unresolved. It was true that some judges were receptive to hearing from critics in censorship matters (and had been as far back as the 1920s), but others paid no attention to critical evaluations of books and movies. In book suppression cases, however, the appellate division justices' colleagues on the New York State Court of Appeals had been admitting the opinions of critics as evidence since 1922.[18] Federal courts were also moving in that direction. In 1934, in one of the most famous book censorship cases, Judge Learned Hand had ruled that the opinions of critics should be considered "persuasive pieces of evidence" in determining obscenity.[19] But courts still routinely ignored critical opinions in deciding film censorship cases. As late as the mid-1950s, film criticism—if mentioned at all in court opinions—was constrained to dissents. As film became more established as a legitimate cultural form, however, film criticism began to affect public opinion. Some critics, like Bosley Crowther, were in the vanguard, pushing for acceptance of film as high culture throughout the 1950s. In the 1960s, what came to be known as "the decade of the Film Generation,"[20] critics would achieve new status as intellectuals. But as Shientag began arguing the critical merits of *La ronde*, neither film nor film critics were fully accepted.

Shientag also went after the statute's vagueness: "Morality is an intangible concept. . . . The federal courts have uniformly held that such intangible moral concepts vary from one period to another." Here Shientag was on solid ground. The New York censors themselves had banned varying film behaviors as "immoral" through the years. Shientag had many instances of case law to cite about changing moral standards. She used the well-known statement from Supreme Court justice Benjamin Cardozo that "a practice considered decent in one period may be indecent in another."[21]

Charles Brind was now in his eighth film censorship appearance at the appellate division in fifteen years. He took the tried-and-true route of invoking judicial reluctance to tamper with administrative bodies, arguing, "In this state the legislature has wisely mandated that the general audiences should not be subjected to such spectacles."[22] The plaintiff had not given sufficient ground, he continued, to justify the court's overruling the judgment of the regents.[23]

But Brind was about to learn that judicial restraint was less dependable than it had been. In the time between his oral argument on *La ronde* and the appellate division's decision, the U.S. Supreme Court changed the rules by extending First Amendment protection to films in *Burstyn v. Wilson*. Thus the *La ronde* case, *Commercial Pictures Corp. v. Regents of the University of the State of New York*, became the first opportunity for a state court to consider film censorship under the new constitutional status of the motion picture.[24]

The appellate division issued its decision in June 1952, less than a month after *Burstyn.* It upheld the regents, but by only three to two, and the majority opinion by Justice Francis Bergan was hardly the ringing endorsement of legislatively empowered administrative bodies that the censors had grown accustomed to. Bergan noted that recent attempts to define legal terms like *immoral* had been unsatisfactory. Administrative determinations were also questionable. "No one has been able clearly to mark out in advance the exact point where a judge will interfere and separate it from the area in which he will not interfere with what the administrator has done." Although questioning where the line should be drawn was good for anticensorites, Bergan was not suggesting that the line should be moved in favor of the film producer or the film critic. Even if some members of the court agreed with the critics about *La ronde*'s artistic merit, Bergan "felt an absence of judicial power to impose those views on the Regents." The New York court had listened to testimony about the opinions of film critics but had decided that such opinions should not override the administrative decisions of state agencies.[25]

Brind and the regents could take some solace in the appellate division's continuing, if weakening, preference for bureaucrat over film critic, but a strong dissenting opinion written by Presiding Justice Sydney F. Foster, joined by Justice O. Byron Brewster, gave them cause to worry. As he had in earlier film censorship cases, Foster saw New York's statute as "an infringement upon freedom of expression." And, unlike Bergan's majority opinion, Foster's dissenting opinion called for an end to the traditional judicial restraint toward administrative bodies, contending that, "in dealing with an issue of free expression, the rule should be quite to the contrary." Here, Foster and Brewster adopted the emerging judicial interpretation first put forth by Justices Stone and Cardozo in the 1930s, and recently promulgated by Justices Hugo Black and William O. Douglas, that governmental restrictions of civil liberties deserved close scrutiny. Foster was in the judicial vanguard when he called the state's film censorship statute unconstitutional. He ignored *Burstyn*'s ambiguities, focusing instead on its statement that censoring be done only under "clearly drawn" statutes. This, said Foster, made New York's statute questionable. "Indefiniteness affords opportunity for arbitrariness," he warned, and he chided the regents for not supplying the motion picture division with clear guidelines. "The lack of proper standards and guidance has led the State Board of Regents into a most surprising record of inconsistency and illustrates at first hand the evils of slap-dash censorship." Frustrated by the uncertainty of censorship's constitutionality, Foster demanded that the court take a definitive stance: "Either motion pictures may be censored or they cannot be."[26]

No doubt cheered by Foster's dissent, Raymond Hakim immediately announced that his company would take the case to the court of appeals. He was not the only one encouraged by the thought that another round in court could shut down the work of the motion picture division. The *New York Times* also wondered if the next court round might "lead eventually to a revision of the state's censorship law."[27] Indeed, the *La ronde* case would turn out to be the last one in which the appellate division upheld the regents.

The ACLU's National Council on Freedom from Censorship, which was looking for the next promising test case, had been watching the *La ronde* situation since October 1951.[28] One of the ACLU attorneys, Herbert Monte Levy, had written to the Hakim brothers requesting a private screening of *La ronde* and offering legal assistance, but the offer was apparently ignored, and Levy dropped the issue.[29] Following the appellate division decision, the ACLU repeatedly tried to make contact with Shientag. One letter from Clifford Forster, executive secretary of the National Council on Freedom from Censorship, reveals that while he may have been in the vanguard for free speech rights, he was not particularly advanced in his thinking about women in the workplace. Forster implored Arthur Garfield Hays to intervene with Shientag. "Like so many women," Forster wrote, Shientag "apparently is having some difficulty in making up her mind and still has not come to a decision as to whether she wants us to file a *brief amicus* in the New York Court of Appeals. She indicated that she would like to discuss the matter of our filing with you, so I wonder if you would be good enough to give her a ring?"[30] Shientag later insisted, however, that she received no such phone call. She would have welcomed ACLU assistance, she remarked, so "I would certainly remember getting a phone call from Arthur Garfield Hays."[31]

As Shientag and the Hakim brothers prepared for the court of appeals, seven states and forty-six municipalities were continuing to censor films, although censorship was under attack almost everywhere. A 1953 ACLU report on censorship in the United States considered Ohio and Maryland quite strict but New York only "moderate" in its control over films. The ACLU characterized Flick as "genial" but worried about New York's unpredictability because of "political pressures on the Board of Regents" (undoubtedly referring to the Catholic pressure on the regents to rescind

The Miracle's license the year before).[32] Any action against the New York censors, then, held great promise for the ACLU, because it would combine two of their major targets: censorship and pressure group influence.

During the same month as the appellate division decision in the *La ronde* case, censorship proponents were on the march. The U.S. House of Representatives had established a select committee to investigate current literature. Several states were considering obscene literature bans. New York's legislature had passed a bill to extend censorship authority over publications to local police, although it was vetoed by Governor Dewey on constitutional grounds. In New York City, the license commissioner had ordered the removal of all nudist publications from newsstands. The publisher of one of the affected magazines, with the misleadingly wholesome title *Sunshine and Health*, appealed the commissioner's ban but managed only a hung jury. The publisher also sued the U.S. Post Office for refusal to deliver the magazine but lost.[33] And the producers of a smash Broadway hit, *Wonderful Town*, canceled a performance after learning that a left-wing publication had bought a block of three hundred seats.[34] The ACLU report questioned, Would the next step be the requiring of loyalty oaths from ticket purchasers? Statutory censorship and its "tireless twin," self-censorship,[35] still had great appeal and great effect in the Communist-fearing United States of the early 1950s as *La ronde* was readied for New York's highest court.

At the court of appeals, the opposing briefs offered only a stark choice. The state, with Brind at the helm, simply dug in its heels, relying on the court's tradition of judicial restraint and maintaining that *La ronde* had been properly rejected as immoral. Shientag claimed that New York's film censorship statute denied legitimate speech rights. She also insisted that the film was not, in any case, immoral. This last assertion provided the court a narrow route to find for her clients, in case the judges found her constitutional arguments unconvincing. It was the same strategy that London had used when he argued that *The Miracle* was not sacrilegious. Although independent distributors' attorneys may have wanted to go for broke constitutionally, they were bound by legal ethics to provide a more practical route by which the judges could rule in favor of their clients. After offering the judges both broad constitutional issues and a narrow route to find *La ronde* moral enough for New York's audiences, Shientag argued that even if a licensing system could be construed as constitutional, prior restraint should be applied only in exceptional cases, such as those presenting a clear and present danger of "some pressing public need."[36]

New York state courts maintained that the *Burstyn* decision did not preclude all motion picture censorship. So the question, unanswered since *Burstyn*, was, Under what circumstances could a film be banned? On this, the New York courts and the U.S. Supreme Court seemed to be heading in different directions. According to the regents and the state courts, films depicting immoral behavior presented a clear and present danger to society. But the Supreme Court seemed less inclined to accept that such films could be sufficiently dangerous to justify censoring them.[37] To ban *La ronde*, Shientag said, the regents needed to prove that it was dangerous, which they had not done.[38]

At oral arguments in January 1953, Shientag drew attention to inconsistencies in the regents' pronounced goals, saying that they routinely licensed films about prostitution, murder, and rape yet would not license this film about love and relationships. Brind defended these variations by pointing out that the censors could determine immorality only in each individual case. Standards, he said, as censors and judges had been saying for four decades, were impossible to delineate.[39] After watching the film, the judges retired, announcing that they would not hand down a ruling that term.

It took five and a half months for the court of appeals to hand down a split decision. The majority opinion, written by Judge Charles W. Froessel and joined by three others, tried to answer three questions. To the first question, whether motion pictures were exempt from prior restraint, Froessel answered no. "Regulation and suppression are not the same," he argued, noting that courts had no trouble in distinguishing the two. He had no doubt that the film was dangerous to society. "That a motion picture which panders to base human emotions is a breeding ground for sensuality, depravity, licentiousness and sexual immorality can hardly be doubted. That these vices represent a 'clear and present danger' to the body social seems manifestly clear." In this interpretation of clear and present danger ring McCarthy-era concerns about freedom versus license. The Supreme Court had been struggling since the 1919 red scare to formulate a doctrine for the permissible control of speech. By 1943, the Court had decided that speech could be controlled only when the danger of its effect was "grave" and "immediate."[40] The presentation by movies of "depravity" and "licentiousness" was a grave enough danger, in the judgment of the majority of New York's highest court, to justify the continuation of prior restraint.

To the second question, whether the term *immoral* was unconstitutionally vague, Froessel answered no. Arguing that New York statutes frequently used the term, he interpreted the legislative intent of *immorality* as relating specifically to sexual immorality. In what seems like painfully contorted logic, Froessel argued that the statute contained a "gradation of language, proceeding from 'obscene' to 'indecent' to 'immoral.' . . . Viewing the statute in its proper setting, then, the words 'immoral' and 'tend to corrupt morals' as used therein relate to standards of sexual morality." Echoing the first film censorship challenge in 1909, Froessel continued, "[The terms] are not vague or indefinite. . . . Every person of ordinary intelligence understands their meaning."[41]

To the third question, whether the statute had been improperly applied to *La ronde*—the narrow route that Shientag had supplied—Froessel answered with a resounding no. The film was immoral. He reminded the appellants that the story, in book form under the title *Hands Around*, had been found obscene by a New York court in 1930.[42] Had *La ronde* received due process of law? "If the Regents err in law," Froessel wrote, "we sit to correct them. If they must exercise their fact-finding powers in a close case and do so honestly and fairly, then due process has been observed."[43]

For Judges Charles S. Desmond and Albert Conway, the majority opinion did not go far enough in endorsing New York's censorship statute. Although Desmond was generally considered a member of the more liberal wing of the court of appeals, he was a social conservative who believed that prior restraint was perfectly permissible under the First Amendment. "We are not so far gone in cynicism that the world 'immoral' has no meaning for us," Desmond wrote. A few months later, he published a law review article promoting censorship. "The essence of the American system," he wrote, was general statutory language, administratively interpreted and judicially reviewed. Moreover, he asserted, the difference between subsequent prosecution (for books, theater, and magazines) and prior restraint (for movies) was of little judicial significance. In a second article, published in 1956, Desmond further argued that since the framers had intended to protect only political speech in the First Amendment, any anticensorship legal arguments based on constitutional protections of artistic speech were baseless. The difficulty with *immoral* as a statutory term, he wrote, was not that it was indefinite but that it had been "robbed of meaning by those who deny that there is any such thing as a changeless code of morals."[44]

Not all the judges agreed with Froessel and Desmond. Marvin R. Dye and Stanley H. Fuld dissented, as they had in the *Miracle* case two years before. Like the appellate division dissenters on *La ronde*, and like Douglas and Black on the Supreme Court, Dye and Fuld found prior restraint flawed in cases involving "fundamental civil rights." The majority opinion had cited *Burstyn* to prove that movies deserved scrutiny because of their unique ability to harm, but the dissenters interpreted *Burstyn* to the contrary. Dye believed that *Burstyn* had extended First Amendment protections "even though" motion pictures possessed greater power than other media. *Burstyn*'s lack of clarity about prior restraint was not an endorsement of movie censorship; it was merely an intermission. The Court was treading water, Dye said, waiting for a case to be presented under a clearly drawn statute so the justices could restrict all motion picture censorship.[45]

Dye and Fuld also willingly accepted film reviews as evidence. As Frankfurter had in his *Burstyn* concurrence, Dye quoted positive evaluations from film critics and recited *La ronde*'s international awards. This was the first time in a film censorship case that a New York state judge held that the opinions of critics mattered. Dye insisted that because film critics and censors could not agree on what constituted an immoral film, the standard was too subjective to meet the Supreme Court's stipulation for censoring only under a clearly drawn statute. Dye and Fuld were also not persuaded by the majority opinion that *immoral* necessarily meant sexually immoral. Dye wanted the statute invalidated on the ground of indefiniteness.[46]

Such disagreements among the court of appeals judges meant that the Hakims were free to apply for certiorari from the U.S. Supreme Court. And the judicial divergence over the meaning of *immoral* would prove crucial to the appeal. Since four judges could not agree on the meaning of the term, the ruling did not have legal validity, and Shientag had a big hole to drive her arguments through on appeal to the Supreme Court.

Companion Case from Ohio

Another film case concurrently litigating in Ohio was also about to ask the Supreme Court for certiorari. Superior Films had been denied an Ohio exhibition license for a Columbia Pictures production. *M* was a remake of the highly regarded 1931 Fritz Lang–Peter Lorre film of the same name, which dealt with the pursuit and execution of a pedophile serial killer. Except for making clear the sexual perversion of the killer and changing the location from Berlin to Los Angeles, director Joseph Losey turned out a faithful retelling of the earlier film. After sailing through the New

York censors,[47] *M* ran into trouble in Ohio "on account of being harmful." Clearly concerned about the Supreme Court's new attitude toward censorship and worried that Ohio's open-ended statute could lead to legal troubles, the reviewers dictated the following for their file: "The showing of this picture, in the judgment of the Department of Education, might quite likely result in the criminal molestation or even the murder of a helpless child. . . . The Department of Education was clearly acting within one of those exceptions which, under the Miracle decision, may be legitimately carved out from the realm otherwise devoted to freedom of expression."[48] This argument, that a film could lead to criminal behavior and thus should be banned, made *M* a promising test case.

When Superior Films appeared before the district court of appeals in Ohio, it came prepared. A brief that was a free speech tour de force showed that every time prior restraint had been recently challenged under the First and Fourteenth amendments, the Supreme Court had struck it down. Superior's attorneys also tried a new tactic: arguing that the license fee was an unconstitutional tax.[49] This was a risky proposition, since Superior had paid the license fee. On the other hand, the Supreme Court had held in 1943 that a fee charged upon a right guaranteed by the Constitution was invalid.[50] But neither the tax argument nor Superior Films' tome on free speech convinced the Ohio appeals court judge. Superior moved on to the Ohio Supreme Court.

Before the state's highest court, Ohio's attorneys called film censorship "a necessary, desired, and long satisfactory institution of Ohio life." They claimed that "foreign producers and fly-by-night producers care little for the crime rate, for the rate of juvenile delinquency, for the morals of Ohio. . . . Ohio does care and should care. Ohio is something more than a market for a tawdry product." To rebut Superior's brief before the appeals court, the state offered its own countervailing free speech lesson. Citing six cases, including *Mutual*, the brief roamed the landscape of decisions unfriendly to free speech.[51]

The state was buttressed by amicus help from the Ohio Congress of Parents and Teachers, a wholesome group that was hard to ignore,[52] and from the Ohio Catholic Welfare Conference, which appealed to the judges' natural reluctance to overturn long-standing precedents and legislative authority. The *Burstyn* decision, attorneys for the Catholic group argued, did nothing to impair the basic right of states to protect their citizens from immoral films,[53] and neither, by implication, should the judges of the Ohio Supreme Court.

In answer, the Ohio Supreme Court cited the recent New York State *Commercial Pictures* decision upholding the regents' ban of *La ronde*. Advancing juvenile delinquency rates, which the court claimed were attributable in part to the "show houses of the country," proved that criminal prosecution after the fact would be "a weak and ineffective remedy to meet the problem at hand." The U.S. Supreme Court had not yet taken away all community control over motion pictures, "and this court will not do so under the claim of complete unconstitutionality of censorship laws."[54] Two Ohio justices dissented, simply stating their opinion that the Ohio statute was now void in the wake of the *Burstyn* and *Gelling* (*Pinky*) decisions.

On to the Supreme Court

While *M* moved through the Ohio courts, in New York the Hakim brothers and Shientag had announced their appeal to the U.S. Supreme Court for *La ronde*. The ACLU then convinced Superior Films to seek certiorari for the Ohio case.[55] Those interested in the film censorship situation must have been delighted when the Supreme Court took both cases and consolidated them for argument and decision. *La ronde* and *M* would become the third and fourth film censorship cases heard by the Supreme Court in three years, suggesting that the justices were ready to make a strong pronouncement on film censorship. The *Motion Picture Herald* predicted that by taking the New York and Ohio cases together, the Supreme Court was ensuring that it would make a far-reaching decision on state film censorship. "It was always possible that as long as the court took only one case, it would decide it on the narrow, technical grounds rather than broad precedent-setting grounds. Taking the two cases," the trade paper argued, "practically makes certain a broader approach since the decision will have to be broad enough to cover both cases."[56]

Since this was her first appearance before the Supreme Court, Sheintag turned to Philip J. O'Brien Jr., a young attorney who had helped to win the *Gelling* case two years before. O'Brien had also coauthored an influential law review article about the status of film censorship in 1951,[57] and he was working on an amicus brief for the MPAA in the *M* case. Oral arguments for that case were set for January 7, 1953, with the *La ronde* arguments the next day. The Court allotted two hours of argument for *M* but only one hour for *La ronde*, supposedly to reduce duplication of argument. Surprisingly, beyond the crossover work of O'Brien, there seems to have been no coordination between the Ohio attorneys and Shientag. Unlike the planned litigation campaigns of other pressure groups, like the NAACP, the anticensorship distributors' campaigns remained unorganized, even when litigating contemporaneous cases before the same court.[58]

Shientag's strategy was to ask the court to ban all prior censorship, calling it a form of "thought control." After filing her brief, she held a press conference in the Supreme Court building—a first—and laid out her case for the press. She argued that motion pictures were not different enough from newspapers and radio to warrant censorship and that films were even less intrusive than television, which existed censor free. "The irony is that *La ronde* could be shown on television in New York and not in a theater for which admission has to be paid," Shientag said. She also compared the censoring of *La ronde* to that of *The Miracle*. The case "turns on 'immoral' as *The Miracle* case turned on 'sacrilegious,'" she explained.[59] The press conference paid off. According to *Variety*, it received "play in many newspapers across the country." The trade publication noted that although the publicity-savvy MPAA had filed a brief in the companion *M* case at the same time, it received no press coverage.[60] But perhaps the MPAA was savvy in maintaining a low profile, given the negative publicity and flak from its membership it would very likely face if the case was lost.

New York used its Supreme Court brief to argue that censorship was a "vital weapon in fighting juvenile delinquency" and that the "artistic merit of a movie had nothing to do with its immorality." In fact, the state implied, artistic merit made the situation worse. "Had the apple in the Garden of Eden not been so attractive, Eve would not have eaten it."[61] Brind succumbed to the temptation of turning the words of the critics around to work against the distributors. He included quotations from several film reviews about *La ronde*'s unseemliness, like this one from Dorothy Kilgallen: "A verree, verree, naughtee French film called La Ronde may get into this country and receive the censor's okay stamp via the simple device of misleadingly innocent English subtitles. . . . Only customers who understand French will catch the stretches of shocking dialogue."[62]

The state went on to warn the judges, "This country has indeed fallen upon evil days" if it could not control the portrayal of "adultery, seduction, fornication, and prostitution." Throwing everything at the justices—juvenile delinquency, the "needs of the decent citizen," the will of the people of New York State, the inefficiency of local regulation, the inevitable time lag between offense and prosecution without prior restraint, and the "clear and present danger" made more appealing by film's artistic allure—the state argued that a film like *La ronde* proved the need for film censorship. The film was "without a single redeeming feature" and was "much more objectionable" than the censored book from which it sprang because of its ending statement, "C'est l'histoire de tout le monde," or as the state's attorneys translated it, "Everybody is doing it."[63]

In her reply brief, Shientag dismissed the juvenile delinquency claim: it was simplistic to blame juvenile delinquency, which was caused by a host of factors, on films. Then she pulled out her best weapon, the judicial disagreements over the meaning of the term *immoral*. Four of the six judges of New York's highest court had not agreed that the term should be limited to sexual immorality. If even New York's highest court could not agree on the meaning of the statutory language, how could any film distributor know what the law required? Even if the term was restricted to sexual immorality, there was no clear definition of that term, either.

The time was now ripe for the ACLU's active involvement. Its National Council on Freedom from Censorship had been watching both the *La ronde* and the *M* situations. Waiting to see what would happen in *Burstyn*, the ACLU had not joined Shientag. When the council did decide to join the *La ronde* case as an amicus before the court of appeals, it was blocked by New York's attorney general.[64] The ACLU's committee then threw its efforts into the Ohio case and prepared a Brandeis brief—a document loaded with more sociology than law. *M* was no more harmful, it argued, than the content of many newspapers freely circulated within the state, and to prove it, the brief included a lengthy appendix of crime-ridden headlines. The ACLU ventured into other new territory by raising the question of artistic and social creativity. "For each picture rejected," the brief asked, "how many more were not submitted through fear of adverse decision?" This circumstance could "effectively stifle all discussion of political, social, or philosophic significance," reducing motion pictures to "intellectual pabulum."[65]

The MPAA, a newcomer to the anticensorship ranks, also filed an amicus brief in the Ohio case. Because *M*, made by MPAA member Columbia Pictures, had also received a code seal, Ohio's censorship could be interpreted as an attack on Hollywood's Production Code. The industry's brief confined itself to the increasing costs of reediting imposed by censors and the restrictions placed on movies by censorship not endured by the uncensored medium of television. After providing a history lesson on

Americans' traditional abhorrence of censorship, the MPAA ended on a rather melodramatic note: "Motion pictures, as part of the press can not remain half slave and half free."[66]

January 6, 1954, was "movie day at the Supreme Court." Chief Justice Warren and Justices Black, Reed, Frankfurter, Douglas, Jackson, Burton, Clark, and Minton watched both *M* and *La ronde*. The double bill caused the justices to miss President Eisenhower's State of the Union speech, a conspicuous absence noted in at least one Washington column.[67]

The case for *M* was heard first. After a rather weak showing by Superior's attorney, John C. Harlor,[68] Shientag opened for Commercial Pictures and *La ronde*. Since Harlor had already covered the issue of prior restraint, Shientag confined her arguments to the statute's vagueness. After insisting that movies should be held to no higher standard than other media, she questioned the ephemeral nature of terms like *immorality*, which were so value laden that even the New York state judges could not agree on their definitions. "'Immoral' is just as hard to define as the word 'beauty,'" Shientag said. Since four of the highest judges in New York State could not agree on what *immoral* meant, the Supreme Court had no choice but to find the term too vague.[69] Brind added nothing new. He repeated his refrain that *immoral* was generally understood and that requiring the state to adopt standards would be impractical.[70]

Most observers expected a lengthy deliberation, but it took just eleven days. On January 18, the Court handed down a per curiam decision that settled nothing. Appellate courts typically hand down decisions either signed (written by a named judge) or per curiam (intended to represent the view of the court as a whole). According to law professor Laura Krugman Ray, the subtext of a per curiam opinion might read like this: "This case is so easily resolvable, so lacking in complexity or disagreement among the Justices, that it requires only a brief, forthright opinion that any member of the Court could draft and that no member of the Court need sign." This seemingly straightforward practice became less so when per curiams began showing up in the 1930s with dissents attached. By the 1950s and 1960s, the per curiam decision had become the instrument of choice for dealing with controversial issues and urgent cases while avoiding messy details.[71]

The decision in *Superior Films* (and *Commercial Pictures*) resolved nothing. In fact, it raised new questions. The opinion, in total, read as follows: "The judgments are reversed. *Joseph Burstyn, Inc. v. Wilson*, 343 U.S. 495."[72] Interestingly—and perhaps tellingly—the per curiam was not based on *Winters v. New York*, the case that had established the "void for vagueness" doctrine, so Shientag's argument had probably not impressed the justices. With only *Burstyn* cited as grounds for reversal, both sides could assume virtually nothing. The ambiguities left by *Burstyn* not only remained unresolved but now had grown even more perplexing, and the new decision left two more censorship standards (immoral and harmful) and two statutes (New York's and Ohio's) in legal limbo.

Hoping to offer a bit of direction, Justices Douglas and Black filed a joint concurring opinion. Seemingly frustrated with the ambiguity of the Court's censorship decisions, Douglas began decisively: "The argument of Ohio and New York that the government may establish censorship over motion pictures is one I cannot accept. . . . [The] chief purpose of the constitutional guaranty of liberty of the press . . . was to prevent previous restraints upon publication." To Douglas, requiring any medium to gain advance approval despoiled the First Amendment. Dismissing the concept that movies were more dangerous than other media, he warned, "[The] First Amendment draws no distinction between the various methods of communicating ideas." He concluded as he had begun: "In this nation, every writer, actor, or producer, no matter what medium of expression he may use, should be freed from the censor."[73] Anticensorites found that they had two solid friends on the Court. Beyond that, there was no certainty for either side.

In the lead article of the next day's *New York Times*, legal affairs reporter Luther Huston reported that the court had overturned the bans on both *La ronde* and *M* but had not overturned all motion picture censorship. Huston interpreted the ruling as meaning that immorality and criminal incitement were now uncensorable concepts. Since obscene pictures were not likely to be submitted to censor boards, he predicted that there remained few grounds upon which censors could act.[74]

In this interpretation, Huston was not alone. The Catholic press also viewed the brusque decision as a major blow to censorship. Archbishop John Francis O'Hara of Philadelphia issued a pastoral letter warning all Catholic parents, "The Supreme Court has underscored your duty of conscience. . . . In effect, the Supreme Court has ruled that the States may label as poison only what affects the body, not that which can destroy the soul."[75] And Auxiliary Bishop Joseph F. Flanelly of St. Patrick's Cathedral wondered whether the Supreme Court had "exploded a moral atomic bomb."[76] Colorado senator Edwin C. Johnson, who three years earlier had advocated undertaking a morals investigation of Hollywood, declared on the Senate floor that the Legion of Decency would now have to take a more active role in protecting the public morals, since the states and cities had been rendered "impotent" by the Supreme Court.[77]

Bosley Crowther's January 24 column exulted: "Freedom of the Screen: The Supreme Court Advances Further the Latitude of a Medium." Crowther optimistically told readers that "the court is out of sympathy with all prior censorship."[78] His colleague Thomas M. Pryor described the rulings as a "staggering blow to state and municipal censor boards."[79]

Between these extreme views, most observers saw the decision as frustratingly vague and insufficient. The stingy per curiam opinion not only failed to deal with prior restraint but made the situation less clear. The ACLU saw no reason for celebration. It was confused by the opinion and issued no press release because it was so unsure what it meant.[80]

Publicly, the states' censors had no doubts about the decision. A meeting of all state censor boards a few weeks afterward issued a statement that they would continue to fulfill their "basic fundamental purpose" of banning objectionable films. The assembled censors reasoned that since only two justices had suggested overturning film censorship, the rest of the court was solidly behind them. The majority, they wrote, "upheld the constitutional rights of the states to exercise pre-regulation of motion pictures."[81] But Hugh Flick sensed the coming end of censorship, and he continued to suggest age classification in place of prior restraint. Invited to a meeting of the National Council on Freedom from Censorship in December 1953, Flick suggested that it was time to automatically license all films, with a review board grading for age suitability. He favored such a plan because it disposed of any constitutional objections while allowing the state to provide some "protection" for the public.[82] Flick put a brave face on the censorship situation, but outside the spotlight he was wondering whether change was inevitable.

Ohio's attorney general, C. William O'Neill, had no doubts. He found the Court's ruling an unambiguous omen. In a letter to the chief Ohio censor, he argued that the decision was far more than just a determination of the censorability of *La ronde* and *M*. To think it affected only those two films was to ignore the jurisdiction of the U.S. Supreme Court, he insisted. Since the Court did not have the power to reverse a decision of any state court on the facts, its only power lay in holding state law up to constitutional scrutiny. Therefore, O'Neill found, the decision did far more than hand exhibition licenses to the distributors of *M* and *La ronde*. It held unconstitutional both Ohio's statutory prohibition against harmful films and New York's prohibition against immoral films.[83] In light of this compellingly clear argument, it seems surprising that there was so little agreement about the meaning of the decision. But even O'Neill was not certain that censoring for a specific type of immorality, like sodomy or incest, would stand a judicial test. He hoped that such a case would turn up so it could be "promptly litigated" and the whole issue disposed of.

Contemporary legal commentators took pronouncedly differing views. David Eardley, writing in the *Maryland Law Review*, found the Court's "inarticulate" opinion "no less enigmatic than the ancient riddle of the Sphinx."[84] Hunter Gholson, writing in the *Mississippi Law Review*, echoed the views of many other commentators when he questioned "whether [the case] completely closes the door on all prior restraint of motion pictures or whether it simply invalidates the prior restraint on broad grounds of immorality."[85] Most agreed that the decision overturned censorship based on the terms *immoral* and *harmful* (rather than overturning merely New York's censorship of *La ronde* and Ohio's of *M*), but the agreement stopped there.[86] Some wondered if the decision threw out film censorship entirely, and others wondered if the decision meant that only specifically drawn statutes could survive judicial scrutiny. This latter position was an interesting one, however, since the decision had not mentioned *Winters v. New York*, the precedent the justices arguably should have used if their concern centered on vagueness.[87]

The *Catholic Lawyer* figured that new statutes needed to be drafted: "It appears that the Supreme Court would uphold the validity of a system of prior restraint [only] if the provisions of the statute were so clear, precise, and unambiguous as to satisfy the requirements of definiteness under the due process clause."[88] Another commentator predicted, "It appears unlikely that the U.S. Supreme Court would uphold prior censorship of movies, except under very rare circumstances, as yet undefined."[89]

A few wondered if the decision would lead to the demise of all state censorship laws. In the *UCLA Law Review*, Edward Lasker raised an interesting point: "When movies are censored, the motion picture industry is at a competitive disadvantage compared to television. This might well create an equal protection problem" under the Fourteenth Amendment. Lasker also believed that the decisions added up to make "almost all of the existing film censorship laws unconstitutional."[90]

For their part, both Charles Brind and the board of regents knew that New York's statute needed to be amended. Their goal was to retain *immoral* by giving it clear definition.[91] By adopting an intentionally ambiguous law in 1921, legislators had been able to pass along to the courts the responsibility for implementation while satisfying the various constituencies that had clamored for control of movie content. As long as the courts of New York had deferred to the legislature's ambiguous language, no incentive existed for clarification. But once the U.S. Supreme Court began to scrutinize the statutory language, beginning with *Burstyn* two years earlier, procensorship legislators needed to revise the statute to forestall further judicial assault. When films previously banned or cut as immoral began showing up for reexamination immediately after the *La ronde* decision, legislators had another reason to develop a new statute.[92] The legislature began work to amend the statute in March. This was not easy. No longer before the Supreme Court justices, Brind admitted that attempting to define *immoral* was like "trying to describe the color red."[93]

Revision of the statute for greater specificity should have appealed to the movie industry. After all, it would make the job of avoiding censorable material easier. But industry groups feared that any attempt to tinker with the law would make it more stringent. The MPAA, the Independent Motion Picture Distributors Association of America, and the NYCLU all pleaded with legislators not to perpetuate the censorship statute.[94] Philip O'Brien, representing the MPAA before the assembly's judiciary committee, suggested that "instead of rehabilitating censorship, which is of doubtful constitutionality . . . the Legislature should be exploring other methods of control which are compatible with constitutional rights."[95] But these pleas went unanswered. In 1954, New York's censorship statute finally carried definitions of the terms *immoral* and *incite to crime*. An immoral film became "a motion picture film or part thereof, the dominant purpose or effect of which portrays acts of sexual immorality, perversion, or lewdness, or which expressly or impliedly presents such acts as desirable, acceptable or proper patterns of behavior." To incite to crime was "to suggest that the commission of criminal acts or contempt for the law is profitable, desirable, acceptable, or respectable behavior; or which advocates or teaches the use of, or the methods of use of, narcotics or habit-forming drugs."[96] (The legislators chose not to define *obscene*, probably because it had a judicially accepted meaning in the common law and because its validity as a censoring standard was almost universally accepted.) Edward Lasker analyzed New York's statutory additions and predicted that they would hold up, but only "if the Supreme Court decides that the Constitution permits any censorship."[97] But the *New York Herald Tribune* foresaw the statute's overturn: "It seems likely to lose out in court tests, just as its predecessor did and, in any case, it is no credit to an enlightened state government."[98] Certainly, New York State was not willing to let go of film censorship in 1954. By redrawing its statute to meet the requirements of the Supreme Court for specificity, the state was trying to breathe new life into its thirty-three-year commitment to film censorship. With juvenile delinquency rates reportedly on the rise and with a Communist threat all around, the idea of someone prescreening movies still had a great deal of political appeal.

New York City theatergoers finally got to see *La ronde* in March 1954. The *New York Times* review by censorship foe Bosley Crowther was headlined "Controversial *La Ronde* Bows at Little Carnegie and Bijou and Proves to Be Innocuous." He referred to the film as "primly moral" but admitted that it consisted of some "quaintly spicy and suggestive little dramas." Finding the movie "confined to pretty little scenes of conversation," he mused, "No wonder the Supreme Court gave it an okay." Out of partisan zeal as a censorship opponent, Crowther may have been just a little less than objective when he downplayed the suggestiveness of *La ronde*'s theme. For example, he euphemistically referred to the woman of the first scene who is clearly a prostitute only as a "strolling girl."[99] Alton Cook's review in the *New York World-Telegram and Sun* also found the fuss much ado about nothing. "Now that the whole censorship fracas is past," Cook wrote, "it hardly seems necessary. . . . *La Ronde* kicks up a merry and dainty heel in blithe mockery of every happy ending ever written. Its topics may be bold, but its laughter and charm are continuously infectious."[100]

But Catholic reviewer William H. Mooring found much to worry about: "There is evidence to connect the infiltration of foreign movie studios by atheistic Communists with the upsurge of offensive movies brought to the USA from abroad. That there is a European Communist plan to 'soften up' America by demoralizing and confusing American youth may not in the present cases interest the Supreme Court. It interests the American people." Perhaps sensing that the Catholic Church and the Legion of Decency were losing their influence as film critics rose in public estimation, Mooring charged that critics were unreliable because they "prostitute their profession to become 'write-up' merchants for the theaters advertising in their papers." He finished by warning, "In the wings, poised for public release, Hollywood has some of the most revoltingly immoral and indecent films I have reviewed in a continuous experience of 30 years."[101] His source for this information he kept to himself.

La Ronde's Impact on Later Decisions

The *La ronde* and *M* cases were not to be the end of the film censorship per curiams. In the five years following the historic *Burstyn* decision in 1952, the Supreme Court heard five more film censorship cases. Each announcement of certiorari kept hopes alive, teasing both sides with the possibility of a definitive pronouncement. But each opinion dashed those hopes when issued as a per curiam, with no opinion. *La ronde* and *M*, the second and third per curiams, were soon followed frustratingly and cryptically by two more. With *Holmby Productions v. Vaughn* (*The Moon Is Blue*) in 1955 and *Times Film Corp. v. City of Chicago* (*The Game of Love*) in 1957, the Court overturned state courts without explaining why and without providing much guidance for state censors, state legislators, or state attorneys general on film censorship questions.

Historian Ira Carmen holds a harsh view of this perplexing string of opinionless per curiams, chastising the justices for their "woeful lack of forthrightness." He believes that Black and Douglas were willing to throw out all prior restraint; Clark was willing to keep censorship, but only to protect the community from real harm; and Frankfurter seemed concerned only with whether the statute was sufficiently narrow. That left five undecided justices. "What better way to shield a breakdown in consensus from public scrutiny," Carmen argued, "than to join hands in drafting one-sentence opinions for the Court!"[102]

Political scientist Richard Randall views the per curiams quite differently: "The exact meaning of these cryptic decisions is less important than the fact that they signaled a willingness of the Court to build upon the *Miracle* decision and closely supervise the prior censorship of motion pictures."[103] But how could the Court review each contested film? Whether the justices intended to adopt a supercensor role or not, one thing was clear: the Court did not want to deal directly with the question of constitutionality. Writing to Hugo Black during deliberation on *La ronde*, Frankfurter suggested that per curiams offered the best way out. He estimated that six of the nine justices would oppose any absolute ban of film censorship, so, he reasoned, it would be better to "*per cur* unanimously" than to allow any one of the hesitant six to offer an opinion that might "however unwittingly" imply that censorship "would pass muster."[104] This may be one way to explain the run of per curiams. Had the Court wished to avoid the issue entirely, it could have denied certiorari. Yet it kept granting film censorship cases oral argument, clearly signaling a willingness to mediate. From the Court's first round with film censorship—the 1915 *Mutual* decision—until the demise of most state censorship statutes, the Supreme Court refused certiorari in only three film censorship cases: *Lost Boundaries*, *Curley*, and a 1954 Chicago ban on *The Miracle*.[105]

Even with hindsight, though, the per curiams are difficult to explain. They left those in the middle, especially the state legal officers, with no clear guidance about motion picture censorship. The situation was so murky that after the next per curiam, the 1955 case against Kansas in *Holmby Productions v. Vaughn*, the Kansas attorney general requested a rehearing for clarification, pleading, "Petitioner does not know and cannot ascertain whether [the Supreme Court] has determined that (1) censorship is *per se* unconstitutional, or (2) the particular standard here applied is indefinite and uncertain as to deny due process, or (3) the judicial review ordered by Kansas is insufficient." Even after such a distinct plea for help from a state attorney general, the Court denied rehearing.[106] The Court was "definitely straining to formulate some sort of answer to the riddle of censorship of protected free speech,"[107] but it was doing so in a most abstruse fashion.

The patience of the anticensorship forces was also strained, but it was the anticensorship litigants' own doing. Although all of the per curiam cases had asked the Court to overturn censorship on First Amendment grounds, they also provided narrower grounds. In lawyer P. D. McAnany's words, "There were always other grounds to give the movie people the victory but not the war."[108]

The unsatisfactory per curiam decision in the *La ronde* and *M* case may have been puzzling to legal commentators, but it was crystal clear for some state courts. It encouraged the courts of Ohio and Pennsylvania to overturn their state censorship statutes entirely, caused Massachusetts to toss out *immoral*, and persuaded the New York state courts to begin overruling their previously undisturbed board of regents. Two years later, another U.S. Supreme Court decision based on both *Burstyn* and *Superior Films* would overturn a Kansas censor board ruling and call that state's entire statute into question.[109]

Perhaps the twin cases brought by *La ronde*'s importers and *M*'s distributors have been overlooked because they left censorship wounded but still breathing. *Mutual* was gone and movies could claim the free speech protection of the First Amendment, but the ghost of the harmfulness concept lingered with at least six of the Supreme Court justices. Nevertheless, their equivocation about the constitutionality of movie censorship was clear. They had considered powerful arguments against prior restraint of movies four times in two years, and each time they had declined the invitation to declare movie censorship unconstitutional. But censors were no longer secure. Their work could now be successfully challenged at all court levels, and they could no longer ban movies for sacrilege, harmfulness, or (except in New York) incitement to crime or riot. Whether they could censor for specifically defined immorality, however, remained to be tested. Censors, movie producers, importers, distributors, and exhibitors continued to work in a most uncertain legal culture.

8

The Tide Turns against the Censors, 1953–1957

As *La ronde* worked its way toward the Supreme Court, the legality of film censorship was beginning to look grim in New York, Pennsylvania, and Ohio. New York's judges, who for three decades had staunchly supported their censors, were starting to question the statute and its application. In the early 1950s, as the judicial attitude toward free speech was shifting at the federal level, New York's appellate division justices became more skeptical about the prior restraint exercised by their motion picture division. In 1953 the board of regents and their counsel, Charles Brind, began a losing streak that never turned around. As the censors tried to hold on to their role as protectors of the state's movie theater screens, the courts of their state and the nation were moving toward a more expansive interpretation of First Amendment rights of speech and press.

Broadway Angels and *Teenage Menace*

While it was working to salvage *immoral* at the U.S. Supreme Court, the board of regents found itself defending the ban of a narcotics film. In 1952, a distribution company with the innocent-sounding name of Broadway Angels asked New York State for a license to show *Teenage Menace*, purportedly to warn young adults about the evils of illegal drug use. Although another film, *The Man with the Golden Arm* (1955), is often considered the groundbreaking movie about drug life, it was preceded by many other films about addiction—including *Teenage Menace*. While Hollywood's Production Code forbade the making of any film about narcotics, independent producers faced no such restrictions.[1] *Teenage Menace* was the twenty-first narcotics film to come before the motion picture division and the twenty-first to be turned down. But Broadway Angels claimed that this film was different because it had been "conceived, produced, and completed as a tool in fighting dope addiction in the interest and welfare of American Youth."[2]

Sensing trouble, the motion picture division sought professional advice from the Federal Bureau of Narcotics. Asking outside experts to review questionable films was a relatively common practice in other censoring states, especially Ohio, Virginia, and Maryland, but it was unusual for New York to ask for backup. In any event, the censors got the advice they wanted when the inspector reported that he found the film dangerous for young people. It would do "irreparable harm if shown to young people," the inspector advised, and it "might cause immature persons to imitate the characters in the film."[3]

William Free of Broadway Angels was secretly hoping for a rejection. His attorney had advised him that a New York ban would be worth an extra $150,000 at the box office.[4] Whereas many of the independent distributors fought film censorship for both monetary and idealistic reasons, Broadway Angels was clearly more interested in profit than free speech. Free must have been a happy man when two reviewers rejected the film "because the use of narcotics is presented in an attractive light . . . [and could] conceivably create a morbid interest in drugs and lead to their use." A second reviewer's report noted, "Of the three drug addicts depicted in this film, only one suffers because of his addiction. His suffering is due mainly to his lack of heroin." The reviewer noted that the other two addicts seemed to be doing fine despite having been mainliners for years. "The roll of greenbacks the pusher flashes about and his big tips to shoeshine boys would certainly not help dispel any teen-agers feeling that a pusher's lot is a happy one."[5]

Broadway Angels acted dumbfounded when the censors rejected *Teenage Menace*. "Obviously," Free replied, "these are the stock terms used as grounds for rejection of all narcotics pictures. . . . There is no written word forbidding exhibition of a picture on the subject of narcotics as such, which would be the only conceivable reason for such license denial of *Teenage Menace*."[6] Broadway Angels was right. New York's statute contained no such prohibition.

The regents found the film to be "immoral (in the sense that it is vicious)" and agreed that it "would tend to corrupt morals." The censors had not yet been hit with the Supreme Court ruling in the *La ronde* case, which would effectively eliminate *immoral* as a censor standard (it was still a year away), so such loose interpretation of the term was still legally valid. So far, Broadway Angels had its rejection, but no publicity yet on which to base hope for a boosted box office. To get that, the case needed airing in the courts.

In November 1953, the appellate division ruled that the censors had been wrong about the picture's ability to corrupt morals. To the contrary, the justices found, the film "taught a moral lesson."[7] For the first time, the appellate division had overturned a censorship determination sustained by the regents. It had taken twenty-five years. And it would prove to be the first of six defeats in a row for the censors. In fact, the last time the appellate division would uphold the regents had already come, with *La ronde* in 1952.

Both Brind and Flick wanted to appeal. Flick was worried that the twenty narcotics-themed movies previously rejected would flood back, demanding licenses. "If we cannot substantiate our position in regard to a film that would encourage the use of drugs according to the best experts in the field," he wrote to the deputy education commissioner, "then our position for control of films at all is extremely shaky."[8] Brind suggested appealing the case but stalling it until the Supreme Court had handed down its decision on *La ronde*.[9] The court of appeals, a more conservative bench, was more likely to agree with the regents and overturn the appellate division. But the censors did not appeal.

So Broadway Angels got its license, and the motion picture division began to realize that the appellate court, which had been its guardian angel, was no longer steadfast. How far the censors' protector would stray from their side would become clear in the next five challenge cases. As each case appeared before the appellate division, adverse opinions continued, growing shorter and more brusque.

A Losing Streak at the Appellate Division

In 1949, a film with the seemingly innocuous title *Mom and Dad* had arrived at the motion picture division. Ostensibly about pregnancy, venereal disease, and social responsibility, the film brought widespread support from seemingly legitimate social welfare and medical agencies. The film was not, however, what it seemed. Though it was labeled as a community service, *Mom and Dad* was marketed as an exploitation film, sensationally promoted by Capitol Enterprises.

The brains of Capitol Enterprises was a huckster who called himself Kroger Babb. He was one of a group who would come to be known as the Forty Thieves, ex–carnival showmen who decided to explore the financial rewards of film promotion. They followed in the footsteps of earlier hustlers who had been peddling sketchy films for years in rural areas, away from censorial powers. Hawking cheaply made, sensational films about miscegenation, abortion, unwed motherhood, venereal disease, drug use—virtually anything taboo—exploitation filmmakers had been adding to the nation's film inventory since 1914. This shadow industry had limped along for decades, but when Hollywood began bleeding in the late 1940s from the one-two punch of the *Paramount* divestment decision and the arrival of television, the "exploiteers" were ready to take advantage.

As we have seen, when *Paramount* forced Hollywood to give up its guaranteed seats in thousands of first-run theaters and, along with them, its market for the cheaply made B pictures, the studios cut back production. Into the vacuum of decreased production stepped dozens of entrepreneurially minded young filmmakers. The nation's screens "suddenly became fair game."[10] Some independent filmmakers made serious artistic films. Some set out to make movies, make money, and have fun doing it. While Hollywood, desperate for audiences, turned out movies with increasingly bloated budgets, this new shadow group made films on a shoestring. High art was not their goal; theater bookings were. To achieve bookings, they had to spot audience trends first and then move fast to get a film in the can and off to theaters before Hollywood could react. Herschell Gordon Lewis, one of the best exploiteers, defined the exploitation film as "a motion picture in which the elements of plot and acting become subordinate to elements that can be promoted."[11] The exploitable elements—sex, aliens, vampires, mutants, serial murderers, demons—then were packaged for sensational advertising.

The Forty Thieves promoted their films using tactics "more like the circus than the movies," according to Joe Bob Briggs.[12] Kroger Babb, the king of these "sleaze merchants," not only used carnival barker techniques but raised them "to the nth degree of perfection."[13] The Forty Thieves chose locations carefully, opting for noncensoring areas or finding ways to move into and out of towns so quickly that they could pocket the profits before local officials could catch up. Babb would book a theater and saturate a town with a publicity blitz about a week before opening. Newspaper ads, radio spots, direct mail flyers, and letters to the editor would proclaim the wholesome, educational benefit of whatever film Babb was promoting that week. Babb even managed to dupe local clergymen and civic officials into endorsing his films, which left several priests in serious trouble with their local bishops. His publicity campaigns were so perfect that *Time* was convinced that they left "only the livestock unaware of the chance to learn the facts of life."[14] Sometimes Babb insisted on sex-segregated showings.[15] Of course, this accomplished exactly what he wanted: he convinced local authorities that he was providing a public service while winking at the audience that there was something truly sensational just inside the theater doors.

State and local censors manhandled exploitation films—when they could get their hands on them. In 1952, Hugh Flick spoke about the "truly surprising number" of movies purportedly devoted to sex education. "Often enough, they'll have a sanctimonious foreword delivered, supposedly, by a clergyman or some other respectable figure," said Flick. "Most of the time the presentation is at the least vulgar, at the most obscene. We're fairly rough on these films, and pass them only after they've been cleaned up considerably."[16]

When *Mom and Dad* appeared at the motion picture division's offices, it had been playing a few performances at a time on the road for several years. Babb's application came with a thick file of endorsement letters from all sorts of groups supporting a variety of social causes. Ministers and satisfied theater owners also sent testimonials. Clearly, *Mom and Dad* was not like other exploitation movies. A group of doctors, lawyers, teachers, and reporters convened by the Virginia censors to pass judgment on *Mom and Dad* responded mostly positively.[17] Depending on one's point of view, the movie itself could be tolerable; it was Babb's marketing and merchandising that were not.

The New York censors had reason to be skeptical about both the film and the promoter. A few months earlier, the Kansas board had shared with Maryland and New York its opinion of Babb's distribution company, Capitol Enterprises. "They are high powered salesmen," wrote the head Kansas censor, "and they will stop at nothing to get their picture across."[18] The New York censors learned that *Mom and Dad* had been rejected in Kansas in 1946 and again in 1947.[19] The Atlanta censor board was so incensed at the reaction to *Mom and Dad* that it banned all sex hygiene pictures. "They are luridly advertised and exploited in a manner which offends the sensibilities and good taste of a majority of the public."[20]

One of the ads Babb used to promote *Mom and Dad* shows a woman scantily clad in an outfit complete with fishnet stockings, high heels, and spaghetti straps, sitting over the film's tagline: "A bold, fearless, shocking expose of teen-age delinquency!" Such a description hardly seemed to fit the film for which the producers claimed endorsements from "educators, clergy, [and] health officials." Later, Babb and Capitol Enterprises claimed that the film had been "praised by 60,000,000 Americans from coast to coast" and that it was "positively the world's most amazing attraction!"[21] It played for twenty-three years (as late as 1977), earning $100 million and collecting more than four hundred court appearances.[22]

Before rejecting the film for the first time in April 1949, Ward Bowen, now motion picture division director, dictated a memo for the files to summarize the film about which there had been so much censor correspondence: "A young girl with a 'prudish' mother gets into trouble. A teacher who'd wanted to include sex hygiene materials in classroom instruction is dismissed, only to be reinstated through the intercession of the girl's father who now realizes the necessity of such education. The film is then interrupted and 'IN PERSON the famous hygiene commentator, Mr. Elliot Forbes . . . presents a lecture (text not submitted to us) on sex hygiene and venereal disease.' The film starts up again with the teacher now reinstated, showing the films that he supposedly shows to his class."[23] The "famous hygiene commentator" was actually one of twenty-six carnival sideshow talkers, who, according to exploitation filmmaker David Friedman, could bring tears to the eyes of all the "suckers" in the audience.[24] According to Bowen's memo, the film included "a diagrammatic explanation of rhythmic sex cycles, ovulation, conception, the growth of a fetus, actual photography of a normal birth . . . and a Caesarian section . . . shots of the horrible tertiary stages of syphilis in adults and babies. One title in this film reads 'Self-Styled Moralists Would Like to Keep These Facts a Secret.' The story resumes and comes to a conclusion with a happy reunion of the family around the daughter's hospital bed. The picture ends with shots of Boy Scouts and Girl Scouts marching with massed flags."[25]

Before the matter could come before the regents for review, Bowen received a telegram from the director of the Health League of Canada advising that Ontario had revoked the license for *Mom and Dad* because large sections were "unfit" for public showing. The director added that the literature that was distributed with the film was "unfit" for public distribution, that the accompanying lecture was "unfit" for public audiences, and that the "entire philosophy of the picture [was] unsound."[26] The New York State Department of Health also took exception to the film's claim of educational value because the sex education was only "half-truths" that, "unaccompanied by a fuller explanation, may impart false impressions rather than knowledge." The venereal disease information, the health department stated, was "grossly misleading as to facts."[27]

Like *Teenage Menace*, *Mom and Dad* presented the New York censors with film content barred by Hollywood's Production Code yet not outlawed by statute. The Production Code specifically rejected any portrayal of birth, whether real or simulated, directly presented or in silhouette. New York had no statutory authority to ban scenes of birth, but since the 1938 controversy spurred by *The Birth of a Baby*, the censors, under their mandate to interpret the statute's provision against indecency, had maintained that realistic representations of childbirth could not be shown in a commercial movie theater with a mixed audience. So, they insisted, Capitol Enterprises must remove the thirty-second childbirth scene, or the film would not be licensed. "The exploitation of the genitals and genital region of men or women in places of public entertainment frequented by mixed audiences of all levels of comprehension is commonly held to be indecent," Hugh Flick told a *Variety* reporter.[28] The Legion of Decency concurred, rating *Mom and Dad* C, "condemned."

When Capitol Enterprises appealed, the motion picture division's response brief before the regents displayed a deeper concern—one also without explicit statutory authorization. The motion picture division took issue with the manner in which the film was presented. The brief argued that Eliot Forbes was no expert commentator; his sole function was to sell books and pamphlets to the audience. (Forbes was reportedly selling between 150 and 200 books per day at showings of *Mom and Dad*.[29]) "The impressions likely to be created by a showing of 'Mom and Dad' under these conditions become a matter of concern to those who are seriously interested in the public welfare," the censors argued.[30] The regents agreed and in July 1949 upheld the rejection of *Mom and Dad*.

Three years later, Capitol Enterprises came back with a revised version, but the censors found it "substantially the same picture."[31] Rather than risk another go at the regents, Capitol's attorneys decided to hitch their wagon to the *La ronde* case, which was then pending before the New York State Court of Appeals. Hygienic Productions, *Mom and Dad*'s producer, filed an amicus brief contending that film censorship was an unconstitutional prior restraint resulting in the "substantially unbridled censorship" that had been struck down in the *Burstyn* case.[32]

In May 1954, when it was clear that *La ronde* was not going to end film censorship entirely, Capitol Enterprises pressed on. Ephraim London, who by now had earned a reputation as the leading anticensorship attorney, took Capitol's case and requested permission to resubmit what he argued was a substantially different film from the 1949 version. Much of the clinical material had been removed, but the objectionable childbirth scene remained. Flick admitted that the scene was brief and that the producers had attempted to cover the mother, but he still found it unacceptable. He was relying on the 1939 appellate division ruling on *The Birth of a Baby* that scenes of childbirth are "indecent when presented to patrons of public entertainment."[33] Only if the venereal disease scenes and the childbirth scene were removed, Flick maintained, could the film be licensed.[34]

Even more correspondence flowed between the censoring states on the revised version of *Mom and Dad*. Sidney Traub, chairman of the Maryland State Board of Censors, which had just lost a court case against Babb, wrote to Flick advising expert testimony. "I earnestly hope that you will take steps to enter expert testimony in the hearing before the Board of Regents. Unless you do, it's dollars to doughnuts that the courts, certainly the U.S. Supreme Court, will decide against you, and then we'll be overrun with these monstrosities throughout the country."[35]

At the same time, the NYCLU weighed in, not to claim any merit in *Mom and Dad* but to express concern for its right to be shown. Taking as its main premise that prior restraint was "alien to the American ideal," the NYCLU argued that banning the film made New York a "laughing stock." It wondered how the film could damage the morals of New Yorkers but had not depraved those living where it had been shown. And it complained that childbirth had recently been shown on NBC-TV, yet censorship was keeping it from movie theaters.[36] Shientag had raised this issue in the *La ronde* case. While television programs were, of course, subject to sponsor control and FCC licensing restrictions, the producers of such shows enjoyed a greater degree of artistic freedom than their Hollywood counterparts. The NYCLU or ACLU could raise this issue, but it would have been dicey for the MPAA to do so. Its member studios were making a great deal of money from made-for-TV movie production.

When *Mom and Dad* came before the appellate division, London tried two new tactics. First, he borrowed Superior Film's argument that the censorship fees were an unconstitutional tax. Brind answered that the fees were not unreasonable and did not constitute a tax, and even if they did, they were not unconstitutional. The justices ignored the whole matter. Second, he tried a major tactical change that represented a frontal assault on all movie censorship. Trying to force a decision on the constitutional issues alone, he conceded that the film was "pornographic" (which it was not) and that the portrayal of human birth would "excite lustful and lecherous desire in the normal viewer" (which clearly it would not). London had been drawn to *The Miracle* for its artistic merit and its principled distributor, but *Mom and Dad* offered neither of those incentives. If he had not moved to the position that all film censorship was unconstitutional, he certainly would not have taken on such an unappealing plaintiff as Capitol Productions. London's strategy, based on his new absolutist position, was to leave the film out and present the court with only two issues: whether the statute's prior restraint was constitutional and whether the fees imposed were a tax on the right of communication.

The appellate division managed to dodge both the question of what the recent Supreme Court decisions meant for New York's statute and London's constitutional questions. Since the justices found nothing exceptional about *Mom and Dad*, they ruled that the censors had gone beyond their authority to interfere only in "an exceptional case." This enabled them to disregard London's admission that the film was pornographic. Taking the narrow route, they also ignored the big constitutional issues, but they did drop a tantalizing hint. Focusing on the "exceptional case" restriction and the "heavy burden" placed on censors' action from *Burstyn*, they openly questioned whether "any area is left open by the decisions of the Supreme Court for the exercise of prior restraint on motion pictures."[37]

And so the appellate division had overturned a second determination of the regents. Again, it was unanimous, but again, it stopped short of the ultimate question, though not for lack of trying on Ephraim London's part. By admitting that the film was obscene, he had attempted to move past the narrow issue and force review of the entire statute. The justices did go further toward that end than any New York court had gone before, but they balked at outright overturn.

Universal Reversal

New York may not have been ready to end film censorship, but other state courts were. The string of tight-lipped per curiams had left state courts unsure of the high court's direction, but film censorship statutes were about to face increasingly robust judicial scrutiny. The Supreme Court was slowly moving toward applying the principle first put forth in the 1930s by Justices Cardozo and Stone that state statutes restricting civil liberties required strong justification. Until this doctrine became part of the justices' overall philosophy, deference to the legislative will and to administrative experts kept state appellate courts from questioning movie censorship. But once a majority of Supreme Court justices accepted in principle that state police power had been used as an excuse for the restriction of individual freedoms, courts began to rethink state interference with the movies. As the Supreme Court moved toward closer scrutiny of state laws infringing the civil liberties of individuals, it began to inspect state film censorship statutes closely, a process begun in 1952 with the *Burstyn* decision. And as the Supreme Court moved in this direction, so too did the state courts, some more rapidly than others.

For the anticensorites, 1955 was a momentous year. While New York wrestled with *Mom and Dad*, the film censorship statutes of two states fell before their own supreme courts and a third statute fell before the U.S. Supreme Court. Barely into 1956, a fourth state's censoring was cut short. In quick succession, four censoring bureaucracies had been struck down, largely because of the U.S. Supreme Court's series of per curiam decisions.

The first statute to fall before a state supreme court was Ohio's. While the Ohio censors were considered stringent, their state courts were not helping. The censors had been facing a tough state bench for several years when they found themselves confronted by RKO Radio Pictures' *Son of Sinbad* in 1954. The nemesis of censors everywhere, Howard Hughes had bought controlling interest in MPAA member studio RKO in 1948. RKO's version of the Sinbad legend included the famous stripper Lili St. Cyr among 250 harem women whose costuming left little to the imagination (a true booborama, as such movies came to be called). When Ohio's censors objected, Hughes sued, and RKO became the first MPAA studio to legally face the censors of any state. It took Hughes two years to negotiate a Production Code seal; even so, the Legion of Decency condemned the film for its "grossly salacious dances." Hughes was delighted and exploited the publicity as only he could. He then made just enough changes in the film to get the legion to reclassify it as B, "morally objectionable in part."

RKO brought suit against Ohio's ban of *Son of Sinbad* at the same time that it was litigating Ohio's ban of another sensational Hughes production, *The French Line*. As if the Ohio attorneys needed more to do, yet another challenge appeared—for *Mom and Dad*. The three suits were combined and heard by the Ohio Supreme Court, which found RKO's arguments—that the state's censor statute violated the First and Fourteenth amendments—persuasive, but the court hesitated to knock the statute down. Citing all the per curiams from the U.S. Supreme Court, the Ohio majority believed that the Supreme Court had invalidated state censorship. But since it had not explicitly done so, Ohio felt unable to make a definitive pronouncement.[38] The per curiams were confusing even the highest court in Ohio. Whatever their bafflement, the Ohio judges were certain that bans on movies like *Son of Sinbad* and *The French Line* were sure to be overturned on appeal.[39] So they ordered that the movies be licensed.

The Ohio censor board lived in this legal limbo for only a few weeks before a lower state court finished it off. Again, the troublemaker was RKO. Like New York's lower appellate court at this time, Ohio's lower appellate court was braver than its higher bench, and it tossed out the statute, saying that Ohio's censoring was repugnant to the "sacred Bill of Rights." Even though the opinion called upon religious and social groups to work with the movie industry against harmful films, the judges were clearly more concerned about harm done to the Constitution than about harm done to moviegoers.[40] An attempt, backed by the governor, to rewrite the censoring statute failed in the Ohio legislature in June 1955, and the board was disbanded in July.

Next to go was Massachusetts. This state had an odd yet effective arrangement for censoring films. Its Lord's Day observance statute required all theatrical performances and cinema exhibitions to obtain permission from the local mayor or his appointee before they could be viewed on Sundays. Massachusetts's Supreme Court went straight to the main issue in 1955, without considering the film in question, and struck down the statute as an unconstitutional prior restraint. It did so, it said, "in light of the controlling decisions of the Supreme Court of the United States."[41]

Kansas was drawn into the reversal trend by a film that was intended to test not the state's censorship but the PCA's. In 1953, when the content regulators of the PCA had been reigning supreme for twenty years, Otto Preminger and United Artists decided to make a film of a hit Broadway play, a verbose light comedy about seduction called *The Moon Is Blue*. When the PCA requested the elimination of six lines of script, Preminger refused. He had intended to buck the code by making the movie, and now he was going to get the chance. Encouraged by the waning influence of the Legion of Decency,[42] the changing mores of the American audience, and the greater availability of non-studio-owned theaters after the 1948 *Paramount* antitrust breakup, Preminger decided to begin distribution without the benefit of a code seal. Releasing the film was bold but not foolhardy. Circumstances were already pointing in the direction Preminger was headed when he began shooting.

Although *The Moon Is Blue* was controversial in its day, today's audiences would search in vain for much to be offended by. Starring William Holden, David Niven, and stage actress Maggie McNamara, it revolves around a "professional virgin" who picks up a bachelor on the observation platform of the Empire State Building and spends the rest of the evening flirting with him and his upstairs neighbor. McNamara steadfastly maintains her virginal virtue while both men pursue her. She is not too innocent, however, to play the men off each other, and in the end she winds up engaged to the more desirable bachelor. The dialogue is peppered with PCA-forbidden words like *virgin* and *pregnant*, and much was made at the time about the film's daring to speak such words out loud. In truth, though, what upset Breen was not the verbiage but the casual treatment of seduction among the film's three unmarried principles.[43]

Such cavalier handling of adult relations earned *The Moon Is Blue* a "condemned" rating from the Legion of Decency, but Catholic leaders in both New York and Philadelphia had little success keeping their congregations away from theaters showing the highly publicized film. Church leaders knew that the success of a noncode film would harm Catholic authority and so fought against *Moon* vigorously. One parish priest in a New York City suburb took up residence outside a Trans-Lux theater at showtime each day, taking down the names of all who dared to go inside. Theater owner and distributor Richard Brandt, an anticensorship crusader, resolutely insisted on continuing the film's run for two weeks, even though it played each time to audiences of ten or fewer.[44]

Trying to keep *Moon* from American screens, the PCA was fighting from a weakened position after *Paramount*. Lack of a PCA seal was no longer the guaranteed financial disaster that it once had been, and Preminger's gamble paid off. *The Moon Is Blue*, the first Hollywood film released without a Production Code seal, became one of the top hits of 1953.[45] The exhibition world was changing; theaters that would not have dreamed of playing a noncode, legion-condemned film ten years earlier now sought out the distributor to get a booking. That people (including Catholics) flocked to theaters to see a film widely publicized as failing to meet PCA and legion standards shows the appeal of the proscribed (something the legion had always worried about), the appetite of American moviegoers for mature movies, and the waning influence of the legion's moral restrictions on moviegoers.

But while the code and the legion were weakening, the Kansas censor board held fast and refused to allow its citizens to see *The Moon Is Blue*. In this period, the Kansas censors operated in a culturally conservative atmosphere, "under a blanket of secrecy."[46] Even the other state boards considered their Kansas colleagues quite strict.[47] The Supreme Court may have been knocking out censoring standards and forcing state censors to approve virtually all nonobscene films, but many Kansans were making their procensorship stance known. And so the board tried, as best it could, to conduct its business, with the Supreme Court on one side and the people of Kansas on the other.[48] When the Kansas board reluctantly licensed *The Case of Dr. Laurents*, a French film that contained a nonobscene portrayal of childbirth, it was hounded by critical letters and phone calls.[49] Bowing to local wishes, the Kansas censors disallowed *The Moon Is Blue* but eventually had to answer to both their state supreme court and the U.S. Supreme Court for their decision.

Their only reasons for disallowing *The Moon Is Blue*, the Kansas censors explained to distributor Holmby Productions, were its "too frank bedroom dialogue" and its "sex scene throughout." After an initial loss before a local judge, who agreed with Holmby that the censorship statute was unconstitutional, the board appealed to the Kansas Supreme Court, which upheld the censors. But the U.S. Supreme Court overturned this ruling, and *Holmby Productions v. Vaughn* became number four of the five post-*Burstyn* per curiams.[50] Kansas's highest court found itself reversed without a single word beyond the citation of *Burstyn* and *Superior Films*. Still, the Supreme Court's intention—that the Kansas statute could no longer stand—should have been clear, since the only issue that had been decided by the Kansas Supreme Court was the statute's constitutionality.

Ironically, the one decision from the U.S. Supreme Court that clearly overruled a state censorship statute did not stop that state from censoring. When Kansas legislators tried to repeal the censor statute, a technical mistake in the repeal legislation left the censor board operational for another eleven years.[51] The unconstitutional yet still functioning censor board of Kansas received no further legal challenges until 1966. In the late 1950s and early 1960s, the anticensorites were saving their efforts for the more lucrative markets of Maryland, Pennsylvania, and especially New York.

Like the Kansas and Massachusetts courts, the Pennsylvania Supreme Court determined that the only question remaining was the basic constitutionality of the statute. Matters of fact and law had been hashed over, and the Pennsylvania justices were ready to deal with the final question when they were faced in 1956 with *She Shoulda Said No*, another iffy production from the makers of *Mom and Dad*. Ostensibly about the evils of marijuana use, *She Shoulda Said No* was really just another exploitation film. But whether the film had any merit was unimportant to the Pennsylvania court. The judges went straight to the constitutional matter and found unanimously that in light of all the recent decisions, both state and federal, the Supreme Court was clearly, if slowly, invalidating state censorship.[52] Pennsylvania's censors were out of business in 1956. A short time later, the Pennsylvania Supreme Court also overturned the only antiobscenity law that could be used by local authorities to prosecute objectionable films after the fact.[53] This was too much for the Pennsylvania legislators, who reenacted statewide film censorship in 1959. Even though the new statute was carefully drawn, allowing the board to review films only after they had been publicly exhibited "at least once" and constraining the board to consider the film in its entirety, the new law was struck down within two years. The legislators had forgotten to consult their own state constitution when drafting the 1959 law: in Pennsylvania, a person can be convicted of an obscene utterance only by a jury. Since the new ordinance carried no provision for appeal or jury trial, the state's supreme court had little choice but to strike the law.[54] Pennsylvania was out of the censoring business for good in 1961.

Between 1954 and 1961, then, the supreme courts of four of the seven censoring states had moved beyond the U.S. Supreme Court. It was an anomalous situation: The Supreme Court had led the way by placing movies under the First Amendment in 1952 and by overturning every film censorship case thereafter. But it had done so without considering the broad constitutional question of prior restraint versus free speech. Rather than wait for the Supreme Court justices to get around to the big question, the state supreme courts stepped into the constitutional vacuum. Pennsylvania, Massachusetts, Kansas, and Ohio each moved beyond the facts on appeal before it, ignored the film in question, and considered the First Amendment issue. Each state found its film censorship statute wanting.

Now the only states left in the censoring business were New York, Maryland, Virginia, and, by legislative fluke, Kansas. New York and Virginia were considered quite moderate, but Maryland was still very much attached to its censoring. The Maryland State Board of Censors complained to the legislature in both 1952 and 1953 that the "morals" of movies were not improving. The following year, the Maryland House of Delegates approved by ninety-one to nine a proposal to investigate strengthening the state's censorship statute in light of the "plague of immorality and indecency spreading through the country through the medium of films."[55] In 1955, as New York had done the year before, Maryland strengthened its statute to withstand constitutional challenges. The new statute limited censorship to films that were obscene, incited to crime, or debased morals. The legislature wisely defined an obscene movie as one whose purpose, "to arouse sexual desires," was so great that it outweighed "whatever other merits the film may possess." Maryland's definition of *immoral*, like New York's, was limited to sexual immorality that was presented as appropriate behavior. And *incitement to crime* meant depicting criminal activity as "profitable, desirable, acceptable, respectable or commonly accepted behavior," or advocating the use of habit-forming drugs.[56] This last part of the new statute caused the Maryland censors to refuse to license *The Man with the Golden Arm*, but in this they were overturned by Maryland's highest court in 1956. The following year, Maryland refused to license *Naked Amazon* because it showed fully nude natives. But Maryland's high court found this a rather silly application of the statute because the film showed no sexual immorality and was neither pornographic nor erotic. The court had been asked to decide both whether the law was constitutional and whether it had been applied correctly to *Naked Amazon*, and since the censors had misconstrued the film as obscene, the judges were able to avoid the larger constitutional question.[57] Once again, the anticensor faction had asked the broad constitutional question but had attached the question to a particular film, thus enabling the judges to evade the big issue. Maryland's censors had lost two rounds in their own state courts, but the basic act of censoring was not yet in jeopardy.

The Epidermis Epidemic

The next decision by New York's appellate division once again contradicted the regents unanimously, but this time the justices did more than overturn the motion picture division on a particular film. They ruled that New York State's censors could henceforth restrict only those films that were demonstrably obscene. The case involved a 1954 nudism film, *Garden of Eden*, that the censors had found indecent. In a nation where the PCA still kept Hollywood producers from showing much more than a bit of cleavage, nudism was sure to sell tickets.

Garden of Eden tells the story of a young widow and her daughter traveling to a new town to find employment. On the way, their car breaks down, and the woman is invited to stay overnight at a nudist camp, an invitation she reluctantly accepts. When her father-in-law learns where she is, he arrives at the camp, indignantly asserting that this is no life for his granddaughter, but he slowly succumbs to the friendliness and the beauty of the Garden of Eden nudist colony, and all live there happily ever after.

Unlike exploitation films, *Garden of Eden* appears to have been carefully researched with the assistance of a pronudism organization, and unlike *Mom and Dad*, it was promoted with tasteful, nonprurient advertising. Its producer, Walter Bibo, a nudist, had assembled a highly qualified production crew. The film was shot on location at an active nudist colony in Florida.[58] But this attention to detail did not save it from film critics, who found it a dull film with mediocre acting.

The regents appeal brought by Excelsior Pictures, *Garden of Eden*'s distributor, to obtain a New York license for the film became more than the usual opinion war because the state tried to argue that the film violated not just the censorship statute but also the New York Penal Law. In 1935, New York State had prohibited the exposure of private parts in public, arguably making nudist colonies illegal.[59] This led Charles Brind to claim that such penal restrictions also applied to films. But Excelsior Pictures argued that no standard of decency had been set for the motion picture division reviewers to go by and that films condemned as indecent "invariably" contained "lewdness, lechery, immorality, corruption of morals, lasciviousness, salaciousness, or similar offense against the public morality," none of which was found in *Garden of Eden*. Excelsior further argued that it had "long been established in law . . . that mere nudity, standing alone, is neither indecent nor obscene, and in this picture besides nudity, there is nothing which could possibly corrupt the morals of its viewers or tend to do so, or could incite lascivious thoughts, or arouse any lustful desires."[60]

From the reviews, it does seem that the movie was quite innocuous. The *New York World-Telegram and Sun* complained of a dull plot, "painful" dialogue, and little nudity. The *Tampa Daily News* wrote, "If you see it in expectation of viewing something sensational, you might as well go to the next exhibit of the Tampa Art Institute and save your money." According to the *New York Daily Mirror*, "It runs only 70 minutes but proves that anything can become boring." The *New York Times* found it "dull" and "prudish," produced "with all the flair of a television commercial."[61]

The New York censors failed to appreciate the film's edification about nudism and to see that such a mediocre film could do little damage. After the film had been exhibited in thirty-six states, the only other state to object was Pennsylvania, yet the regents would not budge. They required that all scenes of nudity be removed, which, of course, stripped the film of its reason for existence.[62]

At the appellate division, the state's position received a unanimous thumbs down. Justice Foster went further, expressing his belief that it was time to review the constitutional question of censorship per se. Noting the "piecemeal" dilution of the statute by the courts, he found it impossible to escape the conclusion that the entire statute was void. Both the Ohio and Pennsylvania supreme courts had taken just such a view and had recently voided their statutes. As far as Foster was concerned, the statute was a "dead letter."[63] His fellow justices, however, were not ready to go that far.

Neither were the judges of the court of appeals, but they were getting closer. Before the court could deliver an opinion on the matter, though, the U.S. Supreme Court altered the judicial landscape by clearing up some of the ground rules. Until the 1930s, o*bscenity* had been defined by the legal doctrine of the *Hicklin* case. Under the *Hicklin* rule, a work of art could legally be labeled obscene based on individual words or passages that might corrupt the most susceptible members of society. This broad definition of what was obscene placed a very narrow limit on what was permissible. Since obscenity remained outside the protections of the First Amendment, attempts at definition were needed. Lower courts had begun to attempt redefinition in the 1930s.

Finally, in 1957, in the case of *Roth v. United States*, the Supreme Court attempted to define what was obscene.[64] Samuel Roth, a "smut-hound," literary pirate, and First Amendment warrior, had been convicted under the federal Comstock law for mailing *American Aphrodite*, his magazine of literary erotica.[65] The magazine contained poems, plays, and short stories about love and sex as well as erotic line drawings. By today's standards, it would certainly not be considered pornography. Rochelle Gurstein characterizes Roth, who was arrested seven times and spent thirteen years in prison lobbying for free expression, as a "disreputable small-time publisher, dealer, and distributor of obscenity."[66] Certainly Roth was a professional troublemaker, but his tactics had a purpose, no less intense than Anthony Comstock's although diametrically opposite. He firmly believed in the right of free expression. Perusal of *American Aphrodite* reveals serious literary pieces and serious art, not titillation for titillation's sake. Either way, when Roth challenged his obscenity conviction, the justices set out to create a more current definition. Although they refused to put obscenity within the protection of the First Amendment (as Roth and others had hoped), they did throw out the ancient *Hicklin* rule. After *Roth*, the new legal definition of *obscenity* boiled down to "whether to the average person" (not the most susceptible person), applying "contemporary community standards" (not just the ideas of individual censors), "the dominant theme of the material, taken as a whole" (not isolated passages), appealed to the "prurient interest."[67] A work's effect on the most susceptible persons of society would no longer suffice as justification to keep it from all; the effect of the entire work had to be considered in relation to its effect upon an average person. The campaign begun in 1909 by the National Board of Censorship to remove children from the censorship discourse had finally born fruit.

Further, to be considered obscene and therefore beyond the protection of the First Amendment, a work had to be "utterly without redeeming social value." The first decision to be made, then, in legally determining obscenity had to be whether the work had any social significance. If it did carry social significance, it could be banned only if it contained some "clear and present danger."

Even though *Roth* reflected an enormous legal change that had been in the works for two decades, it satisfied no one. The decision disappointed those who hoped that the Court would move obscenity under the free speech protection of the First Amendment just as much as it disheartened the procensorites. The Court created two tiers of speech—protected and unprotected—and left itself the only judge of which was which. Furthermore, *Roth* was silent about movies. It mentioned "material," "writing," "matter," "publications," "art, literature, and scientific works," and "advertisements" but not films and obscenity. So the question was, Did the *Roth* test apply to determinations of film obscenity? The Court would remain mum on this issue until 1964.[68] Until then justices at all levels of the judicial system were divided on *Roth*'s applicability to films.

Roth did indicate a sincere effort on the part of the Supreme Court to deal with the obscenity issue and works of art, but the justices failed to produce a precise legal definition. By defining an obscene work as one that appealed to "the prurient interest," the Court essentially stipulated that "the obscene is that which appeals to an interest in the obscene."[69] The Court continued waffling for the next twenty years, reflecting the difficulty of defining *obscenity*—a futility that *Time* magazine compared to "weighing a pound of waltzing mice."[70]

The Court was, however, facing the question. The year before, in

1956, the justices had invalidated a Michigan statute that allowed books to be banned for immorality. Because, the Court argued, the effect of such censorship had reduced the artistic inventory to that which was fit for children, thereby interfering with the individual's liberty to read, "an indispensable condition for the maintenance and progress of a free society" had been curtailed.[71] So by 1957 one of the Progressive Era foundations for censorship—protection of the most innocent—was losing ground in legal discourse.

As the long-standing tenet of judicial deference to legislative will also began to fragment in the 1950s and 1960s, film censorship would meet its greatest challenges. Before the pivotal 1960s, most judges who were asked to overturn a statute on constitutional grounds would question whether the law served a reasonable state function. If it did, it would stand. Beginning in the 1960s, the question would be not whether the state had a reasonable interest but whether that interest limited individual liberty. As the Supreme Court moved in this direction, film censorship challenges grew more successful.

But in 1957, judicial affairs were still moving slowly as far as movie censorship was concerned. In November the Supreme Court reversed a Chicago ban on the French film *The Game of Love*. The decision was the fifth per curiam, and again film censors and legal commentators were left wondering.[72] While the justices showed some willingness to try to define *obscenity* and were beginning to question statutory infringements on individual liberty, their stance on film censorship had changed little. Each challenge film would have to pursue a judicial determination of its censorability.

But even as the judicial tenor concerning obscenity was changing, New York's legislative will concerning censorship—and its statute—was hanging on. Kansas, on the other hand, had sensed the judicial sea change and in 1959 altered its statutory definition of *obscenity*. Still reeling from the U.S. Supreme Court loss on *The Moon Is Blue* and a serious attempt at statute repeal in the 1957 legislative session, the Kansas censor board had been advised by its attorney general to alter its definition of *obscene* to echo the words of the Supreme Court in *Roth*.[73]

Back to *Garden of Eden*

In New York, the first court of appeals case to be decided after *Roth* was that of *Garden of Eden*, Excelsior Pictures' nudism film. Although the issue with *Garden of Eden* was indecency, not obscenity, *Roth* had a major effect on the case because its definition of *obscenity* gave state censors and judges a point of reference. The change in the legal culture can clearly be seen in the attitude of Judge Charles Desmond, who had written two strongly procensorship law review articles in 1953 and 1956. After reading *Roth*, Desmond changed his mind and wrote the majority opinion in favor of *Garden of Eden*. In light of the cumulative Supreme Court decisions, he argued, the only basis left for the censoring of films was obscenity. "It is settled," Desmond wrote, "that 'indecent,' standing alone and read literally, is much too broad and vague a term to make a valid censorship standard." For the first time, twenty-six years after enacting film censorship, a New York state court had declared unconstitutional a term in its own statute; the state could no longer ban a film for indecency.[74]

But anticensorites could take little comfort: *Excelsior* was a bare four-to-three decision with a minority energetically opposing Desmond. In a stinging dissent, Judge Adrian P. Burke harangued the majority for usurping legislative authority. The court's most junior member, Burke was a "politically well connected" Democrat thought of as a political liberal, in part for having helped make New York one of only a few states to constitutionally recognize welfare rights in 1938. During his years on the court of appeals, Burke argued for other liberal positions, like allowing plaintiffs to sue for emotional damages and expanding the rights of defendants in criminal cases. He was, however, also active in several youth welfare organizations and had recently headed an antismut campaign in New York City. His *Garden of Eden* dissent may reflect that experience.[75]

Whereas his colleagues had seen fit to strip the statute of all meaning based on nothing more than "conjecture" about what the U.S. Supreme Court intended, Burke (joined by Conway) argued that since *Garden of Eden* was a depiction of nudism for profit, it fell well within the guidelines of the New York Penal Law. "An oligarchy" of judges, Burke wrote, "cannot be substituted in place of our democracy by judicial fiat." His reading of the law was completely literal. Even though the film did not show private parts, the fact that people were, on film, exposing their private parts to one another was, to him, a clear violation. Burke finished his dissent with some advice for the regents: he suggested that they seek legislative clarification of the term *indecent*. Although Burke had found the term sufficiently narrow—"indecency is not a chameleon term. It speaks not of abstractions, but of objective standards, and its scope is of mathematical precision"—his opinion was a dissent, and he worried that future cases would poke even more holes in the term.[76]

New York's legislators had responded to the *La ronde* loss two years before with a statutory redefinition, but this time they did nothing, even though Hugh Flick also suggested that it was time for New York to reexamine its statute. "If the present statute is not sufficiently clear or definite to allow the legitimate exercising of restraint of material that would have a harmful effect on society," he argued, "then the possibility of an amendment to the statute should be explored."[77] At least one legal scholar was convinced that the ruling left New York without the term *indecent* unless the indecent material in question could be construed as obscene.[78] If the legislature could be persuaded to narrowly define *indecent* as it had *immoral*, the motion picture division might continue its work uninhibited by court challenges. But no such statutory definition came.

Once again, the New York courts had managed to avoid the overall constitutional issue. The supreme courts of Pennsylvania, Kansas, and Ohio had interpreted the Supreme Court decisions as overturning their entire statutes, but the New York State Court of Appeals interpreted the rulings as overturning individual censoring standards only.

Cleared in New York, *Garden of Eden* ran into plenty of censor trouble elsewhere from 1955 to 1959. Just after the Kansas Supreme Court voided its censor statute in 1955, Kansas City tried to use its municipal welfare laws to ban *Garden of Eden*, but a local judge found it neither obscene nor immoral. In 1957, a Fall River, Massachusetts, theater owner was arrested and convicted on obscenity charges, but the Massachusetts Supreme Court overturned the verdict.[79] Theater owners were also arrested in Ohio and Florida.[80] There was so much activity surrounding this nudism film that *Variety* characterized the arrests and prosecutions as "an epidermis epidemic."[81]

In 1959, the New York censors would face another major case like *The Miracle* in another foreign film, a French version of D. H. Lawrence's novel *Lady Chatterley's Lover*. But whereas the *Miracle* decision had left open the possibility of censorship under a narrowly drawn statute, the decision in the *Lady Chatterley's Lover* case would show the censors that even this most cherished of procensorship arguments—that the statutes could be sufficiently narrow—was endangered in the evolving legal culture that questioned state-sponsored invasion of civil liberties.

9

The Seventh Case in Seven Years, 1957–1959

By 1956, only New York, Maryland, Virginia, and Kansas were still censoring. When Kingsley International Pictures submitted a French film version of D. H. Lawrence's sensational novel *Lady Chatterley's Lover* to the New York censors in 1956, only pirated and abridged copies of the book could be found anywhere in the United States because the U.S. Post Office had declared the original novel unmailable. Customs officials confiscated copies at the border.[1] Although shocking for its time, the novel received mostly favorable reviews from sources as varied as the *New York Times*, the *New York Post*, and *Time*. Its 1959 American edition included a preface by Archibald MacLeish, Pulitzer Prize–winning poet and former librarian of Congress, who considered the novel "one of the most important works of fiction of the century."[2]

The French film version starred Danielle Darrieux, one of France's most popular actresses who had also become popular among American foreign film aficionados (she had starred in *La ronde*). The film's scenarist followed the novel's plot closely: When an English nobleman made impotent by war injuries desires an heir for his estate, he urges his young and beautiful wife to become impregnated by another man. At first revolted by this idea, the young noblewoman, Lady Chatterley, becomes physically attracted to the gamekeeper of her husband's estate. After a series of secret trysts, she becomes pregnant with the gamekeeper's child. When she falls in love with the gamekeeper and seeks a divorce, Lord Chatterley insists on keeping the child to raise as his heir. Lady Chatterley refuses and leaves to live with the gamekeeper. Since the film was based on the expurgated version of the novel, with many of the more graphically sexual encounters already removed, today's viewers would find it tame, as did its importer and distributor, Edward Kingsley. Each time the plot approaches the sexual liaison between the two lovers, the screen discreetly fades to black, fading back in only after the tryst has taken place. The lovers are always shown draped by sheets or fully clothed. But such filmic modesty did not help with the New York censors. For them, the issue was not that the film depicted sexual activity, for it did not, but that it revolved around a sexual relationship between people not married to each other.

Two years earlier, *La ronde*, another French film based on another infamous European novel, had forced the New York legislature to redefine immoral content. The new definition of *immorality* allowed censors to continue banning any film that depicted sexual immorality as desirable or proper behavior. Since *Lady Chatterley's Lover* clearly shows two unpunished, unrepentant adulterers, the motion picture division found the film immoral and demanded removal of three romantic scenes.[3] Kingsley refused to make any cuts. The film version already contained many concessions to propriety, and he was ardently opposed to film censorship.[4]

Maybe Kingsley dug in his heels because of the slowly evolving tolerance of mature-themed films and the incipient backlash against censorship restrictions in the mid-1950s. After all, the Supreme Court had knocked down every film censorship case it had heard, and independent producers like Preminger and Kazan were directly attacking the PCA's authority. Breen had retired in 1954 and was replaced by Geoffrey Shurlock, a more liberal-minded regulator who favored code modification and hoped to see age classification take its place. A yearlong soul searching on the issue of the code's relevance in Shurlock's second year led to a revision that allowed some treatment (if tasteful) of previously banned topics like drug trafficking, prostitution, abortion, kidnapping, childbirth, and miscegenation.[5] Words like *hell* and *damn* were also permitted if not used excessively.

Not only was the code losing its grip and loosening its hold, but the list of Hollywood films released without code approval was also growing. Following *The Moon Is Blue*, Preminger released another noncode box office success in 1955, *The Man with the Golden Arm*. More films followed as other independent producers saw Preminger's success. By 1962, three-quarters of all films licensed for exhibition in the all-important New York market did not have a code seal.[6] And the anti-Communist fervor of the immediate postwar period that had propelled both content regulation and governmental censorship was abating in the second half of the 1950s, even among Catholics, the most uniformly anti-Communist group.[7]

Kingsley decided to hire Ephraim London, who had made a name for himself as a censorship expert with his high-profile *Burstyn v. Wilson* win at the Supreme Court and his win for *Mom and Dad* at the appellate division. The partnership of Kingsley and London proved fruitful. Kingsley was, like all the film distributors who had challenged the New York censors, a small businessman with a "hand-to-mouth, film-to-film" existence when he bought the rights to *Lady Chatterley's Lover*. Like Burstyn, he believed that American culture would be enriched through contact with European films.[8] Hiring London made perfect sense, given their mutual opposition to film censorship on moral and artistic grounds.

Kingsley had no financial support, but he had plenty of moral support. In the later 1950s, several New York–based independent film distributors decided to band together to fight the censor board and promote foreign film viewing in the United States. The Independent Film Importers and Distributors Association considered opposition to film censorship its first priority. But its members, mostly in the same financial situation as Kingsley, were in no position to finance a coordinated anticensorship litigation campaign.[9]

Kingsley began his appeal before the board of regents shored up by the good wishes of the International Film Importers and Distributors Association, represented by the nation's foremost film censorship attorney, and sustained by his passionate belief in the benefits of foreign films. Hoping to draw attention to what he called the "legislative humbug" of New York's statute revision on immorality, London invited members of the press to attend the regents' hearing. He managed to attract the *New York Times*, *New York Herald Tribune*, Associated Press, United Press, and *Motion Picture Herald* as well as the *New York Post*, *Newark News*, *Showman's Trade Review*, and *Film Daily*. It was the first time the press had been admitted to a screening and review appeal.[10] London's public relations savvy paid off. The *New York Times* and the *New York Herald Tribune* both ran stories on the appeal, as did several of the trade papers.[11] Anticensorship attorneys saw the press, particularly film critics, as allies in publicizing the secretive work of the state censors.

In front of the regents and the reporters, London argued that the film was "moral in its theme . . . and in the manner of presentation." It dealt, he continued, with the relationships of a woman with her husband and with her lover. The husband was both physically crippled and spiritually corrupt, and the lover represented the simple, decent, natural man. Lady Chatterley's adulterous relationship, although not sanctioned by law, was portrayed as a true marriage, according to London. He insisted that *Lady Chatterley's Lover* was more moral than the motion picture division–approved films whose solution to unhappy marriages involved suicide and murder. He also reminded the regents that because of the *Roth* decision, they were required to judge the film as a whole, not as a collection of scenes. After all, he continued, isolated passages of the Bible, taken out of context, "would be found immoral and obscene." Citing the recent case of *Mom and Dad*, he tried to remind the motion picture division that its power was reduced to censoring only exceptional, flagrant cases. How could the film be exceptional, he asked, given that the Kinsey Institute's recent reports on human sexual behavior had shown that most Americans had committed adultery?[12] The New York censors were clearly out of touch with community mores.[13]

The regents were not swayed by Kinsey or *Roth*. They justified the censors' determination "upon the fundamental recognition by our society that adultery is condemned by both God-given law (Sixth Commandment given to Moses on Mount Sinai) and man-made law (sections 100–103 of the Penal Law). In line after line and in sequence after sequence, this motion picture glorifies adultery and presents the same as desirable, as acceptable and as proper. We can not put our seal of approval upon such a motion picture."[14]

This statement turned out to be a gift. By making it clear that the film had been refused a license because it advocated an idea, the regents had opened a door for Kingsley and London. To use attorney Charles Rembar's words, "The Regents were running blindly, head on, into the barriers of the First Amendment."[15] They had unwittingly moved *Lady Chatterley's Lover* out of the obscenity-immorality continuum and into the center of a heresy debate. *Heresy* has no legal definition in the United States and is usually associated with religious matters, but it also refers broadly to the advocacy of an idea that counters societal norms. A better term might be *dissidence*. Either way, as Rembar notes, "Suppression for heresy has never, under our Constitution, been countenanced."[16] The board of regents had exposed a vulnerable spot in New York's redrafted definition of *immoral*. The statute expressly condemned portraying an act of sexual immorality (in this case, adultery) as an acceptable pattern of behavior. This may have seemed at the time a sufficiently narrow interpretation of immorality, but it actually made the statute more open to legal challenge because distributors could claim that any film advocating an unpopular or unorthodox idea was now censorable. *Lady Chatterley's Lover* provided an excellent example. The case moved out of the murky realm of the constitutionality of film censorship and into the much clearer realm of the censorship of dissident ideas.

When *Lady Chatterley's Lover* came before the courts, three areas of speech were specifically defined as being outside the protection of the First Amendment: libel, obscenity, and speech that threatened order coupled with specific action. In its statutory revision, the state had tried to add a fourth type of unprotected speech: the promulgation of immoral ideas. It looked like a good case for London, but as he prepared for the appellate division, the Supreme Court's position on governmental film censorship lurched along enigmatically. Practically the only thing that could be said for certain was that nonobscene movies were entitled to free speech protection. Whether they could be censored for immorality under a specific definition or for the expression of unwelcome ideas had yet to be tested.

In the New York Courts

At the appellate division, London emphasized that the film was a faithful representation of the expurgated version of *Lady Chatterley's Lover*, not the notorious original version. The themes of *Lady Chatterley's Lover* were well known to the public, he noted, and could not be considered shocking in a filmed version, since more than 160,000 copies of the expurgated version had been sold in New York State. London then struck at the regents where they were most constitutionally vulnerable. Striding through the door they had opened in upholding their censors, he raised the new constitutional issue by questioning whether the revised statute authorized the suppression of opinion. London was bent on showing that the new statutory definition of *immoral* was just as unconstitutional as had been its predecessor. The post–*La ronde* statutory revision, he argued, did nothing but add words to a censoring term that had been declared unconstitutional by the nation's highest court. Since the New York State Court of Appeals had interpreted *immoral* to refer only to sexual immorality, and since that interpretation was binding on the U.S. Supreme Court, when the Supreme Court threw out the use of *immoral* against *La ronde*, it also necessarily rejected *sexual immorality* as a censoring term.[17]

Up to this point, London was asking for constitutional interpretation by the court. Based on what was happening in film censorship cases in other states, he could have stopped there. As we have seen, the highest courts in Massachusetts, Pennsylvania, Kansas, and Ohio had ignored the applications of their censoring laws and had gone directly to the constitutional issue. But London strayed from the abstract question by asking whether the censors were wrong in finding *Lady Chatterley's Lover* immoral, reverting to the usual practice of giving the justices the narrow route. Not until 1961, in *Times Film v. Chicago*, would a film distributor refuse to submit to the licensing process specifically to challenge its basic constitutionality.[18] For *Lady Chatterley's Lover*, London was taking the safer route, probably for the sake of Kingsley, who, though he strongly desired to fight for film freedom, was not a wealthy man.

London and Kingsley were not alone before the appellate division. The NYCLU joined as amicus. Its brief argued the usual points but then got to the heart of the matter, claiming that the revised statute was "aimed directly at dissident opinion. . . . It embodies the very evil the guarantee of free expression was to prevent: the grant of power to State officials to suppress varying or dissident or nonconformist viewpoints." With several nonfilm speech restrictions like this recently struck down, both London and the NYCLU must have felt hopeful.[19]

The state entered the legal battle over *Lady Chatterley's Lover* with two big complicating factors. First, it had just lost the *Garden of Eden* case and was left with no censoring terms but *immorality* and *obscenity* (and the former was highly suspect). Second, the case presented a film that had been censored for presenting not an immoral act but an immoral idea. With the state in this weakened position, London was encouraging the appellate division justices to overturn a statute that had consistently been upheld by their superior court colleagues. Although the justices refused to take this drastic step, they did come closer than any New York state court had come before. They unanimously found in favor of Kingsley, but Presiding Justice Foster abstained, possibly because the court had failed to strike down the entire statute (the gloss that London would put on it when he went before the court of appeals). Writing for the majority minus one, Justice William H. Coon found the legislative attempt to define *immoral* unsatisfactory. The attempt to define such words was helped by adding more words. Coon firmly held that any statute that had as its basis the opinion of a censor was a violation of the Fourteenth Amendment. "If any field of prior restraint is left open," he said, "it would seem clear that the Supreme Court decisions forbid a statute as broad as the one under consideration. . . . It is clear that . . . the presentation of adultery or similar 'immoral' acts as 'desirable, acceptable, proper patterns of behavior' is not a permissible standard under the United States Constitution for prior restraint."[20] So, with its first legal challenge, New York's amended definition of *immoral* was shot down. *Lady Chatterley's Lover* could be shown on New York screens if the state did not appeal.

But the regents did appeal. Given their resounding defeat at the lower court—the fourth unanimous loss in a row—and their loss at the court of appeals in their last appearance, it seemed a risky move at best. But Kingsley had announced that he intended to show *Lady Chatterley's Lover* in New York within the next thirty days.[21] Perhaps the regents appealed to keep the movie from being shown. Perhaps they believed that the court of appeals was home to friendlier judges. Or maybe they saw it as a chance to redeem the last stinging defeat and keep *immoral*. Without it, the New York censors would be left with only *obscenity*. Whatever the motivation, *Lady Chatterley's Lover* was destined for the court of appeals.

Before the film got to New York's highest court, though, there were several important developments at the U.S. Supreme Court. In the 1957 term, the Supreme Court handed down three decisions, all per curiams, yet cumulatively instructive. First the justices reversed the determination that *The Game of Love* was obscene; then they reversed the New York obscenity convictions of two nudist magazines.[22] The three opinions, combined with the three earlier per curiams (in the cases of *La ronde*, *Pinky*, and *The Moon Is Blue*), caused legal commentator George Haimbaugh Jr. to conclude that the Court henceforth would tolerate censoring only for hardcore pornography.[23] Certainly this was true for literary works, but the courts had always accepted the notion that motion pictures were different and somehow more dangerous. In 1958, as the court of appeals heard arguments over *Lady Chatterley's Lover*, it would become clear that film was still not to be treated with the same judicial deference as books, at least not in New York.

At the New York State Court of Appeals

London argued at the court of appeals alone. The NYCLU, for some unknown reason, did not file an amicus. For this more conservative court, London described *Lady Chatterley's Lover* as "a watered version of the expurgated edition of the novel now freely sold throughout the state." The only possible justification for speech suppression, he said, was the possibility of a "clear and probable danger" that would lead to societal harm, and that condition was clearly not present. Shientag had tried this approach successfully four years earlier, and London was banking that it would work again. To prove his point, and to attack the regents where their argument was most vulnerable, London had much case law upon which to rely. "Even if we assume that the picture recommends adultery as Appellant claims," London wrote, "it cannot be seriously contended that any grave, substantial evil will follow from the exhibition of the film." This was particularly true in the case of *Lady Chatterley's Lover*, since the ideas had already been widely read in book form.[24]

London also revisited prior restraint, but this time with a new twist. It had become legally accepted that even though the *Burstyn* decision had brought motion pictures under the umbrella of the First Amendment, prior restraint was still permissible in exceptional circumstances. Legal commentators and states' attorneys general had routinely accepted *Burstyn* as meaning that the Supreme Court accepted prior restraint for movies as a legitimate state right as long as it was done under a "clearly drawn statute." London argued the opposite. He claimed that proper interpretation of the *Burstyn* decision required that suitable attention be paid to the Court's phrasing. When Justice Clark wrote that "it is not necessary for us to decide whether a state may censor motion pictures," the Court was not upholding censorship, it was merely sidestepping the larger constitutional issue. Since *sacrilege* was available to overturn New York's ban of *The Miracle*, the Court had taken that opportunity. What legal experts had interpreted since 1952 as an acceptance of prior restraint by the Supreme Court had actually, according to London, been nothing more than a dodge and had been incorrectly used as proof that the Supreme Court countenanced motion picture censorship. It was a novel argument.

For the final point of his shotgun approach, London argued the unconstitutionality of a tax on speech. Case law showed that no one could be required to purchase the right to speak or to publish. Since movie content had been brought under the free speech and free press protections of the First Amendment in the *Burstyn* case, London asserted, any tax laid upon the exhibition of movies was actually a tax on speech and therefore unconstitutional.

Brind came out swinging. *Immoral* had become unreliable, so Brind tried to characterize the "love making" scenes of *Lady Chatterley's Lover* as "patently pornographic . . . and obscene."[25] The attorney general rebutted London's assertion that the license fee was an unconstitutional tax. This argument had been tried before, he said, but licensing fees were common and had withstood legal tests many times. London's choosing to call the fee a tax did not make it so.[26]

In their decision four months later, the judges reversed the appellate division. The state had won its risky appeal, and *Lady Chatterley's Lover* could be kept from New York screens. But everything else in the case was left muddied, muddled, and perplexing. The complexity was so evident that even the summary of the court's vote is bewildering: "Judges Froessel and Burke concur with Chief Judge Conway; Judge Desmond concurs in result in a separate opinion; Judges Dye and Fuld dissent and vote to affirm, each in a separate opinion in which the other concurs and in both of which dissenting opinions Judge Van Voorhis concurs in part in a separate dissenting opinion."

The majority opinion was written by Chief Judge Albert Conway, a New York City Catholic with strong anti-Communist sentiments. Five years earlier, he had written a majority opinion upholding the dismissal of teachers who refused to answer congressional committee questions about suspected Communist involvement.[27] Conway's lengthy majority opinion about *Lady Chatterley's Lover* began with an homage to the legislative will, then proceeded to denounce the film as an "exaltation of illicit sexual love in derogation of the restraints of marriage." With a nod to the two-year-old *Roth* decision, Conway found not just that the film contained immoral scenes but that its overall message was "utterly immoral" and completely repugnant "by the standards of our community." This theme reverberated throughout the fourteen-page opinion, repeated no fewer than fifteen times. Conway ignored *Roth*. He dismissed London's assertions of statutory vagueness and his "clear and present danger" argument, referring instead to a fifteen-year-old case about "fighting words" (*Chaplinsky v. New Hampshire*) and an 1896 case about involuntary servitude that dealt with free speech only tangentially. Conway was mainly concerned with how society could protect itself from motion pictures, which he believed corrupted public morals. (That movies had such a capacity he accepted without question.) Intent on protecting his state's ability to police its morals, Conway refused to allow the Constitution to be used as "an altar upon which this State, and this nation, must sacrifice themselves to the ravages of moral corruption."[28]

Finally, Conway rejected London's assertion that the Supreme Court had merely declined to consider the basic issue of censorship, since doing so had been unnecessary. Here his interpretation was diametrically opposite London's. Conway claimed that the Court's recent pronouncements had repeatedly held that clearly defined motion picture licensing statutes did not abridge either free speech or free press guarantees. Since the Court had been so unclear, this was not an unreasonable interpretation. Rehashing the harmfulness construct, Conway found prior restraint necessary lest extensive damage result before the penal code could ride to the rescue.

Judge Desmond, upon whom the censors could count until a few years earlier, and who had an intellectual interest in the problems of censorship, filed a concurring opinion in which the black was not so black and the white not so white. Despite his philosophical inclination toward movie censorship, Desmond was troubled by the Supreme Court's refusal to uphold a single case of film censorship since *Mutual*. In fact, he pointed out, just a year earlier, the Court had reversed a Chicago ban on the French film *The Game of Love*, which, he noted, was "sexy in the extreme." He interpreted the Supreme Court's recent rulings as suggesting that censorship for obscenity would have to be "closely confined," especially in regard to works of artistic merit (like *Lady Chatterley's Lover*). He then moved straight to the constitutional question, expressing doubt (for the first time) that New York's statute passed constitutional muster. The only way to find out, he suggested, was to declare it unconstitutional and then "let the Supreme Court have the final say."[29] But he refused to go this far, preferring to let the statute stand.

Conway, then, strongly favored censorship, and Desmond occupied the middle ground, wondering whether his court was out of step with the Supreme Court, but Dye, Fuld, and new judge John Van Voorhis were convinced that New York ought to get out of the censoring business or, at least, allow Kingsley to exhibit *Lady Chatterley's Lover*. However well-intentioned the new definition of *immoral*, Dye wrote, it still suffered from the same ambiguity that had forced the Supreme Court to strike down *sacrilegious* and *harmful*. Because the book version had circulated freely, it made no sense to him that the film version could be banned without violating the First and Fourteenth amendments. Fuld maintained, as he had before, that he could see no legal difference between the rights of a movie and the rights of a newspaper, book, or stage play.[30]

The conservative group in the earlier *Garden of Eden* case—Conway, Froessel, and Burke—remained intact and was joined for *Lady Chatterley's Lover* by Desmond. Jealously protective of the state's right to shelter its citizens from the harm inevitable in movies, this four-man majority ignored the legal trends of four other states as well as the direction of its own junior court. Conway was a dedicated Catholic, anti-Communist, and conservative. Burke was liberal on many issues but was also a New York City Catholic with a lifetime commitment to the welfare of children. Froessel, a lifelong Boy Scout and past grand master of the Masons, favored school prayer and believed that public morality infused with religious faith was necessary for a healthy society.[31] And Desmond, the third Catholic of the group, who had not found any immorality or indecency in *Garden of Eden*, was still concerned by the potential societal harm of movie content, and *Lady Chatterley's Lover* had given him reason for concern. Three of the four were elected from New York City, an area with a strong Catholic presence, which may also help to account for their pro-censorship stances. The dissenters, on the other hand—the more liberal Dye and Van Voorhis—were elected by upstate voters, more heavily Protestant than those of metro New York.

The New York State Court of Appeals had now found for the regents three out of four times (*The Miracle*, *La ronde*, and *Lady Chatterley's Lover*). It had failed to uphold the censors only once (*Garden of Eden*). Unlike the high courts of Massachusetts, Ohio, Pennsylvania, and Kansas, New York's highest court had held that films whose ideas were outside the realm of contemporary moral standards were not protected by the First Amendment or by the state's constitution. But that decision had come from an almost evenly split bench. Decisions seemed to hinge on the vote of one judge. So while New York State would remain in the censoring business, whatever mandate it could claim from the judges of its highest court was slim. Moreover, the state's intermediate court, the appellate division, had gone against the censors three out of five times, and each of those three anticensor decisions had been unanimous. The intermediate appellate court was clearly willing to take more risks and might be ready to strike down the statute.

Surely the state's censors recognized the warning signs. But the legislature seemed content to leave the censorship situation as it stood. After 1933, no repeal bills were introduced, but a new idea was heard in the state capital. As *Lady Chatterley's Lover* began its judicial journey, the legislature began a long but unconsummated flirtation with the idea of classifying films instead of banning them.[32] Assemblyman Luigi R. Marano of Brooklyn introduced classification bills in both the 1957 and 1958 sessions. His bills called for the motion picture division to classify films into three categories: "general patronage," "adults and adolescents," and "adults only." But neither bill made it to the governor's desk.[33] Marano repeatedly introduced such legislation until 1963, when he agreed to withdraw in light of the MPAA's pledge to begin age classification.[34]

At the U.S. Supreme Court

On the day of the court of appeals loss, London announced that he would ask the Supreme Court for review. *Lady Chatterley's Lover* was an excellent test case. It presented the Court with the full range of arguments for and against state film censorship, and it would allow the justices to rule decisively which evils, if any, the state could still ban from theater screens. For the past six years, the trend had not been in the censors' favor.

Nor did the rapidly changing popular culture favor the censors. The reticent, who had started out battling against open sexuality at the end of the nineteenth century and had won (legislatively at least) during the Progressive Era, now were on the defensive seemingly in every aspect of American life. Their last real strongholds were the censor boards of New York, Virginia, Maryland, Kansas, and a smattering of cities.

Lady Chatterley's Lover presented two new issues for the Court to consider. London had already presented the first to the New York courts: whether a state could ban presentation of an idea in film. In a 1957 decision, the justices of the Supreme Court had overturned a conviction for the advocacy of a political idea.[35] Would the Court extend this doctrine to motion picture speech? The second new issue had to do with the requirement that all films submit to prior review. As the *Columbia Law Review* saw it, the Supreme Court had been particularly hostile toward prior restraint on speech. And if the only films that could constitutionally be precensored were obscene films, the requirement that all films go through prior review was overly burdensome and intrusive.[36] So *Kingsley* came to the U.S. Supreme Court in a culturally elastic atmosphere, demanding answers to questions of clear and present danger as applied to speech restriction, the acceptability of statutory vagueness, and the permissible extent of the state's regulatory methods. As the case approached the Supreme Court, *Lady Chatterley's Lover* was being freely exhibited from Boston to San Francisco.[37] Yet in New York it remained taboo.

At the Supreme Court, London argued the usual points—prior restraint, freedom of the press, statutory vagueness—but also ventured into several new areas. Using the newly emerging science of mass communication study, he showed that media presentations affected different people in different ways (a major departure from what was earlier believed). If mass communication experts could not tell which media exposure had created which effects, how could the legal system justify prior restraint for movies but not for books or theater? To satisfy the justices that movies did not have a greater capacity for evil that could justify their control, he used the realities of the film distribution business in the United States. It was supposed that movies had greater ability to affect society because they were distributed en masse and watched by thousands simultaneously and were therefore incapable of being controlled by penal laws. But, London explained, films were not distributed that way. At first run, a film was usually exhibited in only a few theaters within a state. Only after that initial run were more copies distributed to second-run theaters. This first-run time period, with relatively small numbers of viewers, would afford authorities ample time to shut down any criminally offensive film. Thus prior restraint was unnecessary.[38]

London continued to hammer on the inequities of prior restraint by pointing out its inevitable and expensive delay. He used the history of *Lady Chatterley's Lover* as the best example: denied a license in 1956, the film had taken two full years to get a final determination from the New York courts. "It is of little satisfaction," he noted, "to those who would speak or publish, and to those who wish to see and hear, that their rights may be vindicated in several years." He practically implored the Court to put the censorship struggle out of its misery. It had been seven years since the *Burstyn* decision, seven years during which the Supreme Court had obfuscated the issue with its per curiams, causing confusing and contradictory lower-court decisions. London drew attention to the state courts that had completely invalidated their censorship statutes and others that had restricted the censoring activity to obscenity. New York had not made even that much of a limitation.

As he had done at both levels of the New York courts, London brought up the heresy-dissidence issue. The movie could not in any way, he argued, be construed as encouraging people to commit adultery. As he had done in all *Lady Chatterley's Lover* legal appearances, he went after the impossibility of statutory definitions of immorality. *Lady Chatterley's Lover*, he pointed out, had differing meanings for different people. The motion picture division censors had found only three immoral sections, yet the regents had found the entire film immoral. Moreover, only three of the twelve New York judges who had seen the movie had found it immoral. So what did *immoral* mean?

For the state, Brind argued that the sexual immorality of adultery was "without question." But his zeal for censorship defense seemed to be growing thin, and his twenty-one years of defending the regents and the motion picture division were clearly weighing on him. He relied on Conway's opinion: "We do not think that exemplification on our part can add anything to [Judge Conway's] decision. We rest squarely on it."[39]

The Opinions

The Supreme Court unanimously struck down New York's censoring of immorality, but five justices took different paths to the same conclusion.

Justice Potter Stewart, who would later frame the most famous line about pornography (that he could not define it but he knew it when he saw it[40]), wrote the court's opinion. Stewart was a pragmatic, centrist judge, but he often voted with his more liberal colleagues on First Amendment cases. Noting that the court of appeals had not found the film obscene and that the only question was whether the film could be restrained for immorality, Stewart held that New York had prevented *Lady Chatterley's Lover* from being seen purely because it advocated an idea. "The First Amendment's basic guarantee is of freedom to advocate ideas," he maintained, so New York had struck "at the very heart of constitutionally protected liberty." Stewart dismissed the state's claim of justification in protecting itself from ideas that were contrary to the moral standards of its people. This tack "misconceives what it is that the Constitution protects," Stewart stressed. "Its guarantee is not confined to the expression of ideas that are conventional or shared by a majority."[41] Legal expert Harry Kalven Jr. called this statement "one of the Court's clearest and most impressive utterances about free speech in general."[42]

Since New York's transgression of constitutional protection in its definition of *immoral* was so clear, Stewart continued, there was no reason for the Court to go any further and consider the constitutionality of the entire statute. Nor was it necessary to consider the argument that films were unfairly singled out for prior restraint. Stewart's opinion held that any state could censor films for pornographic scenes but could censor for immorality only if it was depicted in an obscene way. Justices Black, Frankfurter, Douglas, Clark, and Harlan agreed but were compelled to offer their own opinions.

Black and Douglas, in separate opinions, carried on their customary arguments against any prior restraints as violative of the First and Fourteenth amendments. Black (who had refused to watch the film since he believed all film censorship unconstitutional) further found that as long as the Court accepted prior restraint on films, it would find itself in the untenable position of the "Supreme Board of Censors." The justices had no expertise in supervising the morals of the nation, he wrote, nor did they have any ability to make value judgments about what movies were good or bad for certain communities. Black found any type of super-review irreconcilable with the rule of law required by the Constitution.[43] Douglas, for his part, could find in the First Amendment "no room for any censor whether he is scanning an editorial, reading a news broadcast, editing a novel or a play, or previewing a movie." The First Amendment, which Douglas continued to find "absolute," was "utterly at war with censorship."[44]

Frankfurter began his concurring opinion in the practical realm, noting that only the "stuffiest of Victorian sensibilities" could have found *Lady Chatterley's Lover* offensive. Because New York's highest court had determined that the film was offensive, Frankfurter had no choice, he wrote, but to agree with his colleagues that the state had "exceeded the bounds of free expression." But that did not mean, Frankfurter argued, that the state could not prohibit some expression, such as pornography. Unlike Black and Douglas, Frankfurter believed that the right to expression was not absolute and that it would necessarily fall to the courts to arbitrate disputes over applicability. "Such an exercise of the judicial function, however onerous or ungrateful," he asserted, "inheres in the very nature of the judicial enforcement of the Due Process Clause [of the Fourteenth Amendment]. We cannot escape such instance-by-instance, case-by-case application of that clause in all the varieties of situations that come before this Court." He compared this situation to the Court's revisiting every year the application of standards to criminal cases, such as coerced confessions and prosecutorial misconduct. The "supreme board of censorship" function that so troubled Black caused Frankfurter no legal trepidation whatsoever. While he did not welcome the task, he viewed it as the very basis of the Court's proper function. Frankfurter here was only carrying on the concept first articulated in the *Burstyn* decision seven years earlier: that the Supreme Court would have to "examine the facts of . . . each case to determine whether the principles of the First Amendment have been honored."[45]

Justice Tom Clark, who had written the *Burstyn* opinion, reminded New York that censors must be equipped with definite language, applied only in exceptional circumstances. Since the New York statute referred to the concept of sexual immorality rather than to acts of sexual immorality, Clark found it far too vague.[46]

Justice Harlan, joined by Frankfurter and Whittaker, also concurred in the result but found his colleagues too eager to strike down New York's definition of *immoral*. He found that only in applying that term to *Lady Chatterley's Lover* had New York exceeded constitutional bounds. Harlan reasoned that if *Lady Chatterley's Lover* or any other film presented an idea—that adultery was permissible, for example—and coupled that idea with scenes that depicted adulterous acts, it could properly be banned by state law as sexually immoral. However, Harlan's assessment of *Lady Chatterley's Lover* diverged from that of the court of appeals. Characterizing the film as "a rather pathetic love triangle," he found nothing obscene or "corruptive of the public morals by inciting the commission of adultery." And Harlan agreed with Frankfurter's opinion that there was no good reason for the Supreme Court not to sit in judgment of particular films since they operated in similar fashion in other areas of the law. Clearly, if *Lady Chatterley's Lover* had not been such an innocuous film, Harlan would have dissented and voted to confirm the court of appeals.[47]

Although the Court had spoken with many tongues, careful consideration of the decision revealed a strong anticensorship statement. The Court had not struck the statute for vagueness, which was the more typical (and more conservative) method of dealing with film censorship problems. That method would have allowed the states to return to the legislative drawing board in search of constitutionally acceptable standards. By overturning the statute based instead on its contravention of the First Amendment's guarantee of free expression, the majority expressly precluded any attempt to redraw.[48]

Overall, then, the majority of the Court had found unconstitutional New York's statute banning any film that presented immoral ideas, while Frankfurter, Harlan, and Whittaker had found the statute itself constitutional but incorrectly applied to this specific film. The Court had restricted itself to two courses of action: either acting as supercensors or deciding the constitutionality of whatever standards had been applied.[49] The decision thus revealed, as had *Roth*, a division among the justices over whether the Court should articulate a clear statement of principle or continue to decide such cases on an individual basis.[50]

The number of justices on either side of the dividing line was almost even. On the side that was more sympathetic to censorship were Frankfurter, Whittaker, Harlan, and Clark. On the side that was less sympathetic to censorship were Stewart, Black, Brennan, and Douglas. Like Warren, Brennan had remained silent on this decision, yet he can be assumed to have been closer to the anticensorship bloc, since it was he who had, in the *Roth* opinion, linked literature and art to freedom of the press for the first time.[51]

New York had taken quite a chance on *Lady Chatterley's Lover*. After all, the regents could have let it drop after their loss at the appellate division. Appeal to the court of appeals had been risky. Even a win there practically guaranteed being dragged into the Supreme Court. So what had begun as a string of unanimous appellate division losses in the mid-1950s now turned into a unanimously negative ruling from the nation's highest court. All New York's attempts to legislatively define an unacceptably immoral movie had failed.

Only Obscenity Left in New York

From 1959 on, the censors of New York would be permitted to watch only for obscenity. But what did *obscene* mean? Would the courts tolerate a different standard of obscenity for films because of their greater capacity for evil? Could the states define what was an obscene film? Words like *immoral*, *indecent*, and *inhuman*, which had had sufficient legal precision in the progressive years, had been struck down, and attempts during the 1950s to provide such connotatively loaded terms with statutory precision had failed. The Supreme Court, after seven years of enigmatic per curiam decisions, had finally spoken, but it had spoken with six voices. On top of all the disagreement from the high court, films were becoming more explicit and daring than ever, and fewer producers and directors were willing to abide by the Production Code or by censor decisions.

It would take more challenge cases, though, to overturn statutory interference with movies, and little help so far had been forthcoming from the MPAA. Edward Kingsley was angered that the MPAA had sat on the sidelines while his small company took on the state censors of New York. Calling the MPAA "guilty of neglect," Kingsley began speaking out. He told a *Variety* interviewer, "They benefit. . . . We pave the way for them and they reap the benefits. But when it comes to helping a small company fight it out, they turn the other way."[52]

Kingsley found the Court's decision to be "most heartening for all of us who have been concerned with the freedom of the screen."[53] Despite the fractured decision, London believed that the case would have far-reaching effects, and not just for New York. He predicted that the remaining state censor laws of Maryland, Kansas, and Virginia would be affected.[54] The ACLU prematurely hailed the decision as having struck down New York's statute.[55] Arch Parsons, writing in the *New York Herald Tribune*, was more circumspect, noting that it was not yet clear how much effect the decision would have, although he believed that it might be "considerable." Louis Pesce, acting director of the motion picture division, withheld comment, but Hugh Flick, who had resigned as director to become assistant to the state education commissioner, commented, "While 'Lady Chatterley's Lover' may now be shown in the state, that doesn't mean that any other movie, any old 'Ten Nights in a Barroom' can now be shown. It can't."[56]

But at least five U.S. senators were worried that *Ten Nights in a Barroom* would soon show up on theater marquees. They recognized that the Court had expressly foiled efforts to redraw statutes to meet objections. So just two days after the ruling, Senate Judiciary Committee chairman James Eastland proposed a constitutional amendment to protect "the right of each state to decide on the basis of its own public policy questions of decency and morality."[57] A stern, staunchly anti-Communist, anti-integration conservative, Eastland was joined by some powerful senators, all southern Democrats: Estes Kefauver, Herman Talmadge, Strom Thurmond, and Olin Johnston. The measure was also supported by Ohio senator Frank Lausche, who as governor of Ohio had in 1954–1955 lobbied tirelessly to reinstate its overturned statute.[58] Calling for the amendment, Lausche tried to rally his colleagues to protest against films like *Lady Chatterley's Lover*. "We believe in the Ten Commandments," he proclaimed. "We believe in the commandment, 'Thou shall not commit adultery.'"[59] Despite Lausche's emotional appeal, the amendment never made it out of the Senate Judiciary Committee.

The six senators were also out of step with the rulings of the state courts. The same day that Eastland and Lausche were trying to rally support for their amendment, the Pennsylvania Supreme Court was invalidating the state's penal statute against the showing of obscene films. The statute, which had been used since the court abolished its prior restraint against films in 1956, had been declared unconstitutional by Pennsylvania's chief justice. He interpreted the 1955 U.S. Supreme Court decision in *Holmby Productions, Inc. v. Vaughn* as having nullified the use of the word *obscene* as a standard against movies and on that basis reversed the penal provisions against "lewd and lascivious" and "obscene" films.[60]

The archenemy of prior restraint, Bosley Crowther, put it best when he wrote six days after the *Lady Chatterley's Lover* decision, "Once more the United States Supreme Court has knocked a substantial prop from under the ever more rickety legal structure upon which official motion picture censorship is based."[61] Legal commentators agreed that the Court had held New York's application of the standard as invalid even though Justices Frankfurter, Whittaker, and Harlan had refused to go that far. John Harvey Whitworth Jr., writing in the *Mississippi Law Journal*, went further than the other commentators, surmising (incorrectly) that the entire New York statute had been overturned and that the statutes of Maryland, Kansas, and Virginia would also fall if the Court were given the chance to rule on them. "Although the Court has consistently refused to hold all precensorship by the states unconstitutional," Whitworth suggested, "it has, in effect, done just that." Calling any redrafting of statutes a "staggering problem," he concluded that until the Court defined *obscenity* more clearly, "efforts at censorship legislation seem futile." Once again the Supreme Court had managed to rule ambiguously—so much so that legal experts could not agree about the Court's meaning despite its unanimity.[62]

Most commentators did agree that films could be censored only for obscenity. The lower federal courts were moving in the same direction. Just one month later, *Lady Chatterley's Lover* was again in the legal news, but this time it was the novel, not the film. U.S. district court judge Frederick van Pelt Bryan, deciding whether the novel could be sent through the mail, held that free expression of ideas in the arts had to be safeguarded. "It is essential to the maintenance of a free society that the severest restrictions be placed upon restraints which may tend to prevent the dissemination of ideas," Bryan held. "It matters not whether such ideas be expressed in political pamphlets . . . or through artistic media. All such expressions must be freely available."[63] The following year, 1960, a circuit court of appeals upheld Bryan's position. The courts had freed *Lady Chatterley's Lover* for viewing in a movie theater and for mailing to customers to read at home.

Legal historians often ponder whether Supreme Court justices reflect, lead, or lag behind public opinion. The case of prior restraint on motion pictures allows no easy analysis, since no polls were taken from which historians could gauge public opinion about movie censorship. Once the Supreme Court took up film censorship in 1952 with *Burstyn*, it considered film cases repeatedly. Whether the justices were ahead of public opinion or not, it is certain that they were ahead of state censors and state legislators. Each film censorship case heard by the Supreme Court overruled the application of state law to an individual film and suggested that statutory terms like *immoral* and *harmful* were unconstitutional. Definition, which in the Progressive Era had been presupposed as unnecessary, became the major legal issue in the censorship battles of the 1950s.

When the Court attempted to deal with literary content in 1957 with *Roth*, it took steps toward a definition of *obscenity*, but each succeeding case seemed to take one step forward and one step sideways. And though the Court declined to place obscenity within the protections of the First Amendment, it did require that those who would determine the obscenity of art do so only by using narrow and clear definitions. But the overall issue of defining *obscenity* was far from settled, and now definition had also become a problem for the content regulators of the PCA. Faced with outright defiance, the MPAA had recast its code in 1956 to reflect societal changes, but fewer producers were willing to submit their films for approval. The court-ordered breakup of the industry worked in these maverick producers' favor, as did the court cases brought by the independent distributors. Content grew ever more daring. Censor and content regulators would face their hardest challenges yet as the 1960s began.

10

The Curtain Coming Down, 1957–1964

While *Kingsley* was less than satisfactory as a solid legal precedent for either side, it was clear to the New York censors that their domain was now limited to obscenity. Since only obscene films could be banned or cut, Charles Brind got a break; he was not bothered by any film challenge cases for two years. But while things were quiet in New York, the anticensorship forces were suffering several worrisome developments: Pennsylvania had reinstated film censorship in 1959 (although, as we have seen, the new statute was struck down by the state supreme court two years later); a major censorship case from Chicago was making its way to the U.S. Supreme Court; and several states were flirting with age classification schemes.

In Ohio, Maryland, and New York, legislators introduced bills to censor films based on age. Procensorship legislators and censors in all three states, incensed by the limitations imposed by the U.S. Supreme Court's rulings, hoped to pass age restrictions on films as a way to regain some authority. Age classification was hardly a new idea: the nation's first film censorship law, the 1907 Chicago ordinance, provided for a special license for films to be seen only by those over twenty-one.[1] The age classification idea had lost favor in the Progressive Era, though, as reformers used protection of the innocent as justification for banning dangerous film content for all. And Hollywood had opposed it since it would restrict potential audience sizes. As the progressive ideas died away and the Supreme Court began to question in the 1950s whether content unsuitable for children should be kept from everyone, the idea of age classification began to reappear. It seemed more modern, fitting in with new ideas about childhood and the teen years as stages of life separate from adulthood. The arrival of rock 'n' roll in the 1950s made marketers realize that media consumption could be based on age. The one-size-fits-all strategy of media production of the 1920s, 1930s, and 1940s seemed passé as Elvis flooded the airwaves and Hollywood began to produce films like *Rock around the Clock* and *Gidget*.[2]

Age classification for movies popped up frequently. When in 1957 the motion picture division reported that fully 20 percent of the films legally required to pass could harm minors, the chair of the New York legislature's Joint Committee on Offensive and Obscene Material, Joseph Younglove, proposed giving the censors authority to rate films on their suitability for those under eighteen. Like many others, Younglove deplored the "lenient attitude of the courts" toward censorship and saw age classification as the cure.[3] Ever wary of attempts to expand film censorship, *New York Times* critic Bosley Crowther called it a "slick idea," since the censor bureaucracy would remain intact along with its "power of arbitrary judgment."[4] Hearings on the proposal drew more criticism than support. Even the General Federation of Women's Clubs, usually a staunch advocate of movie control, was opposed, worried that classification would only intensify youthful curiosity about adult-only films. More opposition came from the NYCLU (represented at the hearings by Ephraim London), the Independent Theatre Owners Association, the Metropolitan Motion Picture Theatres Association, and the MPAA.[5] (In all likelihood, the motion picture organizations probably still resisted classification because they feared losing audience numbers for films rated only for the mature; as late as 1960, fully 50 percent of movie theater attendees were under twenty-one.) After a federal district court judge struck down a similar age-based ordinance in Chicago in 1959,[6] New York's legislative enthusiasm died out and the bill was narrowly defeated.

In 1961, another age classification bill, this time with the backing of the board of regents, surfaced in the New York legislature. Another attempt by Luigi Marano, this proposal required the motion picture division to label those films suitable for viewing by elementary and secondary school children.[7] By itself this classification seemed harmless, but a second proposal called for beefing up the New York Penal Law. If both measures passed, an exhibitor who screened a film not acceptable for children would be liable for criminal prosecution if just one minor attended. Moreover, the restrictions placed on the type of film that could be classified as acceptable for minors were so stringent that films like *West Side*

Story would probably have been excluded.[8] The potential harm to exhibitors from a bill like this was considerable.

Some within the film industry favored age classification. Film authority Arthur Mayer, a censorship opponent since his battle with the motion picture division over *Remous* in the 1930s, pointed out that forty-three countries, including almost every "important" Western country except the United States, classified films. This disparity, he noted, led to the ironic situation that in France, which the New York authorities had referred to so disparagingly in several court cases, a film like *Les liaisons dangereuses* could be seen only by those over eighteen, yet in the United States, except in those places with censorship, it could be seen by everyone.[9]

The interest in age classification shown by many states and organizations indicates the rising frustration of those who believed the Supreme Court and the state courts were going too far in expanding free speech rights to filmmakers. Despite its popularity, though, a modified age classification system was adopted by only one state, Virginia in 1963. The new system allowed a distributor to apply for an over-eighteen rating.

The MPAA remained opposed to age classification as nothing less than another type of governmental censorship. But age classification would have enabled American studios to produce the adult-oriented fare that was sending sophisticated moviegoers to independent and foreign films. It would also have quieted some opposition from pressure groups that had come to favor classification, like the Legion of Decency. To appease the legion, some filmmakers had begun voluntarily labeling their films "suggested for mature audiences only." *Lolita* (1962) escaped a "condemned" rating when its distributors agreed to advertise the film as "for adults only."

The Court Takes a Retrogressive Step

The post-*Burstyn* censor losses had been so consistent that many observers believed it was only a matter of time before the Court overturned prior restraint on movies entirely. When another distributor, Times Film Corporation, decided to bring a case that was designed to test the very basis of prior restraint rather than its application, industry observers held their breath. Times Film was an independent distributor and foreign-film importer whose owner, Jean Goldwurm, was adamantly opposed to film censorship. In the words of International Film Importers and Distributors Association executive director Michael Mayer, Goldwurm had "no hesitation in taking on the censor anywhere—he was anxious to."[10] Goldwurm had already filed suit against Massachusetts in 1955 over its treatment of *One Summer of Happiness* and *The Game of Love* and probably would have won if Brattle Films had not already convinced the Massachusetts Supreme Court to invalidate its statute.[11] In 1961, to test the Chicago censor ordinance (considered one of the strictest in the country), Goldwurm refused to submit *Don Juan*, a film version of Mozart's opera *Don Giovanni*. Goldwurm and Times Film decided that it was time to test the issue of constitutionality without any complicating issues like improper application, statutory vagueness, and denial of due process. By refusing to submit *Don Juan* for review, Times Film denied the court a narrow route on which to base a decision. After five decades of film censorship, the real heart of the matter was about to be tested.

Lower courts held that since *Don Juan* had not been examined or shown, there was no justiciable controversy. But the U.S. Supreme Court agreed to hear the case, signaling its willingness to examine the question of whether motion pictures had the right to be viewed without prior examination.

The Illinois chapter of the ACLU filed an amicus brief before the Supreme Court. The brief restricted itself to the traditional antagonism toward prior restraint, arguing that the potential capacity for evil in film did not justify subjecting all films to "a system of control which for three centuries has been generally condemned as obnoxious to free men." Relying heavily on history, the Illinois ACLU pleaded that the censor, unhampered by presumption of innocence or by evidentiary rules, working in secret, became "a law unto himself." In a clever new tack, the ACLU argued that because Chicago's prior restraint interfered with both protected and unprotected speech, it violated the Constitution.[12]

By not submitting its film for review, Times Film, along with the ACLU, was leveling a "broadside attack" on prior restraint. But during the oral argument, Justices Frankfurter and Clark told the Times Film attorneys, Felix Bilgrey and Abner Mikva, that their case would have been stronger had they exhibited the film without permit and then accepted prosecution. But, Mikva countered, a film company should not have to risk criminal prosecution to test a statute.[13]

Times Film had tried to force the Court to rule on the very basis of film censorship, but a five-man majority on the Court relished the opportunity to slap it down. Those who had wondered how the Court's majority would rule when faced with the pure question of censorship's constitutionality got their answer. "The challenge here," Clark wrote for the majority, "is to the censor's basic authority; it does not go to any statutory standards employed by the censor or procedural requirements." Since the Court had recognized nine years earlier in *Burstyn v. Wilson* that each method of communication presented unique problems (another reference to the harmfulness concept), it refused to knock down prior restraint. Harkening back to the judicial restraint of Justice Holmes, Clark concluded, "It is not for this court to limit the state in its selection of the remedy it deems most effective to cope with such a problem as that presented by obscene films." All those constitutional commentators who were wondering what Clark had meant in his *Burstyn* opinion finally had their answer. He was not, as some had speculated (and as London had argued), waiting for a better case to overturn censorship; he meant that states should be able to censor provided they had well-drawn statutes. Thus the five-man majority denied that prior restraint of motion pictures contravened protected speech.[14]

The four who disagreed with the majority did so vehemently. Chief Justice Earl Warren dissented, joined by Black, Douglas, and Brennan. Whereas he had remained silent on the *Lady Chatterley's Lover* case two years earlier, Warren spoke up on *Times Film* because the case presented the clear-cut issue of prior restraint's constitutionality, with no extraneous issues. His dissent was nothing short of a polemic against censorship. Warren acknowledged that each communication method presented unique circumstances but argued that could not justify censorship of one and not the others. He described the majority opinion as a "full retreat" from the direction begun thirty years earlier in the *Near* decision, in which the Court had removed prior restraint from newspapers. Warren attached a lengthy recitation of what he called "astonishing" examples of censor board excisions over the years. Then he turned to the issue that would become the death knell of motion picture censorship four years later: the problem of delay inherent in any legal proceeding. That the film industry could avail itself of judicial recourse was no help, Warren wrote. "The delays in adjudication may well result in irreparable damage, both to the litigants and to the public." It had taken Times Film three years to get a decision. "This is the delay occasioned by the censor; this is the injury done to the free communication of ideas."[15]

Although the decision came with four dissenters, including the chief justice, even the most optimistic anticensorite saw this as a step backward. The majority had upheld the Chicago censor ordinance—the first time that the Supreme Court had ruled in favor of censorship since *Mutual* in 1915. Even though much scholarship after the Payne Fund's 1930 studies had roundly criticized the belief that movies carried a special capacity for evil, the Supreme Court was hanging on to the harmfulness concept.[16]

Bilgrey was sure that the decision meant nothing more than a rejection of the broad challenge. "We asked for too much," he said, "and if we asked for less, they would probably grant it."[17] Bilgrey was proven right in 1965, when Justice Brennan noted that *Times Film* did not uphold all governmental censorship, as it had been interpreted to do; it held only that prior restraint was "not necessarily unconstitutional under all circumstances."[18] But the important point is that *Times Film* did little to clear up the ambiguity that had existed for nine years. Industry officials and censorship advocates were troubled now, much as they had been almost fifty years earlier with *Mutual*, fearing that the decision could open the floodgates of censorship legislation.

Reaction to the decision came swiftly. The press indicated nearly complete agreement with Warren and the minority.[19] Crowther summed up the reaction of the industry and "liberal minded people in general" as shocked and disappointed, because previous Supreme Court decisions had led them to believe that the Court would declare censorship unconstitutional "the first chance it had." He worried that *Times Film* might "embolden and support the lurking forces that want to legislate more censorship."[20] Legal affairs columnist Anthony Lewis called the "regrettable" decision "a victory for censorship, and a big one."[21] And while in actuality all it did was to continue the *Burstyn* position that censorship was constitutional as long as the censor carried a heavy burden of proof, Lewis was right that the case would reinforce procensorship judges. Three years later, New York's highest court would use the *Times Film* precedent to help bolster its state censors in a major case.

So disturbing was this decision to other media that for the first time, the radio, television, and book industries—represented by the National Association of Broadcasters, the American Book Publishers Council, the American Society of Newspapers Editors, and the Authors League of America—joined the MPAA in a "mutual defense pact" to lobby for greater freedoms. The group's first action was to request a rehearing of the *Times Film* case.[22] Although the action was unsuccessful, Murray Schumach reported this merger of forces as a positive sign that the industry was at last ready to act on the First Amendment protections it had been given nearly nine years earlier in the *Burstyn* decision. He called the multimedia opposition to censorship "a new era" in the history of the film industry.[23]

Schumach was wrong. The newly formed media group generated lots of publicity but remained on the sidelines of the battle, allowing the independent distributors and exhibitors to carry the legal fight forward. The new era Schumach was hoping for came not from the new industry group but from Earl Warren's impassioned dissent. Within fifteen months, the highest courts of Oregon, Georgia, and Pennsylvania (for the second time) invalidated censorship statutes within their states, inspired by Warren.

Although it was not really doing much, the MPAA sought to enhance its reputation as a warrior against prior restraint. President Eric Johnston railed, "Wherever bills are introduced to impose censorship, we shall fight them. Wherever courts shall uphold Government censorship, we shall fight them. Wherever pressures shall be applied to censor motion pictures, we shall fight them."[24] The MPAA, which had not helped Joseph Burstyn and had refused to aid *La ronde* and *Lady Chatterley's Lover* because they were competitive foreign films, had, by the end of the 1950s, decided to fight film censorship, but still preferred to do so only on behalf of its own member studios' productions. The MPAA had allowed Times Film to fight the Chicago ordinance alone but then realized that it could not afford to ignore the damaging outcome. And so it began sending out anticensorship press releases and scheduling speakers. As Schumach noted, the organization left the "heavy fighting" against censorship to the independent distributors, but it could no longer choose only "clean battlegrounds."[25] Even so, it never wholeheartedly supported the anticensorship fight, despite its protestations to the contrary.[26]

Censors were elated at the news of *Times Film*. Vincent Nolan, Chicago's chief censor, hailed the Supreme Court's work as "a victory for movie censorship. . . . Now we can continue to protect the morals of the public."[27] The joy was short lived, though. While the innocuous *Don Juan* was challenging the Chicago censors, so too was the not so innocuous *The Lovers* (*Les amants*). Well reviewed in major newspapers and national magazines, *The Lovers* pushed the boundaries of acceptable content with its theme of extramarital sex, and distributor Zenith International Film was ready to push the boundaries of acceptable procedure. In federal district court, Zenith questioned the process by which the Chicago censors had denied the film an exhibition license. The Chicago ordinance authorized censorship only by the commissioner of police and allowed review only by the mayor, with no hearing or presentation of evidence. Since the commissioner could not personally view all films, he had created a film review board (whose members were usually patronage appointees). When a distributor appealed a denial, the police commissioner and the mayor reviewed only the offending portions of the film. Zenith argued that this process violated the *Roth* requirement that a work be judged in its entirety, and the U.S. Court of Appeals for the Seventh Circuit agreed.[28]

In response, the City of Chicago redrafted its censoring ordinance to create a motion picture appeal board to hear disputes from distributors. Each member of the appeal board was required to be "experienced or educated" in art, drama, literature, philosophy, psychology, history, music, science, or another related field.[29] The new arrangement worked for six years, until it was struck down in 1968.[30]

In Atlanta, the censors had been challenged by independent distributor K. Gordon Murray Productions for stopping *Room at the Top*. The Georgia Supreme Court agreed with the distributor that Atlanta's censor ordinance violated the state constitution's protection of free speech, but the chief judge was clearly unhappy about what he had to do. "As individual citizens, we hate to see the youth of this state . . . subjected to all the evil influence that obscene pictures might exert upon them. But as trusted judges we have no alternative." Atlanta revised its ordinance and in 1962 began classifying films.[31]

Avant-Garde Filmmaking and the "Anglo-Saxon Word"

Back in New York, restricted to censoring only for obscenity, it seemed inevitable that the state censors and film industry would clash over just what that term meant. As new motion picture division director Louis Pesce explained, "It is one thing to read Justice Brennan's definition with its 'dominant theme,' 'prurient interest,' and 'contemporary community standards,' and quite another thing to apply it. Take so-called 'nudist films' like *Garden of Eden*. I think they constitute a 'morbid preoccupation with nudity.' The contemporary community standard so far as public nudity is concerned is self-evident. We'd arrest someone who was nude in public. Yet, the courts overrule us on movies like this. They have made their so-called 'objective' definition very hard to interpret."[32]

When Pesce decided to interpret as obscene the word *shit*, the slang term for heroin, in *The Connection*, a 1961 film about drug addiction, Brind had to defend the state again. Here was another chance for the MPAA to help an independent distributor battle the New York censors.

Considering the film's subject matter and style, however, it is not surprising that the MPAA chose to pass on this one, too. *The Connection* was a gritty, unpleasantly realistic look at the life of eight dope addicts. It had been made and distributed by a group of independent New York filmmakers who called themselves the Connection Company.[33] The film's director, Shirley Clarke, was becoming a well-respected, creative talent.[34] *The Connection* and her next film, *The Cool World* (1962), have been called landmarks of the American new wave.[35] While Hollywood was reeling in the excesses of monumentally budgeted films like *Cleopatra*, some American filmmakers, influenced by the Italian neorealists, like Rossellini and de Sica, were rejecting big budgets and Panavision, replacing them with self-financed films shot with handheld cameras. Clarke was a founder of the movement that came to be known as the new American cinema, a group of twenty-three experimental filmmakers whose goal was to revolt against movie convention. "Who says a film has to cost a million dollars, and be safe and innocuous enough to satisfy every 12 year old in America?" Clarke asked in a 1962 interview. "I want to break away from the other conventions—the idea of heavy production, artificial lighting, all the slickness that plagues the movies. I want to just pick up a camera and go out and shoot the world as it really is."[36]

Clarke made *The Connection* from a hit off-Broadway play that had run for two years without any complaints. Her experimental style made the film look improvised and attracted critical attention, although not always critical approval. Critics from the *New York Post*, *Esquire*, and the *Saturday Review* praised *The Connection*.[37] Others, like Bosley Crowther, found it simply tedious. The film revolves around a group of addicts waiting for their connection to bring them narcotics. According to Crowther's review, "They mumble and rant in the direction of a mostly unseen cameraman who, with his director, has been admitted into the apartment to make an 'honest, human' documentary film. . . . The camera never leaves the bleak apartment. And while it does sweep about a good bit to generate a certain nervous tension under Shirley Clarke's bold direction, its confinement within the one chamber makes for visual monotony." Crowther's overall assessment: "It is deadly monotonous, in addition to being sordid and disagreeable. The actors perform with candor and a brutal clarity, but after a very few minutes of ranting, they've said all they have to say."[38]

For their part, the censors of New York merely found the film's repeated use of the word *shit* unacceptable, and they notified the Connection Company that the film would not be licensed because it was obscene.

The film was screened by the regents in December 1961 and was represented by censor nemesis Ephraim London. Having forced the state to stop censoring for anything but obscenity, he was back before the regents again, this time arguing that the board's interpretation of *obscenity* was wrong. He argued that the state's objection to the word *shit* made no sense because it had not been used in an obscene way and because the same word could freely be published. In response, the regents offered the time-honored argument that film was different from other modes of communication. They also claimed that *shit* was "an obscene term recognized as such universally."[39]

The appellate division heard arguments on *The Connection* in the early summer of 1962. Once again, London argued that the license fee was a tax. He had used this same argument unsuccessfully before, but he was smart to revisit it now. Just a year earlier, the Pennsylvania Supreme Court had agreed that such a license fee was indeed a tax on the right of communication.[40] But because the New York legislature had recently reduced the motion picture license fees, the court was not interested.[41] London argued again that the censors and the regents had erred in applying the standard *obscene* to the use of the word *shit*. The word had been "accepted in English literature since the Fourteenth Century," London argued, and "no legal justification exists for suppression of a film because of its use."[42] Because of the *Roth* decision five years earlier and a recent court of appeals decision, the judges were bound to find as obscene only "the grossly sexual and the lascivious."[43] He concluded with a threat: if the picture was not licensed, it would be exhibited without a license as a "'calculated act of civil disobedience' to test the constitutionality of the state film-licensing law."[44]

The state claimed that use of the word *shit* twenty-eight times in the course of the film offended community standards and made the film "obscene in part."[45] Brind's argument was surprisingly loose. He noted that the Supreme Court had fixed the standard of obscenity as that which appealed to the prurient interest of the general public. "It is our view," he said, "that the term obscenity not only includes sex obscenity, but also other types of obscenity—acts of excretion. We think, without question, that the use of the language in this picture is lewd and obscene and intended to be lewd and said for the purpose of producing lewdness and obscenity."[46] Pesce pointed out that newspapers carrying stories about the controversy went to great lengths to avoid using the word *shit*. The *New York Times* referred to it as "an Anglo Saxon word."[47] Surely, the censors argued, such euphemistic lengths constituted recognition that the word offended community standards.

Once again, however, the appellate division rebuked the regents unanimously, the fourth time since it began reversing the censors in 1953. The very brief decision maintained only three points: that the word *shit* as used in *The Connection* was, at most, vulgar, but certainly not obscene; that the licensing fee, since it had recently been statutorily lowered, constituted not much of an issue; and that the Court would continue to assume the constitutionality of the censorship statute.[48]

London announced that, absent an appeal to the court of appeals by the regents, *The Connection* would open for New York viewers as soon as a theater could be booked. When the regents did announce their appeal, London put into action the advice offered to Times Film by Frankfurter. London announced to the press that *The Connection* would open at New York's D. W. Griffith Theater without a New York State license, making good on his threat before the appellate division to show the film as an act of civil disobedience. "We are convinced," London said, "that the film censors are misapplying the law, which has never been tested in this way, and this affords us a great opportunity to prove it."[49]

The Connection played as promised, but for only two showings for 560 viewers before being stopped by court order. When the theater manager, an arch opponent of censorship, heard about the court order, he locked the projection booth. Pesce arrived to seize the film personally but had to wait fifteen minutes for the door to be unlocked. In the meantime, Ephraim London spoke to reporters and photographers in the theater's lobby. "The picture does not incite lust or pruriency," he said. "There is one woman in the picture and she is 60 years old or more." John Jehu of the regents' legal division told the *New York Herald Tribune* that it was all "a newspaper stunt,"[50] which it undoubtedly was. But London was smart enough to realize that the time was right to bring the anticensorship message out of the courtroom and onto the front page, if he could.

Bosley Crowther had hustled in to see the film before it could be shut down. He was not impressed. His review the next day was liberally sprinkled with words like *repulsive*, *sleazy*, and *sordid*. "As for that controversial language, it scarcely seems out of place or, indeed, any more offensive than anything else in this drab film."[51]

London once again used the press to complain that the board of regents was avoiding the constitutional issue that he had placed in its lap. Clearly, London had hoped for an arrest and criminal prosecution that could have been used to test the New York statute. But the regents were ahead of London on this one and had used the injunctive process instead to avoid any possibility of a jury trial.[52] At the state supreme court hearing on the matter, Justice Kenneth MacAffer made the temporary injunction permanent.[53]

The Connection Company and London had made a valiant attempt to challenge the statute head-on, but the regents stepped aside. They were convinced that London was grandstanding for the press to increase the box office take when the film did open.[54] An injunction rather than criminal charges lessened the amount of publicity London could grab. Also, since a New York State injunction meant a hearing before the court of appeals and not the more liberal appellate division, *The Connection* would come up against the judges who had ruled in the censors' favor three of the last four times.

Despite the injunction, a few hundred more people got to see *The Connection* a week before it reached the court of appeals. London arranged a noncommercial showing at a Greenwich Village church to underscore the "absurdity" of the censoring statute, which allowed review only of films shown commercially.[55] His point was that any film that might harm morality could be publicly exhibited provided that the audience to be thus corrupted saw it for free. If nothing else, London was doing an excellent job of keeping the *Connection* controversy before the public.

When *The Connection* finally made it to the court of appeals, London asked the court to void what was left of New York's censorship statute. He argued again that *The Connection*'s use of the word *shit* should not be construed as obscene, the only statutory standard still left; that the license fee was a tax; and that the entire stature was unconstitutional. Brind told the court that it must not substitute its judgment for that of the censor board and left the constitutional questions unrebutted after Chief Judge Conway intimated that the court might not even consider those issues.[56]

Only one week went by before the court of appeals ruled *The Connection* not obscene. And as Conway had hinted it would, the court upheld the earlier appellate division ruling without opinion, deferring the constitutional issues. So now, without knowing why, New York's censors found their last remaining constitutionally acceptable standard judicially narrowed. With only the opinion of the appellate division to go by, the motion picture division now had only the following guidance: first, that the film the division had branded obscene was not; second, that the fee versus tax issue was no longer a concern; and third, that the censorship law remained constitutional in the eyes of the state's highest court. But Brind advised the censors that he believed the decision went further. Since the court of appeals had overruled the censors' determination that the word *shit* was obscene, no word could be censored except when part of pornographic descriptions that appealed to prurient interests.[57] Even the Anglo-Saxon word for copulation could no longer be censored, provided it was used in a nonerotic fashion, according to Pesce.[58] The handwriting on this wall clearly spelled out pornography as the only acceptable censoring standard.

Intrigues of the Dormitory

In the midst of the controversy over *The Connection*, another film was challenging the censors' determination of obscenity, *Twilight Girls* (1957). The film, yet another French production, dealt with schoolgirls and hinted at homosexual experimentation. Its American distributor, Radley Metzger of Audubon Films, later well known as the director of stylish, erotic films as well as some hardcore pornography in the 1970s, claimed that *Twilight Girls* was about the typical "intrigues of the dormitory" that are "natural and can be expected from girls of their age who are on their journey to womanhood."[59] *Twilight Girls* played in twenty states, but New York rejected the film in 1962 under its one remaining standard of obscenity. Although the Production Code now accepted tactful depictions of homosexuality, *Twilight Girls* would probably not have received a code seal. Metzger was more than just the distributor of this film; he was also an editor and director. He had cut some scenes, then filmed others and added them to increase the film's titillation potential using an actress who was listed under the pseudonym Georgina Spelvin. The final American version in Metzger's possession made explicit what the original French version had suggested. Just how explicit, though, became something for the regents to decide.

Both sides offered up the usual arguments at the regents' review in February 1962. Audubon Films argued that the statute was unconstitutional under the First and Fourteenth amendments and that it was void for vagueness. Parts of the film had been censored, violating the *Roth* requirement that creative works be analyzed for their overall message. The dominant theme, it argued, did not appeal to the prurient interest. In his response before the regents, Pesce countered that scenes of nudity and the "erotic embraces (that) stress undressing and breast exposure 'appeal strongly to the prurient interest.'" The regents agreed with Audubon that the lesbianism alone could not preclude the exhibition of the film. They did find, however, that the manner of presentation in the film was prurient.[60]

More than two years after *Twilight Girls* applied, in 1964, the appellate division handed down a very brief answer to the controversy. For the fifth time in a row, it overturned the regents. Citing only *Kingsley* and *Excelsior*, the per curiam opinion simply found the film nonobscene because it did not appeal to the prurient interest.[61] One month later, the court of appeals declined to hear the case. *Twilight Girls* was licensed; the censors had lost again.

The high courts of four censoring states had thrown their censors onto the unemployment line, but the U.S. Supreme Court continued its obfuscation—offering to hear cases but then refusing to make any definitive pronouncement. So censors in New York, Maryland, Virginia, and Kansas went on, their wings clipped but still able to snip obscenity. Louis Pesce in New York blamed not the courts but his own state legislature for failing to keep up with the times and provide the censors with a workable statute. Like his predecessor, Hugh Flick, Pesce was more worried about violence than sexual content, and he wanted to free all adult movies from prior restraint while censoring films to be shown to children. "The law is not strict enough," he told an interviewer in 1963. "We should be more concerned with the children of the nation."[62] But the legislature did not listen to its chief censor and did not amend its law. Prior restraint for all movies went on, entering its fifth decade.

But the United States was now changing rapidly. American forces were becoming more deeply involved in the conflict in Vietnam. The civil rights movement had grown more deadly with the murder of three civil rights workers in Mississippi. The Warren Commission was trying to soothe ragged nerves after the assassination of President Kennedy. In the cultural arena, millions of young American girls were losing their hearts to the Beatles, and Bob Dylan's protest songs were becoming hugely popular among those under twenty-five. Changing tastes and sensibilities in motion pictures were clear: the 1964 Academy Award for best picture went to the sexually charged *Tom Jones*. Attacks on cultural norms seemed to be everywhere. Soon an enterprising exhibitor in Maryland, a product of these rapidly changing times, would step up to challenge prior restraint. The next film censorship case at the Supreme Court belonged to Ronald Freedman.

11

Fight for Freedom of the Screen, 1962–1965

While New York wrestled with *The Connection* and *Twilight Girls*, Maryland was having its own problems. In November 1962, Baltimore theater owner Ronald Freedman and the brazenly anticensorship Times Film Corporation decided to flout Maryland's law by exhibiting *Revenge at Daybreak* without a license. Freedman had spent much of his career as an exhibitor doing whatever he could to make life difficult for the Maryland censors. He frequently restored excised scenes from films before showing them in his theater, and the board knew it.[1] Like the other independents who fought censorship, Freedman did not intend to become a crusader for anything except, perhaps, avant-garde films. But the interference of censorship, just when many Americans were beginning to experiment with greater societal freedoms, incited Freedman to become a free speech advocate.

Freedman had bought the Rex Theater in 1961, intending to create Baltimore's first "art film" house, showing classic and unusual films. But when he discovered that a sexploitation film called *The Immoral Mr. Teas* (1959) was playing to full houses every night in nearby Washington DC, he decided to look into this new genre.[2] *Mr. Teas* was the first "nudie" to gain mainstream theater distribution without the inclusion of a preachment preamble or doom-and-gloom conclusion (or "square up").[3] Freedman knew an opportunity when he saw one, and he moved to cash in on the burgeoning exploitation film market—and ran afoul of the Maryland censors. Freedman bristled under the censor requirements, particularly because every time the administration changed in Annapolis, the new governor appointed a new chief censor, leaving distributors and exhibitors with little clue as to how the Maryland law would be enforced. Since Freedman was trying to show films with titillating titles like *White Slaves of Chinatown* and *Scanty Panties*, he needed some idea of what might bother the censors. He quickly decided to confront the Maryland censor board, and he became "dedicated and idealistic . . . full of pep and vinegar and very excited about what I was doing." He believed in what he did. "For me, it was a severe battle."[4]

Smarting from its disastrous try at the Supreme Court the year before, Times Film offered Freedman its support. It decided to use a film that even the most conservative censor would approve: *Revenge at Daybreak*, a ten-year-old French film set during the Irish rebellion of 1916. It tells the story of a young woman whose brother is killed by the Irish Republican Army. Vowing to find and murder his killer, the sister becomes drawn into the revolutionary struggle and falls in love with another rebel, only to learn later that he is her brother's murderer. Remaining true to her brother's memory, she carries out her sworn revenge and kills her lover.[5] This film would have no censorship history if it had not been chosen by Ronald Freedman and Times Film as their legal ax against the Maryland censor board.

Freedman showed *Revenge* in November 1962 without a license and was promptly arrested—exactly what he and Times Film wanted. (It was what London had hoped for, too, but did not get, when he exhibited the unlicensed *The Connection* in New York the year before.) Times Film had considerable experience at this sort of thing, having tackled the Chicago censor board twice, winning one case in 1957 and famously losing the other in 1961. According to Edward de Grazia and Roger Newman, Times Film's 1961 loss made the company more determined to fight.[6] Its attorney, Felix Bilgrey, had listened carefully when Supreme Court justices Clark and Frankfurter advised him that he might have prevailed had *Don Juan* been exhibited without a license. So here Bilgrey was, a year later, ready to take on the Maryland censor board in exactly the manner that the justices had suggested: by exhibiting an unlicensed film, a tactic recognized by Maryland's attorney general as a "Trojan horse."[7]

Changes in the Supreme Court's composition seemed promising for the anticensorites. Justices Whittaker and Frankfurter had retired, replaced by the "liberal" Arthur Goldberg and the "usually liberal" Byron White.[8] Not only were two of the *Times Film* 1961 majority group gone, but the four in the anticensorship minority were still on the Court. Some legal commentators guessed that the new Court might reverse the *Times Film* decision if the issue was again brought before it.[9]

Although the judicial balance seemed more encouraging and Freedman's case contained the right elements for a good test (it went straight to the constitutionality of Maryland's statute), the ACLU rebuffed Freedman's request for assistance. "They didn't like the type of movies I was showing," he remarked. True, *Revenge at Daybreak* was nonobscene, but perhaps it was the identity of the plaintiff himself that mattered to the ACLU, as it did to other cause litigators. The NAACP's experiences fighting school segregation proved how important it was to select a perfect plaintiff—one who was earnest, upright, modest, and law abiding—so the cause would appear just and proper. Freedman, an exhibitor of somewhat dubious, off-color films, did not have the sparkling clean image that the ACLU would assuredly have preferred for a censorship test case. The ACLU told Freedman, he said, that it "had bigger fish to fry."[10] Finally, when the case reached the Supreme Court two years later, the ACLU would file an amicus, but, according to Freedman, it did little else. Regardless of the plaintiff's identity, filing late in a case's progress through the court system was far more typical of the ACLU's methods than guiding a case from beginning to end, given that it had limited resources and many fish to fry in other areas of civil liberties litigation.[11]

Freedman and his attorneys had inconsistent support from the MPAA as well. At the state's court of appeals, Freedman had an amicus brief from the association, but it dropped its assistance when the case went to the Supreme Court. According to industry insider Murray Schumach, the MPAA was experiencing a "difference of opinion" over whether to become involved with Freedman's test case, since the group's last support effort in a Times Film case had turned out disastrously.[12]

But Freedman was "a man with a cause." The day he was arrested, he instructed his staff to re-sign the theater marquee to read "Fight for Freedom of the Screen."[13] In his attorney, Richard Whiteford, Freedman found a philosophical soul mate. Just as Ephraim London had tried many of the New York cases, Whiteford tried most of Maryland's. The two men set off to pursue a case that Felix Bilgrey thought the "opportunity of a lifetime."[14] He was right: this would turn out to be the big case in the razing of governmental film censorship.

A Stranger Knocks on the Supreme Court's Door

While Freedman worked his way up the courts of Maryland, back in New York another case was coming up through the court system on its way to the U.S. Supreme Court. The case concerned a prize-winning Danish film, *A Stranger Knocks*. After a yearlong struggle with U.S. Customs officials, which resulted in a single, forty-second cut, the film had begun playing to satisfied crowds in Washington DC and many other U.S. cities. *Variety* reviewed it as "a brooding, explosive and superbly fabricated Danish film" with "only one obvious flaw: it simply is too explicit for exhibition in the U.S."[15]

Independent distributor Trans-Lux had secured the American rights for *A Stranger Knocks* in 1963. Unlike the other independent distributors described in this book, who existed from film to film, Trans-Lux owned a chain of theaters that provided a steady cash flow. Owned by an arch anticensorite who was concerned that the American screen was not free, Trans-Lux under Richard Brandt began importing fine foreign films in the early 1950s. One of Brandt's first was Federico Fellini's first masterpiece, *La strada*, which won the Academy Award for best foreign film in 1957. When Brandt saw *A Stranger Knocks* at the San Francisco film festival in 1963, he bought the American rights.[16]

Notified that New York censors would require two eliminations, Brandt reported to *Variety* that he had no intention of making any further cuts and would fight all the way to the Supreme Court, if necessary. These words were not mere posturing. His refusal to cut anything from the film for the New York censors was "characteristic," according to Michael Mayer. Ten years earlier, Brandt had told *Variety*, "I don't think there should be a Code. I think motion pictures, like the press, should be free of censorship of any kind."[17]

A Stranger Knocks provided many of the principal elements of the censorship controversy. Not only did it make an important test case at the time, but it also sheds significant light on the battle over censorship. A remake of the Cain and Abel story, the film begins with a biblical quotation: "And the Lord set his mark upon Cain lest any finding him should kill him. Therefore whosoever slayeth Cain, vengeance shall be taken from him sevenfold." The story (coincidentally similar to that of *Revenge at Daybreak*) takes place in Denmark just after the end of World War II, when a fugitive approaches an isolated cottage by the North Sea. A solemn young woman lets him in and allows him to sleep by her fire. The fugitive recognizes that the desolation of the cottage and the loneliness of the woman are an excellent setup, and he determines to win her over. They become lovers, and the lonely young woman begins to blossom in the warmth of the new relationship. Slowly, she tells him her story. Her husband, who was in the resistance movement during the war, was tortured and murdered by Nazi collaborators. His captor, we learn from her account, had a large scar on the underside of his right arm. Here the viewer recognizes the Cain and Abel story: the scar on the man's arm is the mark of Cain and the audience's clue that the fugitive is the husband's torturer. The young woman does not see the scar, however, until what *Variety* called one "utterly shocking scene." *Time*'s reviewer noted, "In a scene that is bizarre, to say the least, the heroine discovers the criminal identity of her lover at the erotic climax of their affair. Her scream is a scream of horror—but also a scream of ecstasy."[18] For the last twenty-five minutes of the film, she psychologically plays with him, and then fatally shoots him as he tries to escape. True to the Cain and Abel story, "There can be no doubt that the woman, having erased the stain of the man by killing him, bears within herself the greater guilt of the murder." Noting the film's excellent acting, direction, camerawork, and music, *Variety* concluded that it was a "highly moral film—but the candor of its two seduction scenes makes France's 'The Lovers' seem like a Disney family special. Unfortunately, these two scenes . . . are indispensable to the film's dramatic integrity."[19] Bosley Crowther agreed, calling the movie "a frank and artful realization of the manner in which the urges of the body may be strangled by the tortures of the mind. . . . Anyone who goes to see it expecting to be cheaply entertained is going to find himself looking sadly at a mature and deeply poignant glimpse of life."[20]

In refusing to license *A Stranger Knocks* on the basis of the scenes mentioned above, New York's censors violated the *Roth* requirement that a work be judged as a whole and that obscenity not be charged against a work of artistic integrity. But differing viewpoints about *Stranger* reflect the fuzziness of obscenity law in the mid-1960s. On one hand, the censors found it highly objectionable for its graphic depiction of a man and woman engaged in intercourse (something to which many Americans at the time would probably also have objected). On the other hand, the film had artistic merit, and the scene was integral to the plot. Both sides in the *Stranger* controversy had good, legally sound arguments. The *Roth* decision protected material that had "the slightest redeeming social importance" but allowed the censoring of material that appealed to the prurient interest as defined by contemporary community standards. So even though counsel could argue that *Stranger* had much more than the slightest redeeming social importance, the motion picture division and the regents could claim that it appealed to the prurient interest. The term *ob-*

scene remained defined as "having a tendency to excite lustful thoughts." The censors could argue that scenes of the heroine unmistakably reaching orgasm might be classified as prurient. More important, if the two scenes were integral to the plot, it could be argued that the entire work appealed to the prurient interest and thus could properly be censored.

At the appellate division in November 1963, Trans-Lux's attorney, Harry Rand, recited the usual arguments and added one not heard since *Ecstasy* twenty-seven years earlier—that release by U.S. Customs pre-empted any action by New York. Rand argued that the state statute must "give way" to the federal. The state countered that the censoring done by customs was part of a tax act and was, therefore, not applicable. By this time, Brind had stopped trying to hide his weariness with these film cases. "So many cases have gone through the mill," he wrote, "that I feel that I can add nothing to the Court's grasp of the situation." He reminded the justices about *Times Film v. Chicago*: obscenity was still censorable and no absolute privilege stood against prior restraint.[21]

At oral argument, though, he found a new angle. He told the justices that *Stranger* was the first film in the motion picture division's history that depicted "not only sexual intercourse but also a woman having an orgasm. . . . The cameras are held on this woman for a long period of time." Even *Lady Chatterley's Lover*, with its nudes in bed, had not shown the act of intercourse. "This time," Brind continued, "the line of demarcation has been reached." Intentionally disparaging foreign films, he told the justices that he had just come back from Copenhagen, where he had seen bookstores full of "dirty" books. "Perhaps Copenhagen has a different philosophy than we have."[22]

The justices watched the film and retired to consider their decision. In the meantime, anticensorites were monitoring the progress of two other cases. In Maryland, Freedman had been convicted in the criminal court of Baltimore and was awaiting his appearance before the Maryland court of appeals. In Ohio, an obscenity case concerning exhibition of the French film *The Lovers* was moving even more slowly than Freedman's. After oral arguments in March 1963, the Supreme Court ordered that case (*Jacobellis v. Ohio*) reargued, but it was not heard again until April 1964.

The first judicial pronouncement as to the obscenity of *A Stranger Knocks* came in November 1963 in a very brief opinion. The New York appellate division reported that it was compelled to contradict the censors because the sexual acts were an "integral part of the play." The justices thought they had no choice but to rule in favor of the film in light of recent high court rulings. *Stranger* was, after all, a serious dramatic work with significant artistic merit.[23] So, for the sixth time since 1953, the appellate division ruled against the censors, but this time the justices failed to do so unanimously. For those who had been raised on the restrained and sanitized Hollywood films of the Production Code era, such sexually explicit filmic representation was probably shocking. Even Arthur Mayer, who submitted a lengthy affidavit for the plaintiffs, admitted that the film explored "the close intimacy between a man and a woman, in sexual terms."[24]

Trans-Lux had won. Rand's next step, of course, was to seek a license for his client's film, but that proved to be no easy task. After a lengthy delay, he demanded that the license be issued; the motion picture division, however, did nothing. After several weeks, the regents requested a stay from the appellate division. The court declined. Then after further delay, the regents requested a stay from the court of appeals, which agreed. Even though Trans-Lux had won at the appellate division, Rand had to present his case again to the court of appeals. If ever there was a good case against the delay inherent in prior restraint, this was it. Oral arguments were set for January 1964. Rand and Brandt could not have been pleased about the holdup and expense of another court round: moreover, the court of appeals bench still looked unfriendly to censorship challenges. Desmond and Burke, two of the four procensorship judges, were still sitting, and another conservative Catholic, John F. Scileppi, had been added to the court. If just one more judge joined their position, *Stranger* could lose.

Rand asked the court of appeals to apply to films the same standard that it had applied to magazines just the session before in the *Richmond County News* case—that only hardcore pornography could be curbed. Rand's most persuasive argument, though, came directly from the controlling case in all obscenity challenges, *Roth*. That *sex* and *obscenity* were not synonymous, he argued, was case law, and the judges had before them a perfect example in *A Stranger Knocks*. The sexual relationship was intrinsic to the plot; it advanced characterization and explained motivation. Rand then drove home the point that would eventually overturn film censorship as it had been carried on for four decades: the true costs to film distributors caused by the delay inherent in prior restraint statutes. *A Stranger Knocks* had first requested licensing, he noted, in March 1963. Its appeal to the board of regents was completed in May, but it took the board seven more weeks to render its decision. It was then another five months before the appellate division delivered its opinion that the film was licensable. For another three weeks, the board neither issued a license nor requested a stay. Rand pointed out that Trans-Lux had been unable to show the film for ten months even though the only judicial determination had been that the film was constitutionally protected speech.[25]

Brind was clearly frustrated by the courts' piecemeal removal of censorable themes. Even the charge of obscenity was now under question. "We submit that if this film can be shown, the statement of the Courts relative to regulation of obscenity [*Times Film*] becomes a nullity and the licensing statute for films completely meaningless."[26]

At oral argument, Rand pointed out that the regents' position conflicted with both U.S. Supreme Court decisions and the court of appeals' own recent *Richmond County News* opinion. When Chief Judge Desmond suggested that film was different because of its greater emotional impact, Rand countered that the appellate division had found this film's sex scenes to be integral to the work as a whole. Brind objected to the length of the orgasm scene and the woman's "gyrations." "No man or woman could view these scenes . . . without being sexually stimulated," Brind claimed. Rand did not disagree, but he insisted the Supreme Court had defined *prurient interest* as a "shameful, morbid feeling toward sex," not something that was merely titillating. He insisted that the scenes could not be construed as prurient.[27]

Obscene Scenes

Rand failed to carry the day. The court of appeals split four to three in favor of the regents. In his opinion, Judge Burke (joined by Desmond, Scileppi, and another new judge) ruminated over the distinctions between conduct and speech and the relation of both to the First Amendment. Burke summarily dismissed the *Lady Chatterley's Lover* decision as any sort of precedent because *Stranger* involved not the presentation of an idea but action. And the action was, he said, "just as subject to State prohibition as similar conduct if engaged on the street." Finding that the film represented conduct and not speech left Burke free to dismiss any applicability of *Roth*. So whether the scenes were necessary to the plot made no difference to the court of appeals majority. If *Roth* was applicable to film (a question that would not be answered in *Jacobellis v. Ohio* for another three months), then the grossest type of pornography could be inserted into an otherwise acceptable film and judges would be helpless to act.[28]

In a concurring opinion, Chief Judge Desmond worried that upholding the appellate division on *Stranger* would allow the presentation of a sexual act on stage or screen as constitutionally protected speech. Release of this film, he thought, could pave the way for portrayal of such acts on television. Further, Desmond held, the Supreme Court's *Roth* test did not apply to either stage or screen. "It is unthinkable," he continued, "that a civilized community would permit actors to simulate sexual acts in a play or movie just because the play or movie is said by some critic or other to be an artistic work." A separate concurring opinion by Judge Scileppi went even further, pushing film's progress against censorship back by insisting that any filmic obscenity be judged by the same standards as still photography. Such a position denigrated film as an art form encompassing movement, sound, and the effect of change on the viewer. Just the year before, Scileppi had written the opinion banning Henry Miller's *Tropic of Cancer* from New York bookstores as "dirt for dirt's sake" (the book had been released by courts in Massachusetts and California, and Scileppi's opinion was later overruled by the U.S. Supreme Court). From these opinions, it is clear that the New York State Court of Appeals, with a strong Catholic presence, was clearly more conservative in matters of public exposure than both its counterparts in the other censoring states and its own appellate division.[29]

While each member of the majority agreed that the state could prevent filmic portrayals of acts that were illegal in public, none considered the prior restraint issue beyond a mere mention of the *Times Film* precedent. None answered Rand's contention that the mechanism of prior restraint had caused lengthy delays. New York's highest court ignored years of litigation pounding away on the unconstitutionality of prior restraint on film and pushed the art of film back to the level of photographic pornography.

Dye, Fuld, and Van Voorhis—the usual anticensorship judges—dissented, but none presented an opinion. Perhaps they were growing tired of the "vitriolic" mail that often followed their decisions favoring free speech. After the *Richmond County News* case the year before, one anonymous writer encouraged Fuld to reconsider for the sake of his own soul before making any other free speech decisions. Another wondered if "the children in years to come [will] curse you from the bottom of their smutty minds." Still another wrote, "When the cesspool of obscene literature rises above the floodmark and comes rushing in to cover the city, I hope you are the first to drown."[30]

Trans-Lux had lost at the state's highest court. By approving the removal of purportedly obscene scenes from films, the court of appeals had refused to follow the U.S. Supreme Court's trend of expanding the area of constitutionally protected speech. Whereas a book had to be considered as a whole, a film's scenes could still be considered separately in New York. If this decision, coming from one of the most powerful and respected courts in the nation, were to stand, the cause of the anticensorites would take a staggering blow. Several federal court decisions had suggested a *Roth*-based test that films be examined in their entirety, but the New York State Court of Appeals majority had neatly dodged the issue by construing film scenes as conduct rather than speech.[31]

Anticensorites did not have long to fret, though. Just three months later, the U.S. Supreme Court handed down its decision in *Jacobellis v. Ohio*, which overruled New York's scene-by-scene *Trans-Lux* censorship. *Jacobellis* had been of major interest for beleaguered exhibitors. As the PCA's influence began to decline in the mid-1950s and as state censor boards were gradually shorn of their authority over film, local activists had begun pushing for antiobscenity ordinances (which rapidly appeared in both the former licensing states and those that had never had licensing). These statutes were used to target exhibitors, vulnerable again after losing the veil of protection that came with unrestricted governmental licensing. One such theater manager was Nico Jacobellis, arrested in 1959 for showing *The Lovers*. Jacobellis's situation exemplifies the extreme local pressure starting to creep back in as judges struck down state censorship ordinances (in this case, Ohio's). A recent immigrant to the United States, Jacobellis managed a small, tasteful art house in Cleveland Heights. After his arrest for showing *The Lovers*, he was harassed constantly, even threatened with deportation by his local church. Phone calls in the middle of the night, intimidating letters, unsolicited tradesmen knocking at his door all day, police searches of his home, front-page publicity in the local newspaper, a lengthy judicial process—these were the types of intimidation exhibitors could face.[32]

Fortunately for Jacobellis, who lost both rounds in the Ohio state courts, Ephraim London, the ACLU, and the Ohio Civil Liberties Union came to his aid for the Supreme Court appeal. When that court finally spoke on the issue more than four years after his highly public arrest, Jacobellis's conviction was overturned. Film obscenity, the justices insisted, had to be judged by the same standards used against other media. To be obscene, a film had to lack artistic value, exceed the customary limits of candor, and appeal to an average person's prurient interest when viewed in its entirety by standards of the national community. The Court had finally clarified some of its considerable ambiguity on film censorship: the *Roth* standards, now defined as those of the *national* community, applied to motion picture obscenity allegations. Those allegations now had to be based on an appeal to prurient interest of the overall film, not just isolated sections.[33] So the Supreme Court's ruling in *Jacobellis* and the New York State Court of Appeals' ruling in *Stranger* were completely contradictory. That the Supreme Court, in *Jacobellis*, had also ruled nonobscene a section in *The Lovers* that showed a woman's face during orgasm was not a good sign for the New York censors' case against *A Stranger Knocks*.

Considering Richard Brandt's visceral reaction to New York's censorship statute before the court of appeals decision, no one should have been surprised by his intention to seek review for *Stranger* by the U.S. Supreme Court. He would bring the case to the highest court, he told reporters, "as a protest against recurrent lower court rulings that nibble away at liberties in all fields of the arts."[34] Yet even though Brandt, as a respected businessman, was a good test case litigant, and even though the *Trans-Lux* decision would have been damaging to the industry and to free speech if not explicitly overruled by the Supreme Court, and even though the case seemed assured of overturn in light of *Jacobellis*, Brandt and Trans-Lux went on to the Supreme Court without help from either the MPAA or the NYCLU.[35]

By the time *Trans-Lux* came before U.S. Supreme Court, *Jacobellis* provided an important precedent. And by the time *Trans-Lux* was decided, Freedman's case from Maryland would make the whole issue of filmic obscenity in New York State moot.

The Armageddon of Motion Picture Censorship

Meanwhile, in Maryland, Freedman was waiting for the state court of appeals. Haunted by his failure in the *Times Film* case, Bilgrey needed to prove that this case was different. And there was a significant difference: although neither *Don Juan* nor *Revenge at Daybreak* had been submitted for review, *Don Juan* was never exhibited, whereas *Revenge at Daybreak* was. Bilgrey desperately hoped to disentangle *Revenge at Daybreak* from the specter of *Don Juan* and its disastrous progeny, the *Times Film* precedent. So Freedman went back to the old tactic of questioning not only the process of censoring but also the standards and their application.[36]

The MPAA joined Freedman, but its only new contribution was to attack the statute, which contained so many struck-down standards that the MPAA argued it had to be unconstitutional as a whole.[37]

Ignoring the constitutional arguments and Bilgrey's attempt to force a constitutional pronouncement, the Maryland court of appeals followed the narrower route it had been given: it accepted the state's claim that since Freedman had not submitted the film for licensing, he was able to question the constitutionality only of that part of the statute that required submission, not any of the rest of the statute. And in spite of Bilgrey's impassioned plea to ignore *Times Film*, the Maryland court of appeals specifically cited it as precedent supporting the belief that licensing statutes were not, in themselves, unconstitutional. And so Freedman, after a fourteen-month delay, had finally had his hearing before the state's highest court, where his constitutional questions were summarily dismissed.[38] But he also had ample grounds for reversal by the Supreme Court. Whether he had standing to bring suit on constitutionality issues was certainly open to interpretation, as was the issue of whether *Times Film* properly applied as precedent to Freedman's case.

When Freedman's appeal to the U.S. Supreme Court was granted, the Maryland chapter of the ACLU took notice and filed an amicus brief to bolster Bilgrey's arguments. Bilgrey was arguing that the required submission of films served no valid governmental purpose. Indeed, he argued, it served two invalid purposes: the taxing of free expression and the right to delay. Building on these points, Freedman asked the Court to consider a cost-benefit analysis of film censorship. Since the Maryland censors in recent years had licensed, without cuts, 99.5 percent of all the pictures that had paid the fee, the state's take of $66,000 annually to protect its citizens from one-half of 1 percent of the industry's output was a "gross imposition" for "a microcosmic end."[39]

On the other side, Maryland asked the Court not to be fooled: the case presented was not Ronald Freedman's but actually Times Film's "second round." The state asked the Court not to throw out *Times Film*, claiming that Freedman's case was nothing more than a ruse. Then the state took advantage of Freedman's less than squeaky clean résumé, trying to separate him from those who sincerely labored for film freedom. "Those who hang on the pornographic periphery of the motion picture business," the state's argument ran, "have no communality with those whose confrontations with government have previously established constitutional benchmarks along the survey line of free speech." Without conceding that Freedman had standing to challenge the statute (since he had not submitted his film for review), the brief dismissed the argument that Maryland's statute was constitutionally defective, claiming that it conformed to *Roth* and that most films were not delayed by censorship since they were almost always processed within forty-eight hours. The length of time consumed by judicial review, however, they conveniently overlooked.

Censorship Takes a Left Hook and a Right Upper Cut

Like 1952 and 1953, 1965 was not a good year for censors. On March 1, the U.S. Supreme Court handed down a unanimous decision in favor of Freedman that transformed the course of governmental film censorship. "A left hook and right upper cut," Bosley Crowther called it,[40] but he could not call it a knockout, because the case did not rule prior restraint on film unconstitutional. It did, though, finally make good on the promise dangled before the film industry in the *Burstyn* case thirteen years earlier that the censors should bear the "heavy burden" of proving a film unworthy of exhibition, not the other way around (as it had been since the first censorship ordinance in 1907). The *Freedman* decision put teeth in *Burstyn*'s suggestion about reversing the burden of proof. *Freedman* set up procedural safeguards that kept state and municipal film censorship bodies from delaying exhibition licenses. No longer would they be able to keep a film from public view without first proving to a judge that it was harmful.

Justice Brennan wrote the opinion. Bowing to *Burstyn*, he noted that motion pictures might still be held to a different standard as speech, yet he also called upon the more recent *Bantam Books v. Sullivan*, which held that "any system of prior restraints of expression comes to this Court bearing a heavy presumption against its constitutional validity." Having examined Maryland's statute, Brennan found it lacking procedural safeguards that would minimize the impact of restriction on protected speech while it hunted down unprotected speech. Then Brennan disposed of Maryland's reliance on the *Times Film* precedent. "The only question tendered for decision in that case," he wrote, was "whether a prior restraint was necessarily unconstitutional under all circumstances." Freedman had presented quite a different issue than had Times Film. He suggested that the licensing procedure was invalid because it placed an undue restraint not only on obscenity but also on protected expression and because it placed time restraints on the communication of ideas. "Risk of delay is built into the Maryland procedure," Brennan concluded from the statute. He also worried that censors were, by their nature, far less responsive to free speech concerns than courts. He coupled that concern with the inevitable delay of censorship, especially when judicial review was necessary, and realized that such delay could have a chilling effect on the rights of those communicating protected speech. Recognizing the realities of the business of film distribution, Brennan understood that the stake in a single film might not be enough to make any protracted litigation worthwhile (or even possible). Since only four states and a few cities had active censoring bodies, any distributor would be wiser to take a film elsewhere than to wait for judicial review, which was inevitably lengthy. And so, Brennan argued, "The censor's determination may in practice be final." Accordingly, he insisted that the censor, within a "brief" period, either approve a license or institute legal proceedings to keep the film from exhibition. While Brennan did not mandate specific time periods, he suggested a single day for review and two days for judicial determination. He finished his opinion with the ambiguous warning that adjudication needed to be "considerably more prompt than has been the case under the Maryland statute."[41]

Despite the indefinite close, Brennan's opinion specified three new procedural requirements for anyone who would statutorily censor movies. First, film censors could no longer deny licenses. Henceforth, they would have to institute prompt legal proceedings demonstrating why a film could not be licensed, effectively reversing the backward burden of proof of film obscenity that had stood judicial scrutiny on all levels—local, state, and federal—since it was first questioned in 1909. Censors would have to prove that the film was expression unprotected by the Constitution. Second, they would have to do so promptly. And third, censors had no enforcement authority over a movie until a judicial decision had been made in their favor.

Douglas and Black attached a joint concurring opinion in which they noted that the three new procedural requirements effectively overturned the 1961 *Times Film* decision. Because the censorship ordinance in question in that case would not have met the new procedural requirements, it had to fall. But the majority opinion had not overturned *Times Film*, and therefore prior restraint could go on; it just had to move more quickly and provide legal proof that a film was unworthy. The *Freedman* decision, although it changed the burden of proof, was only another incremental step in the Court's progression of thinking about prior restraint on motion pictures.

Where *Times Film* had held that state and local governments could restrict the freedom to exhibit every picture, *Freedman* now laid out the procedural rules that would make such restriction of freedom conform to due process. As a contemporary legal scholar put it, "Even though prior restraint is not necessarily unconstitutional under all circumstances, it may be if due process is denied in the procedure used to effect the prior restraint. It is a very logical, yet novel, progression."[42]

With yet another loss for the censors at the Supreme Court, the post-*Burstyn* tally now stood at six for the challengers and one for the censors. Only obscenity could be held against a movie's exhibition, and it was difficult for censors to prove: since film had come under the First Amendment, lower courts had heard eighteen obscenity determinations of movies, all decided in favor of the distributors. The censors' losing streak on obscenity challenges was perfect.[43]

Along with shifting the burden of proof, the *Freedman* decision made lengthy waits for court decisions a thing of the past. Freedman had not succeeded in getting censorship declared unconstitutional, but the decades-long presumption that constitutionality existed so long as the banned film had recourse to judicial review—no matter how long that review took—had been recognized as innately unfair.

Stunned, Maryland's attorney general, Thomas J. Finan, called the case "the Armageddon of motion picture censorship."[44] In Maryland, jubilant exhibitor Robert Marhenke sent a telegram to the censor board: "Good Riddance. The unemployment line is just two blocks away. You may join it."[45]

Now Maryland, New York, Virginia, and Kansas, as well as Chicago, Ft. Worth, Providence, and Detroit, all had their censorship statutes overturned. Yet this was not because prior restraint on motion pictures had been found unconstitutional but because the statutes had not set adequate procedure. Although the Supreme Court had refused to acknowledge that prior restraint violated the First Amendment, several state and lower federal courts had already done so. Along with Ohio, Massachusetts, and Pennsylvania, Oregon and Georgia had declared local censorship ordinances in violation of their state constitutions. Perhaps the majority of Supreme Court justices believed that movies, with their potential for obscenity, needed to be reviewed prior to being seen by the public,[46] whereas state courts, closer to political currents (because many state judges were elected), realized that censorship's time was running out.

With film freedom still a legal question, it was clear that any governmental unit that continued to censor motion pictures needed to begin redrafting its legislation. Into this rapidly changing legal environment came another big decision from the U.S. Supreme Court: New York's *Trans-Lux* case. After reading the *Freedman* decision, both sides knew what the *Trans-Lux* decision would be. Two weeks later, the per curiam decision came down: citing only *Freedman*, it reversed the New York State Court of Appeals.[47] By basing the decision on only *Freedman*, the Court made clear that it had invalidated the method of New York's censoring apparatus. But by leaving out any mention of *Roth*, the Court indicated that it preferred not to rule on the obscenity issue presented by *A Stranger Knocks*. The Court also ignored the New York State Court of Appeals' determination that film scenes were conduct and not speech. Thus, rather than striking down prior restraint per se, both *Freedman* and *Trans-Lux* struck down what the Court saw as procedurally defective prior restraint.[48]

So within two weeks came two decisions that had each taken years of litigation, neither one entirely satisfying to its appellants. The people of New York State could see *A Stranger Knocks* and the people of Maryland could see *Revenge at Daybreak*, and the states could either give up or draft new statutes. But neither state censoring authority was ready to concede the game. The Maryland legislature passed a new statute to conform to the *Freedman* requirements within three days, and New York redrafted its regulations within one month.[49] But film censorship's days were numbered: even the ever-cautious MPAA advised its members not to bother submitting films to state censorship boards.[50] Pesce, however, reported that his New York office would "proceed just as before."[51]

12

Denouement, 1965–1981

The 1960s were not kind to movie censors and those who supported them. No other decade, with the possible exception of the 1920s, saw such radical social change. After World War II, those who valued self-reliance, hard work, and patriotism (the group most likely to favor censorship) began to lose cultural authority. The new culture that began to build in the 1950s and prevailed in the 1960s was based more on pacifism, egalitarianism, openness, and individuality.[1] Cultural authority shifted from parents, church leaders, educators, and political leaders to the self.[2] And a culture that emphasized the individual was not likely to tolerate rigid social controls like film censorship.

The growth of this new culture was aided by the rise of national media like movies, radio networks, and television. The transformation to a more nationalized culture that had begun in the 1920s took decades, but with the ascendancy of television in the 1950s, it advanced spectacularly. In the late 1950s, rock 'n' roll also became overwhelmingly popular, helping to bring about the sexual revolution of the 1960s.[3] Rock 'n' roll did more than exacerbate the generation gap; it played a major role in the swing away from the conventional morality of the 1940s, the morality reflected in and encouraged by PCA-dominated Hollywood movies. As the Supreme Court loosened governmental censorship, the PCA's enforcement of the code started to relax. It is no coincidence that when, in 1956, several states overturned their censorship statutes, the MPAA was also redrafting its Production Code. Consequently, in the 1960s, mainstream films grew more daring. *Irma la Douce* (1962) dealt openly (indeed flippantly) with prostitution. *Love with the Proper Stranger* (1963) depicted a young woman seeking an abortion after a one-night stand.

Struggling with films that reflected the new values—the *Lady Chat-*

terley's Lovers and the *Baby Dolls*—the censors and the Legion of Decency epitomized the past. They were losing control of movie content, which they had once held in virtual lockdown. Censorship was an idea born in an era that valued the greater good over the individual, and it was sustained for decades by succeeding groups that for one reason or another also restricted the individual in favor of the majority. But it lost out in a legal culture that began to scrutinize societal controls that infringed individual liberties and in a popular culture that valued individual expression and self-fulfillment above the values of what came to be derisively called "middle America."

March 1965 was a particularly "bad month for governmental censors."[4] After the Supreme Court invalidated both Maryland's and New York's prior restraint statutes in *Freedman v. Maryland* and *Trans-Lux v. New York*, both states took steps to conform to the Court's requirements. Chicago also redrafted its ordinance to comply. In the next three months, these censors would face even more challenges. But even as First Amendment jurisprudence expanded into many new areas and the Supreme Court kept taking on film censorship cases, movie freedom activists still had many more confrontations ahead.

Maryland Revamps Procedures

In 1965, on the day after Maryland received word that the Supreme Court had invalidated the procedures it had used for forty-three years, state legislators received a proposal from the state's attorney general to revise the statute. The new rules gave the censor board five days to review a film and an additional three days to seek a permanent judicial ban on any film deemed obscene. After that, the court had three days to review the case and two additional days to decide whether to uphold the board or to license the film. This tight schedule gave the exhibitor or distributor a maximum of thirteen days to wait. Mindful of *Freedman v. Maryland*, the statute expressly warned, "The burden of proving that the film should not be approved and licensed shall rest on the Board."[5] If the distributor chose to appeal to the Maryland court of appeals, the hearing had to be moved through the calendar as rapidly as possible. The legal officers who drafted the new law had not only worked fast, they had worked well, and the legislature approved. Assistant Attorney General Roger Redden was confident that films that would have been banned under the old statute stood no chance under the new one either.[6]

Constitutional or not, effective or not, Maryland censors had no work coming in. The major film distributors had stopped submitting films to the board for review. Six weeks passed before the first film appeared. More than likely, since it was Trans-Lux applying for a license for *A Stranger Knocks*, the submission was meant as a challenge to Maryland's new statute. And, as expected, the board rejected the film. Trying out its new regulation, it immediately instituted legal proceedings to permanently ban *A Stranger Knocks* from Maryland screens. It seems safe to surmise that the Maryland board was also looking for a confrontation, since it was denying a license to a film cleared by the U.S. Supreme Court just weeks before. After a day of hearings in early May 1965, a judge of the Baltimore circuit court affirmed the board's order.[7]

So *A Stranger Knocks*, the film that ended New York's statute, became the first to challenge Maryland's new procedures. The impact of *Freedman* was clear in the early days of *Trans-Lux Distributing Corp. v. Maryland State Board of Censors*, but the distributor's next move revealed a flaw in the new statute's time scheme. Dissatisfied with the ruling from the Baltimore County court, Brandt had his lawyers appeal to the court of appeals. Maryland's new statute required that the court of appeals expedite film cases but provided no specific guidelines about how much time could elapse.

Trans-Lux's second appeal took two more months. While the case moved more quickly than pre-*Freedman* cases had, it was hardly the swift resolution that the Supreme Court had envisioned. The process took more than five times longer than the thirteen days that had been predicted by the attorney general's office. When the decision did come down, though, it gave both sides something to celebrate. For the Maryland attorney general, the state's highest court validated the new censoring procedures. For Trans-Lux, the judges found the film not obscene and ordered it licensed, citing *Roth* and *Jacobellis*.[8]

New York's New Procedures

Like Maryland, New York had instituted new procedures after the *Freedman* decision, and, as in Maryland, those procedures were immediately challenged by Trans-Lux. Whereas Maryland's statute passed judicial scrutiny, however, New York's new mechanism failed its legal test.

Two days after the U.S. Supreme Court decision on *A Stranger Knocks*, the New York legislature rejected the regents' request for an age classification bill. This rebuff left the state with an unconstitutional apparatus and no new method of film control to replace it. So the regents took it upon themselves to adopt new rules and procedures to comply with the *Freedman* requirements. The new procedures called for the director of the motion picture division to issue a license within five days. If the director refused to license a film because he found it to be obscene, the commissioner of education had seven days to decide whether to uphold or reverse the director's determination. (According to Hugh Flick, the regents wanted to get out of the censoring business, so they turned the appeals over to the commissioner of education.) If the newly empowered education commissioner agreed that the film was obscene, the state had to institute proceedings against the film "forthwith." Although the time limit expressed in "forthwith" was not defined, a spokesman for the education department predicted that banned films would make their way through the state supreme court within one month.[9] The regents had adopted new rules in seeming compliance with the spirit of *Freedman*, but the original New York censoring statute, section 122 of the New York Education Law, remained in place. Its fatal flaw, the decades-old presumption of guilt on the part of the distributor, placed it out of step with the regents' new guidelines. New York had made a good first step toward *Freedman* compliance but had neglected to fix the foundation.

In the meantime, Trans-Lux still wanted to exhibit *A Stranger Knocks*. Although the U.S. Supreme Court had struck down New York's procedures with this film, it had not ruled on the film's alleged obscenity. And New York, with its new regulations, continued to require licenses for film exhibition. Since the censor board had declared *Stranger* obscene in 1963, the film could not be licensed. The motion picture division notified Trans-Lux that it would not receive a license under the new rules and then began legal proceedings to keep *Stranger* off New York screens permanently. Even after spending more than $100,000 (nearly $600,000 today)[10] and winning in the U.S. Supreme Court, Richard Brandt still could not exhibit *A Stranger Knocks* in New York theaters.

New York's Last Challenge

As New York and Trans-Lux squared off again, new trouble was brewing. Another picture was challenging the motion picture division, and this time the MPAA had joined the fight. Though the MPAA had been unwilling to attack censor boards directly after the disastrous 1961 *Times Film* decision, its lawyers were now ready, courtesy of New York's hastily redrawn regulations. Eight member studios of the MPAA filed suit against New York's new procedures. The regents, the MPAA claimed (correctly, as it turned out), had no authority to make sweeping rule changes.[11]

In April 1965, the Trans-Lux case and the MPAA suit were not the only files on Charles Brind's desk. *The Unsatisfied*, a film whose exhibition had been appealed under the old statute, was also demanding Brind's time as it came up against the new procedures. A French import of Cambist Films, *The Unsatisfied* applied for licensing in November 1964. This movie about juvenile delinquency, sexual conquest, and murder concerns a gang of misfits. The voice-over at the beginning of the movie provides a clue about its content: "Throughout the world, youth, restless, eager, and impatient to live, searches for a meaning to its existence. . . . Drugs, murder, violence, and sex are their constant companions. Where do they come from? Where are they going? What will become of the world tomorrow in the thoughtless hands of THE UNSATISFIED? This is the agonizing question to which we seek an answer."

While the film carried a moral that would have made a script reviewer at the old PCA happy, its reality was too gritty and the flesh too exposed for the censors of New York. Even though *The Unsatisfied* had already been shown in eight states, Cambist Films was forced to cut scenes of exposed breasts and buttocks, stripteases, and transparent panties before the film could be shown in New York.[12] Cambist's attorneys placed an appeal before the regents. Relying on *Roth* and *Jacobellis*, the brief argued that the dominant theme of the work did not appeal to the prurient interest of the average person and that the film certainly did not qualify as "utterly without redeeming social importance." Cambist tried to convince the regents that the film was social commentary, pointing out that it dealt with "the complex and frustrating inability of man to come to terms with his environment." It admitted that the film was "stark and candid" but argued that such was the "very substance of gang behavior. . . . This is not a motion picture about youngsters in the Boy Scouts." Relying on *Kingsley*, Cambist argued that material dealing with sex in a "manner that advocates ideas" was constitutionally protected. Use of contemporary standards was even more important in the case of *The Unsatisfied*, Cambist argued, because the film dealt with the contemporary problem of youth alienation.[13]

Before the regents could rule, the Supreme Court mandated the new procedural requirements in *Freedman*. This left the regents scrambling to draw up new procedures while considering what to do about *The Unsatisfied*. Even though they knew that the rules of the game had changed radically, the regents rendered a unanimous decision against Cambist Films on March 26, three weeks after the *Freedman* decision, on the same day as the adoption of their new rules.

Under these new rules, the regents bore the burden of initiating legal action against a film. If they wanted to keep *The Unsatisfied* off New York screens, they were compelled to initiate the legal proceedings. But they failed to do so. Inexplicably, no action followed for more than ten days. Finally Cambist obtained a show-cause order that sent the case to the state's supreme court. Under the old procedures, film censorship cases headed directly to the full appellate division for hearing. With the newly revised statute, however, a speedy hearing could be accomplished only through the lower supreme court, with a single justice sitting. The justice assigned to *The Unsatisfied*, Sidney J. Foster, had been no friend to the censors for the many years that he had been a member of the supreme court. A lifelong Republican, Foster had been one of the first New York State judges to decide that prior restraint on film was unconstitutional.

On May 12, 1965, Foster struck down both the New York censorship statute and the newly adopted Rules of the Board of Regents used to enforce it. He did so not for any of the reasons given by the Cambist attorneys but because he found the regents rules unconstitutional as a matter of law. He found it inconceivable that the regents could change the meaning of a statute through the adoption of different rules by which to implement it. Foster had found the fatal flaw in the regents' procedures: the original New York statute still stood, with the burden of proof still on the license applicant. But *Freedman* had expressly denied forcing the appellant to bear the burden of proof. The regents had hoped that by providing a speedier review, they could appear to be in conformity with the Supreme Court requirements. But only the state legislature, Foster noted, could dictate how quickly any case made it through the court system.

The regents had clearly overstepped their authority in commanding that legal proceedings be instituted "forthwith." Moreover, by leaving the terminology ambiguous, the regents offended the *Freedman* requirements that judicial action be swift. "At the very least," Foster wrote, the regents would need to specify clearly the time frame to be applied to any film challenge. Foster concluded that no censoring statute was in operation in New York, and therefore Cambist's request for a license was moot. According to the New York State Supreme Court, then, both Cambist and

Trans-Lux were free to enter "the marketplace of ideas," subject only to the obscenity restrictions of the penal statutes.[14]

The Censors Are Kaput

A month later, the New York State Court of Appeals reconsidered the *Trans-Lux* case by order of the Supreme Court. On June 10, 1965, forty-three years after the first film distributor challenged New York's censorship statute, the state's highest court declared it null and void.[15] In his regular column, which he had used so frequently over the previous two decades to rail against censorship, Bosley Crowther crowed, "The New York State censor, once powerfully proscriptive, is now kaput."[16]

Reached for comment by a *New York Times* reporter, a spokesman for the MPAA (which had declined to help Brandt and Rand in the *Trans-Lux* case) also gloated: "We are gratified that the Court of Appeals in the Trans-Lux case of *A Stranger Knocks* has today confirmed the position taken by the member companies of the M.P.A.A. in their pending suit against the Board of Regents that the New York State licensing statute is unconstitutional."[17] The MPAA was giving Richard Brandt and the management of Trans-Lux no credit for having carried on the fight. Brandt was apparently not contacted for comment.

As a matter of public interest, the case garnered little attention. Most people had grown weary of the film censorship issue. Aside from articles in the *New York Times*, *Time*, *Newsweek*, and a few major papers of the still censoring states, very little was written about the demise of the watch and ward of the screen. Film censorship, which had lost its appeal in the individually oriented, rights-centered culture of the 1960s, died out not just because judges had moved to a more speech-protective position but also because people had lost interest. Bureaucracies tend to develop their own inertia, which was certainly the case with the censor boards. Institutional momentum kept them going well beyond the days when popular opinion supported their policies. When judges, asked to evaluate the constitutionality of film censoring, began to chip away at the censors' reach, the majority of Americans were not alarmed. Judging by the amount of news coverage devoted to it, the issue of film censorship had become a dud by the early 1960s.[18]

Although censors had been walloped by the courts and enjoyed little public support, they were hardly quiescent. A series of hurriedly drawn bills waited for legislative hearings in New York just a few days after the court of appeals' *Trans-Lux* decision.[19] But the bills all died for lack of interest. Six months later, an upstate legislator asked the regents to continue running the motion picture division until the legislature could take up the issue in the next session. The regents rejected the request, probably quite relieved to be out of the film oversight business.[20] But the people of New York were not without recourse against films deemed unsuitable for minors. As other states had before it, New York expanded its Penal Law in 1965 to criminalize the admission to "harmful" films of those under seventeen.[21]

Like Maryland and New York, Kansas changed its rules after *Freedman* and continued censoring.[22] It should not have been censoring at all, of course, the state's censoring statute having been overturned by its supreme court ten years earlier, but, as we have seen, a legislative error had kept the Kansas board alive. Within a few months of the *Freedman* decision, the Kansas board had been notified by most major film distributors that they had no intention of complying with the state's new rules. To test the constitutionality of the rules, Columbia Pictures began exhibiting without license two 1965 films, a psychological thriller from Otto Preminger called *Bunny Lake Is Missing* and a successful cold war drama about nuclear submarines called *The Bedford Incident*. The films had not run into any trouble anywhere in the United States,[23] mostly because their content was completely unobjectionable. When Kansas sought an injunction to keep the films from the state's theaters, Columbia filed a countersuit, claiming unconstitutional prior restraint.

In July 1966, the Kansas Supreme Court agreed with Columbia Pictures and, just as the New York State Court of Appeals had done, held that any substantive changes in the procedures of censoring needed to be made by the legislature, not the censor board. By invalidating the new rules, the Kansas Supreme Court in essence struck down the entire Kansas statute, since the original law had been invalidated by *Freedman*. This decision left the legislature with a choice. It could rewrite the rules and continue censoring under the *Freedman* requirements, as Maryland had done, or it could let censorship die. It chose the easier course; the legislature made no appropriation for the censors, and they were out of business by October 1966.[24]

Virginia's censorship bureaucracy had recently met the same fate. After the *Freedman* decision was used in *Victoria Films v. Division of Motion Picture Censorship* to declare Virginia's attempt to censor *Traveling Light* an invalid prior restraint,[25] the general assembly ended funding effective June 30, 1966.[26] The only censoring state left was Maryland.

Only Maryland and Municipalities

Most people apparently paid little attention to the new freedom of the screen, but some who had watched Hollywood's Production Code–restrained content grow more and more daring, and who knew that governmental censors were fading away, worried that producers, particularly foreign and independent producers, would quickly seek the lowest common denominator. Stunning societal and cultural changes combined to intimidate many older and culturally conservative Americans, especially those of so-called middle America. It was for middle America that Hollywood had made most of its movies. And it was for middle America and its children that the censors had labored. But some of the films being made in the 1960s were definitely not for them. The censor boards that had protected Americans from such films were dissolving, seemingly with nothing to replace them, save obscenity prosecutions brought before judges who sided increasingly with those who produced the movies.

Hollywood, meanwhile, had been quietly moving away from content regulation and toward age classification. Even though some state censors had been asking for age classification authority for decades, Hollywood moguls had opposed any sort of classification, fearing that restricting audiences would cut too deeply into profits. The code's only real enforcement mechanism had been its ability to withhold theater screens from non-code-approved movies. But the studios controlled far fewer screens once they began their Court-ordered divestment in the 1950s. Moreover, maverick producers continued to release noncode films to profitable runs. By 1966, fully 41 percent of all films released had not bothered to get a code seal.[27] As a stopgap, rather than outlaw the new, more mature themes, the PCA, encouraged by a more lenient Legion of Decency, began to attach a new label, "suggested for mature audiences," thus beginning a de facto age classification system. By 1960, some theaters, like the famous Grauman's Chinese Theatre in Los Angeles, were accomplishing their own age classification by refusing to sell tickets to children for films like *Butterfield 8* and *The World of Suzie Wong*.[28] But in 1965, even though the code was practically defunct, the MPAA was still not ready to plunge into age classification.

With new artistic and legal freedom, and with the theater monopoly of the old PCA days gone, producers were free to create and distribute all manner of film. By 1966, 60 percent of all Hollywood productions released were "suggested for mature audiences."[29] Some commentators began calling for producers to live up to their newfound liberation by producing mature films without obscenity, unnecessary profanity, or gratuitous sex and violence. Bosley Crowther, overjoyed at the censors' demise, nevertheless implored the industry to avoid the trap of making quick money from salacious content.[30] How well he fared in this quest can be judged by the rising number of films like *Blow-Up* (1966), *Darling* (1965), and *Rough Night in Jericho* (1967), followed within a few years by *Deep Throat*, *Behind the Green Door*, and *Last Tango in Paris* (all in 1972). The 1960s Supreme Court decisions freeing obscenity unleashed what Edward de Grazia calls "tides of pornography," seen most clearly in the sexploitation films of the 1960s and 1970s.[31] Against these films, middle America felt defenseless.

In 1965, as film censorship entered its terminal phase, those American parents, educators, and moral guardians who worried about the content of the nation's films—as their Progressive Era counterparts had before them—had good reason for concern. Over the next three years, American movies increased in both violent content and sexual frankness. The pendulum had swung hard in the direction of sex and violence after years of being stuck in the PCA position. Again, movies came under attack. Senators Thomas J. Dodd and Margaret Chase Smith had had enough, decrying the "flood of violence, deviationism, sadism, and an overemphasis on sex."[32]

In New York, with no censoring bureaucracy left, film distributors were free to show any movie without prior restraint. An allegedly obscene film could be shut down and the theater owner prosecuted, however. This discrepancy left the motion picture industry in the strange position of being free to exhibit any film at least once, yet still being subject to the vagaries of police zeal and judicial opinion. Bosley Crowther, one of the few commentators still paying attention to the issue, was concerned. "Judges on the state and federal level are being compelled to act as arbiters of taste and the anomalies are almost as annoying—though not quite as much so—as they were when the function was left almost entirely to the censors who worked behind the scenes."[33] But even though he was drawing attention to a restriction on complete freedom of the screen, Crowther touched upon the crucial distinction between pre- and post-1965 New York exhibition: any censorship now being carried out was an open process. Unfortunately, it could also be a costly one. To seize freedom of expression by exhibiting a possibly objectionable film, an exhibitor risked significant expense.

And censorship was not dead everywhere. Municipal boards continued to restrain films in Memphis, Dallas, and Chicago, as well as a host of other, smaller cities. And Maryland chugged on. Some exhibitors there began a sort of guerrilla warfare against their censor board. As we have seen, Freedman routinely replaced eliminated scenes once he got his films back. Robert Marhenke produced unflattering cartoons of the censors, which he handed out at his theater and published in local newspapers. One day, he scrawled the chief censor's phone number on his screen, along with the suggestion that patrons call her late at night to complain about censorship. That night, the beleaguered censor received twenty calls after 11 PM.[34] Marhenke also brought a series of pestering lawsuits against the censors, and he even hired a sound truck to drive through the chief censor's neighborhood, broadcasting unflattering comments about her for her neighbors' edification.[35] Marhenke had appointed himself the censors' biggest pest, and he frequently hung around the board's offices (required by law to be open to the public), harassing the staff and demanding to read the minutes of board meetings.

In addition to Marhenke's nuisance suits, other court cases continued. In July, the first post-*Freedman* case was decided by a federal district court, invalidating the municipal censorship ordinance of Memphis.[36] Fifteen test cases were still to come in the "still stubbornly censoring" Maryland.[37]

After the initial *Trans-Lux* reversal, Maryland censors got another black eye in October when the distributors of *Lorna* (1964) sought relief at the state court of appeals. *Lorna* was the product of "the King of the Nudies," Russ Meyer. Although it is not full-blown pornography by today's standards, *Lorna* represents a way station on the road to the 1970s' sexploitation films that followed. Each film that Meyer made became a bit more explicit and a bit less taxing on the costume budget. Lorna is a bored housewife who is raped by and then takes up with an escaped convict. When her husband comes home early and finds the two together, he kills them both. The story is punctuated at beginning and end by a mysterious stranger who rants about eternal damnation for such sinners,[38] probably a holdover from the days of the Forty Thieves' "square-up" technique.

The state court of appeals chastised the censors for not presenting any evidence of the film's obscenity; the distributor, on the other hand, had given the court ample evidence for its contention of nonobscenity. This was a far cry from the earlier days of film censorship litigation, when courts refused to consider the testimony of outside experts. The Maryland high court now insisted upon such proof: "Save in the case of the exceptional motion picture which not only speaks for itself but screams for all to hear that it is obscene, the Board under the statute of 1965 will need more than the film to support its opinion in court."[39] The censor board did not pay attention. In three cases that immediately challenged the new Maryland procedures, it failed to defend itself by supplying the requisite expert assessment of obscenity. In each case, the board lost. Whereas some Supreme Court justices and legal commentators had recently argued that judges were as well qualified as any expert to judge the obscenity of an art form, this court clearly wanted to avoid playing the role of obscenity referee.[40]

A case that appeared at the Maryland court of appeals in February 1966 had been through juries, bizarre judicial methods, experts that were no experts, and delay far beyond what the *Freedman* opinion allowed. Distributor William E. Hewitt had submitted the provocatively titled *This Picture Is Censored* for review in October 1965. The film starts with an introduction to film censorship, followed by scenes purportedly cut by state censors (although Hewitt had to admit later that the scenes were recreations). An assortment of women "dressing and undressing, romping around a nudist camp, playing on and in beds, acting as artists' and photographers' models, being seduced, assaulted, tortured and dismembered" followed for about an hour. Promptly pronounced obscene, the film landed in the court of common pleas before a jury. Hewitt and the well-known anticensorship attorney Richard Whiteford argued that the revised statute was unconstitutional and that the film was not obscene. The trial judge, in a wonderful display of initiative, decided to have the twenty-five-member jury pool view the film and then fill out questionnaires. The judge explained that since *Roth* and *Jacobellis* required the use of community standards, he could find no better way to ascertain the average reaction to *This Picture Is Censored* than to ask the citizens empanelled in the jury box. Six of the jurors (preselected by the board of censors) were sworn in as witnesses: a rabbi, a Catholic priest, a Protestant minister, an American Legion adjutant, a probation officer, and a juvenile court consultant. Each found the film obscene. The other nineteen jurors' questionnaires were admitted into evidence. Whiteford repeatedly objected and moved for a mistrial, to no avail. The court of appeals found the entire proceeding unacceptable and ordered the case back to the lower court for rehearing. As to obscenity, the appeals judges seemed rather amused at the Maryland censors: "While there is a most generous display of the female epidermis, both fore and aft, the whole thing is about as titillating and exciting as a ton of coal," wrote Judge J. J. McWilliams for the unanimous court.[41]

The saga of Hewitt and *This Picture Is Censored* continued, remanded for a new hearing. The trial judge again found the film obscene, and Hewitt wound up back at the court of appeals in July. This time the censor board tried to supply corroboration of the film's obscenity, starting with the lower court's jury witnesses. The appeals court was not impressed, finding that not one qualified as an expert who could testify to community standards of decency. The court then looked at the board's experts (two local film critics, a correspondent for movie industry trade magazines, and an English professor) and decided that none of them were qualified, either. To make matters worse for the censor board, the court of appeals found the testimony of its experts more amenable to the film's social value than to its alleged obscenity. Ironically, part of the value of the movie, according to the court of appeals, was its anticensorship message. Once again, even with experts, the censor board was overruled.[42] The highest court of Maryland had refused to uphold its censor board on any case since the inception of the new procedures, a fact noted by some anticensorship legislators.

The Maryland censors did not, however, intend to fade away, nor did the Maryland legislature show any great enthusiasm for repealing the censors' authority despite their judicial setbacks. Maryland's governor, J. Millard Tawes, was a "bureaucrat who believed in bureaucracy." In 1965, when Maryland had to decide what to do in light of *Freedman*, the state was in the midst of an enormous administrative expansion, not a political atmosphere that favored tearing out bureaucratic authority.[43] Maryland continued to censor energetically. According to Ronald Freedman, the new censor board chairman, eighty-two-year-old Egbert L. Quinn, "wanted to stop everything."[44] One year into its new procedures, the board reported an increase in the number of films banned, from nine in 1965 to thirty in 1966, and predicted that it would ban thirty-five in fiscal 1967.[45] In the process of protecting Maryland's young minds, the censor board would inspire many more challenge cases. It found itself before the court of appeals fifteen times from 1965 until the board's demise in 1981.

Since the Maryland legislature had overhauled the statute after *Freedman* rather than merely updating the regulations (as had happened in New York, Kansas, and Virginia), the new procedures were not open to easy attack. And the Maryland censors had picked up a faithful ally in J. Gilbert Prendergast, a judge of the Circuit Court for Baltimore City. He upheld the wishes of the censor board eight times in a row immediately after the new procedures went into effect. Beginning with *A Stranger Knocks* and continuing with *Lorna*, *Warm Days and Hot Nights*, *A French Honeymoon*, and *Dirty Girls*, Prendergast consistently ruled that the censor board had properly refused licenses. He continued his judicial blessing on bans of *Cherry's House of Nudes*, *Dr. Sex*, and *Crazy, Wild and Crazy*.[46] For all their success at the lower court level, however, the censors were startlingly unsuccessful at the appellate level. The only appellate level decision in the censors' favor involved peep shows.[47] This remarkable lack of success led state representative Alexander Stark to call Maryland's censorship "an intellectual insult and a legal anomaly."[48]

Mindful of growing opposition, board chairman Quinn wanted backup to reinforce his conception of what was harmful for children. He asked for and got a panel of psychiatrists, artists, psychologists, and educators.[49] The board also continued its request for age classification authority from the legislature, but this plea, ongoing since 1932, went unheeded.[50] Lobbying to keep their jobs, the censors also began to invite sympathetic groups to private showings of exceptionally horrid film scenes.[51] When they screened a film about strippers for legislators, the *Baltimore Sun* wryly noted, the screening was "well-attended."[52]

Age Classification

Although the Maryland legislature showed no interest in age classification, elsewhere the idea was becoming more popular as a compromise between outright freedom of exhibition and the prior restraint still carried on by Maryland. In 1965, the City of Dallas created a classification board with only two categories, suitable and not suitable for children under sixteen. Municipal lawmakers everywhere watched to see what would happen when Interstate Circuit challenged Dallas three years later over Louis Malle's *Viva Maria* (1965). Even the nine-member classification board had not been able to agree that this comic western with Brigitte Bardot, Jeanne Moreau, and George Hamilton as Central American revolutionaries was problematic for children. *Viva Maria* seems an excellent test case: no overt obscenity or immorality, but scenes some would find questionable for young people. One of the scenes that might have caused concern—Jeanne Moreau making love to a bound George Hamilton—was meant to be humorous, not sexy.[53] The U.S. Supreme Court found that the disagreement among the board supplied good evidence that the statute was void for vagueness. This initially sounded like good news for the free screen forces. But the Court also clearly indicated that age classification under a better statute would survive. Citing both *Burstyn* and

Kingsley, Justice Thurgood Marshall, writing the eight-to-one opinion, held that while the language of a control measure must not be so loose as to leave too much discretion, well-defined language could meet the test of constitutionality. The whole argument was predicated on there being no absolute right to film freedom. Marshall cited *Ginsberg v. New York*, handed down the same day, which judicially blessed state power to keep materials deemed harmful from children.[54]

These two cases, *Interstate Circuit* and *Ginsberg*, were gifts for those who wanted to see classification boards set up in their own cities. The Supreme Court had kept alive the *Burstyn* concept that the First Amendment did not give blanket immunity to movie producers, and it had added authority to the idea that the state's police power could legitimately be used to keep sexually explicit material from minors.

Many cities had been watching this case closely. Jack Valenti, president of the MPAA since 1966 (Eric Johnston had died in 1963), feared that cities across the country would erect classification boards unless the MPAA could beat them to it. Faced again with the threat of federal censorship, the motion picture industry responded as it had more than thirty years before—by insisting it could sweep up its own mess. When the U.S. Senate, at the prodding of Senator Margaret Chase Smith, began hearings on mandatory film classification, Valenti announced that the MPAA was working on a voluntary rating system.[55]

Meanwhile, Maryland's censors not only kept on censoring but often granted interviews and welcomed reporters to their offices. The board was still made up of political appointees who were assisted by civil servant reviewers. Censoring power was usually wielded by one of the governor's cronies. Quinn, the first post-*Freedman* board chair, had been a personal friend and neighbor of the governor. A small-town newspaper publisher, he was estimated by *Baltimore Sun* reporter James Dilts to be Maryland's most experienced censor. Dilts explained that when Quinn was in the state legislature, his good friend, Norman Mason, was chair of the censor board. Whenever he had some free time, Quinn would stop by to see his friend, watch some movies, and listen to the censors' conversations. This, according to Dilts, made Quinn more qualified than any of the other people who had held the chief censor position in Maryland.[56]

In the late 1960s, the other two censors were Margery Shriver, a housewife and part-time college student, and Mary Avara, a Baltimore bail bondswoman and publicly devout Catholic. Avara, who had been criticized in 1963 by a group of theater owners for her lack of education (she dropped out of high school after ninth grade), sounded like the early-twentieth-century maternalists when she claimed that motherhood was her best qualification for the position. "I didn't learn about any of this filth when I was growing up—and I had eleven brothers and sisters," Avara told a *Baltimore Sun* reporter. "When one of my sisters asked where babies come from my mother beat her unmercifully. . . . We led a beautiful, sheltered life."[57] Avara remained on the censor board for twenty years, until its end. She was polite to the distributors but fanatical when she made up her mind that a scene could be harmful. "Every time she cut a picture she thought she was making points to get into heaven," said Freedman.[58]

When Quinn died in 1968, the octogenarian chief censor was replaced by attorney Joseph Pokorny, another friend of the governor. This new chief censor was so morally conservative that he disapproved of *The Graduate* because he thought it degraded motherhood. (*The Graduate* garnered five Golden Globes, including best picture, and seven Academy Award nominations, winning for best director.) Pokorny no doubt opposed the film for other reasons as well, since he believed that films dealing with adultery "could do great harm by lessening respect for the institution of marriage, which is one of the foundations of Western civilization."[59]

Most of the challenges to Maryland's censoring stemmed from arguments about what was obscene, with the Supreme Court insisting that films with any redeeming social value were protected. One Maryland court of appeals case, however, did not challenge the obscenity determination of the board. This case came from William E. Hewitt, who claimed that two of his films had been unconstitutionally delayed in their determinations. Since delay was the issue, not obscenity, the judges did not have to watch the films. And they could hardly contain their elation. The opinion opened, "We have not had to view the suspect film. Our relief at this is great and joy fills our hearts." The court was so glad that it found in favor of the censors, ruling that a two-day delay in the court hearing was not sufficient to judge the case as having offended due process.[60] Any nuisance attempt by disgruntled exhibitors to use the exact letter of the law would not meet with favor at the Maryland court of appeals.

I Am Curious (Yellow)

The Maryland board and film distributors got along uneasily through the next two years, until they were confronted by a Swedish film called *I Am Curious (Yellow)*. It was the first major film to show fully nude actors. A box office success, *I Am Curious* still ranks as the sixth-highest-grossing foreign language film of all time, despite its odd plot and leftist political philosophizing. The film masquerades as a documentary about a young girl, Lena, exploring the realms of sexual relationships and political affairs at the same time, often getting the two confused.[61] While Lena explores politics and conducts interviews, she also engages in frequent sexual trysts with her married lover in unusual places, like the balcony of the Swedish royal palace. The Maryland attorney general told the *Baltimore Sun*, "If the board cannot ban this sort of hard-core pornography masquerading as art, then I suppose it cannot ban anything and should be abolished."[62]

I Am Curious had already had a long legal career. It had been found obscene by U.S. Customs yet had been set free by the U.S. Court of Appeals for the Second Circuit. Since the court did not consider the film "utterly without redeeming social value," its graphic sexual depictions were not enough to render it obscene under *Jacobellis*. But this decision had no bearing on local censors, and the film was under twelve suits and countersuits when it arrived in Maryland in 1969, courtesy of distributor Grove Press and exhibitor Howard Wagonheim. Both sides strutted and postured as they prepared for court. Grove Press crowed that it expected its challenge to abolish the Maryland censor board entirely, and Maryland's chief law enforcer repeated that licensing the film would be tantamount to "unconditional surrender to those who want to exhibit hard-core pornography."[63]

For Grove Press's owner, confronting censorship had become a business staple. Specializing in what he called combat publishing, Barney Rosset had built a publishing house on controversial books, like the unexpurgated version of *Lady Chatterley's Lover* and *Tropic of Cancer*, as well as the magazine *Evergreen Review*. When *Tropic of Cancer* got hung up in U.S. Customs, Rosset hired attorney Edward de Grazia, who succeeded in freeing the book via the U.S. Supreme Court. Rosset was a natural in the anticensorship business; he described himself as "a type of free American spirit, against censorship" by nature. Once he became a publisher, Rosset was more convinced than ever that censorship was wrong and that he should be allowed to publish whatever he wanted. Recognizing the immense potential of European writers like Samuel Beckett, Eugene Ionesco, and Jean Genet, Rosset began importing their lesser-known works. He later would turn to Anglo-American avant-garde writers like Henry Miller, William Burroughs, and D. H. Lawrence and political activists like Malcolm X and Che Guevara. Rosset believed, "If a book has literary merit, you publish it. If you get arrested in the process, you fight it." He later admitted that his publication of the unabridged *Lady Chatterley's Lover* had been a deliberate attempt to provoke an obscenity confrontation.[64] After winning several book censorship battles, Rosset brought Grove Press into the film distribution business. As he purchased the rights to *I Am Curious*, his business was being monitored by the FBI, the CIA, and the U.S. Army.[65] He planned to bring *I Am Curious* to as many states as possible when he ran into the Maryland censor board.

At the circuit court, the censor board, which had finally learned its judicial lesson, presented expert testimony from a psychologist and an educator who both confirmed that *I Am Curious* was obscene. A sculptor also told the judge that the film had no artistic value. But de Grazia explained that the film had been exhibited in twenty-three cities to more than three-quarters of a million viewers, and he brought out a parade of experts with impressive credentials who testified that the film had redeeming social value. Nevertheless, Judge Joseph L. Carter found the film obscene, holding that the time had come "to halt . . . [the pornographers'] program. This does not mean a return to Puritanism by any stretch of the imagination, but it does mean a return to sense and decency."[66]

The court of appeals upheld the lower court by four to three, saying that the film's overriding theme was "sex, *per se*."[67] One justice's dissenting opinion, however, faulted the majority for ignoring the preponderance of expert testimony that the film had social value. Here, in a nutshell, were the distributors' two major dilemmas: first, what would the state of Maryland allow, and second, how could a potential film owner figure that out in advance of purchase?

I Am Curious showed that, as late as 1969, the highest court in Maryland was refusing to follow the U.S. Supreme Court's direction on the determination of obscenity. *I Am Curious* was clearly outside the norm of community standards yet, by most accounts, held at least some social value. It should have met the Supreme Court's standards for a non-censorable film. After the state had won, the attorney general reiterated his earlier statement that if the censors had lost that particular battle, he would have recommended the board's abolition. Asked whether he would feel the same if the U.S. Supreme Court should decide against Maryland, he answered, "It would logically follow, wouldn't it?"[68] Such temptation the anticensorship forces of Maryland could hardly ignore. In Freedman, Wagonheim, Rosset, and Marhenke (dubbed "the everlasting Board's habitual agitator" by the board secretary[69]), the censors had a large contingent of adversaries eagerly awaiting the chance to get the Supreme Court to invalidate Maryland's prior restraint.

Wagonheim managed to get the case of his Swedish film before the U.S. Supreme Court. By the time the Maryland case reached the Supreme Court, *I Am Curious* was in legal trouble in twelve cities. Another case from Massachusetts was also pending before the Supreme Court.

Grove Press and Wagonheim came to the U.S. Supreme Court with lots of friendly assistance. Their case was buttressed by amicus briefs from the International Film Importers and Distributors Association, the National Association of Theatre Owners, the Adult Film Association of America, and the MPAA. At the oral arguments, Maryland attorney general Francis Burch told the Supreme Court justices that the Court must let the states decide obscenity issues at home. Burch put all his eggs into this basket: echoing his earlier statements made for the Maryland press, he told the Court that he would rather see all censorship abolished than have the current state of confusion engendered by the Court's ambiguous rulings. Grove's attorney, de Grazia, explained that the film had been shown in 180 cities, in forty states, to more than five million people. Those numbers alone were clear evidence, he said, that the film was not pornographic. The Court must promise the states, de Grazia said, that it would not interfere with the exhibition of any material short of hardcore pornography, as long as it was available only to consenting adults. According to the *Baltimore Sun*, "Virtually the only thing the two lawyers agreed on was that the law governing obscenity and pornography is in a state of 'confusion,' and that the court should issue a 'clear' mandate."[70]

As they had so many times since 1952, both sides hoped that a decisive ruling by the Supreme Court in this case would "lift the fog" that had come to surround film censorship.[71] But their wish was not to be granted. On March 8, 1970, the Court split evenly (Justice Douglas, who probably would have voted with the liberals, did not participate because of a possible conflict of interest with Grove Press), which meant that the Maryland court of appeals' determination of *I Am Curious (Yellow)* as obscene would stand.[72] And so the two main issues—whether the film and others like it were constitutionally protected speech and whether the Maryland censor statute was unconstitutional—were deferred. In four years, the Maryland censor board had faced and survived eight legal challenges.

The case of *I Am Curious (Yellow)* ended anticlimactically. After another year of haggling with the censor board, Grove Press agreed to make some cuts, and the film was finally licensed in Maryland—but only after a great expenditure of both time and money.[73]

One of the most salient anticensorship issues was how to pay for such lengthy, complex litigation. Despite its three decades of public denunciations of censorship, the ACLU had been able to assist in only a few of the cases. Both the national office and its state affiliates needed promising litigants and local attorneys willing to take on the cause of the motion picture distributors. With the ACLU's resources strained by many civil liberties issues in the mid-twentieth century (separation of church and state, public speech, loyalty oaths, civil rights, defendants' rights), the organization can hardly be faulted for playing a minor role in the fight against motion picture censors. The MPAA also had a surfeit of critical issues to stare down. As a member-driven organization, the association was required to run its affairs through committee. Fighting the censorship of a foreign or independent production or of an allegedly obscene film was not likely to appeal to the dues-paying membership.

And so those who chose to fight the censors were often on their own. Joseph Burstyn had spent a great deal of his own money on his battle because he believed the principle of censorship to be wrong. The Hakim brothers (*La ronde*) also spent their own company finances to fight to the Supreme Court. Richard Brandt used the resources of his theater chain to free *A Stranger Knocks*. Ronald Freedman bankrupted his Baltimore Film Society, a loose collection of film enthusiasts who in the 1960s acquired four theaters and financed his crusade to the Supreme Court. But Grove Press hit on an ingenious financing solution: it took advantage of a plan, set up by de Grazia, that encouraged local attorneys to take local cases for contingency fees based on box office receipts in their area.[74] Thus Grove did not have to shell out cash in advance of a dubious return; local attorneys were given a vested interest in winning the cases, and each local distributor, exhibitor, or bookseller of a Grove product could serve as a test case. Grove Press was able to carry on its extensive cause litigation by convincing attorneys to gamble on the outcome of their own work in their local courts.

Peep Shows

Along with films like *I Am Curious (Yellow)*, the Maryland censors were beset with peep shows, 16 mm exploitation films viewed in coin-operated booths. Because the Maryland court of appeals had interpreted *film* to include peep shows, they had to submit to review. Four peep shows challenged the Maryland censors, with one making it to the U.S. Supreme Court in 1974.[75] In the first case, store owner Al Star delivered a "broadcast attack" in federal district court, arguing that Maryland's 1965 statute did not satisfy the *Freedman* requirements, that the police had acted improperly, that the board was unqualified, and that the statutory language was overbroad. He complained that the process took too long, that it allowed fines for the interim exhibition of a film even if the film was later termed nonobscene, that obscenity was determined without jury trial, that no element of scienter was present (the defendant had no way to know whether the film was obscene or not), and that the board did not have to give its reasons for license denial. The court found all of Star's charges baseless and pronounced the Maryland procedures fully in compliance with the *Freedman* requirements.[76]

Thus rebuked at the district court, Star petitioned for and received certiorari from the U.S. Supreme Court, which upheld the district court without opinion. A dissent by Douglas repeated his oft-made statement that any prior restraint violated the First Amendment. In a separate dissent, Brennan found that as long as questionable materials were not made available to juveniles or to unconsenting adults, neither the state nor the federal government had any business becoming involved. Clearly, he wrote, the Maryland statute was overbroad in its definition (or lack thereof) of *obscene*.[77] The only certainty from this 1974 case was that the U.S. Supreme Court had refused to strike down Maryland's censorship again. The state's newspapers, growing weary of the censorship controversy after fifty-four years, called upon the state legislature to put film censorship out of its misery. "Now that the court has found prior state censorship of obscenity to be constitutionally permissible," the *Baltimore Sun* editorialized, "it will be up to legislators to have the courage to say that it is not wise."[78]

Deep Throat

The same year that the peep shows went to the Supreme Court, the infamous *Deep Throat* (1972) became the latest source of litigation. Starring Linda Lovelace and Harry Reems (both pseudonyms), *Deep Throat* became the first hardcore pornographic film seen by mainstream audiences, launching what has been called the golden era of porn. Before *Deep Throat*, pornographic films were cheap and primitive, usually shot in one day, hastily edited, and then shown to the trench coat crowd. But *Deep Throat* was a new kind of porno film, with a generous $24,000 budget, a six-day shooting schedule, and three months of postproduction, which gave it a decidedly more polished look than its predecessors. In just one week in New York City, it earned more than its production cost. Unlike earlier porno movies, *Deep Throat* had a plot of sorts, some minor character development, and a sense of humor. The plot revolves around Lovelace, a woman who enjoys sex but is unable to achieve orgasm until her doctor discovers that her clitoris is in her throat. After that, Lovelace finds plenty of men willing to help her achieve satisfaction. Mainstream critics like Andrew Sarris of the *Village Voice* and Vincent Canby of the *New York Times* reviewed *Deep Throat* as they would any other Hollywood feature (although Canby's fascination with *Deep Throat* had more to do with its "engineering" than its artistic merit—"How does she do it?" Canby asked).[79]

Whatever created the buzz about this sixty-two-minute oversexed film, it became the hot topic at cocktail parties in major cities, creating a trend that reporter Ralph Blumenthal called "porno chic."[80] Ellen Willis, writing in the *New York Review of Books*, labeled the film "a cultural event," although she found it "about as erotic as a tonsillectomy."[81] Watching *Deep Throat* became the hip thing for cultural liberals to do, and people who had not seen it were considered square.

Deep Throat opened in New York in June 1972. Since New York no longer had a censor board, movies could be subject only to an after-the-fact obscenity prosecution, which for this film happened almost immediately. The movie fell victim to a mayor's campaign to clean up midtown Manhattan, and it also became the source of a second criminal case. When one theater manager was arrested for the misdemeanor of promoting obscenity, the trial judge could hardly contain his vituperative description of the film's sexual content. "There were so many and varied forms of sexual activity one would tend to lose count of them," the trial judge fumed. It was, Judge Joel Tyler said, "a Sodom and Gomorrah gone wild before the fire—all of which is enlivened with the now famous 'four letter words' and finally with bells ringing and rockets bursting in climactic ecstasy." He had certainly never seen a film like *Deep Throat*, so he had only New York law and his own good sense to go by. Noting that many critics had called it hardcore, Tyler found that its only theme was an appeal to the prurient interest, and therefore it was legally obscene.[82] The distributor made cuts and the film played on without incident, probably because the local district attorney had better things to do.[83]

In all, *Deep Throat* would lead to more court battles than any film since *The Birth of a Nation*, surpassing even the record held by *I Am Curious*. Much of the prosecution was pointless: many of the juries refused to find *Deep Throat* obscene.[84] If anything verified the extent to which public opinion had changed in the early 1970s regarding private versus public matters, it was these juries.

Public opinion may have changed, but in 1973 the U.S. Supreme Court abruptly reversed course after years of liberalizing obscenity law. The Court ended its sixteen-year incremental loosening on content restriction in *Miller v. California*, which enabled local authorities to censor under local community standards rather than the previous national standards. *Miller* also revised the definition of *obscenity* from the rather loose "utterly without redeeming social importance" to the more restrictive "without serious literary, artistic, political, or scientific value."[85] Such a test made it easier to find a film like *Deep Throat* obscene.

And that is exactly what happened in Maryland in 1974 when all three censors agreed that *Deep Throat* was "vile," "filthy," "common garbage" and arrested a theater manager for showing the film without a license.[86] At the hearing to restrain the film, circuit court judge James W. Murphy listened to three experts testify that the film did not appeal to prurient interest and that it had redeeming value, but he held to his own opinion, finding the film "much more persuasive than the expert testimony."[87] Once again, a Maryland lower court judge had ignored experts.

Deep Throat would not be licensed in Maryland. The court not only found it obscene but also laid down a definition of *obscenity* for all future cases. Obscenity would be, the Maryland court said, whatever the U.S. Supreme Court had most recently decided it was. To justify this position, the judges pointed out that after *Freedman*, the legislature had not attempted to define *obscenity*. That legislative reticence was a clear indication that it expected the courts to be the final arbiter of the definition.[88] Since the legislature had stepped out of the issue, the court felt that it could hardly be accused of judicial activism.

Not only did the Maryland censors stay at work long after other states had laid their censors off, but their reach was expanded by a 1976 court decision. Having found *Texas Chainsaw Massacre* "obscene," the board was gratified to learn that a Baltimore circuit court judge expanded the definition of *obscene* to include sexually related violence.[89]

Repeated attempts to repeal the statute failed. Barbara Scott, representing the MPAA, lobbied the legislature for repeal every year from

1968 through 1978.[90] Her 1977 effort was thwarted by the censor board's longest-tenured member, Mary Avara, who had become almost legendary in Maryland after her years of censoring. Avara never shied from the spotlight and frequently granted interviews to Baltimore newspapers. Each year when repeal bills were introduced, Avara would trek to the hearings and flamboyantly plead for the life of the censor board. The *Baltimore Evening Sun* called her annual legislative appearances "the Mary Avara Traveling Salvation Show, one of the state's longest running epics."[91] At one of the hearings, Avara told the legislators, "When I came in here today I expected to see everyone nude. That's all I ever see. . . . I have to look at this five days a week. At the end of the week, I say 'Thank you, Jesus.'" The audience broke into laughter and applause.[92] Playing to the house, she continued, "I have to stop eating a lot of foods because of what they do with it in these movies." Speaking of her fellow censors, she reported, "Mrs. Wright goes home and cries. Harrison gets upset, and Andreadakis can't eat his hotdog."[93] In a 1979 interview, she told the *Baltimore News American*, "If [the framers] could have foreseen the future, the Bill of Rights would never have been written."[94] But by 1981, even the quirky annual appeal of Mary Alvara could no longer convince the legislators to fund the censor board. A state sunset law, designed to shake loose unnecessary bureaucracies, brought the censor board to an anticlimactic end.

The U.S. Supreme Court, though it had been slowly chipping away at the procedures and standards of all the governmental censorship bodies, had not ruled prior restraint like Maryland's unconstitutional. The force that set censorship in motion during the Progressive Era—the belief that movies had a special capacity for evil—had still not completely died despite changing notions of public and private and the acceptance of porno chic. The potential harmfulness of movies was still a concern, but it was no longer the hot-button issue it had been from the Progressive Era through the 1950s' anti-Communist hysteria. Even today, experts cannot agree on the effects of films and television on behavior. As long as there is a possibility that young people can be infected with salacious or violent ideas from the movies they watch, some people will want to control their content. This probably accounts for the fact that no censoring state's legislature ever voted to overturn its control statute. Those legislatures that ended their state censoring did so either because their attorneys general advised them to or because a court had forced them to. Even in Maryland, censorship was neither overturned nor repealed. It just faded to black.

The last film submitted to a state censorship agency was the James

Bond installment *For Your Eyes Only*. On her last day at work, Mary Avara, temporarily a celebrity from national talk show appearances, remarked, "I don't think I'll ever look at another movie."[95]

The Legacy of *Freedman*

In the 1950s, the *Burstyn* decision had produced a litter of per curiams. In the 1960s and 1970s, *Freedman* had had more progeny. At the U.S. Supreme Court, *Freedman* served as precedent for ten more cases after it was used to overturn New York's statute in the *Trans-Lux* case.[96] It also served as precedent for twelve U.S. court of appeals decisions and forty-six U.S. district court cases. It overturned the continuing censorship in Memphis[97] and in the two remaining states, Virginia[98] and Kansas.[99]

Sadly, though, thirty-seven years after the *Freedman* decision, Ronald Freedman felt little sense of accomplishment for his troubles. He realized that the decision caused the other censoring states to disband their censor boards but was frustrated with both Maryland's reaction and the lower courts' implementation. "We were disappointed because the Court did not abolish censorship," he explained. "We thought that [Justice] Goldberg would abolish the board. He allowed precensorship to continue. We were jubilant for a moment that the censors were gone, but the legislature was in session and they were back in business in four days. . . . These politicians move fast. . . . They didn't want to lose their jobs." But what really disturbed Freedman was the Maryland lower courts' response. "When you submitted films to the lower courts, they would invariably hold up the censor board. . . . The lower court judges were very fanatic. You just wasted your time in the lower courts. . . . The problem with the Supreme Court's decision was that they assumed that the lower courts would be as knowledgeable of the laws of obscenity as the Supreme Court was, but they weren't. It was useless going to the lower courts. . . . *Freedman v. Maryland* turned out to be a waste of time."[100]

It is true that it took some time for the decision to filter down to the lower courts' level and that it was never used to overturn Maryland's censorship by its highest court. But subsequent film cases benefited from the procedural requirements that the Supreme Court established in *Freedman*, a case, like so many before it, brought by a single man with little support beyond his own opinion that films deserved to be freed from governmental control.

Conclusion

Each time a new mass medium has appeared, it has been welcomed with calls for its restriction: mass market books, magazines, comic books, motion pictures, radio, television, and the Internet. At the beginning of the twentieth century, when moving picture technology allowed the mass dissemination of lifelike moving images for the first time, the result, on the part of some, was moral panic. Motion pictures bore the full brunt of the progressive notion that an educated, bureaucratized elite could best protect the nation and its children. Censorship was a well-established tradition; free speech was not. The era of film censorship shows that, aside from a minority of civil libertarians, most Americans of the early to mid-twentieth century thought little about free speech rights. Few legal scholars and philosophers considered entertainment communication to be speech. Even Zechariah Chafee, one of the leading advocates of free speech rights, as late as 1941 thought "indecent" entertainment speech not worthy of inclusion under the First Amendment.[1] And it took the ACLU until 1962 to adopt an absolutist position on free speech rights. It must have been little surprise to Americans in 1915 when the U.S. Supreme Court denied free speech rights to motion pictures.

At the beginning of the twentieth century, free speech generally meant majoritarian speech. By the middle of the century, that assessment had begun to evolve into the "marketplace of ideas" position that even the "speech we hate" should have the right to be heard. But in the 1970s, as free speech rights were extended to neo-Nazis, smut vendors, and wealthy corporations, some began to rethink the absolutist position and to advance what is now called postmodern free speech theory, raising once again arguments that some speech should be restricted for the public good. Instead of trying to muzzle anarchists, labor organizers, moviemakers, and

Communists as did their forebears, postmodern free speech theorists call for restrictions on indecency, pornography, and hate speech. The subjects of the restrictions have changed; the argument has not.[2]

The issue of speech restriction versus open discourse is not one of conservative versus liberal. The midcentury legal movement to end movie censorship made some strange bedfellows. Take, for example, the sophisticated, urbane Ephraim London arguing for the freedom to exhibit Kroger Babb's *Mom and Dad*. Or consider Luigi Marano, a Republican and Conservative Party member of the New York State Assembly who repeatedly tried to get the state to switch from censoring to age classification. Or consider court of appeals judge Charles Desmond, whose writings reflected the legal transformation of speech. A social conservative in the early 1950s, Desmond so favored censorship that he wrote two law review articles in its support, but he came to view it as unconstitutional just a few years later. His opinions about less than savory movies probably did not change, but his views about the constitutionality of exhibiting such films did.

By 1959, the only standard left to the censors was obscenity. The many court watchers who envisaged the fall of this last censoring standard were mistaken. The Supreme Court never held the prior restraint on film unconstitutional. Indeed, it has never held movie censorship per se unconstitutional. So powerful was censorship's appeal as protection for innocents that no state legislature ever voluntarily repealed its censorship law. Despite massive cultural changes between film censorship's creation and its lingering death, it managed to hold on. In the end, it was terminated by a few state courts and by progressively more constricting procedural requirements demanded by the Supreme Court, combined with state legislatures that had come to care little about film content.

In his study of moral conflict, *Hellfire Nation*, James Morone offers a partial explanation of film censorship's longevity. He identifies a "great cycle of modern moral legislation" and finds that morality policies always outlive the moral panics that inspire them.[3] But this generalization is not completely satisfactory in the case of film. Why, when the Supreme Court was specifically and repeatedly asked to overturn film censorship as contrary to the First Amendment, at a time when the Court was expansively interpreting the First Amendment, did it always refuse? There are two possible explanations, although neither truly suffices. First, since each film censorship case centered on a specific film, the justices could latch on to the specific facts and ignore the broad constitutional issue of whether prior restraint on film violated the First Amendment. Even when Ronald Freedman decided not to allow the Court any narrow route by withdrawing the film's content from consideration, the justices still managed to base their decision on the process of censoring rather than on the justification for examining a film in the first place. The Court, over the span of twenty years and twenty justices, just did not want to deal with the question of constitutionality, and it always managed to find a way not to. A second explanation revolves around the belief that movies carry a special capacity for evil, which has not left the public discourse. That belief is so durable that when the demise of state censorship and the Production Code left movies temporarily free, the MPAA immediately stepped up to fill the vacuum with a brand new, much-ballyhooed rating system in 1968.

For those who oppose censorship on principle, as many in this anticensorship story did, there is no great moment when the justices of the Supreme Court ride the winds of the rights revolution to rescue the beleaguered movie industry and smite the censors. The story of the demise of film censorship is a bit of an anticlimax, actually. There is no great resolution. The plot builds and builds, tension mounts, but the conflict between the characters is never satisfactorily resolved. As a screenplay, it would never work. Moviegoers want suspense, action, conflict, and interesting characters. The slow death by litigation of film censorship has little action or mystery, although it certainly has conflict and a remarkable cast of characters—an unorganized number of small businessmen who took on the censorship bureaucracies starting in 1909 and fought the authority of the seven censoring states and the censoring cities through the 1970s. Some were immigrants with a passionate belief in the American Constitution and its protection of free speech. Some were exhibitors who had problems with authority figures. Some engaged in peddling films of questionable taste or outright exploitation. Some were nearly bankrupted by the precarious business of independent film distribution. Some were moderately successful. But all were unwilling to accept restrictions on their ability to disseminate films they thought should be seen. So they opposed the censors in the only way possible: through litigation. In their suits, they challenged the censors' lack of qualifications, their secretive methods, their lack of standards, their arbitrary decisions, and their violation of free speech rights.

At first the courts were unreceptive to the film men's claims of protection under the First Amendment. Their challenge to statutory vagueness also went nowhere. But following World War II, as the courts slowly began to scrutinize other state laws that abridged individual liberties, and as society began to move away from the communitarian ideals of the Progressive Era toward veneration of individual rights, the distributors felt a bit more welcome in the courts. A hint of what was to come appeared in the 1948 *Paramount* decision, which revealed a new sensibility among some justices as it opened the way for independents to compete fairly in the market. The growing market for foreign films encouraged American filmmakers to consider more daring and more adult topics, and they grew restive under their industry-imposed, Catholic-driven regulation. During the 1950s, prodded by intellectuals, civil libertarians, and film critics, censorship looked less and less like the democratic ideal it had been in the Progressive Era and more like a symbol of repression, the likes of which the nation had seen in Nazi Germany and the Soviet Union.

A turning point—the beginning of the end—came in 1952 when the U.S. Supreme Court brought films under the umbrella of the First Amendment in *Burstyn v. Wilson*. But for the independent distributors, the ruling turned out to be more of a tease than a breakthrough. There was still much litigation left to be done to free the screen. Neither the Supreme Court nor American society was ready to dismantle censorship entirely in the 1950s. But as society changed more rapidly in the late 1950s and 1960s, film censorship came to look not only repressive but old fashioned and out of touch. Censors became targets. In 1964, Murray Schumach was not alone when he called them "the elite among nincompoops."[4]

The distributors began to win, most successfully when they questioned arbitrary and muddy censoring terms like *harmful* and *indecent*, and the censors gradually lost authority. All but one of the major cases brought after *Burstyn* were decided in favor of the film men. Each win knocked a bit off the censors' ability to control the content of the American screen: *sacrilege* was the first to go, then *immorality* and *harmfulness*, then *prejudicial to the best interests of the community*, then *incite to crime*, until all that remained to be censored were films considered obscene. When Joseph Burstyn remarked that his case had opened the door for film to take its "rightful place as a major and adult art form,"[5] he was correct, although a bit premature.

Then in 1965 came another turning point. Mediating the conflict between Ronald Freedman and the Maryland censor board, the Supreme Court set down such rigid procedural requirements for governmental film censorship that all of the remaining states gave up, except—sadly for Freedman—Maryland. Beginning with the *Burstyn* decision and increasing with the *Freedman* decision, the mechanics of governmental film censorship grew to be such an onerous burden that, one by one, the states realized that it was no longer worth the effort. Each of the censoring states, save one, surrendered between 1955 and 1966.

When the state censors finally retired, a rush of increasingly erotic and violent films hit movie theaters across the country. As the PCA came under attack from members of the MPAA, it was forced to loosen its restrictions and then was abandoned. The procensorite predictions of unrestrained smut proved correct. In 1965, the height of shock had been Elizabeth Taylor's screeching "son of a bitch" in *Who's Afraid of Virginia Woolf?* Just six years later, *A Clockwork Orange* included frontal nudity. But only two years after that, the reign of hardcore movie theater pornography ended. In *Miller v. California*, the Supreme Court brought to a close its trend of liberalizing definitions of obscenity, begun in the 1957 *Roth* decision. *Miller* reversed the Court's direction, restoring community-based restrictions on the dissemination of supposedly obscene content.

The MPAA also stepped back into the movie regulation business after its period of liberalization. The PCA's content regulation had staggered on until the late 1960s, although with less clout each year as producers increasingly challenged its restrictions or ignored it entirely. But the PCA was scrapped only when changing social conditions made it clear to Hollywood studios that the code was not only a cultural anachronism but, more important, an economic drain. After giving up the PCA in 1966, the MPAA quickly continued its content regulation with the much-vaunted institution of the movie ratings system, the Code and Rating Administration (CARA). That its name included *code* indicates the degree of continuity between the original Production Code and its successor administration. (Only later was the name changed to the Classification and Rating Administration.) Indeed, the new rating system employed much of the personnel of the old PCA, including its chief, Geoffrey Shurlock. Despite MPAA president Jack Valenti's claim that he voluntarily created the age classification system, it was two major U.S. Supreme Court decisions (*Interstate Circuit v. Dallas* and *Ginsberg v. New York*), combined with the threat of national film classification legislation, that encouraged the MPAA to adopt a classification scheme.[6]

Though CARA rates film rather than restrains it, the effect is quite similar to that of the old PCA. The ratings system is content regulation by another name. Because an X rating (later changed to NC-17) drastically reduced the number of theaters available, producers and directors cut their films to conform to the less controversial R rating to make money. The story of *L.I.E.* (2001) reveals a Hollywood control system every bit as effective as the old Production Code. *L.I.E.* committed the sin of sympathetically portraying a pedophile. Though there is no nudity and no violence (except for one gunshot wound when the pedophile is murdered at the end, something very much like the old "compensating moral values"), no amount of negotiation could convince the CARA raters to reduce the rating to an R. Through CARA, Hollywood has managed to maintain control over its product. As James M. Skinner notes in his study of the Legion of Decency, most Americans would be shocked if art galleries, bookstores, or theater productions were forced to exclude customers based on their age and the ratings of an anonymous private group (or a government agency).[7] Yet few people think to question the movie ratings: movies have always existed under some sort of control.

Informal censorship methods, always available to local pressure groups, declined during the era of governmental censorship. Indeed, part of the PCA's raison d'être had been to forestall such local exhibitor pressure, and it worked. With the demise of both the PCA and the censor boards, though, informal attempts at control began to rise again. Movies like *Dressed to Kill* (1980), *Year of the Dragon* (1985), *Basic Instinct* (1991), and *The Last Temptation of Christ* (1988) were subjected to massive, nationwide interference.[8]

Not only has content regulation continued in Hollywood, but the censorship controversy so evident in the middle years of the twentieth century has not passed, and First Amendment issues have resurfaced as some now call for restrictions on Internet content, film and television, song lyrics, and radio broadcasts. Whereas the midcentury state censors' worries were adultery, childbirth, and gunplay, today's concerns are pornography, terrorism, crime, violence, and both verbal and physical indecency. At base, though, the concerns are the same: immorality and crime. As the FCC fielded complaints from listeners about shock jocks, the nation's largest radio company, Clear Channel Communications, developed what it called its responsible broadcasting initiative. This highly publicized plan, released just as Congress began an investigation, sounded much like the early Hollywood initiatives to stave off federal regulation: the "Don'ts and Be Carefuls" and the Thirteen Points.

In the early days of movies, one of the major criticisms of film addressed its ability to educate viewers in the methods of crime. Concerned citizens, reformers, and censors worried that the 1930s gangster cycle would create a generation of gun-toting thugs. That fear has not died, only dimmed. Movies have grown increasingly violent, frequently displaying criminal activity, and violent movies are immensely popular. The astonishingly violent *Fight Club* (1999), for example, was hugely popular with those in their twenties and thirties. Yet even though Americans seem more accepting of film violence, we are still not sure that it is not harmful. If confronted with evidence that a film might have motivated criminal activity, American legal culture is still likely to accept arguments for its restriction. In 1999, the U.S. Supreme Court allowed Louisiana to deny free speech rights to the film *Natural Born Killers* because it was an "incitement to lawless activity."[9]

Censorship necessarily involves the drawing of a line between what is permissible and what is dangerous. The questions today, as in 1910, are where the line is drawn, who draws it, with what authority, and under what supervision. As Marjorie Heins suggests, until the questions about the best ways to socialize young people about violence and sexuality are answered to the satisfaction of the majority, the "quick fix of censorship to protect the young will continue to have political appeal."[10] But if there is one lesson to be learned from the era of unrestricted governmental censorship of motion pictures, it is that entrusting decisions about questions of morality to bureaucrats—no matter how explicitly drawn the guidelines—means allowing them to decide where to draw the lines. And the results will be neither coherent nor consistent.

The political appeal of censorship may hang on, but the rhetoric has changed. Whereas many progressives were perfectly happy to use the word *censor*, today's moral reformers shy away from its use. Responding to criticism about MPAA ratings, Jack Valenti insisted that CARA did not censor films but merely categorized them (which technically was true, but it was interesting to see how far Valenti would go to avoid being described as a censor). In the 1980s, Tipper Gore was quick to say that she did not want pop music lyrics censored; her group wanted ratings on CDs only for parental guidance. The FCC today does not talk about censoring the airwaves; rather, it uses the rhetoric of indecency and threatens to back its decrees with fines and license suspensions. In 2005, when many people demonstrated their outrage at Janet Jackson, Howard Stern, and Bubba the Love Sponge, congressional investigations centered not on censoring broadcasts but on determining how much it should cost to carry offensive content.

But avoidance of the word *censorship* and the absence of governmental agencies with the power of prior restraint should not blind Americans to the presence of content-altering pressure. Talk show hosts are no more likely to continue speaking today if they are liable for massive fines than movie exhibitors were to face down angry ticket buyers in 1909 or 1949. Movie producers are no more likely to film scenes that might earn an NC-17 rating than they were to risk being denied a PCA seal in 1940.

Most Americans have no idea that the judicially sanctioned right to free speech is a relatively recent concept that was much fought over during the twentieth century. It was a long and complicated road from Justice Jackson's 1943 statement that "no official, high or petty, can prescribe what shall be orthodox in . . . matters of opinion"[11] to Justice Brennan's 1989 opinion that "if there is a bedrock principle underlying the First Amendment, it is that the Government may not prohibit the expression of an idea simply because society finds the idea itself offensive or disagreeable."[12] Many deserve credit for pushing the Court to adopt the speech-protective position Americans today take for granted, including the NAACP and the ACLU, to name just two easily identifiable organizations.

But the independent film distributors and exhibitors, because they were unorganized and carried on an unplanned and uncoordinated effort, have gone unrecognized. It is time to acknowledge Joseph Burstyn, Ronald Freedman, Jean Goldwurm, Edward Kingsley, Richard Brandt, and the others who refused to submit to a licensing procedure that most Americans today would find offensive to liberty.

Today, the marketplace—audiences and bankers—largely determines which films will be made and which will not. While the self-restrictions and the content regulations are still alive in the United States today, as evidenced by CARA, the prior restraint of governmental censorship is gone. We can safely speculate that film censorship statutes would eventually have been overturned. But bureaucratic inertia and profitability kept state legislatures from voluntarily disbanding censor boards. Only when pushed by the courts, which had been pushed by the independent distributors, did the states give up. Ending state film censorship may have been the goal of Burstyn, Brandt, and Freedman, but the expansion of First Amendment rights to free speech and free press was the by-product.

For those who mourn the collapse of modesty and public decency, there is no comfort in free speech for moviemakers. Movies like *Natural Born Killers* and *Kill Bill* display a level of unprecedented movie violence, as does *The Passion of the Christ*. Sexual content has become so normal that what used to be considered soft porn now gets an R rating. Yet there is little doubt that with the end of censorship and the end of Hollywood's content regulation came the freedom for filmmakers to deal with subjects that would previously have been banned. And while postmodern free speech theorists wish to see public speech controlled for the good of all and some long for taste arbitration, history reveals how difficult those propositions will always be. In the earliest years of film, the National Board of Review, a nongovernmental agency, tried to serve as a taste arbiter of film, but it never fully satisfied anyone, and within two decades it was virtually defunct. Industry self-regulation has not worked either. The Production Code stifled the serious contemplation of many ideas. Nor can the governmental route work absent an amendment to the U.S. Constitution repealing part of the First Amendment. Although we may not have figured out how to deal with free speech and mass media, and outrage at offensive content has reached another peak, and censorship by other names still lurks, Americans are not falling back on the quick fix of governmental censorship. We have been there; we have done that.

Notes

Abbreviations

ACLUA	American Civil Liberties Union Archives, 1950–1995, Public Policy Papers, Department of Rare Books and Special Collections, Princeton University Library, Princeton, NJ
AGHP	Arthur Garfield Hays Papers, Seeley G. Mudd Manuscript Library, Princeton University, Princeton, NJ
MC	Maryland Collection, Enoch Pratt Free Library, Baltimore
MSBC	Maryland State Board of Censors, Department of Licensing and Regulation, Maryland State Archives, Annapolis
NYMPD	New York State Motion Picture Division, New York State Archives, Albany
ODFC	Ohio Division of Film Censorship, Ohio Historical Society, Columbus
PCAR	Motion Picture Association of America Production Code Administration Records, Special Collections, Margaret Herrick Library, Academy of Motion Picture Arts and Sciences, Beverly Hills, CA
PSBC	Pennsylvania State Board of Censors (Motion Pictures), Records of the Department of Education, RG 22, Pennsylvania State Archives, Harrisburg
VDMPC	Virginia Division of Motion Picture Censorship, Library of Virginia, Richmond

Introduction

1. Leonard W. Levy, *Legacy of Suppression: Freedom of Speech and Press in Early American History* (New York: Harper and Row, 1960).

2. See Paul S. Boyer, *Purity in Print: The Vice-Society Movement and Book Censorship in America* (New York: Scribner, 1968).

3. See John Springhall, "Censoring Hollywood: Youth, Moral Panic and Crime/Gangster Movies of the 1930s," *Journal of Popular Culture* 32, no. 3 (1998): 135–36.

4. Florida also enacted a censorship statute but did no original censoring, so I do not include it in the censoring states.

5. These figures are approximations and represent the film censorship situation between 1950 and 1964. The actual number is probably higher.

6. No fewer than sixty-three Supreme Court cases have used the exact phrase "marketplace of ideas." It is usually used to invoke the idea of a free exchange of all ideas so that the best will surface but none will be repressed.

7. See Rochelle Gurstein, *The Repeal of Reticence: A History of America's Cultural and Legal Struggles over Free Speech, Obscenity, Sexual Liberation, and Modern Art* (New York: Hill and Wang, 1996).

8. Gregory D. Black, *Hollywood Censored: Morality Codes, Catholics and the Movies* (Cambridge: Cambridge University Press, 1994), 239–60.

9. Elmer Rice, "Entertainment in the Age of McCarthy," *New Republic*, April 13, 1953.

10. The Hollywood Production Code Administration has been the subject of much scholarship. See, for example, Gregory D. Black, *The Catholic Crusade against the Movies, 1940–1975* (Cambridge: Cambridge University Press, 1997); Black, *Hollywood Censored*; Una M. Cadegan, "Guardians of Democracy or Cultural Storm Troopers? American Catholics and the Control of Popular Media, 1934–1966," *Catholic Historical Review* 87 (2001): 252–82; Richard Corliss, "The Legion of Decency," *Film Comment*, Summer 1968, 24–61; Leonard J. Leff and Jerold L. Simmons, *The Dame in the Kimono: Hollywood, Censorship, and the Production Code from the 1920s to the 1960s* (New York: Grove Weidenfeld, 1990); Jon Lewis, *Hollywood v. Hard Core: How the Struggles over Censorship Saved the Modern Film Industry* (New York: New York University Press, 2000); Frank Miller, *Censored Hollywood: Sex, Sin and Violence in Hollywood* (Atlanta: Turner, 1994); Murray Schumach, *The Face on the Cutting Room Floor: The Story of Movie and Television Censorship* (New York: Morrow, 1964); Stephen Vaughn, "Morality and Entertainment: Origins of the Motion Picture Code," *Journal of American History* 77 (1990): 39–65; and Frank Walsh, *Sin and Censorship: The Catholic Church and the Motion Picture Industry* (New Haven, CT: Yale University Press, 1996).

11. Lewis, *Hollywood v. Hard Core*, 6. Two other terms were suggested in a 1970 law review article: "private ordering" and "private lawmaking." Douglas Ayer, Roy E. Bates, and Peter J. Herman, "Self-Censorship in the Movie

Industry: An Historical Perspective on Law and Social Change," *Wisconsin Law Review*, 1970, no. 3:791.

12. Nancy J. Rosenbloom, "Between Reform and Regulation: The Struggle over Film Censorship in Progressive America, 1909–1922," *Film History* 1 (1987): 307–25; Nancy J. Rosenbloom, "From Regulation to Censorship: Film and Political Culture in New York in the Early Twentieth Century," *Journal of the Gilded Age and Progressive Era* 3 (2004): 369–406; Janet Staiger, *Bad Women: Regulating Sexuality in Early American Cinema* (Minneapolis: University of Minnesota Press, 1995), 86–115.

13. Richard S. Randall, *Censorship of the Movies: The Social and Political Control of a Mass Medium* (Madison: University of Wisconsin Press, 1968), 162–78.

14. The first Hollywood studio production to be involved in challenging governmental censorship was *Curley*, a 1947 film by Hal Roach Studios. The distributor, United Artists, brought suit against the censors of Memphis, Tennessee. A second case came in 1950 when an exhibitor played the 20th Century–Fox film *Pinky* without a censor license from municipal officials in Marshall, Texas. But 20th Century–Fox did not bring the case; it came from the prosecution of the local exhibitor, W. L. Gelling. The first MPAA member studio to challenge a state censor decision was Howard Hughes's RKO Radio Pictures in 1954, in *RKO Radio Pictures, Inc. v. Department of Education*, 162 Ohio St. 263 (1954). The second was United Artists, which brought suit over *The Man with the Golden Arm* in 1956 in *United Artists v. Maryland State Board of Censors*, 210 Md. 586 (1956).

15. I use the term *determination* here to indicate the final judgment of the state censor boards because that is the term used in their records and their correspondence.

16. Zechariah Chafee, *Free Speech in the United States* (Cambridge, MA: Harvard University Press, 1941), 542.

17. Robert Reich, review of *The Republic of Choice: Law, Authority and Culture*, by Lawrence M. Friedman, *American Political Science Review* 84 (1990): 1383.

18. John Izod, *Hollywood and the Box Office, 1895–1986* (New York: Columbia University Press, 1988), 148.

19. Alan Brinkley, *The End of Reform: New Deal Liberalism in Recession and War* (New York: Vintage Books, 1996), 164–65.

20. Majority opinion, *Commonwealth v. Blumenstein*, 396 Pa. 417 (1959).

21. Black, *Hollywood Censored*, 296.

22. See Richard A. Brisbin, "Censorship, Ratings, and Rights: Political Order and Sexual Portrayal in American Movies," *Studies in American Po-*

litical Development 16 (2002): 1–27; Francis G. Couvares, introduction to "Hollywood, Censorship, and American Culture," special issue, *American Quarterly* 44 (1992): 509–24; Ernest David Giglio, "Prior Restraint of Motion Pictures," *Dickinson Law Review* 69 (1965): 379–90; and Garth Jowett, "Moral Responsibility and Commercial Entertainment: Social Control in the U.S. Film Industry, 1907–1968," *Historical Journal of Film, Radio, and Television* 10 (1990): 3–32. Richard Brisbin's article, which deals mostly with the later period of film censorship, credits producers, directors, the ACLU, legal realist judges, and Jesuit intellectuals for ending film censorship activity yet neglects to mention the independent distributors who brought the significant cases.

23. Flick quoted in Otis L. Guernsey, "Film Censor's Dilemma," *New York Herald Tribune*, February 27, 1955.

24. Bosley Crowther, *New York Times*, August 13, 1961.

1. The Origins of Governmental Film Censorship, 1907–1923

1. Robert Sklar, *Movie-Made America: A Cultural History of American Movies* (New York: Vintage Books, 1994), 175.

2. Gurstein, *Repeal of Reticence*, 32–60.

3. Walter Kendrick, *The Secret Museum: Pornography in Modern Culture* (New York: Viking, 1987), 134–35.

4. "Social sewage" comes from drama professor Fred Eastman, quoted in David A. Horowitz, "An Alliance of Convenience: Independent Exhibitors and Purity Crusaders Battle Hollywood, 1920–1940," *Historian* 59, no. 3 (1997), http://www.ebscohost.com. For a description of the films that so worried reformers, see Kevin Brownlow, *Behind the Mask of Innocence: Sex, Violence, Prejudice, Crime; Films of Social Conscience in the Silent Era* (Berkeley and Los Angeles: University of California Press, 1990), and Thomas Doherty, *Pre-Code Hollywood: Sex, Immorality, and Insurrection in American Cinema, 1930–1934* (New York: Columbia University Press, 1990).

5. "Moral panic" comes from Springhall, "Censoring Hollywood," 136.

6. James A. Morone, *Hellfire Nation: The Politics of Sin in American History* (New Haven, CT: Yale University Press, 2003), 15–17.

7. Helen Lefkowitz Horowitz, *Rereading Sex: Battles over Sexual Knowledge and Suppression in Nineteenth-Century America* (New York: Knopf, 2002), 121–43.

8. John Wertheimer, "The *Mutual Film* Reviewed: The Movies, Censorship and Free Speech in Progressive America," *American Journal of Legal History* 37 (1993): 162.

9. Much has been written about the cultural upheaval from these new forms of recreation. See, for example, Lewis A. Erenburg, *Steppin' Out: New York Nightlife and the Transformation of American Culture, 1890–1930* (Chicago: University of Chicago Press, 1981); Harvey Green, *The Uncertainty of Everyday Life, 1915–1945* (Fayetteville: University of Arkansas Press, 2000); David Nasaw, *Going Out: The Rise and Fall of Public Amusements* (New York: Basic Books, 1993); Kathy Peiss, *Cheap Amusements: Working Women and Leisure in Turn-of-the-Century New York* (Philadelphia: Temple University Press, 1986); Burton W. Peretti, *The Creation of Jazz: Music, Race, and Culture in Urban America* (Urbana: University of Illinois Press, 1994); and Robert W. Snyder, *The Voice of the City: Vaudeville and Popular Culture in New York* (New York: Oxford University Press, 1989).

10. Garth Jowett, "A Capacity for Evil: The 1915 Supreme Court Mutual Decision," *Historical Journal of Film, Radio, and Television* 9 (1989): 59; Lary May, *Screening Out the Past: The Birth of Mass Culture and the Motion Picture Industry* (New York: Oxford University Press, 1980), 58.

11. R. Laurence Moore, *Selling God: American Religion in the Marketplace of Culture* (New York: Oxford University Press, 1994), 222.

12. Paul Starr, *The Creation of the Media: Political Origins of Modern Communications* (New York: Basic Books, 2004), 295–326. See also Brownlow, *Behind the Mask of Innocence*, 374–75; Steven Alan Carr, *Hollywood and Anti-Semitism: A Cultural History up to World War II* (Cambridge: Cambridge University Press, 2001); Andrea Friedman, *Prurient Interests: Gender, Democracy, and Obscenity in New York City, 1909–1945* (New York: Columbia University Press, 2000); Garth Jowett, *Film: The Democratic Art* (Boston: Little, Brown, 1976), 87–88; and May, *Screening Out the Past*, 169–75.

13. Couvares, introduction to "Hollywood, Censorship, and American Culture," 3; Friedman, *Prurient Interests*, 63. Friedman freely adopts Couvares's term "vulnerable viewer."

14. Peiss, *Cheap Amusements*, 146.

15. Sharon R. Ullman, *Sex Seen: The Emergence of Modern Sexuality in America* (Berkeley: University of California Press, 1997), 8–23. For more on this and on movies in the 1920s, see Brownlow, *Behind the Mask of Innocence*, 26–94.

16. David M. Rabban, *Free Speech in Its Forgotten Years* (Cambridge: Cambridge University Press, 1997), 213.

17. Quoted in *Literary Digest*, May 14, 1921, 32.

18. Molly Ladd-Taylor, *Mother-Work: Women, Child Welfare, and the State, 1890–1930* (Urbana: University of Illinois Press, 1994), 3.

19. Leigh Ann Wheeler, *Against Obscenity: Reform and the Politics of Womanhood, 1873–1935* (Baltimore: Johns Hopkins University Press, 2004), 60.

20. Robin Gallagher, "Public Educators and Hollywood, 1900–1922," *High School Journal* 82 (1999): 195–208.

21. Friedman, *Prurient Interests*, 28.

22. *New York Times*, "Moving Picture Shows Win," January 7, 1909.

23. Friedman, *Prurient Interests*, 30–32.

24. Rosenbloom, "Between Reform and Regulation," 311.

25. Friedman, *Prurient Interests*, 47–49.

26. Ibid.

27. See Mark Lynn Anderson, "Regulating Racism: Americanism, Identity Politics, and the Battle for Film Censorship in New York State" (paper presented at Researching New York, University at Albany, State University of New York, November 21, 2003); May, *Screening Out the Past*, 58; and Sklar, *Movie-Made America*, 124. Sklar maintains that the moral reformers were motivated by class concerns, whereas May emphasizes the more specific fear of immigrants and their apparent takeover of the cities.

28. *New York Times*, August 14, 1910.

29. Joseph Levenson (secretary, New York State Motion Picture Commission) quoted in *New York Times*, February 5, 1922.

30. A search of the *New York Times* from 1909 to 1913 reveals no arrests for indecent motion picture exhibitions. See also Alison M. Parker, *Purifying America: Women, Cultural Reform and Pro-Censorship Activism, 1873–1933* (Urbana: University of Illinois Press, 1997), 123.

31. Black, *Hollywood Censored*, 15; Richard Carl Saylor, "The Pennsylvania State Board of Censors (Motion Picture)" (master's thesis, Pennsylvania State University at Harrisburg, 1999), 5.

32. Appeal of Metro Film Exchange, September 1917, box 10, PSBC.

33. Kansas's censors were to "disapprove such moving picture films or reels as are sacrilegious, obscene, indecent, or immoral, or such as tend to corrupt morals." Quoted in Linda K. Warner, "Movie Censorship in Kansas: The Kansas State Board of Review" (master's thesis, Emporia State University, 1988), 1.

34. Majority opinion, *Mutual Film Corp. v. Industrial Commission of Ohio*, 215 F. 138 (1914).

35. Starr, *Creation of the Media*, 238–42.

36. Richard Nunez, "In Search of a Legislative Definition: The Judicial and Legislative History of State Film Censorship in New York" (master's thesis, Syracuse University, 1960), 48–49.

37. Friedman, *Prurient Interests*, 51.

38. Ibid. Also see the court's opinion in *People ex rel. Schwab* v. *Grant*, 12 N.Y.S. 889 (1890 N.Y. Misc.).

39. In thirty-five years, the courts overruled the license commissioner's

determinations about the morality of films only once, in the case of a film called *The Ordeal*, in *Life Photo Film Corp. v. Bell*, 90 Misc. 469, 154 N.Y.S. 763 (1915). For more information on the case and the film, see Edward de Grazia and Roger K. Newman, *Banned Films: Movies, Censors and the First Amendment* (New York: Bowker, 1982), 183–84, and Dawn B. Sova, *Forbidden Films: Censorship Histories of 125 Motion Pictures* (New York: Facts on File, 2001), 232–34. The case that would finally overrule a license commissioner determination was *Burstyn v. McCaffrey* in 1951. See ch. 6 for details. New York City's license commissioner was also sustained by the federal courts, but not without an initial loss. In 1919, an anti-VD film called *Fit to Win* was challenged by License Commissioner Gilchrist. Bringing suit in federal district court, Commissioner Gilchrist lost in the first round but was upheld on appeal to the U.S. Court of Appeals for the Second Circuit. *Silverman v. Gilchrist* 260 F. 564 (2d Cir. 1919).

40. *New York Times*, "Unaccompanied Children," January 12, 1913.

41. Nunez, "In Search of a Legislative Definition," 67.

42. Report of the New York State Conference of Mayors quoted in Charles Matthew Feldman, *The National Board of Censorship (Review) of Motion Pictures, 1909–1922* (New York: Arno Press, 1977), 164–65.

43. Ibid., 168–82.

44. *New York Times*, April 12, 1921.

45. Quoted in Feldman, *National Board of Censorship*, 190.

46. *New York Times*, April 12, 1921.

47. Starr, *Creation of the Media*, 317–18.

48. Ira H. Carmen, *Movies, Censorship and the Law* (Ann Arbor: University of Michigan Press, 1966), 127; *State ex rel. Cummins v. Coleman*, Circ. Ct., 11th Jud. (1937).

49. Virginia's statutory standards were identical to New York's: a film was to be disallowed if it was "obscene, indecent, immoral, inhuman or is of such character that its exhibition would tend to corrupt morals or incite crime." Agency History, DMPCR.

50. J. Douglas Smith, "Patrolling the Boundaries of Race: Motion Picture Censorship and Jim Crow in Virginia, 1922–1932," *Historical Journal of Film, Radio, and Television* 21 (2001): 273, 277.

51. Randall, *Censorship of the Movies*, 17.

52. For the colorful story of this masterful public relations campaign, see Wheeler, *Against Obscenity*, 67–72.

53. *New York Times*, July 7, 1955.

54. Morton Keller, *Regulating a New Society: Public Policy and Social Change in America, 1900–1933* (Cambridge, MA: Harvard University Press, 1994), 89. The Catholic Church estimated that there were as many as three

hundred municipalities censoring films in one way or another in 1929. See Walsh, *Sin and Censorship*, 57. Gregory Black estimates that there were two hundred. Black, *Catholic Crusade against the Movies*, 100. As late as 1957, one estimate put the number at ninety. See Carmen, *Movies, Censorship and the Law*, 184.

55. Black, *Hollywood Censored*, 191.

56. Parker, *Purifying America*, 35–36.

57. For more on early methods of film distribution, see Suzanne Mary Donahue, *American Film Distribution: The Changing Marketplace* (Ann Arbor, MI: UMI Research Press, 1987); Gorham Kindem, ed., *The American Movie Industry: The Business of Motion Pictures* (Carbondale: University of Illinois Press, 1982); and David Puttnam, *Movies and Money* (New York: Knopf, 1998), 29–44.

58. J. A. Aberdeen, "The Early Film Business: Distribution; States Rights or Road Show," Hollywood Renegades Archive, http://www.cobbles.com/simpp_archive/statesrights.htm.

59. Donahue, *American Film Distribution*, 16.

60. Ibid., 21.

61. Quoted in Randall, *Censorship of the Movies*, 126.

62. *New York Times*, July 21, 1928.

63. Oberholtzer quoted in Richard C. Saylor, "Banned in Pennsylvania!" *Pennsylvania Heritage*, Summer 1999, 15.

64. *Philadelphia Evening Bulletin*, April 27, 1954.

65. Warner, "Movie Censorship in Kansas," 8.

66. The personnel files are missing from the New York Motion Picture Division archives. However, the reviewers' note sheets contain initials, so their longevity can be estimated.

67. *New York Times*, November 27, 1949.

68. In 1948, the film reports deleted the identity of the reviewers. Eliminations files, 1932–1948, series A-1417, NYMPD.

69. Series 1581, box 50,737, ODFC.

70. Quoted in Frederick Marshall Wirt, "State Film Censorship with Particular Reference to Ohio" (PhD diss., Ohio State University, 1956), 212.

71. Draft of article that was to appear in the *Roanoke (Va.) Times* on March 8, 1964, series 1441, box 50,744, file 97, VDMPC.

72. *New York Times*, September 4, 1921.

73. George H. Cobb to Samuel Cummins of Social Welfare Pictures Inc., May 27, 1925, file 3221-2565, series A-1418, NYMPD.

74. Douglas W. Churchill, "Hollywood Heeds the Thunder," *New York Times*, July 22, 1931.

75. Quoted in Ruth Inglis, *Freedom of the Movies: A Report on Self-*

Regulation from the Commission on Freedom of the Press (Chicago: University of Chicago Press, 1947), 19.

76. Temporary State Commission on Coordination of State Activities, *Report on the Motion Picture Division, New York State Education Department* (Albany, NY: Temporary State Commission on Coordination of State Activities, 1949), 1. An act passed May 8, 1929, amended Pennsylvania's censorship statute to exempt newsreels. *In re* Spain in Flames, 36 Pa. D. & C. 285 (1937); *State v. Smith*, 108 N.E. 2d 582 (1952).

77. New York State Motion Picture Division, annual reports, 1927–1940, series A-1415, NYMPD.

2. The Courts Provide No Relief, 1909–1927

1. *Regina v. Hicklin*, L.R. 3Q.B. 360 (1868).
2. *Block v. Chicago*, 239 Ill. 251, 87 N.E. 1011 (1909).
3. Rabban, *Free Speech in Its Forgotten Years*, 121.
4. See, for example, David Yassky, "Eras of the First Amendment," *Columbia Law Review* 91 (1991): 1699–755. Also see Bruce Ackerman, "Constitutional Politics/Constitutional Law," *Yale Law Journal* 99 (1989): 453–547.
5. Rabban, *Free Speech in Its Forgotten Years*, 131.
6. Aitken quoted in Wertheimer, "*Mutual Film* Reviewed," 177.
7. Ibid., 175.
8. For more on the original package doctrine, see Richard F. Hamm, *Shaping the Eighteenth Amendment: Temperance Reform, Legal Culture, and the Polity, 1880–1920* (Chapel Hill: University of North Carolina Press, 1995).
9. *Buffalo Branch, Mutual Film Corp. v. Breitinger*, 250 Pa. 225 (1915).
10. Wertheimer, "*Mutual Film* Reviewed," 166.
11. *Buffalo Branch, Mutual Film Corp. v. Breitinger.*
12. *Mutual Film Corp. v. Industrial Commission of Ohio*, 215 F. 138.
13. *Mutual Film Corp. of Missouri v. Hodges*, 236 U.S. 248 (1915).
14. Randall, *Censorship of the Movies*, 20.
15. Appellants' brief, *Mutual Film Corp. v. Industrial Commission of Ohio*, 236 U.S. 230 (1915).
16. *Mutual Film Corp. v. Industrial Commission of Ohio*, 236 U.S. 230.
17. Rabban, *Free Speech in Its Forgotten Years*, 175.
18. David Post, "Understanding the Techno Evolution," *American Lawyer*, September 1996, 104.
19. Wertheimer, "*Mutual Film* Reviewed," 160.
20. Rabban, *Free Speech in Its Forgotten Years*, 175.
21. *Hannegan v. Esquire*, 327 U.S. 146 (1946).
22. Puttnam, *Movies and Money*, 39.

23. Starr, *Creation of the Media*, 314.
24. Jowett, *Democratic Art*, 121.
25. Horowitz, "Alliance of Convenience."
26. Jowett, "Capacity for Evil," 73.
27. *New York Times*, August 16, 1921.
28. *Pathe Exchange Inc. v. Cobb*, 202 A.D. 450 (1922).
29. *Pathe Exchange Inc. v. Cobb*, 236 N.Y. 539 (1923).
30. Leslie DeBauche Midkiff, *Reel Patriotism: The Movies and World War I* (Madison: University of Wisconsin Press, 1997), 105–11.
31. Jowett, *Democratic Art*, 465.
32. *New York Times*, November 19, 1921.
33. *Goldwyn Distributing Corp. v. Cobb*, 199 A.D. 913 (1921).
34. Francis Bergan, *The History of the New York Court of Appeals, 1847–1932* (New York: Columbia University Press, 1985); Arthur Karger, *The Powers of the New York Court of Appeals*, 3rd ed. (Rochester, NY: Lawyers Cooperative, 1997).
35. File 9989-2721, series A-1418, NYMPD. *The Night Rose* was also known as *Voices of the City* and *Flowers of Darkness*.
36. *New York Times*, November 19, 1921.
37. Brownlow, *Behind the Mask of Innocence*, 153–55.
38. *In re Weathers*, 203 A.D. 896 (1922).
39. *New York Times*, May 18, 1922.
40. From the motion picture commission annual reports, it is impossible to determine how many films were required to make cuts each year. The reports indicate how many cuts were required for each category—for example, in 1926 there were 442 scenes eliminated as "inhuman" and 141 eliminated as "immoral"—but there is no way to tell how many films these eliminated scenes occurred in.
41. The numbers of films requesting reconsideration of a license refusal during these years were as follows: eighty-three in 1924, thirty-two in 1925, sixteen in 1926, nineteen in 1927, forty-nine in 1928, thirty-three in 1929, and thirty-one in 1930. The rate of rejection dipped only in 1926 and 1927. New York State Motion Picture Division, annual reports, NYMPD.
42. *In re* Spain in Flames.

3. Hollywood and the Legion of Decency, 1922–1934

1. Randall, *Censorship of the Movies*, 13–14.
2. Margaret A. Blanchard, "The American Urge to Censor: Freedom of Expression versus the Desire to Sanitize Society—from Anthony Comstock to 2 Live Crew," *William and Mary Law Review* 33 (1992): 779.

3. *New York Times*, January 12, 1923, September 13, 1921.

4. Hays quoted in *New York Times*, July 25, 1922.

5. Ford H. MacGregor, "Official Censorship Legislation," *Annals of the American Academy of Political and Social Science* 128, no. 1 (1926): 164–66.

6. Leff and Simmons, *Dame in the Kimono*, 7.

7. In New York, 1928 and 1929 were busy years for the censors: in 1928, the censors stopped 661 films before exhibition, and in 1929, they intercepted 448. New York State Motion Picture Division, annual reports, NYMPD.

8. Parker, *Purifying America*, 143–45.

9. Wheeler, *Against Obscenity*, 86.

10. Tino Balio, *Grand Design: Hollywood as a Modern Business Enterprise, 1930–1939* (New York: Scribner, 1993), 56.

11. Wheeler, *Against Obscenity*, 163–65.

12. Frank Walsh offers examples of Catholic clergy who favored governmental censorship, but most opposed it. Walsh, *Sin and Censorship*, ch. 1.

13. *New York Times*, July 25, 1934; Harold C. Gardiner, *Catholic Viewpoint on Censorship* (Garden City, NY: Hanover House, 1958), 88. Also see Friedman, *Prurient Interests*, 134–54.

14. See Vaughn, "Morality and Entertainment," and Jowett, "Moral Responsibility and Commercial Entertainment."

15. Quoted in Black, *Hollywood Censored*, 167.

16. Paul W. Facey, *The Legion of Decency: A Sociological Analysis of the Emergence and Development of a Social Pressure Group* (New York: Arno Press, 1974), 40.

17. For more on the Production Code and its provisions, see Black, *Hollywood Censored*; Leff and Simmons, *Dame in the Kimono*; and Walsh, *Sin and Censorship*.

18. Quoted in "Censorship of Motion Pictures," *Yale Law Journal* 49 (1939): 104.

19. Doherty, *Pre-Code Hollywood*, 6.

20. Blanchard, "American Urge to Censor," 743.

21. Black, *Catholic Crusade against the Movies*, 17.

22. Dialogue quoted in Frank Thompson, "Pre-Code Parlance," *American Film* 15, no. 2 (1989): 13. For more on Joy and Wingate, see Black, *Hollywood Censored*.

23. Black, *Hollywood Censored*, 101.

24. For more on these films, see Lea Jacobs, *The Wages of Sin, 1928–1942* (Madison: University of Wisconsin Press, 1991).

25. Quoted in Walsh, *Sin and Censorship*, 73.

26. See Doherty, *Pre-Code Hollywood*.

27. Ibid., 324.

28. Sarah J. Smith, *Children, Cinema and Censorship: From Dracula to the Dead End Kids* (London and New York: I. B. Tauris, 2005), 79.

29. Mark May quoted in Garth S. Jowett, Ian C. Jarvie, and Kathryn H. Fuller, *Children and the Movies: Media Influence and the Payne Fund Controversy* (New York: Cambridge University Press, 1996), 104.

30. Henry James Forman, *Our Movie Made Children* (New York: Macmillan, 1934). For more on Forman's digest of the studies, see Jowett, Jarvie, and Fuller, *Children and the Movies*, 102–8.

31. Arthur R. Jarvis Jr., "The Payne Fund Reports: A Discussion of Their Content, Public Reaction, and Affect [*sic*] on the Motion Picture Industry, 1930–1940," *Journal of Popular Culture* 25, no. 2 (1991): 127–40.

32. Florence Finch Kelly, "A Study of the Movies' Effects on Children," *New York Times*, June 18, 1933.

33. Jowett, Jarvie, and Fuller, *Children and the Movies*, 104.

34. Ohio's brief against the film *M* in 1952 referred to films as "a complex combination of these things which achieves titanic impact on the viewer because it draws him *into* the very action it portrays." Defendant's brief, *Superior Films, Inc. v. Department of Education of Ohio*, 159 Ohio St. 315, 112 N.E. 2d 311 (1953).

35. Rodney A. Wambeam, "Lights! Camera! Policy! Regulating the Morality of American Entertainment" (PhD diss., University of Nebraska, 1999). The number of magazine articles about movie morality increased sharply in the early 1920s, again in 1933 and 1934, and again from 1952 through 1954. Interest in the topic tapered off in the 1960s. The *New York Times* index also shows a peak in 1933 and 1934.

36. Quoted in *New York Times*, February 11, 1934.

37. *New York Times*, February 11, March 22, 24, 1934.

38. *New York Times*, January 3, 1935.

39. *New York Times*, July 22, 1934.

40. Black, *Hollywood Censored*, 156; *New York Times*, June 11, 1934. For a brief discussion about the writing of the codes of fair competition, see Colin Gordon, *New Deals: Business, Labor, and Politics in America, 1920–1935* (Cambridge: Cambridge University Press, 1994), 174–80. For information on Hollywood and the National Recovery Administration, see Giuliana Muscio, *Hollywood's New Deal* (Philadelphia: Temple University Press, 1996).

41. Hays quoted in James M. Skinner, *The Cross and the Cinema* (Westport, CT: Praeger, 1993), 36–37.

42. Ibid., 37.

43. Facey estimates the number at between 7 and 9 million of the 20 million Catholics in the country. Facey, *Legion of Decency*, 60. Other estimates

range as high as 11 million. Jowett places the number at 9 to 11 million. Jowett, "Moral Responsibility and Commercial Entertainment," 62.

44. Leff and Simmons, *Dame in the Kimono*, 44.

45. Gerald Gardner, *The Censorship Papers: Movie Censorship Letters from the Hays Office, 1934–1968* (New York: Dodd, Mead, 1987), xix.

46. Skinner, *Cross and the Cinema*, 38–39.

47. In New York State, problem films declined by 70 percent between 1934, the year the PCA was founded, and 1940. New York State Motion Picture Division, annual reports, NYMPD.

48. "Censorship of Motion Pictures," 106.

49. Quoted in Eric Hodgins, "A Round Table on the Movies," *Life*, June 27, 1949.

50. Gardner, *Censorship Papers*, xx–xxi.

51. New York State Motion Picture Division, annual reports, NYMPD.

52. The *New York Daily News* reported that *Polygamy* was the first movie with a "Hays purity seal" to be rejected in New York—the "first setback suffered by an American film here since Joseph I. Breen joined Hays' office as official purifier." *New York Daily News*, "State Censors Bar 'Polygamy' Film from N.Y.," June 13, 1939.

53. Black, *Hollywood Censored*, 238.

54. Hodgins, "Round Table on the Movies."

55. Black, *Catholic Crusade against the Movies*, 5.

56. Andre Sennwald, "The Screen Comes to Grips with Life," *New York Times*, December 16, 1934.

57. Gregory Black's *Catholic Crusade against the Movies* details the extent to which Catholic pressure influenced the content of Hollywood films. See also Facey, *Legion of Decency*.

4. Early Challenges to State Censors, 1927–1940

1. Pennsylvania and Ohio each faced three, Virginia faced only one (a case that was simultaneously challenged in New York), and Maryland and Kansas had none.

2. *In re Fox Film*, 295 Pa. 461, 145 Atl. 514 (1929); *Vitagraph, Inc.'s Application*, 295 Pa. 471, 145 Atl. 518 (1929).

3. Randall, *Censorship of the Movies*, 21.

4. Series 1581, box 50,737, ODFC.

5. *In re* Spain in Flames.

6. *In re* The Ramparts We Watch, 39 Pa. D. & C. 437 (1940); legal briefs, box 10, PSBC.

7. Annual reports, NYMPD.

8. The genre of the "clap opera" had developed following the production of the sensational 1914 play *Damaged Goods*, a story of a bridegroom who contracts syphilis at his bachelor party, then infects his wife and unborn child. The film version grossed $2 million, an amazing amount for the time. Filmmakers soon realized that they could disguise lots of taboo topics under the cloak of public service messages, and they kept at it for thirty more years. Joe Bob Briggs, *Profoundly Disturbing: Shocking Movies That Changed History* (New York: Universe, 2002), 32–33. For more on social hygiene films, see Joe Bob Briggs, "Kroger Babb's Roadshow," *Reason*, November 2003, http://www.reason.com/news/show/28934.html, and Eric Schaefer, *Bold! Daring! Shocking! True! A History of Exploitation Films, 1919–1959* (Durham, NC: Duke University Press, 1999).

9. Sova, *Forbidden Films*, 215.

10. Appellant's brief, *Public Welfare Pictures Corp. v. Lord*, file 3221-2565, series A-1418, NYMPD.

11. *Public Welfare Pictures Corp. v. Lord*, 224 A.D. 311 (1928).

12. Special cases files, "Social Diseases," boxes 2565–69, series A-1418, NYMPD.

13. The movie was *Dr. Ehrlich's Magic Bullet*, a well-reviewed and highly regarded film today. "Censorship of Motion Pictures," 108.

14. The first sex education film to be passed by the censors was *Birthright*, which dealt with venereal disease and was produced as a Columbia University educational film. *New York Times*, February 8, 1952.

15. File 27099-2555, series A-1418, NYMPD.

16. Reminiscences of Arthur Loeb Mayer (1958), 28–29, Oral History Research Office Collection, Columbia University, New York.

17. *New York Herald Tribune*, June 27, 1935.

18. *New York Herald Tribune*, November 22, 1935.

19. Irwin Esmond to Eureka Productions, March 12, 1936, file 30766-2555, series A-1418, NYMPD.

20. The film was so chopped up for various censor boards that the original version has not survived in the United States. A version available on VHS includes both of the added scenes mentioned here.

21. *Eureka Productions, Inc. v. Lehman*, 17 F. Supp. 259 (S.D. N.Y., 1936).

22. *United States v. One Book Entitled* Ulysses, 72 F.2d 705 (1934).

23. See Raymond J. Haberski Jr., *It's Only a Movie! Films and Critics in American Culture* (Lexington: University Press of Kentucky, 2001).

24. De Grazia and Newman, *Banned Films*, 49.

25. *Eureka Productions, Inc. v. Byrne*, 252 A.D. 255 (1937).

26. Breen quoted in Gardner, *Censorship Papers*, 74.

27. De Grazia and Newman, *Banned Films*, 49.

28. Gardner, *Censorship Papers*, 75.

29. Thomas Pryor, *New York Times*, November 28, 1937.

30. File 36341-2556, series A-1418, NYMPD.

31. *Film Daily*, May 29, 1939.

32. Irwin Esmond to Eureka Productions, April 18, 1940, file 38589-2556, series A-1418, NYMPD.

33. File 39118-2556, series A-1418, NYMPD.

34. *Tomorrow's Children*, file 27387-296, series A-1418, NYMPD.

35. Appellant's memorandum, *Matter of Foy Productions before the Commissioner of Education*, file 28361-333, series A-1418, NYMPD.

36. Respondent's statement, ibid.

37. Appellant's memorandum, ibid.

38. *Foy Productions v. Graves*, 253 A.D. 475 (1938).

39. For more on totalitarianism's influence on American legal culture during World War II, see Brinkley, *End of Reform*, 154–64; William E. Nelson, *The Legalist Reformation: Law, Politics, and Ideology in New York, 1920–1980* (Chapel Hill: University of North Carolina Press, 2001), 121–47; and Edward A. Purcell, "American Jurisprudence between the Wars: Legal Realism and the Crisis of Democratic Theory," in *American Law and the Constitutional Order: Historical Perspectives*, ed. Lawrence M. Friedman and Harry N. Scheiber (Cambridge, MA: Harvard University Press, 1988), 359–74.

40. Dissent by James P. Hill, *Foy Productions v. Graves*, 253 A.D. 475.

41. *Matter of Foy Productions v. Graves*, 278 N.Y. 498 (1938).

42. *Tomorrow's Children* entered the debate over propriety just after a significant change in the legal culture. In 1930, a sex education pamphlet by Mary Ware Dennett had been cleared of the charge of obscenity, opening the way for public dissemination of what had previously been considered unacceptable—at least in print. *United States v. Dennett*, 39 F.2d 564 (1930).

43. Morris L. Ernst and Alexander Lindey, *The Censor Marches On: Recent Milestones in the Administration of the Obscenity Law in the United States* (New York: Doubleday, Doran, 1940), 86.

44. New York State Motion Picture Division, internal memorandum, file 31582-465, series A-1418, NYMPD.

45. Burstyn and Mayer to New York State Motion Picture Division, September 9, 1936, file 31582-465, series A-1418, NYMPD. Burstyn and Mayer insisted that members of the Legion of Decency previewed the film and had no objection. There is no response to their letter in the NYMPD records.

46. Biographical sketch, AGHP, http://infoshare1.princeton.edu/libraries/firestone/rbsc/finding_aids/hays.html#bio.

47. Box 33, folder 16, AGHP. This statement, made in celebration of *Jo-*

seph Burstyn, Inc. v. Wilson in 1952, reflects the culture of the ACLU in the Baldwin years. Roger Baldwin frequently expressed the view, as paraphrased by Paul L. Murphy, that "civil liberties might not win in an immediate fight, but in the long run it never lost when an issue was dramatized." Paul L. Murphy, *The Meaning of Freedom of Speech: First Amendment Freedoms from Wilson to FDR* (Westport, CT: Greenwood, 1972), 228.

48. *The Captive*: *Horace B. Liveright v. Waldorf Theatres Corp.*, 220 A.D. 182 (1927). See Friedman, *Prurient Interests*, 106–11, and Haberski, *It's Only a Movie*, 67–80.

49. File 34068-578, series A-1418, NYMPD; Russell Potter to Arthur Garfield Hays, January 25, 1938, box 5, folder 6, AGHP.

50. Appellant's brief, *Mayer v. Byrne*, file 34068-578, series A-1418, NYMPD.

51. Ibid.

52. *Near v. Minnesota*, 283 U.S. 697 (1931).

53. Mark A. Graber, *Transforming Free Speech: The Ambiguous Legacy of Civil Libertarianism* (Berkeley and Los Angeles: University of California Press, 1991), 25.

54. Hays quoted in Boyer, *Purity in Print*, 178.

55. *Palko v. Connecticut*, 302 U.S. 319 (1937); *United States v. Carolene Products Co.*, 304 U.S. 144 (1938).

56. Respondent's brief, *Mayer v. Byrne*.

57. *Mayer v. Byrne*.

58. Bosley Crowther, *New York Times*, October 8, 1940.

59. Newspaper clippings, file 34068-578, series A-1418, NYMPD.

60. For an interesting summary of the fate of several foreign films of the 1930s, see Ezra Goodman, "Notes for a Geography of Morals," *New York Times*, July 10, 1938.

61. Irwin Esmond, internal memorandum, March 5, 1938, file 33320-2553, series A-1418, NYMPD.

62. Appellant's brief before the board of regents, file 33320-2553, series A-1418, NYMPD.

63. *New York Post*, April 12, 1938; *New York Times*, April 12, 1938.

64. Appellant's brief, file 33320-2553, series A-1418, NYMPD.

65. *New York Times*, March 17, 1938.

66. *Nation*, March 19, 1938; *Time*, April 4, 1938; Ernest L. Meyer, "Those Odd Censors: Murder Approved, Maternity Taboo," *New York Post*, March 11, 1938. There is no evidence in the NYMPD files that the censors responded to such charges.

67. Appellant's brief, *American Committee on Maternal Welfare v. Mangan*, file 33320-2553, series A-1418, NYMPD.

68. Respondent's brief, ibid.

69. Kellogg quoted in "Calf Birth Scene Kills New Disney Movie for State," unidentified newspaper clipping, n.d., Alexander C. Flick Family Papers, Syracuse University Archives, Syracuse, NY.

70. Disney quoted in de Grazia and Newman, *Banned Films*, 85.

71. Appellant's reply brief, *American Committee on Maternal Welfare v. Mangan*, file 33320-2553, series A-1418, NYMPD.

72. Majority opinion, ibid.

73. Dissenting opinion, ibid.

74. For the full story of the creation of the "separate classification" (sometimes called "special category"), see Skinner, *Cross and the Cinema*, 58–64.

75. National Council on Freedom from Censorship, *What Shocked the Censors: A Complete Record of Cuts in Motion Picture Films Ordered by the New York State Censors from January, 1932 to March, 1933* (New York: National Council on Freedom from Censorship, 1933).

76. *State ex rel. Midwestern Film Exchange v. Clifton*, 118 Ohio St. 91 (1928); *In re Appeal from Board of Censors, Phila.*, C.P. Ct. no. 6 (1937). The Circuit Court of the City of Richmond overturned its censors on *The Birth of a Baby* in 1939.

77. The New York state constitution's provision on free speech rights states, "Every citizen may freely speak, write, and publish his or her sentiments on all subjects, being responsible for the abuse of that right, and no law shall be passed to restrain or abridge the liberty of speech or of the press." New York constitution, art. 1, sec. 8. Pennsylvania, Ohio, Virginia, Maryland, Massachusetts, and Kansas all had free speech provisions within their state constitutions.

5. The First Amendment Resurfaces, 1946–1950

1. Richard W. Steele, *Free Speech in the Good War* (New York: St. Martin's Press, 1999), 11.

2. Henry J. Abraham and Barbara A. Perry, *Freedom and the Court: Civil Rights and Liberties in the United States*, 6th ed. (New York: Oxford University Press, 1994), 163.

3. *Hannegan v. Esquire*; *Thomas v. Collins*, 323 U.S. 516 (1945); *Pennekamp v. Florida*, 328 U.S. 331 (1946).

4. G. Edward White, "The First Amendment Comes of Age: The Emergence of Free Speech in Twentieth Century America," *Michigan Law Review* 95 (1996): 308–9. See also Reuel E. Schiller, "Free Speech and Expertise: Administrative Censorship and the Birth of the Modern First Amendment," *Virginia Law Review* 86 (2000): 11–20.

5. Samuel Walker, *In Defense of American Liberties: A History of the ACLU* (New York: Oxford University Press, 1990), 232–35.

6. One exception was in Portland, Oregon, where the ACLU tried to induce a theater owner to exhibit *The Bicycle Thief* without submitting to local censorship. Herbert Monte Levy to Dwight L. Schwab, June 5, 1950, file 757-24, ACLUA. The case was dropped when a local judge issued an injunction that allowed the movie to be shown.

7. Walker, *In Defense of American Liberties*, 35; Frank Eugene Beaver, *Bosley Crowther: Social Critic of the Film, 1940–1967* (New York: Arno Press, 1974), 20.

8. Sova, *Forbidden Films*, 15–16.

9. Minutes of the New York Civil Liberties Union, June 10, 1947, file 562-18, ACLUA.

10. For Hughes's highly publicized problems with *Scarface*, see Doherty, *Pre-Code Hollywood*, 148–50, and Sova, *Forbidden Films*, 259–62.

11. James M. Skinner, "The Tussle with Russell: *The Outlaw* as a Landmark in American Film Censorship," *North Dakota Quarterly* 49 (1981): 6.

12. For more about the making and the selling of *The Outlaw*, see de Grazia and Newman, *Banned Films*, 65–76, 225–27, and Skinner, "Tussle with Russell."

13. Skinner, "Tussle with Russell," 9.

14. *New York Post*, October 24, 1946.

15. Skinner, *Cross and the Cinema*, 77.

16. Annual report, 1945–1946, box 1, 2-70-23, MSBC.

17. Quoted in Gardner, *Censorship Papers*, 30.

18. File 47913-2564, series A-1418, NYMPD.

19. *New York Times*, October 23, 1946; *Film Daily*, October 24, 1946.

20. *United Artists Corp. v. Amity Amusement Corp.*, 188 Misc. 146 (1946), 271 A.D. 825 (1946).

21. Peter Dart, "Breaking the Code: A Historical Footnote," *Cinema Journal* 8, no. 1 (1968): 41.

22. *Hughes Tool Co. v. MPAA*, 66 F. Supp. 1006 (1946).

23. Ibid.

24. File 47913-2564, series A-1418, NYMPD.

25. *City of Lynchburg v. Dominion Theatres*, 175 Va. 35 (1940), quoted in the opinion of *Hughes Tool Co. v. Fielding*, 188 Misc. 947, 73 N.Y.S.2d 98 (1947).

26. *Hughes Tool Co. v. Fielding*, 188 Misc. 947.

27. Osmond Fraenkel to Clifford Forster, March 9, 1948, state correspondence 1948, reel 252, ACLUA.

28. Amicus curiae brief of the American Civil Liberties Union, *Hughes Tool Co. v. Fielding*, 297 N.Y. 1024 (1948).

29. Sherwin Kane, *Motion Picture Daily*, January 27, 1947.

30. The only substantive changes were that block booking had to be limited to five features, blind selling had to cease (exhibitors were to have the opportunity to view films before agreements were drawn up), and the chains could not acquire large numbers of new theaters. In exchange, the government agreed not to pursue divorcement of exhibition from the studios. For more on the consent decree, see Muscio, *Hollywood's New Deal*, 187–89. Also see Michael Conant, *Antitrust in the Motion Picture Industry* (Berkeley and Los Angeles: University of California Press, 1960), 85–106.

31. *United States v. Paramount Pictures, Inc.*, 334 U.S. 131 (1948).

32. Conant, *Antitrust in the Motion Picture Industry*, 107–12.

33. *United States v. Paramount Pictures, Inc.*

34. Annual report, 1957, record series 1802-E5, box 1, SBTSR.

35. Conant, *Antitrust in the Motion Picture Industry*, 112–14, 200.

36. *New York Times*, June 14, 1949.

37. Thomas F. Brady, "Hollywood Issue," *New York Times*, November 26, 1950.

38. *Allen B. Dumont Laboratories v. Carroll*, 86 F. Supp. 813 (E.D. Pa. 1949).

39. *Allen B. Dumont Laboratories v. Carroll*, 184 F.2d 153 (3d Cir. 1950).

40. *Carroll v. Allen B. Dumont Laboratories*, 340 U.S. 929 (1951).

41. Douglas quoted in Theodore Kupferman and Philip O'Brien, "Motion Picture Censorship—the Memphis Blues," *Cornell Law Quarterly* 36 (1951): 300.

42. *Kovacs v. Cooper*, 336 U.S. 77 (1949).

43. *New York Times*, October 15, 1950.

44. Quoted in *United Artists Corp. v. Board of Censors of City of Memphis*, 189 Tenn. 397 (1949).

45. John Dales Jr. (executive secretary of the Screen Actors Guild) to Eric Johnston, October 1, 1947, *Curley*, PCAR.

46. Press release, September 19, 1947, *Curley*, PCAR.

47. *New York Times*, "Johnston Backs Production Code," May 21, 1955.

48. They had ruled that, since there was no contract to exhibit *Curley* and United Artists was a non-Tennessee corporation, it had no standing to question the laws of the state.

49. *United Artists Corp. v. Board of Censors of City of Memphis*, 339 U.S. 952 (1950), refusing to review 189 Tenn. 397 (1949).

50. Richard Griffith, Arthur Mayer, and Eileen Bowser, *The Movies* (New York: Simon and Schuster, 1981), 381.

51. Jowett, *Democratic Art*, 367.

52. *RD-DR Corp. v. Smith*, 183 F.2d 562 (1950).

53. Melvin I. Urofsky, *Division and Discord: The Supreme Court under Stone and Vinson, 1941–1953* (Columbia: University of South Carolina Press, 1997), 155.

6. The Strange Case of *The Miracle*, 1950–1952

1. *New York Times*, December 16, 1950.

2. See Thomas Doherty, *Cold War, Cool Medium: Television, McCarthyism, and American Culture* (New York: Columbia University Press, 2003), 68, and Amy Kiste Nyberg, *Seal of Approval: The History of the Comics Code* (Jackson: University of Mississippi Press, 1998).

3. Blanchard, "American Urge to Censor," 788–96, 798–802.

4. Walker, *In Defense of American Liberties*, 231.

5. I borrow "celebration of the state" from Brinkley, *End of Reform*, 164.

6. *New York Times*, February 8, 1950; letters, files 24–26, box 1, Seattle Board of Theatre Supervisors records, Seattle Municipal Archives, Seattle; Ivan Brychta, "The Ohio Film Censorship Law," *Ohio State Law Journal* 13 (1952): 361.

7. *New York Times*, March 26, 1950.

8. Johnson quoted in *New York Times*, March 15, 1950, and Leff and Simmons, *Dame in the Kimono*, 162.

9. *Film Daily*, March 16, 1950.

10. *New York Times*, April 16, 1950.

11. Jackson had served as acting PCA chief for fifteen months in 1947 and 1948. Ibid.

12. *New York Times*, April 23, 1950. Jackson refused to accept the assignment unless his knowledge of Hollywood insider information remained confidential.

13. *New York Times*, "Filmland Breathes Easier: End of Inquiry Removes the Fear of Some New Form of Federal Censorship," April 30, 1950.

14. *New York Times*, May 15, 1950.

15. S Res. 321, 81st Cong., 2d sess. (1950), quoted in *New York Times*, August 24, 1950.

16. Charles R. Morris, *American Catholic: The Saints and Sinners Who Built America's Most Powerful Church* (New York: Times Books, 1997), 196–97.

17. Record series 1802-E5, box 1, file 26, SBTSR.

18. Haberski, *It's Only a Movie*, 104.

19. Renoir quoted in Walsh, *Sin and Censorship*, 247.

20. Hodgins, "Round Table on the Movies."

21. Bosley Crowther, *New York Times*, December 13, 1950.
22. Wanda Hale, *New York Daily News*, December 13, 1950.
23. Seymour Peck, *New York Daily Compass*, December 13, 1950.
24. Frank Quinn, *New York Daily Mirror*, December 13, 1950.
25. *Newsweek*, December 18, 1950.
26. Crowther, *New York Times*, December 13, 1950.
27. Truman quoted in *New York Times*, December 16, 1950.
28. Hugh Flick, interview by Shawn Purcell, September 30, 1989, New York State Oral History Project, New York State Library.
29. Hugh Flick, memorandum to Dr. James E. Allen, January 10, 1951, file 2 of 4, 55250-2561, series A-1418, NYMPD; *New York Times*, December 24, 1950.
30. Black, *Catholic Crusade against the Movies*, 94.
31. Bosley Crowther, "The Strange Case of 'The Miracle,'" *Atlantic Monthly*, April 1951.
32. Quoted in Thomas M. Pryor, *New York Times*, December 3, 1950.
33. Lillian Gerard provides some insight into McCaffrey's motivation: McCaffrey was a political leftover from the previous city administration, and he might have hoped that adopting a high moral tone would assure that the newly elected mayor could not replace him. Lillian N. Gerard, "'Ways of Love' or a History of the Ways of Censorship" (unpublished manuscript, 1977), pt. 2, pp. 27–38. Parts of this manuscript were printed in *American Film*, vol. 2, nos. 10–11 (1977).
34. Quoted in *New York Times*, December 27, 1950.
35. Quoted in *New York Times*, December 28, 1950.
36. *Variety*, December 27, 1950.
37. *New York Post*, "Civic Censor," December 27, 1950; Max Lerner, "The Shadow on the Screen," *New York Post*, December 27, 1950.
38. Robert Hatch, *New Republic*, January 1, 1951.
39. Andrea Friedman notes that the topics of Communist infiltration and pornography were an "almost natural fit." Friedman, *Prurient Interests*, 185.
40. *Catholic News*, December 30, 1950.
41. *Brooklyn Tablet*, January 6, 1951. The *Tablet* was published in Brooklyn but had a national circulation.
42. See John T. McGreevy, "Thinking on One's Own: Catholicism in the American Intellectual Imagination, 1928–1960," *Journal of American History* 84 (1997): 97–131.
43. John T. McGreevy, *Catholicism and American Freedom: A History* (New York: Norton, 2003), 166–69.
44. Walker, *In Defense of American Liberties*, 98.
45. Black, *Catholic Crusade against the Movies*, 1–2, 65. According to

Thomas Doherty, to see a movie at this time was "to see the world through Joe Breen's eyes." Doherty, *Pre-Code Hollywood*, 342.

46. William P. Clancy, "The Catholic as Philistine," *Commonweal*, March 16, 1951, 567–69. Clancy was fired from his position at the University of Notre Dame immediately after writing this article. Walsh, *Sin and Censorship*, 254.

47. *Joseph Burstyn, Inc. v. Edward T. McCaffrey, as Commissioner of Licenses of the City of New York*, 198 Misc. 884 (1951).

48. The only other reversal had come in 1915, in *Life Photo Film Corp. v. Bell.*

49. Gerard, "History of the Ways of Censorship," pt. 1, p. 50.

50. Spellman quoted in *New York Times*, January 8, 1951. The cardinal never saw the film. John Cooney, *The American Pope: The Life and Times of Francis Cardinal Spellman* (New York: Times Books, 1984), 196.

51. Flick liked to recite a story about a film that he felt had incited to crime: "The bad guys had caught the chief detective. They put him down in a basement and the chief of the bad guys turns to his lieutenant and says, 'Now give him the works, but keep it legal.' So the lieutenant . . . looked around and saw one of his people had a hearing aid. . . . He took the hearing aid, plugged it into the ear of the detective who was sitting in the chair, turned the radio on full blast, and he went on and left him there. It was two days later he was stark mad and they turned him loose and he was no trouble anymore. They had kept it legal. There was no scratch on him. I kept book that summer and I had a number of cases where people were mugged, their hearing aids were taken, and nothing else after this film was opened in New York City. I'm sure there's a correlation between those who saw the film and those who said 'let's keep it legal.' That's the sort of clear and present danger." Hugh Flick, interview by Esperanza Cintrón, "In Retrospect," *Insights: A Quarterly Magazine for Employees of the New York State Education Department*, August 1990, 6–8.

52. Guernsey, "Film Censor's Dilemma."

53. Hugh M. Flick, "Censorship, Logic and the Law," *New York Times*, August 28, 1955.

54. Flick quoted in Guernsey, "Film Censor's Dilemma."

55. Spellman quoted in *New York Times*, January 8, 1951.

56. *New Republic*, "Catholic Censorship," January 29, 1951.

57. Cooney, *American Pope*, 181.

58. Crowther, "Strange Case."

59. Quoted in Alan Westin, *The* Miracle *Case: The Supreme Court and the Movies* (Inter-university Case Program, 1961), 9–10.

60. *New York Times*, January 10, 1951.

61. Robert Wohlforth, "People and Pickets," *New Republic*, February 5, 1951.

62. Crowther, "Strange Case."

63. Gerard, "History of the Ways of Censorship," pt. 2, p. 4. The *New York Times* January 15 edition carried this headline on p. 31: "Miracle Picketed by 1,000 Catholics."

64. *New York Times*, January 9, 1951.

65. Alton Cook, unidentified clipping, January 25, 1952, Joseph Burstyn file, Billy Rose Collection, New York Public Library for the Performing Arts, New York City.

66. *Cue*, December 16, 1950.

67. Arthur Pollock, "Movie Talk," *New York Daily Compass*, January 28, 1952.

68. Westin, Miracle *Case*, 5.

69. Arthur Mayer, *Simply Colossal: The Story of the Movies from the Long Chase to the Chaise Longue* (New York: Simon and Schuster, 1953), 216.

70. Westin, Miracle *Case*, 5; appellant's supporting petition, *Joseph Burstyn, Inc. v. Wilson*, 278 A.D. 253 (1951).

71. Joseph Burstyn, prepared remarks (typescript), file 55250-2561, series A-1418, NYMPD.

72. Burstyn quoted in *New York Times*, January 8, 1951.

73. *New York Times*, January 15, 1951.

74. Quoted in *New York Times*, January 18, 1951.

75. Quoted in *New York Herald Tribune*, January 20, 1951.

76. *New York Times*, January 18, 1951.

77. *New York Times*, January 12, 1951.

78. Flick, memorandum to Allen, January 10, 1951.

79. Gilbert Seldes, "Pressures and Pictures," pt. 1, *Nation*, February 3, 1951.

80. Folder 3 of 4, file 55250-2561, series A-1418, NYMPD.

81. Thomas A. Duffy to Dr. Hugh Flick, January 12, 1951, file 55250-2561, series A-1418, NYMPD. This file contains many letters both supporting and attacking the film. File 3 of 4 contains letters from clergy supporting the film; file 1 of 4 contains the "stack" of letters of criticism that New York State's attorney would refer to in court, although he never produced the documents.

82. *New York Times*, January 9, 1951.

83. *New York Times*, February 17, 1951. Ohio, Virginia, and Maryland gave their censors the right to rescind any license.

84. See the opinion in *Jewel Productions v. Esmond*, 168 Misc. 838 (1938).

85. *New York Herald Tribune*, January 21, 1951.

86. *New York Post*, January 22, 1951.

87. Cooney, *American Pope*, 196, 203.

88. *New York Times*, January 23, 1951.

89. Burstyn quoted in *New York Times*, January 29, 1951.

90. Beaver, *Bosley Crowther*, 96.

91. Bosley Crowther, *New York Times*, February 25, 1951.

92. Crowther, "Strange Case."

93. *Gelling v. Texas*, 343 U.S. 960 (1952).

94. *Palko v. Connecticut*; *United States v. Carolene Products Co.*; *Hannegan v. Esquire*; *Pennekamp v. Florida*; *Thomas v. Collins*; *Winters v. New York*, 333 U.S. 507 (1948); *Saia v. New York*, 334 U.S. 558 (1948).

95. *Kunz v. New York*, 340 U.S. 290 (1951).

96. *New York Times*, January 20, 1951; *New York Herald Tribune*, January 20, 1951.

97. *Joseph Burstyn, Inc. v. Wilson*, 278 A.D. 253, transcript of the hearing, file 55250-2561, series A-1418, NYMPD.

98. According to London, Burstyn had first asked him to represent him in his censor difficulties over *The Bicycle Thief*. After that success, London became Burstyn's personal attorney, and the two grew to be good friends. Ephraim London, interview by Mary Batten, "There Must Be Freedom to Expound All Ideas," *Film Comment*, Winter 1963, 2–19. For *The Miracle*, however, Burstyn had been advised to retain Catholic counsel, and so he chose Farber to represent him. By the time the case got to the New York State Court of Appeals, though, London would take over as counsel.

99. *New York Times*, January 31, 1951.

100. Gerard, "History of the Ways of Censorship," pt. 2, 42–43.

101. Quoted in *New York Times*, February 5, 1951.

102. *New York Times*, April 17, 1951.

103. Hollis Alpert, "Talk with a Movie Censor," *Saturday Review*, November 22, 1952.

104. *New York Times*, February 17, 1951.

105. Burstyn quoted in *Film Daily*, February 15, 1951.

106. ACLU, press release, February 16, 1951, file 1274, ACLUA.

107. Cooney, *American Pope*, 200.

108. The MPAA's files contain very little about *The Miracle* and Joseph Burstyn. Breen did write to Kenneth Clark in the MPAA's Washington office, "I have heard, from a responsible source, that a movement is on foot right now, with the favorable disposal of Governor Dewey, to completely re-arrange, and re-set, the business of film censorship in New York State. My information is that, for a long number of years, various people in New York

have contended that the censor board there is a farce, and completely ineffective. It may be that we shall wake up some day and find the board there functioning in such a way as to give us enormous difficulty." Joseph Breen to Kenneth Clark, January 11, 1951, *The Miracle*, PCAR.

109. "Notes: Motion Pictures and the First Amendment," *Yale Law Journal* 60 (1951): 696–719.

110. Appellant Joseph Burstyn's brief, *Joseph Burstyn, Inc. v. Wilson*, 278 A.D. 253, 21–22.

111. Appellant Joseph Burstyn Inc.'s brief, ibid., 31, 39.

112. "Censorship Battle, 1953–55," box 10, PSBC.

113. Respondents' brief, *Joseph Burstyn, Inc. v. Wilson*, 278 A.D. 253. The Frankfurter opinion Brind refers to is from *Kovacs v. Cooper*.

114. Opinion, *Joseph Burstyn, Inc. v. Wilson*, 278 A.D. 253. See also *New York Times*, March 13, June 2, 1951.

115. Amici curiae brief of the New York Civil Liberties Union and National Council on Freedom from Censorship, *Joseph Burstyn, Inc. v. Wilson*, 303 N.Y. 242 (emphasis in original). The Jackson quotation is from *West Virginia State Board of Education v. Barnette*, 319 U.S. 624 (1943).

116. *Joseph Burstyn, Inc. v. Wilson*, 303 N.Y. 242.

117. Ibid.

118. Stanley Fuld, speech given before the Federation of Bar Associations, Oneonta, NY, July 1946, box 17, Stanley H. Fuld Collection, Rare Book and Manuscript Library, Columbia University, New York City.

119. *Albany (NY) Times-Union*, October 23, 1966, B2.

120. *Joseph Burstyn, Inc. v. Wilson*, 303 N.Y. 242.

121. Westin, Miracle *Case*, 22.

122. *New York Times*, October 19, 1951.

123. *New York Times*, February 27, 1949.

124. Jowett, "Moral Responsibility and Commercial Entertainment," 3.

125. Garth Jowett, "A Significant Medium for the Communication of Ideas: The Miracle Decision and the Decline of Motion Picture Censorship, 1952–1968," in *Movie Censorship and American Culture*, ed. Francis G. Couvares (Washington, DC: Smithsonian Institution Press, 1996), 272.

126. *Variety*, February 28, 1951.

127. C. Herman Pritchett, *Civil Liberties in the Vinson Court* (Chicago: University of Chicago Press, 1954), 182.

128. When *Pinky* appeared at the Supreme Court, it was without an amicus brief from the MPAA, although Philip O'Brien, counsel to the MPAA, was listed "of counsel" to Gelling.

129. *Variety*, "Pix Lawyers Dubious on High Court Censorship Test: 'Suppose We Lose?'" February 28, 1951.

130. Burstyn quoted in Herbert Mitgang, "Transatlantic 'Miracle Man,'" *Park East*, August 1952. Actually, *ladri di biciclette* means "bicycle thieves," but the film title is not translated this way.

131. *Box Office*, March 12, 1952.

132. For the story of the pressure Monsignor Kellenberg placed on the Catholic Committee for Cultural Action, see Westin, Miracle *Case*, 24–25.

133. Reminiscences of Arthur Loeb Mayer, 26–27.

134. Unknown newspaper clipping, June 7, 1950, file 757-24, ACLUA.

135. Burstyn paraphrased in Archer Winsten, "Reviewing Stand," *New York Post*, January 6, 1952.

136. Mayer, *Simply Colossal*, 233.

137. Leff and Simmons, *Dame in the Kimono*, 145–66.

138. Burstyn quoted in Ezra Goodman, *The Fifty-Year Decline and Fall of Hollywood* (New York: Simon and Schuster, 1961), 423.

139. *New York Times*, February 5, 1952.

140. *New York Times*, obituary of Ephraim London, June 14, 1990.

141. Ephraim London, "The Freedom to See: With or without Glasses," *Nation*, December 19, 1953.

142. Michael F. Mayer, interview by the author, June 9, 2003.

143. Walker, *In Defense of American Liberties*, photo caption.

144. *New York Times*, obituary of Morris Ernst, May 23, 1976.

145. *New York Times*, obituary of Emanuel Redfield, January 24, 1983.

146. *New York Times*, obituary of Shad Polier, July 1, 1976.

147. *United States Law Week*, April 29, 1952.

148. Ibid.

149. Amicus curiae brief of the New York State Catholic Welfare Committee, *Joseph Burstyn, Inc. v. Wilson*, 343 U.S. 495 (1952).

150. Amici curiae brief of the American Civil Liberties Union and American Jewish Congress, ibid.

151. Peter Irons, *A People's History of the Supreme Court* (New York: Penguin Books, 1999), 367.

152. Opinion, *Joseph Burstyn, Inc. v. Wilson*, 343 U.S. 495.

153. Mitgang, "Transatlantic 'Miracle Man.'" As early as 1916, judges had worried that they would be forced into the role of supercensor. This was one of the reasons that they so steadfastly refused to interfere with the determinations of statutorily empowered bureaucracies. That the Supreme Court would have to assume the role of supercensor became the subject of several opinions in *Kingsley International Pictures Corp. v. Regents of the University of the State of New York* (see ch. 9).

154. *New York Times*, May 27, 1952.

155. Anthony Lewis, "Sex and the Supreme Court," *Esquire*, June 1963.

156. *New York Times*, May 28, 1952.

157. *Variety*, May 28, 1952.

158. Andrew James Driggs, "*The Miracle*: The Controversy and the Constitution" (master's thesis, Brigham Young University, 1986), 126.

159. The news release quoted affirmations of the Supreme Court's wisdom from the *Christian Science Monitor*, *Boston Herald*, *Washington Post*, *Los Angeles Times*, *New York Herald Tribune*, *Cincinnati (OH) Post*, *Toledo (OH) Blade*, *Providence (RI) Bulletin*, and thirty other daily newspapers. *Motion Picture Bulletin*, June 17, 1952.

160. ACLU, press release, file 1274, ACLUA.

161. Malin quoted in Bosley Crowther, "Hollywood Hails Action," *New York Times*, May 27, 1952; Burstyn quoted in ibid.

162. *New York Times*, May 28, 1952.

163. *Brooklyn Tablet*, May 31, 1952.

164. Corliss, "Legion of Decency," 44.

165. Chafee, *Free Speech in the United States*, 215.

166. Luncheon program, file 55250-2561, series A-1418, NYMPD.

167. *New York Herald Tribune*, November 30, 1953. Westin cites the figure as $60,000. Westin, Miracle *Case*, 33.

168. Burstyn quoted in Cook, *New York World-Telegram*, January 25, 1952.

169. Gerard, "History of Ways of Censorship," pt. 1, 16.

170. Burstyn quoted in Mitgang, "Transatlantic 'Miracle Man.'"

171. Black, *Catholic Crusade against the Movies*, 102.

172. Joseph Burstyn to the Kansas State Board of Censorship, June 9, 1953, quoted in Thomas Michael Gaume, "Suppression of Motion Pictures in Kansas, 1952 to 1975" (master's thesis, University of Kansas, 1976), 40.

173. *Variety*, "Joseph Burstyn Left No Will," December 2, 1953.

174. De Grazia and Newman, *Banned Films*, 77; Carmen, *Movies, Censorship and the Law*, 50–54; Black, *Catholic Crusade against the Movies*, 100; Jowett, "Significant Medium," 267; Randall, *Censorship of the Movies*, 32; Gerard, "History of the Ways of Censorship," pt. 1, 4.

175. *Gelling v. Texas*.

176. The Maryland and New York statutes were virtually identical. Annual report, 1951–1952, box 1, 2-70-23, MSBC.

177. *RKO Radio Pictures, Inc. v. Department of Education*, 162 Ohio St. 263; *Holmby Productions, Inc. v. Vaughn*, 350 U.S. 870 (1955); *Hallmark Productions v. Carroll*, 384 Pa. 348 (1956).

178. Leonard W. Levy, *Blasphemy: Verbal Offense against the Sacred, from Moses to Salman Rushdie* (New York: Knopf, 1993), 527.

179. Bosley Crowther, *New York Times*, December 13, 1953.

7. *La Ronde*, 1951–1954

1. Mathews, *Censored*, 127.

2. For a pictorial view of the film's plot, see "*La Ronde* Has Censor Trouble," *Life*, January 21, 1952.

3. The cast included France's most brilliant stars: Simone Signoret, Anton Walbrook, Danielle Darrieux, Simone Simon, Jean-Louis Barrault, Gerard Philipe, Serge Reggiani, Daniel Gelin, and Isla Miranda.

4. *Daily Mail* (London), April 27, 1951.

5. *London Sunday Express* quoted in *Variety*, March 5, 1952.

6. *Times* (London) quoted in Commercial Pictures Corp., appeal to board of regents, file 56139-2562, series A-1418, NYMPD.

7. *Variety*, March 5, 1952.

8. *Time*, October 22, 1951.

9. Kilgallen quoted in appellees' brief, *Commercial Pictures Corp. v. Regents of the University of the State of New York*, 346 U.S. 274 (1954).

10. *New York Times*, November 5, 1951.

11. File 56139-2562, series A-1418, NYMPD.

12. Alpert, "Talk with a Movie Censor."

13. Kate Cameron, "Banned Comedy Is Enchanting," *New York News*, April 13, 1952.

14. *New York Times*, December 18, 1953; Florence Perlow Shientag, interview by the author, April 12, 2001; *Who's Who in American Law*, 2002.

15. Commercial Pictures Corp., appeal to board of regents.

16. Opinion of the board of regents, file 56139-2562, series A-1418, NYMPD.

17. Shientag quoted in *Film Daily*, May 15, 1952.

18. *Raymond D. Halsey v. The New York Society for the Suppression of Vice*, 234 N.Y. 1 (1922).

19. *United States v. One Book Entitled* Ulysses, 72 F.2d 705 (1934).

20. Stanley Kauffman quoted in Haberski, *It's Only a Movie*, 165.

21. Petitioner's brief, *Commercial Pictures Corp. v. Regents of the University of the State of New York*, 280 A.D. 260 (1952).

22. Brind quoted in *Film Daily*, May 15, 1952.

23. *Commercial Pictures Corp. v. Regents*, 280 A.D. 260.

24. Carmen, *Movies, Censorship and the Law*, 56.

25. *Commercial Pictures Corp. v. Regents*, 280 A.D. 260.

26. Ibid.

27. *New York Times*, June 15, 1952.

28. *ACLU Weekly Bulletin*, July 28, 1952, box 767, file 19, ACLUA. The National Council on Freedom from Censorship had members from the

business, arts, and journalistic communities. Their roster included Bosley Crowther; authors Eugene O'Neill, Lewis Mumford, H. L. Mencken, Clifton Fadiman, and Fannie Hurst; actor Melvyn Douglas; Congresswoman Helen Gahagan Douglas; and commentator H. V. Kaltenborn. The council was supported by fifty-seven organizations and publishers, including the MPAA, Actors Equity, Screen Writers Guild, National Board of Review, American Newspaper Guild, American Booksellers Association, American Book Publishers Council, National Association of Magazine Publishers, American Federation of Radio Artists, and American Society of Composers, Authors and Publishers.

29. The ACLU took no action on *La ronde* because the "censorship point was being handled in 'Miracle' case, then undecided . . . trying to get copy of decision to see if our intervention is now warranted." PMM to AR and HML, May 16, 1952, file 767-19, ACLUA.

30. Clifford Forster to Arthur Garfield Hays, n.d., box 767, file 19, ACLUA.

31. Shientag, interview by the author. Shientag received a condolence note from Hays after her husband's death. At the end, Hays notes that he would like to speak with her about assisting her on *La ronde*. Shientag believes that in her grief, she did not read to the bottom of the note. Ibid.

32. "Report on Censorship, September 1952–June 1953," box 78, folder 39, ACLUA.

33. *Sunshine Book Co. v. Summerfield*, 128 F. Supp. 564 (1955).

34. *New York Times*, March 26, 1953. Although the producer of *Wonderful Town* refused to reveal the name of the publication, the *National Guardian* reported that it had purchased the tickets. The editors charged that a Broadway columnist who did not like the *National Guardian*'s views had demanded that the theater drop the April 8 performance.

35. "Without its tireless twin, self-censorship, censorship could not work." Hans Magnus Enzensberger quoted in "Introductory Notes to *The File Room*," http://www.thefileroom.org/documents/Intro.html.

36. *Commercial Pictures Corp. v. Regents of the University of the State of New York*, 305 N.Y. 336 (1953).

37. See Morris Mondschein, "Constitutional Law: Motion Picture Censorship," *Cornell Law Quarterly* 44 (1959): 411–19.

38. *Commercial Pictures Corp. v. Regents*, 305 N.Y. 336.

39. *New York Times*, January 8, 1953.

40. *West Virginia State Board of Education v. Barnette*.

41. *Commercial Pictures Corp. v. Regents*, 305 N.Y. 336.

42. *People v. Pesky*, 230 A.D. 200 (1930); *People v. Pesky*, 254 N.Y. 373 (1930).

43. *Commercial Pictures Corp. v. Regents*, 305 N.Y. 336.

44. Charles Desmond, "Censoring the Movies," *Notre Dame Lawyer* 29 (1953): 27–36; Charles Desmond, "Legal Problems Involved in Censoring the Media of Mass Communication," *Marquette Law Review* 40 (1956): 38–56.

45. *Commercial Pictures Corp. v. Regents*, 305 N.Y. 336.

46. Ibid.

47. File 54906-1544, series A-1418, NYMPD.

48. Series 1591, box 50,733, ODFC.

49. Brief on behalf of plaintiffs-appellants, *Superior Films, Inc. v. Department of Education*, Court of Appeals of Franklin County, Ohio, series 1591, box 50,733, ODFC.

50. "A state may not impose a charge for the enjoyment of a right granted by the Federal Constitution." *Murdoch v. Pennsylvania*, 319 U.S. 105 (1943).

51. Brief on behalf of the defendant, *Superior Films, Inc. v. Department of Education*, 159 Ohio St. 315. The other five cases cited were *Kovacs v. Cooper*, *Cox v. New Hampshire*, *Chaplinsky v. New Hampshire*, *Fox v. Washington*, and *Feiner v. New York*.

52. Amicus curiae brief of the Ohio Congress of Parents and Teachers, *Superior Films, Inc. v. Department of Education*, 159 Ohio St. 315.

53. Amicus curiae brief of the Ohio Catholic Welfare Conference, ibid.

54. *Superior Films, Inc. v. Department of Education*, 159 Ohio St. 315.

55. Clifford Forster to Ephraim London, May 19, 1953, box 766, folder 5, ACLUA.

56. *Motion Picture Herald*, October 13, 1952.

57. Kupferman and O'Brien, "Motion Picture Censorship."

58. File 3 of 3, 56139-2562, series A-1418, NYMPD.

59. Shientag quoted in *Film Daily*, December 18, 1953.

60. *Variety*, December 23, 1953.

61. Quoted in *New York Times*, December 29, 1953.

62. Kilgallen quoted in appellees' brief, *Commercial Pictures Corp. v. Regents*, 346 U.S. 274. Kilgallen's French may not have been as good as she thought it was. French film scholar Michelle Scatton-Tessier of the University of North Carolina Wilmington contends that the film's subtitles accurately reflect both the dialogue and the action on the screen. Michelle Scatton-Tessier, personal communication with the author, October 18, 2006.

63. Appellees' brief, *Commercial Pictures Corp. v. Regents*, 346 U.S. 274.

64. Forster was notified that the ACLU would not be allowed to file amicus based on the number of other requests. The state claimed that it denied all. Clifford Forster to Charles Brind, December 22, 1953, file 767-19, ACLUA.

65. Amicus curiae brief of the American Civil Liberties Union, *Superior Films, Inc. v. Department of Education of Ohio*, 346 U.S. 217, series 4, box 1724, ACLUA.

66. Amici curiae brief of the Motion Picture Association of America and the Independent Theatre Owners of Ohio, *Superior Films, Inc. v. Department of Education of Ohio*, 346 U.S. 217.

67. George Dixon, *Washington (DC) Times-Herald*, January 12, 1954.

68. Harlor was put on the defensive several times by Justice Frankfurter, Chief Justice Warren, and Justice Burton. Frankfurter seemed quite annoyed with Harlor's inability to answer a question concerning the enjoining of libel. Frankfurter chided him, "It is relevant to this problem." When Harlor responded that all censorship should be banned, Frankfurter complained, "Why lawyers insist on absolutes is something I'll never understand." *United States Law Week*, January 12, 1954.

69. Shientag quoted in *New York Herald Tribune*, January 8, 1954.

70. *United States Law Week*, January 12, 1954.

71. Laura Krugman Ray, "The Road to *Bush v. Gore*: The History of the Supreme Court's Use of the Per Curiam Opinion," *Nebraska Law Review* 79 (2002): 519–20.

72. Opinion, *Superior Films, Inc. v. Department of Education of Ohio*, 346 U.S. 587.

73. Concurring opinion, ibid.

74. *New York Times*, January 19, 1954.

75. O'Hara quoted in *Brooklyn Tablet*, January 20, 1954.

76. Flanelly quoted in *New York Times*, February 8, 1954.

77. Johnson quoted in ibid.

78. Bosley Crowther, "Freedom of the Screen: The Supreme Court Advances Further the Latitude of a Medium," *New York Times*, January 24, 1954.

79. Thomas M. Pryor, "Hollywood Dossier: Supreme Court's Decision Tops Busy Movie Week," *New York Times*, January 24, 1954.

80. Alan Reitman (ACLU publicity director) to Varian Fry (ACLU member), February 8, 1954, file 767-19, ACLUA.

81. Quoted in *New York Herald Tribune*, January 22, 1954.

82. Minutes of the National Council on Freedom from Censorship, December 17, 1953, series 1, box 78, file 39, ACLUA. Indeed, had Flick's recommendation been adopted by New York State, its censoring would have met even the mid-1960s Supreme Court demands and withstood all constitutional scrutiny.

83. C. William O'Neill to Clyde Hissong, n.d., file 2562-56139, folder 3 of 3, series A-1418, NYMPD.

84. David J. Eardley, "Motion Picture Censorship—a Constitutional Dilemma," *Maryland Law Review* 14 (1954): 284–85.

85. Hunter M. Gholson, "Recent Decisions," *Mississippi Law Journal* 25 (1954): 274.

86. See ibid.; Constantine D. Kasson, *Michigan Law Review* 52 (February 1954): 599–602; "Movie Censorship Standards Held Invalid Because of Vagueness," *University of Pennsylvania Law Review* 102 (1954): 671–74; Joseph Kolmacic, "Prior Restraints on Motion Pictures," *Catholic University of America Law Review* 4 (May 1954): 112–18; Edward Lasker, "Censorship of Motion Pictures Pursuant to Recent Supreme Court Decisions," *UCLA Law Review* 1 (1954): 582–92; David J. Eardley, "Recent Decisions," *Notre Dame Lawyer* 29 (1954): 663–66.

87. *Winters v. New York*; Mondschein, "Constitutional Law."

88. "Legislation: New York Motion Picture Censorship Law," *Catholic Lawyer* 1 (January 1955): 58–59.

89. Gholson, "Recent Decisions," 274.

90. Lasker, "Censorship of Motion Pictures," 584, 592.

91. *Motion Picture Daily*, January 29, 1954; *New York Times*, January 21, 1954.

92. *New York Times*, March 10, 1954.

93. Brind quoted in ibid.

94. *New York Times*, March 6, 10, 1954.

95. O'Brien quoted in *New York Times*, March 10, 1954.

96. Quoted in "Legislation: New York Motion Picture Censorship Law," 59. The amendment was signed into law by Governor Dewey on April 12, 1954.

97. Lasker, "Censorship of Motion Pictures," 587.

98. *New York Herald Tribune*, March 23, 1954.

99. Bosley Crowther, "Controversial *La Ronde* Bows at Little Carnegie and Bijou and Proves to Be Innocuous," *New York Times*, March 17, 1954.

100. Alton Cook, *New York World-Telegram and Sun*, March 17, 1954.

101. William H. Mooring, *Brooklyn Tablet*, January 30, 1954.

102. Carmen, *Movies, Censorship and the Law*, 62–65.

103. Randall, *Censorship of the Movies*, 52.

104. Frankfurter quoted in de Grazia and Newman, *Banned Films*, 84.

105. *Lost Boundaries*: *RD-DR Corp. v. Smith*, 340 U.S. 853 (1950) (certiorari was denied though Justice Douglas wanted to hear the case); *Curley*: *United Artists Corp. v. Board of Censors of City of Memphis*, 189 Tenn. 397; *The Miracle*: *American Civil Liberties Union v. City of Chicago*, 3 Ill.2d 334 (1954). From 1935 through the end of New York's censorship statute in 1965, no case from New York or Maryland was denied certiorari.

106. Gaume, "Suppression of Motion Pictures in Kansas," 51.

107. P. D. McAnany, "Motion Picture Censorship and Constitutional Freedom," *Kentucky Law Journal* 50 (1962): 438.

108. Ibid., 441.

109. *Holmby Productions, Inc. v. Vaughn*, 177 Kan. 728 (1955).

8. The Tide Turns against the Censors, 1953–1957

1. The PCA rescinded its ban on narcotics themes in 1946 but, responding to pressure from the Federal Bureau of Narcotics, reinstated it in 1951. *New York Times*, March 28, 1951.

2. Broadway Angels to Motion Picture Division, December 3, 1952, file 58385-2559, series A-1418, NYMPD.

3. Daniel A. Belmont to Motion Picture Division, November 17, 1952, file 58385-2559, series A-1418, NYMPD.

4. Miss Farrell, memorandum to Director Flick, November 28, 1952, file 58385-2559, series A-1418, NYMPD.

5. LMP and JD, review notes, December 1, 1952, file 58385-2559, series A-1418, NYMPD.

6. Broadway Angels to Motion Picture Division, December 3, 1952.

7. *Broadway Angels v. Wilson*, 282 A.D. 643 (1953).

8. Hugh Flick to James E. Allen, November 20, 1953, file 58385-2559, series A-1418, NYMPD.

9. Charles Brind to Chancellor William J. Wallin, November 20, 1953, file 58385-2559, series A-1418, NYMPD.

10. John McCarty, *The Sleaze Merchants: Adventures in Exploitation Filmmaking* (New York: St. Martin's Griffin, 1995), vii. For the story of the exploitation industry, see also Briggs, *Profoundly Disturbing*.

11. Lewis quoted in McCarty, *Sleaze Merchants*, 38.

12. Briggs, *Profoundly Disturbing*, 26.

13. McCarty, *Sleaze Merchants*; Skinner, *Cross and the Cinema*, 79.

14. Quoted in Briggs, *Profoundly Disturbing*, 26.

15. For a summary of Babb's tactics, see Skinner, *Cross and the Cinema*, 78–83.

16. Alpert, "Talk with a Movie Censor."

17. *Mom and Dad*, file 56, general correspondence and controversial films, accession no. 26515, box 54, VDMPC.

18. Mrs. Francis Vaughn to Maryland State Board of Censors, August 11, 1948, file 53258-2567, series A-1418, NYMPD.

19. Handwritten note, file 53258-2567, series A-1418, NYMPD.

20. File 53258-2567, series A-1418, NYMPD.

21. *National Social Hygiene League News*, file 53258-2567, series A-1418, NYMPD.

22. Briggs, *Profoundly Disturbing*, 27.

23. Ward Bowen, memorandum, March 31, 1949, file 53258-2567, series A-1418, NYMPD.

24. Briggs, *Profoundly Disturbing*, 28; David F. Friedman, interview by David Chute, "Wages of Sin," *Film Comment*, July–August 1986, 42–43.

25. Bowen, memorandum, March 31, 1949.

26. Gordon Bates, telegram to Ward Bowen, May 1, 1949, file 53258-2567, series A-1418, NYMPD.

27. William A. Brumfield Jr. to Ward Bowen, June 16, 1949, file 53258-2567, series A-1418, NYMPD.

28. *Variety*, October 20, 1954.

29. *Middletown (NY) Times Herald*, June 22, 1956.

30. Respondents' brief, file 53258-2567, series A-1418, NYMPD.

31. File 58580-2568, series A-1418, NYMPD.

32. Amicus curiae brief of Hygienic Productions in support of petitioner-appellant's position, *Commercial Pictures Corp. v. Regents*, 305 N.Y. 336, *New York Court of Appeals Cases and Briefs*, vol. 13, 336–85.

33. Hugh Flick, memorandum, November 10, 1954, file 62738-2569, series A-1418, NYMPD.

34. Motion Picture Division to Ephraim London, June 13, September 9, 1954, file 62738-2569, series A-1418, NYMPD.

35. Sidney Traub to Hugh Flick, September 17, 1954, file 62738-2569, series A-1418, NYMPD.

36. Carl Rachlin (on behalf of the NYCLU) to Charles Brind, November 8, 1954, file 62738-2569, series A-1418, NYMPD.

37. *Capitol Enterprises, Inc. v. Regents of the University of the State of New York*, 1 A.D.2d 990 (1956).

38. Opinion, *RKO Radio Pictures, Inc. v. Board of Education*, 162 Ohio St. 263 (1954).

39. Judge John H. Lemneck to Frank Lausche (governor of Ohio), December 3, 1954, legal files, series 1591, box 50,732, ODFC.

40. *RKO Radio Pictures, Inc. v. Board of Education*, 130 N.E.2d 845 (1955).

41. *Brattle Films, Inc. v. Commissioner of Public Safety*, 333 Mass. 58 (1955).

42. Black, *Catholic Crusade against the Movies*, 144.

43. See Leff and Simmons, *Dame in the Kimono*, 190–208.

44. Richard Brandt, interview by the author, October 2005. According to Jon Lewis, priests also lurked in the lobbies of theaters that dared to play the legion-condemned film *Baby Doll* in 1955. Lewis, *Hollywood v. Hard Core*, 125–26.

45. Jowett, *Democratic Art*, 415. See also Sova, *Forbidden Films*, 210.

46. Warner, "Movie Censorship in Kansas," 61.

47. See the censor interviews at the end of Carmen, *Movies, Censorship and the Law*, appendices 2–7.

48. Warner, "Movie Censorship in Kansas," 77.

49. Ibid., 79.

50. *Holmby Productions, Inc. v. Vaughn*, 350 U.S. 870.

51. Warner, "Movie Censorship in Kansas," 70–71.

52. *Hallmark Productions, Inc. v. Carroll.*

53. Saylor, "Pennsylvania State Board of Censors," 101.

54. *William Goldman Theatres, Inc. v. Dana*, 405 Pa. 83 (1961).

55. Annual report, 1953–1954, box 1, 2-70-23, MSBC.

56. Quoted in *United Artists v. Maryland State Board of Censors.*

57. *Maryland State Board of Censors v. Times Film Corp.*, 212 Md. 454, 129 A.2d 833 (1957).

58. *Garden of Eden* (promotional brochure), file 64633-2560, series A-1418, NYMPD.

59. The state's response brief before the regents cites the New York Penal Law of 1935, sec. 1140-b. The law was enlarged to include public and private nudism after a sensational 1935 court of appeals decision held that the state's current decency law did not preclude nude exercises in a public gymnasium. *People of New York v. Burke*, 267 N.Y. 571 (1935).

60. Appellant's memorandum before the regents, file 64633-2560, series A-1418, NYMPD.

61. *New York World-Telegram and Sun*, December 18, 1957; *Tampa Daily News*, January 27, 1955; *New York Daily Mirror*, December 18, 1957; *New York Times*, December 18, 1957.

62. Regents review, file 64633-2560, series A-1418, NYMPD.

63. *Excelsior Pictures Corp. v. Regents of the University of the State of New York*, 2 A.D.2d 941 (1956).

64. *Roth v. United States*, 354 U.S. 476 (1957).

65. Michael Bronski, "Hero with a Dirty Face," *Boston Phoenix*, August 15, 2002, http://www.bostonphoenix.com/boston/news_features/other_stories/multi-page/documents/02397916.htm. Bronski explains that the term *smuthound* was in use at the time.

66. Gurstein, *Repeal of Reticence*, 249.

67. *Roth v. United States.*

68. *Roth* was applied to movies in *Jacobellis v. Ohio*, 378 U.S. 184 (1964). See John T. O'Mara, "Obscenity: *Roth* Goes to the Movies," *Buffalo Law Review* 14 (1965): 512–24.

69. Harry Kalven, "The Metaphysics of the Law of Obscenity," *Supreme Court Review*, 1960, 15.

70. *Time*, December 9, 1946, 24–25.

71. *Butler v. Michigan*, 352 U.S. 380 (1957). See also Bosley Crowther, "All for the Kids: Viewing an Anomaly of Film Censorship," *New York Times*, March 3, 1957.

72. Anthony Lewis, "Justices Viewed Censored Movie," *New York Times*, November 14, 1957.

73. Gaume, "Suppression of Motion Pictures in Kansas," 60.

74. *Excelsior Pictures Corp. v. Regents of the University of the State of New York*, 3 N.Y.2d 237 (1957).

75. Obituary of Adrian P. Burke, *New York Times*, September 9, 2000; *The New York Red Book*, 1956.

76. Dissenting opinion, *Excelsior Pictures Corp. v. Regents of the University of the State of New York*, 3 N.Y.2d 237.

77. Flick quoted in *Variety*, October 30, 1957.

78. *St. John's Law Review* 32 (December 1957): 126–31.

79. *Variety*, June 12, 1957.

80. *Film Daily*, November 26, 1958; *Hollywood Reporter*, October 6, 1955.

81. *Variety*, September 14, 1955.

9. The Seventh Case in Seven Years, 1957–1959

1. Dawn B. Sova, *Banned Books: Literature Suppressed on Sexual Grounds* (New York: Facts on File, 1998), 101.

2. MacLeish quoted by Judge Bryan of the U.S. district court in Manhattan in his opinion in the case against the postmaster general's ban, *Grove Press v. Christenberry*, 175 F. Supp. 488 (1959).

3. File 66580-2563, series A-1418, NYMPD.

4. Brandt, interview by the author; Mayer, interview by the author.

5. *New York Times*, December 12, 1956.

6. Walsh, *Sin and Censorship*, 321.

7. Thomas W. Spalding, *The Premier See: A History of the Archdiocese of Baltimore, 1789–1994* (Baltimore: Johns Hopkins University Press, 1995), 402.

8. Mayer, interview by the author.

9. Ibid.

10. *Film Daily*, August 8, 1956.

11. *New York Times*, August 8, 1956; *New York Herald Tribune*, August 8, 1956; *Film Daily*, August 8, 1956.

12. Petition to the board of regents, exhibit A, *Kingsley International Pictures Corp. v. Regents of the University of the State of New York*, 4 A.D.2d 348 (1957).

13. Paul V. Beckley, "Regents Group Reviews Ban on 'Chatterley' Film," *New York Herald Tribune*, August 8, 1956.

14. Opinion of the regents, file 66580-2563, series A-1418, NYMPD.

15. Charles Rembar, *The End of Obscenity: The Trials of* Lady Chatterley, Tropic of Cancer, *and* Fanny Hill (New York: Harper and Row, 1968), 146.

16. Charles Rembar, introduction to *Obscenity: The Complete Oral Arguments before the Supreme Court in the Major Obscenity Cases*, ed. Leon Friedman (New York: Chelsea House, 1970), xv.

17. Petitioner's brief, *Kingsley International Pictures Corp. v. Regents*, 4 App. Div.2d 348.

18. This case, *Times Film Corp. v. City of Chicago*, 365 U.S. 43 (1961), dealt with a distributor's refusal to submit a nonobscene film to the Chicago board of censors. It is not to be confused with *Times Film Corp. v. City of Chicago*, 355 U.S. 35 (1957), which dealt with the supposed obscenity of *Game of Love*.

19. Amicus curiae brief of the New York Civil Liberties Union, *Kingsley International Pictures Corp. v. Regents*, 4 A.D.2d 348.

20. *Kingsley International Pictures Corp. v. Regents*, 4 A.D.2d 348.

21. *New York Times*, July 25, 1957.

22. *One, Inc. v. Olesen*, 355 U.S. 71 (1958); *Sunshine Book Co. v. Summerfield*, 355 U.S. 372 (1958).

23. George Haimbaugh Jr., "Film Censorship since Roth-Alberts," *Kentucky Law Journal* 51 (1963): 656–66.

24. Appellee's brief, *Kingsley International Pictures Corp. v. Regents of the University of the State of New York*, 4 N.Y.2d 349 (1958).

25. Appellant's brief, ibid.

26. Brief of attorney general for respondents-appellants, ibid.

27. Obituary of Albert Conway, *New York Times*, May 19, 1969. See also *New York Times*, "Women Are Urged to Aid Democracy," September 16, 1951.

28. *Kingsley International Pictures Corp. v. Regents*, 4 N.Y.2d 349.

29. Concurring opinion, ibid.

30. Dissenting opinions, ibid.

31. *New York Times*, May 7, 1956.

32. *New York Times*, February 16, 24, 1962.

33. Nunez, "In Search of a Legislative Definition," 90.

34. *New York Times*, April 3, 1963.

35. *Yates v. United States*, 354 U.S. 298 (1957).

36. "State Court Upholds Constitutionality of Refusal to License *Lady Chatterley's Lover* under Recently Amended Motion Picture Licensing Statute," *Columbia Law Review* 59 (1959): 350.

37. *Newsweek*, July 13, 1959.

38. Appellant's brief, *Kingsley International Pictures Corp. v. Regents of the University of the State of New York*, 360 U.S. 684 (1959).

39. Appellees' brief, ibid.

40. Concurring opinion, *Jacobellis v. Ohio*, 378 U.S. 184 (1964).

41. Opinion, *Kingsley International Pictures Corp. v. Regents*, 360 U.S. 684.

42. Kalven, "Metaphysics of the Law of Obscenity," 30.

43. Concurring opinion by Black, *Kingsley International Pictures Corp. v. Regents*, 360 U.S. 684.

44. Concurring opinion by Douglas, ibid.

45. Concurring opinion by Frankfurter, ibid.

46. Concurring opinion by Clark, ibid.

47. Concurring opinion by Harlan, ibid.

48. Edward de Grazia, *Girls Lean Back Everywhere: The Law of Obscenity and the Assault on Genius* (New York: Random House, 1992), 736–37.

49. John R. Verani, "Motion Picture Censorship and the Doctrine of Prior Restraint," *Houston Law Review* 3 (1965): 28–31.

50. Kalven, "Metaphysics of the Law of Obscenity," 34.

51. De Grazia, *Girls Lean Back Everywhere*, xii.

52. *Variety*, July 15, 1959.

53. Kingsley quoted in ibid.

54. *Box Office*, July 6, 1959.

55. *New York Times*, June 30, 1959.

56. Arch Parsons, "'Chatterley' Film Ban Held Unconstitutional," *New York Herald Tribune*, June 30, 1959; Flick quoted in ibid.

57. *New York Times*, July 3, 1959.

58. Wirt, "State Film Censorship," 102–4.

59. Lausche quoted in *New York Times*, July 3, 1959.

60. *New York Times*, July 3, 1959.

61. Bosley Crowther, "Victory for Ideas," *New York Times*, July 5, 1959.

62. "Decisions—Constitutional Law—Motion Picture Censorship," *Brooklyn Law Review*, December 1959; B.P.W., "Constitutional Law—Motion Picture Licensing Statute—Validity Of," *Albany Law Review*, January 1960; "New York Statute Censuring 'Sexual Immorality' in Motion Picture Film Held Unconstitutional," *Temple Law Quarterly*, Winter 1959, 243; John Harvey Whitworth Jr., "Constitutional Law—'Lady Chatterley's Lover': Death to Motion Picture Censorship?" *Mississippi Law Journal* 31 (1959): 96–97.

63. *Grove Press v. Christenberry*.

10. The Curtain Coming Down, 1957–1964

1. Jowett, "Capacity for Evil," 64.

2. Glenn C. Altschuler, *All Shook Up: How Rock 'n' Roll Changed America* (New York: Oxford University Press, 2003), 186.

3. *New York Times*, February 18, 1959.

4. Bosley Crowther, "Censors Carry On: New Measures to Put More Curbs on Films," *New York Times*, February 8, 1959.

5. *New York Times*, February 27, 1959.

6. *New York Times*, March 25, 1959.

7. *New York Times*, February 24, 1962.

8. Bosley Crowther, "On Guard Again: New Film Restraints Loom in Albany," *New York Times*, March 4, 1962.

9. Arthur Mayer, "How Much Can the Censors Say?" *Saturday Review*, November 3, 1962.

10. Mayer, interview by the author.

11. *New York Times*, "Censoring of Films in Bay State Voided," July 7, 1955.

12. Amicus curiae brief of the American Civil Liberties Union, *Times Film Corp. v. City of Chicago*, 365 U.S. 43.

13. *New York Times*, October 21, 1961.

14. Opinion, *Times Film Corp. v. City of Chicago*, 365 U.S. 43.

15. Dissenting opinion, ibid.

16. Giglio, "Prior Restraint of Motion Pictures," 379–90.

17. Bilgrey quoted in *New York Times*, January 24, 1964.

18. Majority opinion, *Freedman v. Maryland*, 380 U.S. 51 (1965).

19. Verani, "Motion Picture Censorship," 40.

20. Bosley Crowther, "A Hurtful Decision," *New York Times*, January 29, 1961.

21. Anthony Lewis, "A New Lineup on the Supreme Court," *Reporter*, August 17, 1961; Anthony Lewis, "Censor Upheld," *New York Times*, January 29, 1961.

22. Murray Schumach, "Film, Radio, TV and Book Men Will Join in Censorship Fight," *New York Times*, February 21, 1961.

23. Murray Schumach, "Hollywood Fight: United Industry Enlists Other Media to Combat Censorship Pressures," *New York Times*, February 26, 1961.

24. Johnston quoted in ibid.

25. Schumach, "Hollywood Fight."

26. Only four challenges were assisted by either the MPAA or its counsel,

Philip J. O'Brien Jr. or Sidney A. Schreiber: *Gelling v. Texas* (*Pinky*), *Superior Films, Inc. v. Department of Education of Ohio* (*M*), *Freedman v. Maryland* (*Revenge at Daybreak*), and *United Artists Corp. v. Board of Censors of City of Memphis* (*Curley*). The MPAA requested leave to file a brief for the second Times Film case but apparently did not follow through.

27. Nolan quoted in *New York Times*, March 7, 1965.

28. *Zenith International Film Corp. v. City of Chicago*, 291 F.2d 785 (1961).

29. Randall, *Censorship of the Movies*, 132.

30. *Teitel Film Corp. v. Cusack*, 390 U.S. 139 (1968).

31. *K. Gordon Murray Productions, Inc. v. Floyd*, 217 Ga. 784 (1962). Under the new ordinance, any film rated "objectionable" by Atlanta's single reviewer would be subject to obscenity prosecution if exhibited. See Carmen, *Movies, Censorship and the Law*, 315–24.

32. Louis Pesce, interview, in Carmen, *Movies, Censorship and the Law*, 270.

33. File 70321-2563, series A-1418, NYMPD.

34. Bev Zalcock, "Not Forgetting Shirley Clarke," *Filmwaves* 2 (1997): 14–15.

35. Shirley Clarke, interview by Dee Dee Halleck, New York City, 1985, The Early Video Project, http://www.davidsonsfiles.org/shirleyclarkeinterview.html.

36. Shirley Clarke, interview by Eugene Archer, "Woman Director Makes the Scene," *New York Times*, August 26, 1962.

37. Writing in 1997, a film historian termed *The Connection* "almost a parody of the cinema verite approach to filmmaking" and called it "both technically and theoretically fascinating." Zalcock, "Not Forgetting Shirley Clarke," 15.

38. Bosley Crowther, *New York Times*, October 4, 1962.

39. Regents review, January 25, 1962, file 70321-2563, series A-1418, NYMPD.

40. *William Goldman Theatres v. Dana*.

41. *Variety*, July 11, 1962.

42. London quoted in *Motion Picture Daily*, February 23, 1962.

43. The case London referred to was *People v. Richmond County News, Inc.*, 9 N.Y.2d 578 (1961).

44. London quoted in *Box Office*, October 22, 1962.

45. *Variety*, November 1, 1961.

46. Brind quoted in *Box Office*, May 14, 1962.

47. *New York Times*, July 3, 1961, September 28, 1962.

48. *Matter of the Connection Co. v. Regents of the University of the State of New York*, 17 A.D.2d 671 (1962).

49. Quoted in *New York Times*, September 28, 1962.

50. *New York Herald Tribune*, October 4, 1962.

51. Bosley Crowther, "'Connection' Here and Gone," *New York Times*, October 4, 1962.

52. Milton Esterow, "Unlicensed Film of 'Connection' Stopped by Court on First Day," *New York Times*, October 4, 1962.

53. *Matter of the Application of the Connection Co. v. the Regents of the University of the State of New York*, Supreme Court, Albany County (calendar 51), file 70321-2563, series A-1418, NYMPD.

54. *Variety*, October 3, 1962.

55. *New York Times*, October 18, 1962.

56. *New York Times*, October 24, 1962.

57. Louis Pesce, memorandum to Motion Picture Division, November 2, 1962, file 70321-2563, series A-1418, NYMPD.

58. Ernest David Giglio, "The Decade of *The Miracle*, 1952–1962: A Study in the Censorship of the American Motion Picture" (PhD diss., Syracuse University, 1964), 120.

59. Appeal before the board of regents on *Twilight Girls*, file 73186-2536, series A-1418, NYMPD.

60. Ibid.

61. *Metzger v. Couper*, 21 A.D.2d 920 (1964).

62. Pesce, interview, in Carmen, *Movies, Censorship and the Law*, 266–75.

11. Fight for Freedom of the Screen, 1962–1965

1. The records of the Maryland censor board, particularly its minutes, reflect the censors' consternation at Freedman's refusal to follow the rules. Minutes, box 11, MSBC; Ronald Freedman, interview by the author, September 11, 2002.

2. Charles Cohen, "Porn Free," *Baltimore City Paper*, October 11, 2000, http://www.citypaper.com/news/story.asp?id=2463.

3. Friedman, interview by Chute, 34.

4. Freedman, interview by the author.

5. Sova, *Forbidden Films*, 251.

6. De Grazia and Newman, *Banned Films*, 112.

7. Appellee's brief, *Freedman v. Maryland*.

8. De Grazia, *Girls Lean Back Everywhere*, 566.

9. See Giglio, "Decade of *The Miracle*," 110.

10. Freedman, interview by the author.

11. For more on litigation strategy, see David J. Garrow, *Liberty and Sexuality: The Right to Privacy and the Making of Roe v. Wade* (New York: Mac-

millan, 1994); Mark V. Tushnet, *The NAACP's Legal Strategy against Segregated Education, 1925–1950* (Chapel Hill: University of North Carolina Press, 1987); and Stephen L. Wasby, *Race Relations Litigation in an Age of Complexity* (Charlottesville: University Press of Virginia, 1995).

12. Murray Schumach, *New York Times*, November 10, 1962.

13. Freedman, interview by the author; de Grazia and Newman, *Banned Films*, 112.

14. Bilgrey quoted in de Grazia and Newman, *Banned Films*, 112.

15. *Variety*, May 8, 1963.

16. Brandt, interview by the author.

17. Brandt quoted in Black, *Catholic Crusade against the Movies*, 134.

18. *Time*, February 15, 1963.

19. *Variety*, November 2, 1960.

20. *New York Times*, April 1, 1965.

21. *Trans-Lux Distributing Corp. v. Board of Regents of the University of New York*, 19 A.D.2d 937 (1963).

22. Brind quoted in *Film Daily*, September 23, 1963.

23. *Trans-Lux Distributing Corp. v. Regents*, 19 A.D.2d 937.

24. Affidavit of Arthur Loeb Mayer in support of petition, *Trans-Lux Distributing Corp. v. Board of Regents of the University of New York*, 14 N.Y.2d 88 (1964).

25. Brief on behalf of respondent, ibid.

26. Brief on behalf of appellant, ibid.

27. *Box Office*, January 27, 1974. *Box Office* apparently had a reporter in the courtroom.

28. Opinion, *Trans-Lux Distributing Corp. v. Regents*, 14 N.Y.2d 88.

29. Concurring opinions, ibid.

30. In all, Fuld received 126 postcards and letters after the *Richmond County News* case. Box 6, Stanley H. Fuld Collection, Rare Book and Manuscript Library, Columbia University, New York City.

31. See Richard J. Lyons, "Constitutional Law—Board of Regents May Ban Removal of Obscene Scenes from Motion Picture," *Syracuse Law Review* 16 (1964): 131–32, and *Columbia Pictures Corp. v. City of Chicago*, 184 F. Supp. 817 (1959).

32. Randall, *Censorship of the Movies*, 162–66.

33. *Jacobellis v. Ohio*, 378 U.S. 184.

34. *New York Times*, March 27, 1964.

35. Brandt spoke to the MPAA. Although they were interested, they did not help. Brandt, interview by the author. Brandt appealed to the U.S. Supreme Court on June 5, 1964, and the *Jacobellis* decision came on June 22, 1964. There would have been ample time for the MPAA or the NYCLU to file an amicus brief.

36. *Freedman v. State*, 233 Md. 498 (1964).

37. Amicus curiae brief of the Motion Picture Association of America, Inc., ibid.

38. *Freedman v. State*, 233 Md. 498. The case was decided in February, one month after the *Trans-Lux* court of appeals decision.

39. Brief for appellant, *Freedman v. Maryland*, 380 U.S. 51.

40. Bosley Crowther, *New York Times*, June 20, 1965.

41. Majority opinion, *Freedman v. Maryland*, 380 U.S. 51.

42. Rudolph G. Hasl, "Constitutional Law—Procedural Safeguards Necessary for Valid Prior Restraint of Motion Pictures," *Saint Louis University Law Journal* 10 (1965): 145.

43. For the list of cases, see Randall, *Censorship of the Movies*, 245n54.

44. Finan quoted in *Baltimore Sun*, March 2, 1965.

45. Marhenke quoted in minutes of Maryland State Board of Censors, March 4, 1965, box 11, MSBC.

46. Verani, "Motion Picture Censorship," 40.

47. *Trans-Lux Distributing Corp. v. Board of Regents of the University of New York*, 380 U.S. 259 (1965). The Court returned the case to the state courts for "further proceedings not inconsistent with this ruling." *New York Times*, June 11, 1965.

48. Verani, "Motion Picture Censorship," 49.

49. Murray Schumach, "Film Censorship Shifted by State," *New York Times*, March 27, 1965.

50. Fred P. Graham, "Movies and the Court: The State Must Streamline Its Procedure If Censorship of Films Is to Continue," *New York Times*, March 16, 1965.

51. *New York Times*, March 17, 1965.

12. Denouement, 1965–1981

1. David Steigerwald, *The Sixties and the End of Modern America* (New York: St. Martin's Press, 1995), 154.

2. David Farber, *The Age of Great Dreams: America in the 1960s* (New York: Hill and Wang, 1994), 65. See also Lawrence M. Friedman, *Republic of Choice: Law, Authority and Culture* (Cambridge, MA: Harvard University Press, 1990).

3. Altschuler, *All Shook Up*, 67–68.

4. *New York Times*, March 21, 1965.

5. *Trans-Lux Distributing Corp. v. Maryland State Board of Censors*, 240 Md. 98 (1965).

6. *Baltimore Sun*, March 2, 1965.

7. Minutes, May 3, 1965, box 11, MSBC.

8. *Trans-Lux Distributing Corp. v. Maryland State Board of Censors.*

9. *New York Times*, March 27, 1965.

10. Brandt, interview by the author.

11. *New York Times*, June 11, 1965.

12. File 73479-2549, series A-1418, NYMPD.

13. Appeal to the board of regents, ibid.

14. *Cambist Films, Inc. v. Board of Regents of the University of New York*, 46 Misc.2d 513 (1965).

15. *Matter of Trans-Lux Distributing Corp. v. Board of Regents of the University of New York*, 16 N.Y.2d 710 (1965). Also see *New York Times*, June 11, 1965.

16. Bosley Crowther, "Obscenity Is a Dirty Word," *New York Times*, December 5, 1965.

17. *New York Times*, June 11, 1965.

18. The number of articles on film censorship in *The Reader's Guide to Periodical Literature* declined through the censoring years. For 1955–1957, thirty-five articles appeared. In the next issue, 1957–1959, fourteen articles appeared. By 1963–1965, only five articles appeared. The only periodicals that carried any mention of the *Freedman* decision were *Time* and *Newsweek*.

19. Bosley Crowther, "Goodbye to the Censor," *New York Times*, June 20, 1965.

20. *New York Times*, October 30, 1965.

21. New York Penal Law of 1965, sec. 484-h. See *Variety*, May 1, 1968.

22. The new rules were adopted on April 26, 1965, to take effect on January 1, 1966. They required the board to approve a film within two days or to notify the distributor that the film would not be approved within one day. Within two days of receiving a nonapproved film, the board had to institute legal proceedings unless the film was withdrawn by the distributor. After filing, the board could request a four-day restraint on distribution. *State of Kansas ex rel. Londerholm v. Columbia Pictures Corp.*, 197 Kan. 448 (1966).

23. Sova, *Forbidden Films*, 38, 64.

24. The statute remained on the books until it was formally repealed in 1968. Warner, "Movie Censorship in Kansas," 90.

25. Attorney general correspondence, file 54, box 53, VDMPC.

26. John S. Salmon, *A Guide to State Records in the Archives Branch, Virginia State Library* (Richmond: Virginia State Library, 1985).

27. Black, *Catholic Crusade against the Movies*, 221.

28. Schumach, *Face on the Cutting Room Floor*, 260–61.

29. Dorothy Hamilton, "Hollywood's Silent Partner: A History of the Mo-

tion Picture Association of America Movie Rating System" (PhD diss., University of Kansas, 1999), 49.

30. Bosley Crowther, "The Heat Is on Films," *New York Times*, January 17, 1965.

31. De Grazia, *Girls Lean Back Everywhere*, xii. The most notable case of freeing obscenity was that of Henry Miller's *Tropic of Cancer*. Here expression "not utterly without" literary, artistic, scientific, or social value was to be protected. Such a test made proof of obscenity extraordinarily difficult. Edward de Grazia refers to this test of obscenity as "the Brennan doctrine." Ibid.

32. *New York Times*, June 12, 1968; Frederic J. Wertham, "Are Movies Teaching Us to Be Violent?" *New York Times*, June 30, 1968.

33. Crowther, "Obscenity Is a Dirty Word."

34. Minutes, November 26, 1969, box 11, MSBC.

35. Ibid., December 1, 1969.

36. *Embassy Pictures Corp. v. Hudson*, 242 F. Supp. 975 (1965). The film involved was *Women of the World*. Ephraim London assisted a Memphis attorney.

37. Crowther, "Obscenity Is a Dirty Word."

38. Sova, *Forbidden Films*, 186–87.

39. *Dunn v. Maryland State Board of Censors*, 240 Md. 249 (1965).

40. See, for example, William B. Lockhart and Robert C. McClure, "Censorship of Obscenity: The Developing Constitutional Standards," *Minnesota Law Review* 45 (1960): 5–121.

41. *Hewitt v. Maryland State Board of Censors*, 241 Md. 283 (1966).

42. *Hewitt v. Maryland State Board of Censors*, 243 Md. 574 (1966).

43. George H. Callcott, *Maryland and America, 1940 to 1980* (Baltimore: Johns Hopkins University Press, 1985), 178.

44. Freedman, interview by the author.

45. *Baltimore Evening Sun*, n.d., MC.

46. Minutes, May 25–October 20, 1965, box 11, MSBC.

47. *Sanza v. Maryland State Board of Censors*, 245 Md. 319 (1967).

48. Minutes, August 10, 1965, box 11, MSBC.

49. Ibid., June 30, 1967.

50. Annual report, 1932–1933, box 1, 2-70-23, MSBC.

51. Minutes, February 13, 1968, box 11, MSBC.

52. *Baltimore Sun*, June 25, 1967.

53. Sova, *Forbidden Films*, 302.

54. *Interstate Circuit, Inc. v. City of Dallas*, 390 U.S. 676 (1968); *Ginsberg v. New York*, 390 U.S. 629 (1968).

55. Vincent Canby, "Plan to Classify Movies Debated," *New York Times*, June 12, 1968; Hamilton, "Hollywood's Silent Partner," 52.

56. James Dilts, *Baltimore Sun*, June 25, 1967.

57. *Baltimore Sun*, undated clipping [December 1968], MC.

58. Freedman, interview by the author.

59. Pokorny quoted in *Baltimore Sun*, undated clipping [October 1968], MC.

60. *Hewitt v. Maryland State Board of Censors*, 255 Md. 528 (1969).

61. Matt Langdon, review of *I Am Curious (Yellow)*, 2003, http://www.filmcritic.com/misc/emporium.nsf/reviews/I-Am-Curious-(Yellow).

62. *Baltimore Sun*, July 9, 1969.

63. Ibid.

64. De Grazia, *Girls Lean Back Everywhere*, 368–69.

65. De Grazia and Newman, *Banned Films*, 123.

66. *Baltimore Sun*, August 1, 1969.

67. *Baltimore Sun*, October 23, 1969; *Wagonheim v. Maryland State Board of Censors*, 255 Md. 297 (1969).

68. *Baltimore Evening Sun*, November 1, 1969.

69. Minutes, March 4, 1965, box 11, MSBC.

70. *Baltimore Sun*, November 11, 1970.

71. *Baltimore News American*, November 12, 1970.

72. *Grove Press, Inc. v. Maryland State Board of Censors*, 401 U.S. 480 (1971). The Supreme Court's composition had changed since the 1964 *Jacobellis* decision. Warren, Goldberg, and Clark had been replaced by Warren Burger, Thurgood Marshall, and Harry Blackmun.

73. *Baltimore Sun*, September 4, 1972.

74. De Grazia and Newman, *Banned Films*, 125.

75. The four cases were *Modern Social Education, Inc. v. Preller*, 353 F. Supp. 173 (1973); *Ebert v. Maryland State Board of Censors*, 19 Md. App. 300 (1973); *Sanza v. Maryland State Board of Censors*; and *Star v. Preller*, 352 F. Supp. 530 (1972).

76. *Star v. Preller*, 352 F. Supp. 530.

77. *Star v. Preller*, 419 U.S. 956 (1974).

78. *Baltimore Sun*, October 31, 1974.

79. Vincent Canby, "What Are We to Make of 'Deep Throat'?" *New York Times*, January 21, 1973.

80. Ralph Blumenthal, "Porno Chic," *New York Times Magazine*, January 21, 1973.

81. Ellen Willis, "Hard to Swallow," *New York Review of Books*, January 25, 1973.

82. *People of New York v. Mature Enterprises, Inc.*, 73 Misc. 2d 749, 343 N.Y.S.2d 911 (1973).

83. De Grazia and Newman, *Banned Films*, 141.

84. Ibid.; Sova, *Forbidden Films*, 95.

85. *Miller v. California*, 413 U.S. 15 (1973).
86. *Baltimore Evening Sun*, May 25, 1974.
87. *Baltimore Sun*, June 25, 1974.
88. *Baltimore Sun*, November 26, 1974; *Mangum v. Maryland State Board of Censors*, 273 Md. 176 (1974).
89. *Baltimore Sun*, April 5, 1976.
90. *Baltimore News American*, July 1, 1981.
91. *Baltimore Evening Sun*, February 24, 1977.
92. Avara quoted in ibid.
93. Avara quoted in *Baltimore Sun*, February 1, 1979.
94. *Baltimore News American*, December 5, 1978.
95. Avara quoted in *Baltimore News American*, June 26, 1981.
96. *Interstate Circuit, Inc. v. City of Dallas*; *Vance v. Universal Amusement Co.*, 445 U.S. 308 (1980); *Teitel Film Corp. v. Cusack*; *Lee Art Theatre, Inc. v. Virginia*, 392 U.S. 636 (1968); *Paris Adult Theatre I v. Slaton*, 413 U.S. 49 (1973); *Heller v. New York*, 413 U.S. 483 (1973); *Byrne v. Karalexis*, 401 U.S. 216 (1972); *Southeastern Promotions, Ltd. v. Conrad*, 420 U.S. 546 (1974); *Star v. Preller*, 419 U.S. 956; *M.I.C., Ltd. v. Bedford Township*, 463 U.S. 1341 (1983).
97. *Embassy Pictures, Corp. v. Hudson*.
98. *Victoria Films v. Division of Motion Picture Censorship*, April 15, 1965, Circuit Court of the City of Richmond, file 54, box 53, VDMPC.
99. *State of Kansas ex rel. Londerholm v. Columbia Pictures Corp.*
100. Freedman, interview by the author.

Conclusion

1. Chafee, *Free Speech in the United States*, 150.
2. Steven G. Gey, "The Case against Postmodern Censorship Theory," *University of Pennsylvania Law Review* 145 (1996): 193–298. Gey's article attacking the postmodern speech theories of Richard Delgado, Cass Sunstein, Catherine MacKinnon, Mari Matsuda, and others was answered by Delgado two years later. Richard Delgado, "Are Hate Speech Rules Constitutional Heresy? A Reply to Steven Gey," *University of Pennsylvania Law Review* 146 (1998): 865–73.
3. Morone, *Hellfire Nation*, 239.
4. Schumach, *Face on the Cutting Room Floor*, 185.
5. *New York Times*, May 27, 1952.
6. Hamilton, "Hollywood's Silent Partner," 19, 51–52.
7. Skinner, *Cross and the Cinema*, 1.
8. See Charles Lyons, *The New Censors: Movies and the Culture Wars* (Philadelphia: Temple University Press, 1997).

9. The Supreme Court refused certiorari and so let stand the Louisiana decision in *Byers v. Edmondson*, 712 So.2d 681 (1998). See also "Supreme Court Denies Review of Free Speech Issue over *Natural Born Killers*," *Sports and Entertainment Litigation Reporter*, November 1999, 5.

10. Marjorie Heins, *Not in Front of the Children: "Indecency," Censorship, and the Innocence of Youth* (New York: Hill and Wang, 2001), 12.

11. *West Virginia State Board of Education v. Barnette*.

12. *Texas v. Johnson*, 491 U.S. 397 (1989).

Selected Bibliography

Aberdeen, J. A. "The Early Film Business: Distribution; States Rights or Road Show," Hollywood Renegades Archive, http://www.cobbles.com/simpp_archive/statesrights.htm.

Abraham, Henry J., and Barbara A. Perry. *Freedom and the Court: Civil Rights and Liberties in the United States*. 6th ed. New York: Oxford University Press, 1994.

Ackerman, Bruce. "Constitutional Politics/Constitutional Law." *Yale Law Journal* 99 (1989): 453–547.

Alpert, Hollis. "Talk with a Movie Censor." *Saturday Review*, November 22, 1952, 21, 50–54.

Altschuler, Glenn C. *All Shook Up: How Rock 'n' Roll Changed America*. New York: Oxford University Press, 2003.

Anderson, Mark Lynn. "Regulating Racism: Americanism, Identity Politics, and the Battle for Film Censorship in New York State." Paper presented at Researching New York, University at Albany, State University of New York, November 21, 2003.

Ayer, Douglas, Roy E. Bates, and Peter J. Herman. "Self-Censorship in the Movie Industry: An Historical Perspective on Law and Social Change." *Wisconsin Law Review*, 1970, no. 3:791–838.

Balio, Tino. *Grand Design: Hollywood as a Modern Business Enterprise, 1930–1939*. New York: Scribner, 1993.

Beaver, Frank Eugene. *Bosley Crowther: Social Critic of the Film, 1940–1967*. New York: Arno Press, 1974.

Bergan, Francis. *The History of the New York Court of Appeals, 1847–1932*. New York: Columbia University Press, 1985.

Black, Gregory D. *The Catholic Crusade against the Movies, 1940–1975*. Cambridge: Cambridge University Press, 1997.

———. *Hollywood Censored: Morality Codes, Catholics and the Movies*. Cambridge: Cambridge University Press, 1994.

Blanchard, Margaret A. "The American Urge to Censor: Freedom of Expression versus the Desire to Sanitize Society—from Anthony Comstock to 2 Live Crew." *William and Mary Law Review* 33 (1992): 741–851.

Boyer, Paul S. *Purity in Print: The Vice-Society Movement and Book Censorship in America.* New York: Scribner, 1968.

Briggs, Joe Bob. "Kroger Babb's Road Show." *Reason*, November 2003, http://www.reason.com/news/show/28934.html.

———. *Profoundly Disturbing: Shocking Movies That Changed History.* New York: Universe, 2002.

Brinkley, Alan. *The End of Reform: New Deal Liberalism in Recession and War.* New York: Vintage Books, 1996.

Brisbin, Richard A. "Censorship, Ratings, and Rights: Political Order and Sexual Portrayal in American Movies." *Studies in American Political Development* 16 (2002): 1–27.

Bronski, Michael. "Hero with a Dirty Face." *Boston Phoenix*, August 15, 2002, http://www.bostonphoenix.com/boston/news_features/other_stories/multi-page/documents/02397916.htm.

Brownlow, Kevin. *Behind the Mask of Innocence: Sex, Violence, Prejudice, Crime; Films of Social Conscience in the Silent Era.* Berkeley and Los Angeles: University of California Press, 1990.

Brychta, Ivan. "The Ohio Film Censorship Law." *Ohio State Law Journal* 13 (1952): 350–411.

Cadegan, Una M. "Guardians of Democracy or Cultural Storm Troopers? American Catholics and the Control of Popular Media, 1934–1966." *Catholic Historical Review* 87 (2001): 252–82.

Callcott, George H. *Maryland and America, 1940 to 1980.* Baltimore: Johns Hopkins University Press, 1985.

Carmen, Ira H. *Movies, Censorship and the Law.* Ann Arbor: University of Michigan Press, 1966.

Carr, Steven Alan. *Hollywood and Anti-Semitism: A Cultural History up to World War II.* Cambridge: Cambridge University Press, 2001.

"Censorship of Motion Pictures." *Yale Law Journal* 49 (1939): 87–113.

Chafee, Zechariah. *Free Speech in the United States.* Cambridge, MA: Harvard University Press, 1941.

Clarke, Shirley. Interview by Dee Dee Halleck. New York City, 1985. The Early Video Project. http://www.davidsonsfiles.org/shirleyclarkeinterview.html.

Conant, Michael. *Antitrust in the Motion Picture Industry.* Berkeley and Los Angeles: University of California Press, 1960.

Cooney, John. *The American Pope: The Life and Times of Francis Cardinal Spellman.* New York: Times Books, 1984.

Corliss, Richard. "The Legion of Decency." *Film Comment*, Summer 1968, 24–61.

Couvares, Francis G. Introduction to "Hollywood, Censorship, and American Culture." Special issue, *American Quarterly* 44 (1992): 509–24.

Crowther, Bosley. "The Strange Case of 'The Miracle.'" *Atlantic Monthly*, April 1951, 35–39.

Dart, Peter. "Breaking the Code: A Historical Footnote." *Cinema Journal* 8, no. 1 (1968): 39–41.

de Grazia, Edward. *Girls Lean Back Everywhere: The Law of Obscenity and the Assault on Genius*. New York: Random House, 1992.

de Grazia, Edward, and Roger K. Newman. *Banned Films: Movies, Censors and the First Amendment*. New York: Bowker, 1982.

Delgado, Richard. "Are Hate Speech Rules Constitutional Heresy? A Reply to Steven Gey." *University of Pennsylvania Law Review* 146 (1998): 865–73.

Desmond, Charles. "Censoring the Movies." *Notre Dame Lawyer* 29 (1953): 27–36.

———. "Legal Problems Involved in Censoring the Media of Mass Communication." *Marquette Law Review* 40 (1956): 38–56.

Doherty, Thomas. *Cold War, Cool Medium: Television, McCarthyism, and American Culture*. New York: Columbia University Press, 2003.

———. *Pre-Code Hollywood: Sex, Immorality, and Insurrection in American Cinema, 1930–1934*. New York: Columbia University Press, 1990.

Donahue, Suzanne Mary. *American Film Distribution: The Changing Marketplace*. Ann Arbor, MI: UMI Research Press, 1987.

Driggs, Andrew James. "*The Miracle*: The Controversy and the Constitution." Master's thesis, Brigham Young University, 1986.

Eardley, David J. "Motion Picture Censorship—a Constitutional Dilemma." *Maryland Law Review* 14 (1954): 284–98.

Erenburg, Lewis A. *Steppin' Out: New York Nightlife and the Transformation of American Culture, 1890–1930*. Chicago: University of Chicago Press, 1981.

Ernst, Morris L., and Alexander Lindey. *The Censor Marches On: Recent Milestones in the Administration of the Obscenity Law in the United States*. New York: Doubleday, Doran, 1940.

Facey, Paul W. *The Legion of Decency: A Sociological Analysis of the Emergence and Development of a Social Pressure Group*. New York: Arno Press, 1974.

Farber, David. *The Age of Great Dreams: America in the 1960s*. New York: Hill and Wang, 1994.

Feldman, Charles Matthew. *The National Board of Censorship (Review) of Motion Pictures, 1909–1922*. New York: Arno Press, 1977.

Flick, Hugh. Interview by Esperanza Cintrón. "In Retrospect." *Insights: A*

Quarterly Magazine for Employees of the New York State Education Department, August 1990, 6–8.

Forman, Henry James. *Our Movie Made Children*. New York: Macmillan, 1934.

Friedman, Andrea. *Prurient Interests: Gender, Democracy, and Obscenity in New York City, 1909–1945*. New York: Columbia University, 2000.

Friedman, David F. Interview by David Chute. "Wages of Sin." *Film Comment*, July–August 1986, 31–47.

Friedman, Lawrence M. *Republic of Choice: Law, Authority and Culture*. Cambridge, MA: Harvard University Press, 1990.

Friedman, Leon, ed. *Obscenity: The Complete Oral Arguments before the Supreme Court in the Major Obscenity Cases*. New York: Chelsea House, 1970.

Gallagher, Robin. "Public Educators and Hollywood, 1900–1922." *High School Journal* 82 (1999): 195–208.

Gardiner, Harold C. *Catholic Viewpoint on Censorship*. Garden City, NY: Hanover House, 1958.

Gardner, Gerald. *The Censorship Papers: Movie Censorship Letters from the Hays Office, 1934–1968*. New York: Dodd, Mead, 1987.

Garrow, David J. *Liberty and Sexuality: The Right to Privacy and the Making of Roe v. Wade*. New York: Macmillan, 1994.

Gaume, Thomas Michael. "Suppression of Motion Pictures in Kansas, 1952 to 1975." Master's thesis, University of Kansas, 1976.

Gerard, Lillian N. "'Ways of Love' or a History of the Ways of Censorship." Unpublished manuscript, 1977.

Gey, Steven G. "The Case against Postmodern Censorship Theory." *University of Pennsylvania Law Review* 145 (1996): 193–298.

Gholson, Hunter M. "Recent Decisions." *Mississippi Law Journal* 25 (1954): 273–74.

Giglio, Ernest David. "The Decade of *The Miracle*, 1952–1962: A Study in the Censorship of the American Motion Picture." PhD diss., Syracuse University, 1964.

———. "Prior Restraint of Motion Pictures." *Dickinson Law Review* 69 (1965): 379–90.

Goodman, Ezra. *The Fifty-Year Decline and Fall of Hollywood*. New York: Simon and Schuster, 1961.

Gordon, Colin. *New Deals: Business, Labor, and Politics in America, 1920–1935*. Cambridge: Cambridge University Press, 1994.

Graber, Mark A. *Transforming Free Speech: The Ambiguous Legacy of Civil Libertarianism*. Berkeley and Los Angeles: University of California Press, 1991.

Green, Harvey. *The Uncertainty of Everyday Life, 1915–1945*. Fayetteville: University of Arkansas Press, 2000.

Griffith, Richard, Arthur Mayer, and Eileen Bowser. *The Movies*. New York: Simon and Schuster, 1981.

Gurstein, Rochelle. *The Repeal of Reticence: A History of America's Cultural and Legal Struggles over Free Speech, Obscenity, Sexual Liberation, and Modern Art*. New York: Hill and Wang, 1996.

Haberski, Raymond J., Jr. *It's Only a Movie! Films and Critics in American Culture*. Lexington: University Press of Kentucky, 2001.

Haimbaugh, George, Jr. "Film Censorship since Roth-Alberts." *Kentucky Law Journal* 51 (1963): 656–66.

Hamilton, Dorothy. "Hollywood's Silent Partner: A History of the Motion Picture Association of America Movie Rating System." PhD diss., University of Kansas, 1999.

Hamm, Richard F. *Shaping the Eighteenth Amendment: Temperance Reform, Legal Culture, and the Polity, 1880–1920*. Chapel Hill: University of North Carolina Press, 1995.

Hasl, Rudolph G. "Constitutional Law—Procedural Safeguards Necessary for Valid Prior Restraint of Motion Pictures." *Saint Louis University Law Journal* 10 (1965): 142–47.

Heins, Marjorie. *Not in Front of the Children: "Indecency," Censorship, and the Innocence of Youth*. New York: Hill and Wang, 2001.

Hodgins, Eric. "A Round Table on the Movies." *Life*, June 27, 1949, 90–97+.

Horowitz, David A. "An Alliance of Convenience: Independent Exhibitors and Purity Crusaders Battle Hollywood, 1920–1940." *Historian* 59 (1997): 553–72.

Horowitz, Helen Lefkowitz. *Rereading Sex: Battles over Sexual Knowledge and Suppression in Nineteenth-Century America*. New York: Knopf, 2002.

Inglis, Ruth. *Freedom of the Movies: A Report on Self-Regulation from the Commission on Freedom of the Press*. Chicago: University of Chicago Press, 1947.

Irons, Peter. *A People's History of the Supreme Court*. New York: Penguin Books, 1999.

Izod, John. *Hollywood and the Box Office, 1895–1986*. New York: Columbia University Press, 1988.

Jacobs, Lea. *The Wages of Sin, 1928–1942*. Madison: University of Wisconsin Press, 1991.

Jarvis, Arthur R., Jr. "The Payne Fund Reports: A Discussion of Their Content, Public Reaction, and Affect [*sic*] on the Motion Picture Industry, 1930–1940." *Journal of Popular Culture* 25, no. 2 (1991): 127–40.

Jowett, Garth. "A Capacity for Evil: The 1915 Supreme Court *Mutual* Decision." *Historical Journal of Film, Radio, and Television* 9 (1989): 59–78.

———. *Film: The Democratic Art*. Boston: Little, Brown, 1976.

———. "Moral Responsibility and Commercial Entertainment: Social Control in the U.S. Film Industry, 1907–1968." *Historical Journal of Film, Radio, and Television* 10 (1990): 3–32.

———. "A Significant Medium for the Communication of Ideas: The Miracle Decision and the Decline of Motion Picture Censorship, 1952–1968." In *Movie Censorship and American Culture*, edited by Francis G. Couvares, 258–76. Washington, DC: Smithsonian Institution Press, 1996.

Jowett, Garth S., Ian C. Jarvie, and Kathryn H. Fuller. *Children and the Movies: Media Influence and the Payne Fund Controversy*. New York: Cambridge University Press, 1996.

Kalven, Harry. "The Metaphysics of the Law of Obscenity." *Supreme Court Review*, 1960, 1–45.

Karger, Arthur. *The Powers of the New York Court of Appeals*. 3rd ed. Rochester, NY: Lawyers Cooperative, 1997.

Keller, Morton. *Regulating a New Society: Public Policy and Social Change in America, 1900–1933*. Cambridge, MA: Harvard University Press, 1994.

Kendrick, Walter. *The Secret Museum: Pornography in Modern Culture*. New York: Viking, 1987.

Kindem, Gorham, ed. *The American Movie Industry: The Business of Motion Pictures*. Carbondale: Southern Illinois University Press, 1982.

Kupferman, Theodore, and Philip O'Brien. "Motion Picture Censorship—the Memphis Blues." *Cornell Law Quarterly* 36 (1951): 273–300.

Ladd-Taylor, Molly. *Mother-Work: Women, Child Welfare, and the State, 1890–1930*. Urbana: University of Illinois Press, 1994.

Lasker, Edward. "Censorship of Motion Pictures Pursuant to Recent Supreme Court Decisions." *UCLA Law Review* 1 (1954): 582–92.

Leff, Leonard J., and Jerold L. Simmons. *The Dame in the Kimono: Hollywood, Censorship, and the Production Code from the 1920s to the 1960s*. New York: Grove Weidenfeld, 1990.

"Legislation: New York Motion Picture Censorship Law." *Catholic Lawyer* 1 (January 1955): 58–59.

Levy, Leonard W. *Blasphemy: Verbal Offense against the Sacred, from Moses to Salman Rushdie*. New York: Knopf, 1993.

———. *Legacy of Suppression: Freedom of Speech and Press in Early American History*. New York: Harper and Row, 1960.

Lewis, Anthony. "A New Lineup on the Supreme Court." *Reporter*, August 17, 1961, 42–46.

———. "Sex and the Supreme Court." *Esquire*, June 1963, 82–83+.

Lewis, Jon. *Hollywood v. Hard Core: How the Struggles over Censorship Saved the Modern Film Industry*. New York: New York University Press, 2000.

Lockhart, William B., and Robert C. McClure. "Censorship of Obscenity: The Developing Constitutional Standards." *Minnesota Law Review* 45 (1960): 5–121.

London, Ephraim. "The Freedom to See: With or without Glasses." *Nation*, December 19, 1953, 544–45+.

Lyons, Charles. *The New Censors: Movies and the Culture Wars*. Philadelphia: Temple University Press, 1997.

Lyons, Richard J. "Constitutional Law—Board of Regents May Ban Removal of Obscene Scenes from Motion Picture." *Syracuse Law Review* 16 (1964): 131–32.

MacGregor, Ford H. "Official Censorship Legislation." *Annals of the American Academy of Political and Social Science* 128, no. 1 (1926): 163–74.

May, Lary. *Screening Out the Past: The Birth of Mass Culture and the Motion Picture Industry*. New York: Oxford University Press, 1980.

Mayer, Arthur. "How Much Can the Censors Say?" *Saturday Review*, November 3, 1962, 18–20+.

———. *Simply Colossal: The Story of the Movies from the Long Chase to the Chaise Longue*. New York: Simon and Schuster, 1953.

McAnany, P. D. "Motion Picture Censorship and Constitutional Freedom." *Kentucky Law Journal* 50 (1962): 427–58.

McCarty, John. *The Sleaze Merchants: Adventures in Exploitation Filmmaking*. New York: St. Martin's Griffin, 1995.

McGreevy, John T. *Catholicism and American Freedom: A History*. New York: Norton, 2003.

———. "Thinking on One's Own: Catholicism in the American Intellectual Imagination, 1928–1960." *Journal of American History* 84 (1997): 97–131.

Midkiff, Leslie DeBauche. *Reel Patriotism: The Movies and World War I*. Madison: University of Wisconsin Press, 1997.

Miller, Frank. *Censored Hollywood: Sex, Sin and Violence in Hollywood*. Atlanta: Turner, 1994.

Mitgang, Herbert. "Transatlantic 'Miracle Man.'" *Park East*, August 1952, 32–36.

Mondschein, Morris. "Constitutional Law: Motion Picture Censorship." *Cornell Law Quarterly* 44 (1959): 411–19.

Moore, R. Laurence. *Selling God: American Religion in the Marketplace of Culture*. New York: Oxford University Press, 1994.

Morone, James A. *Hellfire Nation: The Politics of Sin in American History*. New Haven, CT: Yale University Press, 2003.

Morris, Charles R. *American Catholic: The Saints and Sinners Who Built America's Most Powerful Church*. New York: Times Books, 1997.

Murphy, Paul L. *The Meaning of Freedom of Speech: First Amendment Freedoms from Wilson to FDR*. Westport, CT: Greenwood, 1972.

Muscio, Giuliana. *Hollywood's New Deal*. Philadelphia: Temple University Press, 1996.

Nasaw, David. *Going Out: The Rise and Fall of Public Amusements*. New York: Basic Books, 1993.

National Council on Freedom from Censorship. *What Shocked the Censors: A Complete Record of Cuts in Motion Picture Films Ordered by the New York State Censors from January, 1932 to March, 1933*. New York: National Council on Freedom from Censorship, 1933.

Nelson, William E. *The Legalist Reformation: Law, Politics, and Ideology in New York, 1920–1980*. Chapel Hill: University of North Carolina Press, 2001.

Nunez, Richard. "In Search of a Legislative Definition: The Judicial and Legislative History of State Film Censorship in New York." Master's thesis, Syracuse University, 1960.

Nyberg, Amy Kiste. *Seal of Approval: The History of the Comics Code*. Jackson: University of Mississippi Press, 1998.

O'Mara, John T. "Obscenity: *Roth* Goes to the Movies." *Buffalo Law Review* 14 (1965): 512–24.

Parker, Alison M. *Purifying America: Women, Cultural Reform and Pro-Censorship Activism, 1873–1933*. Urbana: University of Illinois Press, 1997.

Peiss, Kathy. *Cheap Amusements: Working Women and Leisure in Turn-of-the-Century New York*. Philadelphia: Temple University Press, 1986.

Peretti, Burton W. *The Creation of Jazz: Music, Race, and Culture in Urban America*. Urbana: University of Illinois Press, 1994.

Pritchett, C. Herman. *Civil Liberties in the Vinson Court*. Chicago: University of Chicago Press, 1954.

Purcell, Edward A. "American Jurisprudence between the Wars: Legal Realism and the Crisis of Democratic Theory." In *American Law and the Constitutional Order: Historical Perspectives*, edited by Lawrence M. Friedman and Harry N. Scheiber, 359–74. Cambridge, MA: Harvard University Press, 1988.

Puttnam, David. *Movies and Money*. New York: Knopf, 1998.

Rabban, David M. *Free Speech in Its Forgotten Years*. Cambridge: Cambridge University Press, 1997.

Randall, Richard S. *Censorship of the Movies: The Social and Political Control of a Mass Medium*. Madison: University of Wisconsin Press, 1968.

Ray, Laura Krugman. "The Road to *Bush v. Gore*: The History of the Supreme Court's Use of the per Curiam Opinion." *Nebraska Law Review* 79 (2002): 517–76.

Reich, Robert. Review of *The Republic of Choice: Law, Authority and Culture*, by Lawrence M. Friedman. *American Political Science Review* 84 (1990): 1382–84.

Rembar, Charles. *The End of Obscenity: The Trials of* Lady Chatterley, Tropic of Cancer, *and* Fanny Hill. New York: Harper and Row, 1968.

Rice, Elmer. "Entertainment in the Age of McCarthy." *New Republic*, April 13, 1953, 14–17.

Rosenbloom, Nancy J. "Between Reform and Regulation: The Struggle over Film Censorship in Progressive America, 1909–1922." *Film History* 1 (1987): 307–25.

———. "From Regulation to Censorship: Film and Political Culture in New York in the Early Twentieth Century." *Journal of the Gilded Age and Progressive Era* 3 (2004): 369–406.

Rosset, Barney. Interview by John Oakes. "Barney Rosset and the Art of Combat Publishing." *Review of Contemporary Fiction* 10, no. 3 (1990): 20–57.

Salmon, John S. *A Guide to State Records in the Archives Branch, Virginia State Library*. Richmond: Virginia State Library, 1985.

Saylor, Richard C. "Banned in Pennsylvania!" *Pennsylvania Heritage*, Summer 1999, 12–21.

———. "The Pennsylvania State Board of Censors (Motion Picture)." Master's thesis, Pennsylvania State University at Harrisburg, 1999.

Schaefer, Eric. *Bold! Daring! Shocking! True! A History of Exploitation Films, 1919–1959*. Durham, NC: Duke University Press, 1999.

Schiller, Reuel E. "Free Speech and Expertise: Administrative Censorship and the Birth of the Modern First Amendment." *Virginia Law Review* 86 (2000): 1–102.

Schumach, Murray. *The Face on the Cutting Room Floor: The Story of Movie and Television Censorship*. New York: Morrow, 1964.

Seldes, Gilbert. "Pressures and Pictures." Pt. 1. *Nation*, February 3, 1951, 104–6.

Skinner, James M. *The Cross and the Cinema*. Westport, CT: Praeger, 1993.

———. "The Tussle with Russell: *The Outlaw* as a Landmark in American Film Censorship." *North Dakota Quarterly* 49 (1981): 5–12.

Sklar, Robert. *Movie-Made America: A Cultural History of American Movies*. New York: Vintage Books, 1994.

Smith, J. Douglas. "Patrolling the Boundaries of Race: Motion Picture Censorship and Jim Crow in Virginia, 1922–1932." *Historical Journal of Film, Radio, and Television* 21 (2001): 273–91.

Smith, Sarah J. *Children, Cinema and Censorship: From Dracula to the Dead End Kids*. London and New York: I. B. Tauris, 2005.

Snyder, Robert W. *The Voice of the City: Vaudeville and Popular Culture in New York*. New York: Oxford University Press, 1989.

Sova, Dawn B. *Banned Books: Literature Suppressed on Sexual Grounds*. New York: Facts on File, 1998.

———. *Forbidden Films: Censorship Histories of 125 Motion Pictures*. New York: Facts on File, 2001.

Spalding, Thomas W. *The Premier See: A History of the Archdiocese of Baltimore, 1789–1994*. Baltimore: Johns Hopkins University Press, 1995.

Springhall, John. "Censoring Hollywood: Youth, Moral Panic and Crime/Gangster Movies of the 1930s." *Journal of Popular Culture* 32, no. 3 (1998): 135–54.

Staiger, Janet. *Bad Women: Regulating Sexuality in Early American Cinema*. Minneapolis: University of Minnesota Press, 1995.

Starr, Paul. *The Creation of the Media: Political Origins of Modern Communications*. New York: Basic Books, 2004.

"State Court Upholds Constitutionality of Refusal to License *Lady Chatterley's Lover* under Recently Amended Motion Picture Licensing Statute." *Columbia Law Review* 59 (1959): 337–51.

Steele, Richard W. *Free Speech in the Good War*. New York: St. Martin's Press, 1999.

Steigerwald, David. *The Sixties and the End of Modern America*. New York: St. Martin's Press, 1995.

"Supreme Court Denies Review of Free Speech Issue over *Natural Born Killers*." *Sports and Entertainment Litigation Reporter*, November 1999, 5.

Temporary State Commission on the Coordination of State Activities. *Report on the Motion Picture Division, New York State Education Department*. Albany, NY: Temporary State Commission on the Coordination of State Activities, 1949.

Thompson, Frank. "Pre-Code Parlance." *American Film* 15, no. 2 (1989): 13.

Tushnet, Mark V. *The NAACP's Legal Strategy against Segregated Education, 1925–1950*. Chapel Hill: University of North Carolina Press, 1987.

Ullman, Sharon R. *Sex Seen: The Emergence of Modern Sexuality in America*. Berkeley: University of California Press, 1997.

Urofsky, Melvin I. *Division and Discord: The Supreme Court under Stone and Vinson, 1941–1953*. Columbia: University of South Carolina Press, 1997.

Vaughn, Steven. "Morality and Entertainment: Origins of the Motion Picture Code." *Journal of American History* 77 (1990): 39–65.

Verani, John R. "Motion Picture Censorship and the Doctrine of Prior Restraint." *Houston Law Review* 3 (1965): 11–57.

Walker, Samuel. *In Defense of American Liberties: A History of the ACLU.* New York: Oxford University Press, 1990.

Walsh, Frank. *Sin and Censorship: The Catholic Church and the Motion Picture Industry*. New Haven, CT: Yale University Press, 1996.

Wambeam, Rodney A. "Lights! Camera! Policy! Regulating the Morality of American Entertainment." PhD diss., University of Nebraska, 1999.

Warner, Linda K. "Movie Censorship in Kansas: The Kansas State Board of Review." Master's thesis, Emporia State University, 1988.

Wasby, Stephen L. *Race Relations Litigation in an Age of Complexity*. Charlottesville: University Press of Virginia, 1995.

Wertheimer, John. "The *Mutual Film* Reviewed: The Movies, Censorship and Free Speech in Progressive America." *American Journal of Legal History* 37 (1993): 158–89.

Westin, Alan. *The* Miracle *Case: The Supreme Court and the Movies*. Inter-university Case Program, 1961.

Wheeler, Leigh Ann. *Against Obscenity: Reform and the Politics of Womanhood, 1873–1935*. Baltimore: Johns Hopkins University Press, 2004.

White, G. Edward. "The First Amendment Comes of Age: The Emergence of Free Speech in Twentieth Century America." *Michigan Law Review* 95 (1996): 299–392.

Whitman, Alden, ed. *American Reformers: An H. W. Wilson Biographical Dictionary*. New York: H. W. Wilson, 1985.

Wirt, Frederick Marshall. "State Film Censorship with Particular Reference to Ohio." PhD diss., Ohio State University, 1956.

Wohlforth, Robert. "People and Pickets." *New Republic*, February 5, 1951, 13.

Yassky, David. "Eras of the First Amendment." *Columbia Law Review* 91 (1991): 1699–755.

Zalcock, Bev. "Not Forgetting Shirley Clarke." *Filmwaves* 2 (1997): 14–15.

Index